The World
We Have Lost

The World
We Have Lost
further explored

Peter Laslett

PUBLISHED BY
CHARLES SCRIBNER'S SONS • NEW YORK

Copyright © 1965, 1971, 1984 Peter Laslett

Library of Congress Cataloging in Publication Data

Laslett, Peter.
  The world we have lost.

  Bibliography: p.
  Includes index.
  1. Great Britain—Social conditions   2. Great
Britain—Civilization.   I. Title.
HN385.L35   1983   306'.0941   84-1242
ISBN 0-684-18080-4
ISBN 0-684-18079-0 (pbk.)

1 3 5 7 9 11 13 15 17 19   F/C   20 18 16 14 12 10 8 6 4 2
1 3 5 7 9 11 13 15 17 19   F/P   20 18 16 14 12 10 8 6 4 2

PRINTED IN THE UNITED STATES OF AMERICA

Contents

List of figures

List of tables

Introduction to the third edition, 1983

The World We Have Lost was first published in London in 1965 and in New York in 1966. It was revised to some extent in each of its subsequent English language printings and in its foreign translations up to 1971. A more extensively amended text was issued in that year as a second edition, and the same process of revision as to some details has gone on in subsequent printings of this edition. As a result, the text now exists in numerous variants and shows progressive deterioration. When it was resolved to replace that text by a third edition brought entirely up to date, so much rewriting became necessary that the title itself has had to be elongated into *The World We Have Lost further explored.*

What is in front of the reader, then, is a work of the 1960s which has evolved into a work of the 1980s. Its first three chapters are much amended versions of those in the final English printing (1979) of the second edition, but the following four in that edition have been rewritten almost entirely. The chapters on births, marriages and deaths and on patterns of authority have been divided into halves, the new chapters bearing the titles: 'Misbeliefs about our ancestors' (Chapter 4 of the present book) and 'The politics of exclusion and the rule of an élite' (Chapter 10). No completely new chapter has been contributed, but the book is 15,000 words longer.

This had to be so if anything like proper account was to be taken of research results published since 1965 on the topics discussed in the original book. Some of these topics had never been previously broached in historical writing and several of them have developed a literature of some size written in several countries. As might be expected, however, not all of the lines of investigation suggested have been subsequently pursued.

The author is aware that these changes may have given to *The World We Have Lost* a more academic cast than it possessed before or than it was originally intended to possess. An essay addressed to a readership far wider than that of a class in school or university, which began in a series of broadcasts on the old, original, incomparable Third Programme of the BBC in the days of sound, has become much more of an exposition of the textbook kind to be used by the student as well as by the professor. The change had come about well before this rewriting was in contemplation and the form and content of the work now published are designed to accommodate that change.

The second part of the volume which contains the guide to the files of the Cambridge Group for the History of Population and Social Structure, along with the notes, has been lengthened and brought up to the minute, and the references extended as far as seems useful. This is especially so for the demographic discussions and those on the family, on famine and on illegitimacy. Nevertheless, this reference section is still independent of the essay itself. There are no notes on the pages of the essay and it is hoped that its contents remain a good read for everyone, and not only for those instructing or under instruction.

No sympathetic reader, though the history of the book shows that not all of its readers have been sympathetic, will fail to appreciate that to update a work in this way and to alter its identity to some degree must be a difficult and risky business. I have undertaken the task because the book is still in demand for teaching and for other purposes in English-speaking countries and because translations are still being undertaken. It seemed wrong, in leaving it uncorrected, to perpetuate misinformation by permitting inaccuracies to go on being printed and lacunae to remain. Furthermore it is obviously of importance that the entirely new results bearing on the themes of the book which have been reported in learned and often technical form in academic volumes and journals should take their place here.

A determined effort has been made to present these results as lucidly as possible, in a form which can be appreciated by the reader with little or no previous information, and without a taste for technical demonstration. He or she must accept the fact that such simplification is always to some degree also distortion and that results pared down in this fashion cannot be understood by the reader in quite the same sense as they were understood by the originator. I have tried to guard against the danger of misrepresentation by asking the scholars in question to read what I have written. This has usually been possible only in the case of the results issued by the Cambridge Group itself, and I am particularly indebted to Roger Schofield for his careful monitoring and unflagging interest.

It should therefore be evident how far what follows consists in the work of members of the Cambridge Group other than myself. This is in spite of the fact that *The World We Have Lost* was written in the first place before 1964, when the Group was founded, and in spite of the fact that efforts were made in the earliest of the introductions to dissociate its contents from the researches of the Group itself. I have been forced to recognize the extent to which the volume has become identified with the Group, and this has meant accepting into the text results which are in no way my own. This is especially the case of course with the contents of the most important title published from the Group, *The Population History of England, 1541–1871: A Reconstruction* by E. A. Wrigley and R. S. Schofield, my two fellow directors of the Group, issued in 1981 by Edward Arnold, London, and in 1982 by Harvard University Press in the United States.

I hereby acknowledge my debt to these two friends and fellow researchers, collaborators now for nearly twenty years, and to all of the rest of our membership: Richard Wall, Richard Smith, James Oeppen, Rosalind Davies, Karla Oosterveen, Leslie Pepper and the many others who have now left us. There are also those who have worked and still work as research students: Keith Wrightson, Vivien Brodsky, Emmanuel Todd, David Thomson, Graham Kerby, Martin Clarke, David Levine, Keith Snell, David Souden and others, as well as our visitors and associates. The list of these is far too long to reproduce but I should like to name Alan Macfarlane, Kenneth Wachter, James E. Smith, Peter Czap, Ann Kussmaul, Hervé le Bras and Osamu Saito.

I hope that those acknowledged in previous introductions, for the debt which I still owe them, will accept this renewed assurance. Perhaps I may be allowed to thank my critics too, and my friends Jean-Louis Flandrin in France, and Hans Medick in Germany as well as those in Britain and America. I hope they all will be pleased to recognize that there is enough here to justify their having another go at *The World We Have Lost* even though it now has a slightly different name.

The continued vitality of the original controversy, addressed almost entirely to the political chapters, is well illustrated by the content of *Class in English History*, published by R. S. Neale in 1981. The fact that the issues are still alive and the differences still pronounced, if considerably less than they once were, puts the writer of a reformulated essay into a position of constraint. He is not at liberty to omit or even much to modify the original opinions or even the theoretical positions with which he has become identified. The reader interested in the controversy will expect to find these positions written out in their pristine form, and he or she will do so. The statements presenting the theory of the one-class society which were perhaps the most contentious of them all, are reproduced unaltered, in no way extenuated but with some extension. Those on the inappropriateness of a revolutionist ideology to the explanation of events in England in the seventeenth century are now rounded off with a plea for the erasure of the phrase 'the English Revolution' altogether.

Matters of informational fact, however, have been revised, omitted, replaced and multiplied. It is obvious that the implied distinction between theory and fact is finally untenable. But I have done my best. I hope that it will be evident that *The World We Have Lost* is still present in its entirety in *The World We Have Lost further explored* but along with much else besides.

Langley, British Columbia and
3 Clarkson Road, Cambridge
May 1983

Introduction to the first edition, 1965

This essay has been six years in the making, and is on the way to being overtaken by events. It began as an attempt to write out in a straightforward way the introductory facts about the structure of English society as it was before the Industrial Revolution, and to make some comparison with its structure in the twentieth century. But the idea of an introduction to a subject of this kind turned out to be peculiarly elusive. Even the choice of the point at which to start is a problem, for it may determine the view of the whole which will be taken. Every descriptive remark after that may also mask the reality it aims to convey. Accordingly I have found that the task of working out an intelligible plan of a complete social structure is extraordinarily formidable; putting it down in clear, readable form has been even more so.

Hence a whole series of successive provisional drafts of the text over the six years, of which the one printed here is the last. The difficulties have not been entirely intellectual and literary. Since 1959, when a casual reference brought *The Rector's Book, Clayworth, Nottinghamshire* up out of the vaults of the Library of Congress, sources for this study have been coming to light so rapidly that it has been almost impossible to decide when the time had come to pause and write down a summary of knowledge acquired to date. In this situation resort was had to the Third Programme of the British Broadcasting Corporation, and some of the material of *The World We Have Lost*, as well as its title, appeared as talks and in the *Listener* in the years 1960, 1962 and 1963.

It became clear quite early that two much more important things were wanted in addition to an introductory essay to the subject as a whole. One was an arrangement for collaborative research, which would make it possible to undertake tasks no man could hope to carry out on his own. The second was the fund of information and the necessary time to write a large and something like a definitive study of the social structure of pre-industrial England, and perhaps of Europe generally.

The first of these objects has been happily attained, and the Cambridge Group for the History of Population and Social Structure began its official life in 1964, with the generous support of the Calouste Gulbenkian Foundation of Lisbon,

London branch. This should secure the second object as well. One of the titles in the series of works to be published by the Cambridge Group will be the full treatise of which the present essay is merely a foretaste. This wholly more academic treatise will print as much of the evidence as seems to be required, and others of the monographs which we are planning, together with various articles, will also contain instalments of the full facts and figures which have been used so sketchily here.

But though *The World We Have Lost* is in a sense a collaborative work, and could never have been written if only one man had been at work, it is emphatically not a publication of the Cambridge Group for the History of Population and Social Structure and does not appear under that imprint. The first of the series to be issued by the Group will in fact come out early in 1966, *An Introduction to English Historical Demography*, edited by E. A. Wrigley, with contributions from him, from the present author and others. That work, and other publications, will contain instalments of precisely those findings which are repeatedly mentioned in this book as being urgently needed and probably obtainable, since some of them have already been worked out in France, mainly statistics of population. In this sense it is possible to say that *The World We Have Lost* is fortunately about to be overtaken, in respect at least of the research results which it presents.

The rougher facts and figures used here belong to an earlier and less regular period in the initial stages of this departure in historical and social research. The present essay has been dedicated to three of the volunteers who undertook the wearisome tasks of working through the newly found documents to find out if the newly worked-out hypotheses were of any value. Several other volunteers should also be thanked for their part in the investigations and in the consultations which took place in Cambridge: Mr Newman Brown, Mr John Montgomery, Mrs Bessie Maltby and Mr F. G. Emmison. Nearly all these historians are still working in correspondence with the Cambridge Group, but in the more advanced and regular way which has now become possible.

The list of those to whom I owe thanks and acknowledgements is so long that it could only be unreadable in full. There are first of all the French scholars, without whose achievements and example many of the activities reported here could never have gone forward. I hope Louis Henry and Pierre

Goubert will accept this tribute to their pre-eminence, and my thanks for their friendliness and forbearance with an awkward English visitor. M. Alfred Sauvy, the *doyen* (now in the English sense only) of the Institut National d'Études Demographiques and of demographic studies all over the world, has been very obliging, and I owe much to J.-N. Biraben and other members of the staff of the Institut.

The social scientists nearer home who have been good enough to guide me are also a large company, and I wish that I had been a better pupil. David Glass, Tom Marshall, Max Gluckman, Meyer Fortes, Jack Goody, Audrey Richards, David Lockwood, John Goldthorpe and Edmund Leach are some of them, and I owe a great deal to Edward Shils, my caustic mentor now for nearly twenty years. David Eversley has been an unfailing source of help and friendliness. Many people have given quite unlooked for assistance far in excess of what a researcher has a right to expect; there are Mr and Mrs Gooder of the Birmingham Extra-Mural Board as one instance, or the many clergy of the English Church who have responded to queries and given access to the documents in their care. A number of literary scholars have assisted too; there are Mrs Florence Trefethen, of Lexington, Massachusetts, and Professor Muriel Bradbrook.

Like every other writer with a case I have learnt a lot from those with whom I wish to disagree, at least to some extent; here Eric Hobsbawm and Christopher Hill are two names to mention, whilst Brough Macpherson has been a most friendly and useful collaborator and critic. E. H. Carr has encouraged me a great deal too and I should like to record my gratitude to him. Sir Charles Snow, Sir Anthony Wagner and Asa Briggs have been amongst the patrons of social structural research, and I can only hope that they may like this first instalment of its results.

Even this may seem an inordinate list of debts for so short a book, but I have still to reach my more personal acknowledgements. There is Anna Kallin, late and for so long acknowledged as the reigning princess of the Third Programme. There is Maurice Ashley, editor of the *Listener*, a long-standing, faithful friend to studies of this kind. There are those who took the trouble to write to me after hearing broadcast talks. There is Trevor Dannatt, the architect, whose friendship is so valuable to me and his opinion so important. He introduced me to Douglas Merritt, who designed this book, and has shown an extraordinary insight and sympathy with the work reported upon. My long-suffering wife, after all those rejected drafts, set to and made out the index in two weeks, amidst everything else.

Trinity College, Cambridge – *August 1965*

The World
We Have Lost

English society
before and after the
coming of industry
Chapter 1

The passing of the patriarchal
household: parents and children,
masters and servants

In the year 1619 the bakers of London applied to the authorities for an increase in the price of bread. They sent in support of their claim a complete description of a bakery and an account of its weekly costs.[1] There were thirteen or fourteen people in such an undertaking: the baker and his wife, four paid employees who were called journeymen, two apprentices, two maidservants and the three or four children of the master baker himself. Six pounds ten shillings (£6.50) a week was reckoned to be the outgoings of this establishment, of which only eleven shillings and eightpence (58p) went for wages: half a crown (25p) a week for each of the journeymen and tenpence (4.5p) for each of the maids. Far and away the greatest expense was for food: two pounds nine shillings (£2.45) out of the six pounds ten shillings, at five shillings (25p) a head for the baker and his wife, four shillings (20p) a head for their helpers and two shillings (10p) for their children. It cost much more in food to keep a journeyman than it cost in money; four times as much to keep a maid. Clothing was charged up too, not only for the man, wife and children, but for the apprentices as well. Even school fees were claimed as a justifiable charge on the price of bread for sale, and sixpence (2.5p) a week was paid for the teaching and clothing of a baker's child.

A London bakery was undoubtedly what we should call a commercial or even an industrial undertaking, turning out loaves by the thousand. Yet the business was carried on in the house of the baker himself. There was probably a 'shop' as

part of the house, 'shop' as in 'workshop' and not as meaning
a retail establishment. Loaves were not ordinarily sold over
the counter: they had to be carried to the open-air market and
displayed on stalls.[2] There was a garner behind the house, for
which the baker paid two shillings a week in rent, and where
he kept his wheat, his 'sea-coal' for the fire and his store of
salt. The house itself was one of those high, half-timbered
overhanging structures on the narrow London street which we
always think of when we remember the scene in which
Shakespeare, Pepys, or even Christopher Wren lived. Most of
it was taken up with the living-quarters of the dozen people
who worked there.

It is obvious that all these people ate in the house, since the
cost of their food helped to determine the production cost of
the bread. Except for the journeymen they were all obliged to
sleep in the house at night and live together as a family.

The word generally used at that time to describe such a
group of people was 'family', though household is found as
well. The man at the head of the group, the entrepreneur, the
employer, or the manager, was then known as the master or
head of the family. He was father to some of its members and
in place of father to the rest. There was no sharp distinction
between his domestic and his economic functions. His wife
was both his partner and his subordinate, a partner because
she ran the family, took charge of the food and managed the
women-servants, a subordinate because she was woman and
wife, mother and in place of mother to the rest.[3]

The paid servants of both sexes had their specified and
familiar position in the family household, as much part of it
during their residence as the sons and daughters, but not quite
in the same situation of course. At that time the family was
thought of not as one society only, but as three societies fused
together. There was the society of man and wife, that of
parents and children, and that of master and servant. The
first of these was for the life of husband and of wife; only death
could put an end to their being members of each other, though
this society could be and often was renewed by remarriage.
The second association bound father and mother to son and to
daughter until the time came for the child to leave home,
though he or she could return at will, at least up until marriage.
But a servant did not enjoy permanent membership of the
household in which he served. When a servant left, the rela-

tionship was over. Most households, moreover, had no servant
at all, so that the society of master and servant did not exist
for them.

A period of service began with an undertaking to serve, the
best-known of such undertakings being the binding out, as it
was called, of a youth as an apprentice. Here the agreement is
made between the parents of a boy about to become an
apprentice and his future master. The boy covenants to dwell
with his master for seven years, to keep his secrets and to obey
his commandments.[4]

> Taverns and alehouses he shall not haunt; dice, cards or any
> other unlawful games he shall not use; fornication with any
> woman he shall not commit; matrimony with any woman he
> shall not contract. He shall not absent himself by night or
> by day without his master's leave but be a true and faithful
> servant.

On his side, the master undertakes to teach his apprentice his
'art, science or occupation with moderate correction'.

> Finding and allowing unto his said servant meat, drink,
> apparel, washing, lodging and all other things during the
> said term of seven years, and to give unto his said appren-
> tice at the end of the said term double apparel, to wit, one
> suit for holydays and one suit for worken days.

Apprentices, therefore, and many other servants, were
workers who can be thought of in a sense as extra sons or extra
daughters (for girls could be apprenticed too), clothed and
educated as well as fed, obliged to obedience and forbidden to
marry, often unpaid and dependent until after the age of
twenty-one or even considerably longer. If such servants were
workers in somewhat the position of sons and daughters, the
sons and daughters of the house were workers too. John Locke
laid it down in 1697 that the offspring of the poor had to work
for some part of the day when they reached the age of three.[5]
The children of a London baker were not likely to go to school
for many years of their young lives, or even to play as they
wished when they came back home. Soon they would find
themselves doing what they could in 'bolting', that is sieving
flour, or in helping the maidservant with her panniers of loaves

on the way to the market stall, or in playing their small parts in preparing the never ending succession of meals for the whole household.

We may see at once, therefore, that the world we have lost, as I have chosen to call it, was no paradise, no golden age of equality, tolerance or of loving kindness. Once into their teens, not often earlier, they might become servants too and leave the parental home to work in another family, work for a living. The coming of industry cannot be shown to have brought economic oppression and exploitation along with it. It was there already. The patriarchal arrangements which we have begun to explore were not new in the England of Shakespeare and Elizabeth. They were as old as the Greeks, as old as European history, and not confined to Europe. The institution of life-cycle service, as we have come to call it, was a peculiarly western European one, nevertheless. And it may well be that such relationships as we have described abused and enslaved people quite as remorselessly as the economic arrangements which had replaced them in the England of Blake and Victoria.[6]

Perhaps every servant in the old social world was confident enough that he or she would some day get married and be at the head of a new family, keeping others in subordination. In this they were deceiving themselves to some extent, for by no means all persons found spouses in pre-industrial western society, and some stayed subordinate to a master in a master's house for the whole of their lives. If it is legitimate to use the words exploitation and oppression in thinking of the economic arrangements of the pre-industrial world, there were nevertheless differences in the manner of oppressing and exploiting. The ancient order of society was felt to be eternal and unchangeable by those who supported, enjoyed and endured it. There was no expectation of reform. How could there be when economic organization was domestic organization, and relationships were rigidly regulated by the social system, by the content of Christianity itself?

Here is a vivid contrast with social expectation in Victorian England, or in industrial countries everywhere today. Every relationship in our world which can be seen to affect our economic life is open to change, is expected indeed to change of itself, or if it does not, to *be* changed, made better, by an omnicompetent authority. This makes for a less stable social

world, though it is only one of the features of our society which
impels us all in that direction. All industrial societies, we may
suppose, are far less stable than their predecessors. They lack
the extraordinarily cohesive influence which familial relationships carry with them, that power of reconciling the frustrated
and the discontented by emotional means. Social revolution, meaning an irreversible changing of the pattern of
social relationships, never happened in traditional, patriarchal,
pre-industrial human society. It was almost impossible to
contemplate.

Almost, but not quite. Sir Thomas More, in the reign of
Henry VIII, could follow Plato in imagining a life without
privacy and money, even if he stopped short of imagining a
life where children would not know their parents and where
promiscuity could be a political institution. Sir William Petty,
150 years later, one of the very first of the political sociologists,
could speculate about polygamy; and the English of the
Tudors and the Stuarts already knew of social structures and
sexual arrangements, existing in the newly discovered world,
which were alarmingly different from their own. But it must
have been an impossible effort of the imagination for them to
suppose that they were anything like as satisfactory.[7]

It will be noticed that the roles we have allotted to all the
members of the capacious 'family' of the master-baker of
London in the year 1619 are, emotionally, all highly symbolic
and highly satisfying. We may feel that in a whole society
organized like this, in spite of the subordination, the exploitation and the obliteration of those who were young, or female,
or in service, everyone belonged in a group, a family group.
Everyone had his or her circle of affection: every relationship
could be seen as a love-relationship. This in spite of the fact that
demography prevented everyone from belonging to a familial
unit in the literal sense, a family of his own or her own, or the
family of a parent. In spite also of the further fact that the
social rules actually tended to exclude the orphaned and the
widowed from the familial group and from the support of
kinsfolk not immediate in their relationship to the victim of
circumstances.

But with us, the social world is such that no sentiment of the
familial kind is likely to attach itself to work relationships.
Who could love the name of a limited company or of a government department as an apprentice could love his superbly

satisfactory father-figure master, even if he were a bully and a beater, a usurer and a hypocrite? If a family is a circle of affection, we must remember that it can also be the scene of hatred. The worst tyrants among human beings, the murderers and the villains, are jealous husbands and resentful wives, possessive parents and deprived children. In the traditional, patriarchal society of Europe, where practically everyone lived out his whole life within the family, though not usually within one family, tension like this must have been incessant and unrelieved, incapable of release except in crisis. Conflict in such a society was accordingly between individual people, on the personal scale. There could scarcely be a situation such as that which makes our own time, as some say, the scene of perpetual revolution, social revolution.

All this is true to history only if the little knot of people making bread in Stuart London was indeed the typical social unit of the old world in its size, composition and scale. There are reasons why a baker's household might have been a little out of the ordinary, for baking was a highly traditional occupation in a society increasingly subject to economic change. A 'family' of thirteen people, which was also a unit of production of thirteen, less the children still incapable of work, was quite big for English society at that time and in a way exceptional as well.

In fact the town and the craft probably bulk too large in the folk-memory we still retain from the world we have lost. Agriculture and the countryside do not dominate our recollections to anything like the extent that they dominated that vanished world. We have all heard about the apprentices who married their master's daughter: these are the heroes. Or about the outsider who married the widow left behind by the father/master when he came to die: these unwelcome strangers to the family are the villains. We refer to bakers as if they really baked in their homes; of spinsters who really sat by the fire and span. A useful, if a rather arbitrary and romantic guide to the subject in hand, is the famous collection of fairy tales compiled by the brothers Grimm in Germany a century and a half ago and more, where the tales we tell to our children mostly have their source.[8] Even in the form given to them by Walt Disney and his successors, the makers of television programmes and picture-books for the youngest members of our rich, leisurely, powerful, puzzled world of successful industrialization, stories like Cinderella are a sharp reminder of what life was once like for the apprentice, the journeyman, the master and all his family in the craftsman's household. Which means, in a sense, that we all know it all already.

We know, or half-remember, that a journeyman might sometimes have to spend a year or two on his journeys, serving out that difficult period after he was trained and capable of his craft, but before he had made, or inherited, or had the prospect of marrying, enough money to set up as master by himself. It takes a little reflection to recognize in this practice a reason why so many heroes of the nursery rhymes and stories are on the road, literally seeking their fortunes. We have to go even further to search here for the origin of the picaresque in literature, perhaps for the very germ of the novel. And conscious analysis, directed historical research of a kind only recently supposed to be possible and necessary, has had to be done before even a few fragmentary facts about the tendency of young people to move about could be recovered. It has been found that most young people in service, except, of course, the apprentices, seem to have looked upon a change of job bringing them into a new family as the normal thing every few years.[9]

We shall have more to say about the movement of servants from farmhouse to farmhouse in the old world, and shall return to the problem of understanding ourselves in time, in contrast with our ancestors. Let us emphasize again the scale of life in the working family of the London baker.

Few persons in the old world ever found themselves in groups larger than family groups, and there were not many families of more than a dozen members in any locality. But at the very top of the society family households could be huge, even larger than in parts of the world where the generations often lived together. Apart from the royal court and the establishments of the nobility, lay and spiritual, a resident gentleman like Sir Richard Newdigate, Baronet, could have dozens of people around him. In his house of Arbury within his parish of Chilvers Coton in Warwickshire, in the year 1684, there were thirty-seven in the 'family': himself; Lady Mary Newdigate, his wife; seven daughters, all under the age of sixteen; and twenty-eight servants: seventeen men and boys and eleven women and girls.[10] This was still a family, not an institution, a staff, an office or a firm.

Everything physical was on the human scale, for the

commercial worker in London, and the miner who lived and
toiled in Newdigate's village of Chilvers Coton. No object in
England was larger than London Bridge or St Paul's Cathedral,
no structure in the western world to stand comparison with the
Colosseum in Rome. Everything temporal was tied to the
human life-span too. The death of the master baker, head of
the family, ordinarily meant the end of the bakery. Of course
there might be a son to succeed, but the master's surviving
children would frequently be young if he himself had lived
only as long as most men. Or an apprentice might fulfil the
final function of apprenticehood, substitute sonship, that is to
say, and marry his master's daughter, or even his widow.
Surprisingly often, the widow, if she could, would herself carry
on the trade.

This, therefore, was not simply a world without factories,
without firms, and for the most part without economic continuity. Some partnerships between rich masters existed,
especially in London, but since nearly every activity was
limited to what could be organized within a family, and within
the lifetime of its head, there was an unending struggle to
manufacture continuity and to provide an expectation of the
future. 'One hundred and twenty family uprising and down-
lying, whereof you may take out six or seven and all the rest
were servants and retainers': this was the household of the
Herberts, Earls of Pembroke in the years before the Civil War,
as it was remembered a generation later by the sentimental
antiquarian of the West Country where the Herberts were
seated, John Aubrey of the *Lives*. It is wise to be careful of
what men liked to report about the size and splendour of the
great families in days gone by: £16,000 a year was the Herbert
revenue, so John Aubrey claimed, though 'with his offices, and
all' the earl 'had £30,000 per annum. And, as the revenue
was great, so the greatness of his retinue and hospitality were
answerable.' These are improbably large figures, but we know
that Lord William Howard kept between forty and fifty
servants at Naworth Castle in Cumberland in the 1620s on a
much smaller revenue. And as late as 1787, the Earl of Lonsdale, a very rich, mine-owning bachelor, lived in a household
of fifty at Lowther in Westmorland, himself that is and forty-
nine servants. All this illustrates the symbolic function of
aristocratic families in a society of families, which were
generally surprisingly small. They were there to defy the

limitation on size, and to try to maintain a patriline which should last indefinitely.

We may pause here to point out that our argument is not complete. There was an organization in the social structure of Europe before the coming of industry which enormously exceeded the family in size and endurance. This was the Christian Church. It may be true to say that the ordinary person, especially the female, never went to a gathering larger than could assemble in an ordinary house except when going to church. When we look at the aristocracy and the church from the point of view of the scale of life and the impermanence of all man-made institutions, we can see that their functions were to some degree compensatory. The calendar itself underlined the great age and the continuity of the church. The rules of succession permitted a cousin, however distant, to succeed to the title and to the headship of a noble house, provided only he was in the male line. Even then, as we shall see, extinction was an ever present possibility and we can expect that a half of all lines of male succession would die out within a hundred and fifty years. But here the final remedy lay in the power of the Crown, the fountain of honour, to declare that an anomalous succession should take place. Nobility was for ever.[11]

The symbolic provision of permanence is only the beginning of the social functions of the church. At a time when the ability to read with understanding and to write much more than a personal letter was confined for the most part to the ruling minority, in a society which was otherwise oral in its communications, the lettered parson was the great link between the illiterate mass and the political, technical and educated world.

Sitting in the 10,000 parish churches of England at every service, Sundays and Saints Days, holy days, that is, or holidays as we now call them, in groups of 20, 50, 100 or 200, the illiterate mass of the people were taking part in the single group activity which they ordinarily shared with others outside their own families. But they were doing more than this. They were informing themselves in the only way open to them of what went on in England, Europe and the world as a whole. The priesthood was indispensable to the religious activity of the old world, at a time when religion was still of primary interest and importance. But the priesthood was also indispensable because of its functions in social communication. This, perhaps, was one reason why the puritan layman insisted so strongly upon a preaching clergy.

When we insist on the tiny scale of life in the pre-industrial world, especially on the small size of the groups in which nearly everybody spent their lives, there are, of course, certain occasions and institutions which we must not overlook. There were the military practices, an annual muster of the able-bodied men from every county, which took place after harvest in Tudor times.[12] There were regular soldiers too, though not very many of them; variegated bands of the least promising of men straggling behind the banner of some noble adventurer. Much more familiar to Englishmen, at least in the maritime areas, must have been the sailors; twenty, thirty, even fifty men at sea, sometimes for days or even weeks on end.

Lilliputian, we must feel, when we compare such details with the crowds we meet in our society. The largest crowd recorded for seventeenth-century England, that is the parliamentary army which fought at Marston Moor, would have gone three, four or even five times into the sporting stadium of today.[13] Other organizations and purposes which brought groups of people together were the assizes in the county towns; the quarter sessions of the county justices; the meetings of the manorial courts in the villages, of the town councils in the towns, of the companies or craftsmen there, each one to a trade or occupation; the assemblies which sometimes took place of clergy or of nonconformist ministers. Most regular of all, and probably largest in scale and most familiar to ordinary men and women, were the weekly market days and the annual fairs in each locality. Then there were the 2000 schools in England, one for every fifth parish but very few large enough to have more than a single teacher, and the two universities, with less than 10,000 men between them.[14] Then there was Parliament itself. All these occasions and institutions assembled men in some numbers for purposes which could not be called familial. Women too assembled; though, save to the markets and to protests against prices, they came as spectators rather than as participants.

The fact that it is possible to name most of the large-scale institutions and occasions in a sentence or two makes the contrast with our own world more telling than ever. We have only to think of the hundreds of children sitting in their classrooms every weekday, for most of the year, all over the country, of the hundreds and thousands together in the factories, the offices, the shops, to recognize the difference. The detailed study of the pre-industrial social world makes this question of scale more critical still. Wherever the facts of economic life and technology required a working group different in size and constitution from the working family, there was discontinuity. Hence the crew of a ship, the team of workers on a building, the fifty or sixty grown men who might be required to work a mine or an armaments manufactory, were all looked upon as exceptional. As indeed they were, so much so that the building trade had had its own society from medieval times, and the miners were a community apart wherever they were found.[15]

Not only did the scale of their work and the size of the group which was engaged make them exceptional, the constitution of the group did too. In the baking household we have chosen as our standard, sex and age were mingled together. Fortunate children might go out to school, but most adults did not usually go out to work. There was nothing to correspond to the thousands of young men on the assembly line, the hundreds of young women in the offices, the lonely lives of housekeeping wives, which we now know only too well. But we shall see on the other hand that those who survived to old age in the much less favourable conditions for survival which then were prevalent, were sometimes left to live and die alone, in their tiny cottages or sometimes in the almshouses which were being built so widely in the England of the Tudors and the Stuarts.[16] Poor-law establishments, parochial in purpose and in size, had begun their melancholy chapter in the history of the English people. But institutional life was otherwise almost unknown. There were no hotels, hostels or blocks of flats for single persons, very few hospitals and none of the kind we are familiar with, extremely few young men and women living on their own. The family unit where so great a majority lived was what we should undoubtedly call a 'balanced' and 'healthy' group.

When we turn from the hand-made city of London to the hand-moulded immensity of rural England, we may carry the same sentimental prejudice along with us. To every farm there was a family, which spread itself over its portion of the village lands as the family of the master-craftsman filled out his manufactory. When a holding was small, and most were small as are the tiny holdings of European peasants today, a man tilled it with the help of his wife and his children. No single man, we must remember, would usually take charge of the land, any more than a single man would often be found at the head of a workshop in the city. The master of a family was expected to be a householder in the town or in the country. In the city of Coventry in the sixteenth century, if he was not a householder he was outside civil society, classed as a cottager. Marriage we must insist, and it is one of the rules which gave its character to the society of our ancestors, was the entry to full membership, in the enfolding countryside, as well as in the scattered urban centres.

But there was a difference in scale and organization of work on the land and in the town. The necessities of rural life did require recurrent groupings of households for common economic purposes, occasionally something like a crowd of men, women and children working together for days on end. Where the ground was still being tilled as open fields, and each household had a number of strips scattered all over the whole open area and not a compact collection of enclosures, ploughing was co-operative, as were many other operations, above all harvesting, and this continued even after enclosure. We do not yet know how important this element of enforced common activity was in the life of the English rural community on the eve of industrialization, or how much difference enclosure made in this respect. But whatever the situation was, the economic transformation of the eighteenth and nineteenth centuries destroyed communality altogether in English rural life. The group of men from several farmsteads working the heavy plough in springtime, the bevy of harvesters from every house in the village wading into the high standing grass to begin the cutting of the hay, had no successors in large-scale economic activity. For the arrangement of these groups was entirely different in principle from the arrangement of a factory, or a firm, or even of a collective farm.

Both before and after enclosure, some peasants did well: their crops were heavier and they had more land to till. To provide the extra labour needed then, the farming householder, like the successful craftsman, would extend his working family by taking on young men and women as servants to live with him and work the fields. This he would have to do, even if the land which he was farming was not his own but rented from the great family in the manor house. Sometimes, we have found, he would prefer to send out his own children as servants and bring in other children and young men to do the work. This is one of the few glimpses we can get into the quality of the emotional life of the family at this time, for it shows that parents may have been unwilling to submit children of their own to the discipline of work at home. It meant, too, that servants were not simply the perquisites of wealth and position. A quarter, or a third, of all the families in the country contained servants in Stuart times, and this meant that very humble people had them as well as the titled and the wealthy. Most of the servants, moreover, male or female, in the great house and in the small, were engaged in working the land.[17]

The boys and the men would do the ploughing, hedging, carting and all the heavy work. The really skilled tasks were often reserved to the labourers or to craftsmen in rural matters like thatchers. The women and the girls would keep the house, prepare the meals, make the butter and the cheese, the bread and the beer, and would also look after the cattle and take the fruit to market. At harvest-time, from June to October, every hand was occupied and every back was bent. These were the decisive months for the whole population in our damp northern climate, with its single harvest in a season and reliance on one or two standard crops. So critical was the winning of the grain for bread that the first rule of gentility (a gentleman never worked with his hands for his living) might be abrogated.

We have hinted that a fundamental characteristic of the world we have lost was that the scene of labour was universally supposed to be the home. It has been implied in the case of industry and in towns that the hired man who came in to work during the day and went home to his meals and at night was looked on as exceptional. Such workers existed, nevertheless, as did other divisions between household and workplace. In Coventry in the 1520s there were large numbers of journeymen at work, when they were able to find work, in the establishments of entrepreneurs, establishments whose claim to be described as families can only be called strained. These men, often married, were able to spend only their sleeping time, their Saturday evenings and their Sundays with their own families. Their hours on the job were exceedingly long, and their situation resembled nothing so much as that of the worker on the factory floor or in the office in our own industrial

era.[18] But when all is said, the journey to work, the lonely
lodger paying his rent out of a factory wage or office salary,
are the distinguishing marks of our society, not of theirs.

The level of activity in agriculture is fundamentally
rhythmic, and its labour demands inevitably vary with the
time of the year, the weather in the week, as well as with the
prices of its products on the market. To work the land at all,
especially as we have already hinted with the climate and
geology of England, provision had to be made for a pool of
labour, which the farming family could use or not as the
farmer himself should decide. The manner in which this
economic necessity was provided for shows how well the
traditional, patriarchal structure of society could be adapted
to meet the needs of a particular economy. It has to be traced
in the life stories of the men and the women who lived in the
villages and worked the land, or who pursued those occupations which were settled in the countryside, and were as much
a part of its life as what went on in the stables and the barns.
Let us begin with the life cycle of a poor inhabitant of an
English village.

A boy, or a girl, born in a cottage, would leave home for
service at any time after the age of ten. A servant-in-hus-
bandry, as he might be called if he were a boy, would usually
stay in the position of servant, though very rarely in the same
household, until he or she got married. Marriage, when and if
it came, would quite often take place with another servant.
All this while, and it might be twelve, fifteen or even twenty
years, the servant would be kept by the succession of employers in whose houses he dwelt. He was in no danger of
poverty or hunger, even if the small landholder with whom he
lived could be very badly placed. 'His landlord's horses',
wrote a contemporary of the lowly husbandman, 'lie in finer
houses, than he, and his meanest servant wears a cloth beyond
him.' But the husbandman had his own servant, nevertheless,
for when he said family prayers after a day's exhausting toil
'the wife is sleeping in one corner, the child in another, the
servant in a third'.[19]

Poverty awaited the husbandman's servant when he got
married, and went himself to live in just such a labourer's
cottage as the one in which he had been born. Whoever had
been his former master, the labourer, late servant in husbandry, would be liable to fall into want directly his wife

began to have children and he lost the earnings of his companion. Once he found himself outside the farming household
his living had to come from his wages, and he, with every
member of his family, was subject for his labour to the local
vagaries in the market. Day-labourer was now his full description, for he earned what money came his way by contracting
for work a day at a time with the gentlemen, yeomen and
husbandmen of his village. This was a source of the variable
casual labour needed to keep agriculture going, and the poor
cottager could expect mainly seasonal employment at a wage
fixed, as indeed his wage as a servant had been fixed, by the
justices of the peace. Two forms of wage were laid out in the
published tables, with and without meat and drink. The day-
labourer visiting a farm for his work could claim his place at
the table along with the servants living in; it might be said
that he was made a member of the working family for that day
by breaking bread with the permanent members. It was almost
a sacramental matter.

But his own casual earnings were not the only fund on which
the labourer had to live. There was the produce of the little
plot of land lying round his cottage to begin with, if he had
such a thing. Elizabeth's government had decreed that it
should be four acres in size, though this cannot have been
anything like a general rule. Then there were the pennies
thrown to his children for bird scaring, or catching vermin, or
minding sheep – the little boy blue who burst into tears in the
nursery rhyme might easily have been of nursery age. But
above all, there were the earnings of his wife and the whole of
his little family at 'industrial' occupations.[20] A little family
because every grown child would have to leave, and because
death came quickly. It was the cottagers of England who
carried on the great woollen industry of England, spinning the
yarn which the capitalist clothiers brought to their doors.
Industry, in fact, kept the poor alive in the England of our
ancestors, and the problem of poverty in their own opinion
could only have been solved by the spread of industrial activity.

The men and women whose livelihood came from crafts,
agricultural and industrial, lived under the same system of
servanthood until marriage. So indeed did the merchants and
the shopkeepers. Not all households took part in the interchange all the time. At any moment a quarter or a third of the
households of a community would contain servants, and a

similar proportion would have children absent from home and
in service. The households which remained would at that point
in time be unaffected by the system of service, but many of
them, perhaps most, would at other stages of their development either yield up or take in servants. This is the sense in
which it could be said that service was practically a universal
characteristic of pre-industrial English society. Because so
many of those who became servants were between the age of
sexual maturity and the age of marriage we have come to call
them life-cycle servants. We now know that the number of
servants went up when marriage age went up in the later
seventeenth century.

Industry at this time was carried on not only by individual
productive units, like the bakery in London, but by the
'putting-out' system, in which several households were set on
work by one middleman, the clothier-capitalist we have referred to. Much of it was done in the spare time of the farming
population, not simply by the labourers, but by the farmers
and their families as well, the simpler operations, that is to
say, the sorting and carding and spinning of the wool. But the
weaving, the dyeing and dressing of the cloth was usually the
work of families of weavers, shearmen or dyers who did
nothing else for nine months of the year. If they worked on
the land of the villages where they lived it was only in harvest-
time, from late June, when the haymaking began, till late
September when the last of the wheat or the barley would be
brought home.

Hence it came about that the English village contained not
simply the husbandmen, the labourers and their families, with
the smith, the ploughwright, the miller and the men who plied
the agricultural trades, but textile workers too. In the Midlands there were nailers and miners, and everywhere everyone
might also work on the land during the crisis of harvest-time.

Such are the rough outlines of the system whereby the unity
if not the full economic independence of the household was
preserved, yet each was made to collaborate with other households in the working of the land, and in the production of
manufactures. Capitalism, we must notice, was a conspicuous
feature of the system, that store of wealth and raw materials
in the hands of the clothier which made it possible for him to
give work to the villagers and yet not move them from the
village. That this was a form of exploitation has been amply

demonstrated by recent students of this system, which has been renamed proto-industrial to distinguish it from factory production. Its possible effects on family life will concern us in due course. In the world we have lost, it can still be said, however, industry and agriculture lived together in some sort of symmetry, and the unity of the family was in no way in jeopardy.

> The bourgeoisie, wherever it has got the upper hand, has put an end to all feudal, patriarchal, idyllic relations. It has pitilessly torn asunder the motley feudal ties that bound man to his *natural superiors*, and has left remaining no other nexus between man and man than naked self-interest, than callous *cash-payment*. It has drowned the most heavenly ecstasies of religious fervour, of chivalrous enthusiasm, of philistine sentimentalism, in the icy water of egotistical calculation. It has resolved personal worth into exchange value, and in place of the numberless indefeasible chartered freedoms, has set up that single, unconscionable freedom – Free Trade. In one word, for exploitation veiled by religious and political illusions, it has substituted naked, shameless, direct, brutal exploitation.
>
> The bourgeoisie has stripped of its halo every occupation hitherto honoured and looked up to with reverent awe. It has converted the physician, the lawyer, the priest, the poet, the man of science, into its paid wage-labourers.
>
> The bourgeoisie has torn away from the family its sentimental veil, and has reduced the family relation to a mere money-relation.

These were the fervent words used by the most penetrating of all observers of the world we have lost when they came to pronounce on its passing. The idyllic patriarchalism and the exploitation which Marx and Engels had in mind in this passage from the *Communist Manifesto*[21] written in 1848 is recognizable in the arrangements we have been discussing in this introductory chapter. And it was England which they had first and foremost in their minds. Ours was the society which first ventured into the industrial era, and English men and women were the first who had to try to find a home for themselves in a world where the working family, the producing household, seemed to have no place.

But Marx and the historians who have followed him were surely wrong to call this process by the simple name of the triumph of capitalism, the rise and victory of the bourgeoisie. The presence of capital, we have seen, was the very circumstance which made it possible in earlier times for the working family to preserve itself as a working unit both on the land and in the cities, linking together the scattered households of the workers in such a way that no one had to make the daily double journey from home to workshop, from suburb to office and factory. Capitalism, however defined, did not begin at the time when the working household was endangered by the beginnings of the factory system, and economic inequality was not the product of the social transformation which so quickly followed after. Though the enormous, insolent wealth of the new commercial and industrial fortunes emphasized the iniquity of the division between rich and poor, it is doubtful whether Victorian England was any worse in this respect than the England of the Tudors and the Stuarts. It was not the fact of capitalism alone, not simply the concentration of the means of production in the hands of the few and the reduction of the rest to a position of dependence, which opened wide the social gulf, though the writers of the eighteenth and nineteenth centuries give us ample evidence that this was observed and was resented – by the dispossessed peasantry in England especially. As important, it is suggested, indeed perhaps a more likely source for the feeling that there is a world which once we all possessed, a world now passed away, is the fact of the transformation ˉof the family life of everyone which industrialism brought with it.[22]

In the vague and difficult verbiage of our own generation, we can say that the removal of the economic functions from the patriarchal family at the point of industrialization created a mass society. It turned the people who worked into a mass of undifferentiated equals, working in a factory or scattered between the factories, the mines and the offices, bereft for ever of the feeling that work was a family affair, done within the household. Marxist historical sociology presents this as the growth of class consciousness amongst the proletariat, and this is an important historical truth. But because it belongs with the large-scale class model for all social change it can also be misleading, as we shall hope to show. Moreover it has tended to divert attention from the structural function of the family in the pre-industrial world, and has impeded a proper, informed contrast between our world and the lost world we have to analyse.

But this is not the only consequence of the failure to look realistically at the familial texture of society at the time of our ancestors, and Marxist historical convention is not the only source of the distortions. Historians have to talk all the time about nations, countries, the units of historical narrative, the arena of historical change. The logical difficulties of defining change in such a way that nations can change autonomously, like chemical compounds, are formidable by themselves. But the historian does not seem to have got even as far as this before he loses his realism. What does the word 'England' mean, for the year 1640, shall we say, the England of politics and political history, the England of the older textbooks?

Not every single person alive in the country in that year: no historian could possibly suppose such a thing. But only the recognition that people came not as individuals, but as families, families conceived of in the way we have described, makes it possible to begin to come closer to the facts. England was an association between the heads of such families, but an association largely confined to those who were literate, who had wealth and status, those, in fact, who belonged, with their families as part of them, to what we have already called the ruling minority. Almost no woman ever belonged to England as an individual, except it be a queen regnant – scarcely a woman in the ordinary sense – or a noble widow and heiress or two, a scattering of relicts of successful merchants and yeomen. No individual under the age of thirty was likely to be a member, except in the very highest reaches of society, and very few men who had never been married.

It is problematical how far the mature male heads of families amongst the mass can be counted as part of England for such historical purposes: in so far as they had a role at all, it was a negative rather than a positive one, a limitation on what the ruling minority could do rather than an independent source of action and of attitude. We shall return to the relationship between the gentry and the rest, and attempt to make a rough sketch of what the whole was like, though much will have to be left uncertain. It goes without saying, of course, that no one in a position of 'service' was an independent member of society, national or local, political or otherwise,

with the outstanding exception of 'The King's Servants' who
were the civil service. All those in life-cycle service, all women,
all unmarried persons were caught up, so to speak, 'subsumed'
is the ugly word we shall use, into the personalities of their
fathers and masters. 'Subsumption' was a very widespread
characteristic of traditional society and it could well be extended to cover the relationship between the great household
in a village community and the ring of smaller households
ranged around it, sited on the landlord's estate, engaged for
the most part in working his land. That same contemporary
whose words we have quoted on the husbandman and his
servants had this to say about the husbandman and his lordly
neighbour:

> A just fear and respect he must have for his landlord, or the
> gentleman his neighbour, because God hath placed them
> above him and he hath learnt that by the father he ought to
> honour [the reference here is to the Fifth Commandment,
> Honour thy Father . . .] is meant all his superiors.[23]

We can claim with confidence that anyone who uses the
word 'England' without remembering the existence of subsumption is scarcely using it with understanding. A very
considerable number of existent English individuals must be
looked upon as null, as having no function, not even as subsumed into units which did have a function. These were the
paupers, anyone who was in receipt of charity for his upkeep,
or who had ever been in such a position. This body was surely
as much a proletariat as ever there has been in the age of
industrialism. Growing in the sixteenth and seventeenth
centuries, a great mass by the year 1800, such persons had
nevertheless existed at all previous times.

Capitalism, then, is an incomplete description and historians' language is marked by many other incomplete descriptions too, of which their use of the names of countries is but
one example. The historical distortions which come about
from the uncritical use of 'capitalism', 'the rise of the
bourgeoisie', and so on, have arisen from an obliquity which
we can only now begin to correct. With the 'capitalism
changed the world' way of thinking goes a division of history
into the ancient, feudal and bourgeois eras or stages. But the
facts of the contrast which has to be drawn between the world

we have lost and the world we now inhabit tends to make all such divisions as these into subdivisions. The time has now come to divide our European past in a simpler way with industrialization as the point of critical change.

The word 'alienation' began its career as an attempt to describe the separation of the worker from his world of work. We need not accept all that this expression has come to convey in order to recognize that it does point to something vital to us all in relation to our past. Time was when the whole of life went forward in the family, in a circle of loved, familiar faces, known and fondled objects, all to human size. That time has gone for ever. It makes us very different from our ancestors.

A one-class society
Chapter 2

Social divisions and power relations amongst nobility, gentry, townsmen and peasants

---

A one-class society may appear at first sight to mean one where there is no inequality, because everyone belonged to the same class. But it has already been laid down that this cannot have been so in the pre-industrial world, at least in Europe. The *ancien régime*, as the historians call it, was marked by a very sharply delineated system of status, which drew firm distinctions between persons and made some superior, most inferior. There were various gradations, all authoritatively established and generally recognized. If class were simply a matter of social status, of the various degrees of respect in which men are held by their fellows, then it could not be said that the world we have lost was a one-class society. On the contrary, it would have to be described as a society with a considerable number of classes, as many as there were distinct steps in the graduated system of status.

But when the word 'class' is used, in conversation and by historians, it does not merely refer to status or to respect. The distribution of wealth and power is also at issue. This is obvious when the phrase 'class-conflict' appears. For it nearly always seems to imply the clash of groups of persons defending and enhancing not simply a common status but also interest and power. The emphasis is on the solidarity of classes as groups of persons which act in championship of their conflicting aims. Such classes have a further characteristic in ordinary usage: they are nation-wide.

It is in this sense that we shall claim that there was, in England at least, only one class in pre-industrial society. A distinction will be drawn between a status group, which is the number of people enjoying or enduring the same social status, and a class, which is a number of people banded together in the exercise of collective power, political and economic. The argument will be that there was a large number of status groups but only one body of persons capable of concerted action over the whole area of society, only one class in fact.

It is unfortunate that an introductory study of this character should have to be concerned with anything as difficult, contentious and technical as the question of class. It is unfortunate also that the only vocabulary which is open to us to discuss it should be that designed for nineteenth- and twentieth-century society. 'Status groups' and 'class' do not fit at all well as descriptions of sets of people belonging to Stuart England, and most of the rest of the terminology used by sociologists is inappropriate too. The word 'group' is misleading when coupled with status, because it conveys a solidarity, a readiness to act together, which is quite inappropriate. These expressions have implications belonging to rather different social structures.

But literary critics, even novelists, have talked about traditional England in these terms, as well as historians and sociologists. We cannot direct our attention to the everyday life of our ancestors and the scale on which they lived it out without any notion of the overall shape of their society, its macro-structure as it might be called, in contrast to its micro-structure where, as we have seen, the family was the key. The macro-structure of Stuart society moreover has become a subject of world-wide discussion because a good part of the contemporary world has to believe in a particular version of what is called 'the English Revolution' for political reasons. Class conflict in the age of Charles I and Cromwell is not simply a matter of social antiquarianism. In the self-proclaimed socialist states of the late twentieth century, from the USSR to Rumania, from China to many of the new African states and to Cuba, the dogma that the English Civil War and the English Revolution represent the first national victory of the bourgeoisie is a part of political belief, or of its historical legitimation. We shall consider the implications of this in Chapter 8.

There is a sense in which the phrase 'class-conflict' might be appropriate to pre-industrial society, even if it did contain only one class. For the conflict could be between those who were included within it and everyone else. Perhaps if the expression were always used in this very restricted sense, it would be acceptable as a rough description

of what went on. It is certainly no part of our purpose to deny
that conflict existed at this time. But historians have not in
fact used the phrase in such a restricted way, or in any very
closely defined fashion at all. When they have discussed rising
and falling classes they have obviously had in mind interaction
of a very different kind. Sometimes, perhaps not very often
because their language has been so vague, they have made the
precise error of confusing a status group with a class and have
proceeded as if status groups could rise, fall, conflict, be self-
conscious, have a policy. Let us leave these generalities for a
moment and look more closely at status symbols and systems
in our industrial society as well as in that of our ancestors.

We now inhabit a world wealthy on a scale quite unknown
before industrialization, and many of us are possessed of a
power and a consequence never known in earlier times. Our
society is therefore marked by an intense search after status
and after symbols to express it. The most important of those
symbols is a personal title, an addition to a man's name, pro-
claiming who he is, how much success he has had and how
much he ought to be respected. There is a whole study of the
part which titles and other less satisfactory and specific symbols of status have to play in our contemporary world and on
its social, economic, even its political stage. The difficult
problem for us in our day is to find out how status and its
symbols are to do their necessary psychological work unless
they belong to a recognizably coherent system. This used to
exist in pre-industrial times but change since then has been so
rapid and profound that it survives today only in a form so
attenuated that it can hardly fulfil its functions any longer.

The reasons for this are complex, but the most obvious is
that we want contradictory things – a system of status and
universal social equality. It is easy to illustrate the difficulties.
Some issues of relative social importance can still be settled
fairly simply; we can put a managing director, for example, on
a level with a lieutenant-colonel, though it begins to be a little
puzzling when we consider whether the executive secretary of
a professional society, say of electrical engineers, is in the same
category of status. When it comes to extremes, our status
system breaks down altogether. We have no intelligible
method for relating a world-ranking pop artist and a cardinal-
archbishop. We know that they are both influential people,
and must be treated with due deference, even though when it

comes to election time each should have only one vote and each must be equal with the other before the law, and equal to everyone else in such respects. Nevertheless we cannot relate them satisfactorily one to another.

We cannot weigh them up against each other, but even if we could we have no set of symbols universally recognized which could give even a rough expression of their relative importance. The pop-star can, and will, collect as many signs of superiority as possible, of an enormously variegated sort, but none of them help very much when we compare them to the traditional titles of the senior and successful cleric. For the symbolic superiority of a cardinal-archbishop belongs to an ordering which the master of the media of our day can never hope to share. This ordering is an inheritance from the world we have lost.

'Lost' may not be quite the proper word here, and for two reasons. One is that in some contemporary societies and for certain purposes, the status system of the traditional, pre-industrial world is still in use with all its necessary symbols: near imaginary use perhaps we ought to say, since the effectiveness of both the traditional status and its trappings are so much reduced. Just as the English still seem to want to live in the structures of the pre-industrial world, prizing the thatched cottage and the half-timbered house as the proper place for the proper Englishman to dwell in, so also do the British go on awarding the symbolic titles which belong to the status system of the world we have lost. We still recognize the titles inherited by our blue-blooded contemporaries from the world of our forefathers, and we still like to distinguish between the really ancient, really aristocratic family lines and the upstarts of recent preferment. We even go on creating knights and life peerages and calling entertainment tycoons, cricketers and jockeys 'My lord' or 'Sir'. We do so in spite of the fact that we no longer understand the system which once informed these honorifics and are uneasily aware that their distribution may not correspond to the true distribution of consequence in our society. This is typical of the way in which the world we have lost is in some sense still present with us, or at least of the difficulty we have in becoming conscious of its ghostly persistence, and so addressing ourselves to the problem of putting something else in its place.

But the second reason why the word 'lost' is somewhat

paradoxical when we talk of the system of status and its symbols in the pre-industrial world is that elsewhere it was not a case of losing but of rejecting. Titles of honour were deliberately obliterated, first in the United States, then in France and so successively in other European countries, at their 'revolutions'. Great Britain is one of a handful of countries which has not yet found it proper to abolish them by law. The subject of status and its symbols is, therefore, of particular interest to English historians. Here is something in our present which we know to affect the lives of everybody, since the hierarchy of status we preserve so meticulously is by no means confined to titles of nobility and marks of gentility, yet which can only be explained by reference to a past we have nearly forgotten. This is one of the ways in which our country, which was the first to be industrialized and to lose most of the economic institutions of traditional Europe, has nevertheless clung for longest and with most affection to little, unrelated fragments of the world we have lost.

We live, in England, among the material remains of a patriarchal society of peasants and craftsmen: those stately castles, spacious manor houses, splendid churches, farmsteads, cottages, mill-houses, bridges, all built for itself by the familial social order which is the subject of this essay. We only dimly understand what they were for, just as we only half recognize the original import of the names of our towns, or of some of the older streets within them. It is difficult to appreciate that Oxford was a particular site on the muddy banks of a widening Thames where cattle could be moved across because the water was shallow and the riverbed firm underfoot. Still less are we likely to recognize that the Haymarket in the West End of London was a wide street where fodder for horses could be bought, and for the numerous cows kept within the city. We find these things mildly interesting when they are pointed out to us, often quaint and picturesque, and always, if we are honest, a little puzzling too.

We are puzzled in exactly the same way when we try to decide whether to put 'Esq.' or 'Mr' on a letter. If we ask ourselves why we use these abbreviations at all, we find that we do not quite know. Yet these are the most common of all status symbols and we use them every day.

We call each other 'gentlemen' as well, although we have some difficulty in deciding what the word means. Defining 'gentleman' indeed, and disputing about the qualities which go to make one, is a favourite pastime of those who write impressionists' accounts of social history. The rest of us, if ever it occurs to us to decide, dismiss the expression as having by now no meaning at all. It can no longer be defined by contrast since everybody expects to be called a gentleman, and to be addressed in writing as 'esquire'. So it is not difficult to guess that the descriptions 'Mister' and 'Esquire' must once have implied that the person addressed was in fact a gentleman. But further than that we usually cannot go.

There could be no more vivid illustration of our dim and partial understanding of the pre-industrial world. In that society of peasants, craftsmen, labourers, husbandmen and a very few gentry and nobility, the word 'gentleman' meant something tangible, substantial enough, if uncertain in precise definition. It was a grade amongst other grades in a carefully graduated system of social status and had a critically important use.

The term gentleman marked the boundary at which the traditional social system divided up the population into two extremely unequal sections. About a twenty-fifth, at most a twentieth, of all the people alive in the England of the Tudors and the Stuarts, the last generations before the coming of industry, belonged to the gentry and to those above them in the social hierarchy. This tiny minority owned a third, or even up to a half of all the land in the country, and an even greater proportion of all the wealth. They wielded the power and made all the decisions, political, economic and social for the national whole. If you were not a gentleman, if you were not often or ordinarily called 'Master' by the commoner folk, or 'Your Worship'; if you, like nearly all the rest, had a Christian and a surname and nothing more; then you counted for little in the world outside your own household, and for almost nothing outside your small village community and its neighbourhood.

'Nothing' is too strong a word perhaps, and in every society, however constituted, even the smallest unit, the weakest influence, is of some account, has to be allowed for in the general social process. The plain Richard Hodgsons, Robert Boswells, Humphrey Eltons and John Burtons of the English villages, the labourers and husbandmen, the tailors, millers, drovers, watermen, masons, could become constables, parish clerks, churchwardens, ale-conners, even overseers of the poor.

They had something of a public life, within the tiny boundaries of the village, and this might give them a minor consequence in the surrounding villages. If they happened to be technically qualified, they might cast a vote at an election.

But in none of these capacities did their opinion matter very much, even in the last. They brought no personal weight to the modest offices which they could hold. As individuals they had no instituted, recognized power over other individuals, always excepting once again those subsumed within their families. Directly they acquired such power, whether by the making or the inheriting of wealth, or by the painful acquisition of a little learning, then they became 'worshipful' by that very fact. Then and then only could they know anything substantial of the world, which meant everything which went on outside their own localities, everything rather which was inter-local, affecting more communities and localities than one.

To exercise power, then, to be free of the society of England, to count at all as an active agent in the record we call histori- cal, you had to have the status of a gentleman. When you came to die you had to hold one of those exceptional names in a parish register which bore a prefix or a suffix; about one name in fifteen or twenty seems to have been the average. The commonest addition to a name to be read in a register is 'Mr', for the word 'Master', and 'Mrs', for the word 'Mistress', applied to the maidens as well as the wives and widows. 'Gent.' and 'Esq.' are rare amongst the additions, as is the word 'Dame', the designation of their wives, and 'Knight' and 'Baronet' are, of course, much rarer still. The reader with the whole population in his mind, as distinct from the reader with an eye only for the interesting and attractive, will, of course, occasionally come across the titles 'Lord' or 'Lady', and the ceremonious phrase 'The Right Honourable the . . .' which was often used to introduce them. But the higher titles of nobility are absent for all practical purposes when the whole population is under review. They are rather like the four- leaved clover to the collector of flowers, or perhaps the winning ticket numbers in a national lottery; one knows they must exist because the system demands it, but one never sees them. Nevertheless, page after page, year after year, decade after decade in the books recording, conscientiously, the burials in an ordinary English parish church will show some title or other for 3 per cent, 5 per cent or at most 10 per cent of the names, never very much more unless the parish had extraordinarily aristocratic or even royal connections. All the rest of the entries are for simple names and surnames.

We should not exaggerate the precision with which our ancestors ascribed status, and the titles or descriptions which went with status, to each other. No doubt the clerks and parsons wrote down 'gentleman' in the parish register against many a name which in other documents would be marked 'yeoman', or left without a suffix. A rigorous analysis of all the recorded descriptions of all the individuals who ever held office in the county of Cheshire in the later sixteenth and earlier seventeenth centuries reveals a marked inconsistency in the use of titles for the same individual. Such inconsistency was at its most pronounced at the boundary between what is here termed the gentry, or the gentry and above, and the rest of the society. This is perhaps what we should expect, but it implies that there must have been quite a considerable intermediate area of uncertain status between the élite and the mass. It implies also that the people of the time did not always bother with their honorifics, even though their honorific hierarchy was so carefully specified at law and in the writings of that day. We must be on our guard against the authors of those writings, some of them professionals in the matter, heralds that is to say, and all of whom must be supposed to have possessed a highly developed sense of rank and grade, conveying an impression of too much clarity and rigidity in the status system.[1]

However this may be, the concept of gentry in that social structure conveyed a distinction which could be of great importance. Here was an economy conspicuously lacking in those devices for the saving of exertion which are so marked a feature of our own everyday life. The simplest operation needed effort; drawing the water from the well, striking steel on flint to catch the tinder alight, cutting goose-feather quills to make a pen, they all took time, trouble and energy. The working of the land, the labour in the craftsmen's shop, were infinitely taxing. The surviving peasantry in western Europe still shock us with their worn hands and faces, their immeasurable fatigue. Yet the primary characteristic of the gentleman was that he never worked with his hands on necessary, as opposed to leisurely, activities.

The simple fact of leisure dividing off this little society of the privileged – it had to be little at a time when the general resources were so small – is the first step in comprehending the attitude of our forefathers to rank and status. The law of the land laid it down how long common men should work and how little they should rest:

> And be it further enacted by the authority aforesaid, That all artificers and labourers being hired for wages by the day or week shall, betwixt the midst of the months of March and September, be and continue at their work, at or before five of the clock in the morning, and continue at work, and not depart, until between seven and eight of the clock at night (except it be in the time of breakfast, dinner or drinking, the which times at most shall not exceed two and a half hours in a day, that is to say, at every drinking one half-hour, for his dinner, one hour, and for his sleep, when he is allowed to sleep, the which is from the midst of May, to the midst of August, half an hour at the most, and at every breakfast one half-hour). And all the said artificers and labourers, between the midst of September, and the midst of March, shall be and continue at their work from the spring of the day in the morning, until the night of the same day, except it be in time afore appointed to breakfast and dinner.

This was laid down in 1563 in the famous Elizabethan Statute of Artificers,[2] as it is usually called, which made compulsory by law the common practice of the time. At the county assizes, the judges had to inquire whether there were workers who 'do not continue from Five of the Clock in the Morning till Seven at Night in the Summer and from Seven till five in the Winter'.[3] No mention of sleeping-time here, even in the heat of the harvest. Still Breughel's sleeping harvester was an ordinary working man acting on his rights; he was no visionary, no drowsy peasant drunkard.

Although those in work for wages lived a life of rough, incessant toil – no Saturday afternoons, none even of the safeguards of the early Factory Acts – not all the common people were caught up in productive work. This is outstandingly evident from Gregory King's famous table of the structure of English society, reproduced on pages 32–3. It was drawn up in the 1690s and applied to the year 1688. It divides up the population of the country in such a way as to show that more than half the people when alive were to some degree dependent – 'Decreasing the Wealth of the Kingdom' is the expression appearing in King's *General Account*.[4]

King's calculation was the only one ever worked out by a contemporary for a European society in wholly pre-industrial times. As with everything else which he committed himself to, however, it has to be considered as part of a traditionalist, indeed something like a reactionary, general argument, and his figures treated accordingly. Gregory King was a herald; Rouge Dragon Pursuivant-at-Arms from 1677 onwards.

It is now supposed that the reason why so large a proportion of the population could not wholly support itself was because there was not enough productive work to do.[5] The more impressionistic writers in Gregory King's time and before it did not hesitate to call everyone below a certain level by insulting names: the 'rascal', or 'rascality', the 'proletarii'. In the 1560s Sir Thomas Smith, a respected lawyer, spoke his mind in this way, and his is an instructive comment on the common people of England in their relation with their social superiors.

For this observer, English society had a fourfold division:

1. 'The first part of the Gentlemen of England called *Nobilitas Major*.' This is the nobility, or aristocracy proper.
2. 'The second sort of Gentlemen called *Nobilitas Minor*.' This is the gentry and Smith further divides it into Knights, Esquires and gentlemen.
3. 'Citizens, Burgesses and Yeomen.'
4. 'The fourth sort of men which do not rule.'

We shall concern ourselves in due course with the relationship between these four divisions. Our present interest is in Smith's detailed description of the lowest of them. These are his words:

> The fourth sort or class amongst us is of those which the old Romans called *capite sensu proletarii* or *operarii*, day labourers, poor husbandmen, yea merchants or retailers which have no free land, copyholders, and all artificers, as tailors, shoemakers, carpenters, brick-makers, brick-layers, etc. These have no voice nor authority in our commonwealth and no account is made of them, but only to be ruled and not to rule other, and yet they be not altogether neglected. For in cities and corporate towns, for default of yeomen,

Table 1: *Gregory King's 'Scheme of the income & expence of*

Number of families	Ranks, degrees, titles and qualifications	Heads per family	Number of persons
160	Temporal Lords	40	6,400
26	Spiritual Lords	20	520
800	Baronets	16	12,800
600	Knights	13	7,800
3,000	Esquires	10	30,000
12,000	Gentlemen	8	96,000
5,000	Persons in greater Offices and Places	8	40,000
5,000	Persons in lesser Offices and Places	6	30,000
2,000	Eminent Merchants and Traders by Sea	8	16,000
8,000	Lesser Merchants and Traders by Sea	6	48,000
10,000	Persons in the Law	7	70,000
2,000	Eminent Clergy-men	6	12,000
8,000	Lesser Clergy-men	5	40,000
40,000	Freeholders of the better sort	7	280,000
120,000	Freeholders of the lesser sort	$5\frac{1}{2}$	660,000
150,000	Farmers	5	750,000
15,000	Persons in Liberal Arts and Sciences	5	75,000
50,000	Shopkeepers and Tradesmen	$4\frac{1}{2}$	225,000
60,000	Artizans and Handicrafts	4	240,000
5,000	Naval Officers	4	20,000
4,000	Military Officers	4	16,000
500,586		$5\frac{1}{3}$	2,675,520
50,000	Common Seamen	3	150,000
364,000	Labouring People and Out Servants	$3\frac{1}{2}$	1,275,000
400,000	Cottagers and Paupers	$3\frac{1}{4}$	1,300,000
35,000	Common Soldiers	2	70,000
849,000		$3\frac{1}{4}$	2,795,000
	Vagrants; as Gipsies, Thieves, Beggars, &c.		30,000
	So the general Account is		
500,586	Increasing the Wealth of the Kingdom	$5\frac{1}{3}$	2,675,520
849,000	Decreasing the Wealth of the Kingdom	$3\frac{1}{4}$	2,825,000
1,349,586	Neat Totals	$4\frac{1}{13}$	5,500,520

the several families of England' calculated for the year 1688*

Yearly income per family		Yearly income in general	Yearly income per head			Yearly expense per head			Yearly increase per head			Yearly increase in general
£	s.	£	£	s.	d.	£	s.	d.	£	s.	d.	£
3,200		512,000	80	0	0	70	0	0	10	0	0	64,000
1,300		33,800	65	0	0	45	0	0	20	0	0	10,400
800		704,000	55	0	0	49	0	0	6	0	0	76,800
650		390,000	50	0	0	45	0	0	5	0	0	39,000
450		1,200,000	45	0	0	41	0	0	4	0	0	120,000
280		2,880,000	35	0	0	32	0	0	3	0	0	288,000
240		1,200,000	30	0	0	26	0	0	4	0	0	160,000
120		600,000	20	0	0	17	0	0	3	0	0	90,000
400		800,000	50	0	0	37	0	0	13	0	0	208,000
198		1,600,000	33	0	0	27	0	0	6	0	0	288,000
154		1,540,000	22	0	0	18	0	0	4	0	0	280,000
72		144,000	12	0	0	10	0	0	2	0	0	24,000
50		400,000	10	0	0	9	4	0	0	16	0	32,000
91		3,640,000	13	0	0	11	15	0	1	5	0	350,000
55		6,600,000	10	0	0	9	10	0	0	10	0	330,000
42	10	6,375,000	8	10	0	8	5	0	0	5	0	187,500
60		900,000	12	0	0	11	0	0	1	0	0	75,000
45		2,250,000	10	0	0	9	0	0	1	0	0	225,000
38		2,280,000	9	10	0	9	0	0	0	10	0	120,000
80		400,000	20	0	0	18	0	0	2	0	0	40,000
60		240,000	15	0	0	14	0	0	1	0	0	16,000
68	18	34,488,800	12	18	0	11	15	4	1	2	8	3,023,700
								Decrease				_Decrease_
20		1,000,000	7	0	0	7	10	0	0	10	0	75,000
15		5,460,000	4	10	0	4	12	0	0	2	0	127,500
6	10	2,000,000	2	0	0	2	5	0	0	5	0	325,000
14		490,000	7	0	0	7	10	0	0	10	0	35,000
10	10	8,950,000	3	5	0	3	9	0	0	4	0	562,500
		60,000	2	0	0	4	0	0	2	0	0	60,000
68	18	34,488,800	12	18	0	11	15	4	1	2	8	3,023,700
10	10	9,010,000	3	3	0	3	7	6	0	4	6	622,500
32	5	43,491,800	7	18	0	7	9	3	0	8	9	2,401,200

* See note 4 of Chapter 2.

inquests and juries are impanelled of such manner of people.
And in villages they are commonly made churchwardens,
aleconners, and many times constables, which office touch-
eth more the commonwealth.[6]

Even though Smith was prepared to use the word '*proletarii*'
of these people, the old Roman expression meaning those able
to produce nothing but offspring, *proles*, as their contribution
to society, it does not appear that this description includes the
humblest of all. These 'low and base persons', as Smith goes
on to call them, may not have made up the complete whole of
the majority of the population which was 'decreasing the
wealth of the kingdom' and some of them may have been
increasers. The really large groups of lowly persons are not
mentioned by Smith. Though King's 'labouring people'
appear, his 'cottagers and paupers' are not mentioned at all.
The truly poor, the begging poor, had no craft and could never
have become constables or ale-conners, as could the proletariat
of Sir Thomas Smith. They were truly nobodies: *gens de néant*,
the French called them.

Begging was universal, as it is today in some of the countries
of Asia; beggars at the door, outside the churches, in the
market-places and wandering along the roads. Men sometimes
took fright at their numbers, especially in Tudor times, and
the savage laws against sturdy vagabonds have become notorious in the textbooks. Everyone knows that the poor law made
each parish responsible for its own indigent persons, and that,
when a pauper could be identified as from another community,
he or she was sent along the highway from place to place until
the place of settlement was reached.

Yet crowds of destitute people were not typical of poverty
in the old world in quite the way that queues of unemployed
are typical of industrial poverty. The trouble then, as we have
hinted, was not so much unemployment as under-employ-
ment, as it is now called, and once more the comparison is
with the countries of Asia in our own century. Too many members of a family were half-busied about an inadequate plot of
infertile land; not enough work could be found for the women
and children to do round the cottage fire, in some districts
none at all, for there was no rural industry in them. Everywhere work of all kinds varied alarmingly with the state of
the weather and of trade, so that hunger was not very far

away, as we shall see. Starvation itself, we perhaps ought to add at once, cannot be shown to have been an omnipresent menace to the poor in Stuart times.

No one could call a life of this sort a life of leisure, even if it was not a life of ceaseless toil for everybody, and leisure as has been said was a mark of the gentleman. The most celebrated Elizabethan definition of a gentleman comes from Harrison's *Description of England,* published in 1577. Besides the sons of gentlemen already recognized, he says:

> Whosoever studieth the laws of this realm, who so abideth in the university giving his mind to his books, or professeth physic [that is medicine of course] and the liberal sciences, or beside his service in the room of captain in the wars, or good counsell given at home, whereby his common-wealth is benefitted, can live without manual labour, and thereto is able and will bear the port, charge and countenance of a gentleman, he shall for money have a coat and arms [coat of arms etc.] bestowed upon him by the heralds (who in the charter of the same do of custom pretend antiquity, service and many gay things) and thereunto being made so good cheap, be called master, which is the title that men give to esquires and gentlemen, and reputed for a gentleman ever after.[7]

Any professional man, any university graduate, any officer in the royal forces, therefore, was a gentleman in England by that very fact, and the business of coats of arms, ancestry and public service could all be assumed; the heralds who were responsible would make it all up if required. Harrison is a little obscure when it comes to the matter of the money necessary to attain gentility, but popular opinion was much more straightforward: 'In England gentry is but ancient riches.' The historian is always coming across families which obey this simple rule. If a family had the money for long enough – just over one succession was generally sufficient – it graduated to the gentry. By money here is meant means sufficient to enable a family to live without doing manual work.

Gentility and its ranks were real enough to those who worked out taxation systems. The Poll Tax, imposed in 1660 for the first time, was graduated according to rank: a really ordinary person paid only 6*d.* a year, but a gentleman paid £5, an esquire paid £10, a knight £20, a baronet £30, a baron paid £40 and his heir £30, a viscount £50 (£35), an earl £60 (£40) and a duke £100 (£60).[8] The time when you could be legally compelled to dress according to your rank was passing, though private correspondence is full of resentment at common people wearing the clothes reserved to the socially superior. But the distinction between those who were and those who were not within the gentry was still of overriding importance.

The system of status does not seem to have prevented social mobility, however. The scale of this movement, we shall see in Chapter 10, may have been small and it undoubtedly varied from time to time. But it went on in both directions, downwards as well as upwards, and demography was one of the reasons why this had to happen. In fact rather more people may have descended than ascended in society. Social mobility is always most conspicuous at the frontiers, so to speak, and in traditional society this meant at the crucial divide between the minority which ruled and the mass which did not rule. The fact that this movement was constantly happening was one of the circumstances which made it possible for the single ruling group to maintain its supremacy and to adapt its membership to changing conditions.

In spite of the elaborate arrangements to maintain the community of the privileged in their position, easier to ensure in that agrarian society than it is in our own industrial society, interchange due to economic influences could not be prevented, and presumably happened most often at times of pronounced economic development. It is possible therefore that periods of particularly intense economic change might have been marked by unusually pronounced social mobility, and this might conceivably have led to unrest and conflict, particularly if there was any blockage, so to speak, any threat of resistance from those unwilling to be replaced.

But if what is called the English Revolution was like this, then it was very different from a conflict of classes as that term has ordinarily been used. It leaves little room for the rise of a class, the capitalist or middle class as a group of persons. Even some of those who wish to retain a modified version of the rise-of-a-capitalist-class view of social development in pre-industrial times have begun to recognize that the capitalists as a group of persons capable of coming into conflict with other groups of persons are unlikely ever to be identified in England under pre-industrial conditions. Rather it is now supposed that the whole of the English gentry, in our own terminology the whole of the ruling segment, was imbued with bourgeois values by the middle years of the seventeenth century.[9] According to this view the world of gentleman, parson, peasant, craftsman and pauper was already a 'fully possessive market society', where conflict must presumably have been due to the internal contradictions of capitalism rather than to the clash of bourgeoisie and aristocrats. If this was so, the rivalries and clashes between Englishmen in Stuart and even Tudor times, intellectual, political and military, can hardly have been of an inter-class character. They must have gone on within the one class.

Social change and development in the pre-industrial world need not, therefore, be thought of in terms of classes which rise, conflict and fall.[10] It perhaps ought to be emphasized once again that this does not mean that opposition of economic interest was absent from that society. No sharper clash of interest, material, economic or even biological, can be easily imagined than that between those with and those without access to the land or the means to buy food when scarcity raised prices. In an agrarian economy not far removed from the subsistence level in some areas and in some periods, this might have meant that when harvests were bad some men could count on surviving, whilst others, the landless, and those with few resources could not be so sure. But this confrontation of class interest in the sense that whole unorganized masses of persons were on the one side and a few, concerted persons were on the other, is very different from an overt or covert collision between the rising bourgeoisie on the one hand and the falling feudality on the other.

The graduated ladder from top to bottom of the social scale has already been referred to as the status system. Status depended for the most part on the position a man occupied on that ladder, though there was some admixture of status which arose from his actual function in society and his personal achievement. Status, that is to say, did not come exclusively from the title a man had inherited, or had conferred on him with a greater or lesser degree of consistency by his fellows. Nearly all the height of the social ladder was to be found within the ruling minority, within that part of the whole society which contained the nobility and the gentry, though

Table 2: *Chart of rank and status – Stuart England*

	Grade	Title	Form of address	Status name	Occupational name
G E N T R Y — *Nobilitas Major* (Greater Nobility) LORDS AND LADIES	1. Duke, Archbishop 2. Marquess 3. Earl 4. Viscount 5. Baron, Bishop	Lord, Lady	The Right Honourable The Honourable The Lord The Lady My Lord My Lady Your Grace (for Grade 1) Your Lordship Your Ladyship, etc.	Noble-man	None
Nobilitas Minor (Lesser Nobility) GENTLEMEN	6. Baronet 7. Knight 8. Esquire 9. Gentleman	Sir Dame*† Mr ‡Mrs	The Worshipful, Your Worship, etc.	Gentle-man	[*Professions*] Army Officer, Doctor of Medicine, Doctor of Law, Merchant, etc.
	Clergyman		[†Sir]		[Your Reverence]
	10. Yeoman 11. Husbandman	†Goodman †Goodwife (Goody)	†Worthy Yeoman		Husband-man
	12. Craftsman / Tradesman / Artificer	None	None	Name and Surname only	Name of Craft (Carpenter, etc.)
	13. Labourer				Labourer
	14. Cottager / Pauper				None

* Often called 'Lady' by courtesy.
† Occasional, obsolescent usage.
‡ For unmarried as well as married women.

General note to scheme of ranks

The common tendency for a person to be called by a rather higher title than the one to which he was strictly entitled was already present. For example the wives of Knights and Baronets were called 'Lady' rather than 'Dame'. Usage was stricter amongst the nobility and also somewhat complicated.

Any nobleman might be called 'Lord' (Lord Norfolk, Lord Shaftesbury), but in the higher ranks the actual grade was almost always specified on each occasion (the Duke of Norfolk, the Earl of Shaftesbury). Most noblemen had titles of honour different from their family names (Anthony Ashley Cooper, Earl of Shaftesbury). Occasionally however the family and the title were identical (Ralph Montagu, Duke of Montagu). Some courtesy titles were in use for their heirs: more usually, the heirs to noble titles would be called 'Lord' followed by the family name, but the brothers and sisters of heirs of noble titles were often called plain 'Mr' or 'Mrs'. They were all entitled of course to the general designation 'Honourable' as an additional form of address. The grandsons of holders of titles were quite usually called 'Mr' without the 'Honourable' and so came to be recognized as plain gentry. Usage below the line of gentry, as is emphasized in the text, was very much more uncertain because what status there was was associated with occupation.

The clerical equivalents given above represent usage, but status was uncertain and some clerics (especially those without benefices) were often regarded as below the line of gentry. The status name applied to all members of a family, that is to say the wife and children of a nobleman, were all noble, and of a knight, all gentle. In the case of the clergy, wives and children were always in an equivocal position. There was a tendency for the occupational name of a professional man to be associated with his status name, so that the son of a merchant might be described as a merchant. Below the gentry line this tendency seems to have taken the form of associating the children with the status below that of the head of the family, so that a yeoman's sons would call themselves husbandmen and husbandmen's sons labourers.

---

the men below that line did share to some extent in the status system. I have tried to represent the facts in Table 2 on page 38, drawing the dividing line below Gentleman.

At the very top of the society came the monarchy, but it was related to the whole in many other ways than that of status and its very special position is not our present concern. Under the Throne came the nobility, two hundred families, a thousand people or so, in a population of some five and a half million – by 1688 in Gregory King's reckoning (see Table 1 on page 32). Yet most of the gradations in the system of honour were contained within this little gilded network; his Grace the Duke (or the Archbishop), the Marquis, the Earl, the Viscount, and lowest of all, his Lordship the Baron (or the Bishop). These were the *nobilitas major* of Sir Thomas Smith, but described by him as belonging to the gentlemen of England all the same.[11] Every step in the honorific grading was meticulously marked and every noble family strove to mount the next one upwards of the glittering steps. Difference in wealth sometimes made the distinctions unrealistic, for even in Stuart times a viscount on the fertile plains of southern England might outweigh a marquis on the northern moors. But it could not obliterate them.

It cannot be said that the whole society of the nobility ever acted as a group; their identification with the gentry as a whole was reality, not a piece of legal fancy. We now know for certain that a majority of all marriages made by the English nobility from the sixteenth century until the twentieth were made with commoners, mainly with the gentry.[12] This may mark off our English titled families from their continental counterparts, and hierarchy was notoriously less rigid in England than elsewhere in western Europe.

But our nobility had a remarkable privilege of their own nevertheless which gave them a defined, active institution and consolidated political power. They had the House of Lords. It may seem extraordinary to assert that in spite of this the peerage in England was for all purposes except the details of their status at one with the rest of the ruling segment, the gentry as a whole, yet this was undoubtedly the case. To look on the peerage as a class apart, to see it simply as an element surviving from the feudal age, resenting, and in rivalry with, the humbler members of the privileged order, would be a serious misunderstanding of the society and of what happened.

Every system of this type must have its rewards, its goals, its upper reaches, otherwise it will not work. This, then, was the important function of the English peerage, to provide the topmost placements in a society of privileged persons all of whom were gentry and all of whom were members of a different order from the whole mass of the people. The language of 'The Estates of the Realm', which made of the Lords Spiritual, the Lords Temporal and the Commons the constituent parts of Parliament, might seem to imply that the function of nobility was much more extensive than this. It is true that in the highly conventional activity of politics, both at the centre of society round the throne and in the localities, titles of nobility had considerable political potential and did not operate simply as the final goal of political success. It is true also that the traditional division of Parliament was of structural importance to its workings and did give the nobles an additional purchase over political decisions because they had their own House.

But the Estates of the Realm never had corresponded at all closely to divisions in English society as a whole and the general history of Parliaments might make a fascinating study in the complicated relationships between social structures and the political systems which they generate. In seventeenth-century England the whole arrangement was recognized as archaic and there was even some confusion about what the Estates were, for the Crown rather than the Lords Spiritual was already being referred to as one of them. What might seem to us the most critical division of all, that between members for the boroughs and members for the counties, was passed over and all members of the Lower House referred to as the Commons. Whatever distinction historians of our own day have seen between the bourgeoisie of the urban areas and the gentry of the countryside, it was decidedly not reflected in the constitution of the Estates. It was less so in Stuart times in fact than it had been earlier, for the gentry had taken over the representation of the boroughs from their retained, wage-receiving MPs by the year 1700. Andrew Marvell, poet and (what was typical of his age) politico as well, is traditionally pointed out as the last Member of Parliament who received his pay, for representing the borough of Kingston-upon-Hull, until his death in 1678. It is wholly confusing to think, as sociologists tend to do, of class systems of subsequent societies, including our own, as descended in any simple way from the medieval Estates of the Realm.

During the Commonwealth, at the height of what is usually called the English Revolution, the House of Lords was abolished. It is a remarkable fact that the peers as a status group were entirely unaffected by the fundamental change in the political constitution of the country. Those who did not go into exile with the royalists went on living in their magnificent seats, enjoying their social and apparently all their other privileges, even some of their political eminence as individuals. Cromwell's government continued to address them by their titles and ended by attempting to create its own class of peers. This is eloquent testimony to the apparently indispensable function of the English peerage in the traditional English social structure and to the extent to which their order existed independently of the House of Lords itself. Though as a society, as a political group, the peers did not exist under Cromwell, within a century, by the middle of the Hanoverian

Age, the English nobility had come to make up a palpable
block of political power. These vicissitudes seem to me to
indicate that none of the events which occurred to those
occupying positions of the highest social status at this time,
did much to threaten the solidarity of the ruling minority as
a whole, that consolidated block of 'gentlemen', including the
nobility, who virtually constituted English political society.[13]

It always seems to have been true that the gap between
those who were within and those who were outside the ruling
group was greater than the gap between any two orders
within the ruling group itself. The differences between say a
baronet and an ordinary baron (the lowest type of lord), who
stood above the baronet in the status system, were always
smaller in number and degree than the differences between
the man who was, and he who was not, often or usually referred to as a gentleman.[14]

Baronet, knight, esquire, gentleman – these were the grades
below the peerage in Tudor and Stuart times, Smith's *Nobilitas
Minor*. All these titles, like the titles of nobility, were honorifics only, not descriptions of function. But we have seen that
Harrison does talk of a man's function as qualifying him for
gentle status, since a physician, a don, a military officer were
gentlemen, he thought, by virtue of doing what they did. An
Act of Parliament passed in 1694,[15] which goes into status to a
degree of minuteness which has to be read to be believed, is
even more straightforward about who was and who was not a
gentleman. It imposed a tax to be collected 'upon burial of
every Gentleman or reputed Gentleman, or owning or writing
himself such'. Phrases of this sort are quite common in legal
discussion of the crucial difference between those who belonged
to the privileged and ruling minority. In fact a man's reputation as a gentleman depended to a considerable degree on what
he did, when it was not obvious to all who knew him that he
had been born to that status. The Acts imposing the Poll Tax
list a whole range of holders of legal, ecclesiastical and even
commercial offices as being liable to taxation at levels corresponding to grades of the nobility and gentry. The equivalent
grades were usually rather modest ones, except for certain
lucrative legal offices.[16]

Such provisions as these amount to an overt, legal recognition of movement into the gentry, even deliberate provision
for ensuring that anyone making money or attaining any form

of social consequence should succeed to gentle status. Let us
pursue the hierarchy of status below the critical divide, and
into the largely undifferentiated mass of ordinary people.
Before we do so we may notice that the lowest grades of gentry
enormously outnumbered the titled grades. With less than 200
noble families in his table (p. 32), it was reckoned by Gregory
King that there were in 1688 800 families of baronets and 600
of knights, but 3000 families of esquires and 12,000 of gentlemen. These figures may be too small, but it would be difficult
to make them add up to more than a third of the number of
those who must be reckoned to have composed the ruling
segment at that time, a third of the one in twenty we referred
to earlier. The other two-thirds must have been those with the
title 'master' ('Mr' on our letters), self-reputed or locally
recognized gentlemen rather than those living on landed
estates. This was what might be called the penumbra of the
privileged group and again will concern us when we come to
social mobility.

Status amongst the common people, the vast majority, went
with occupation, in so far as it was marked at all; it was a
matter of function, not description. The only status name as
such which men recognized below the line, so to speak, was the
name 'yeoman' (see Table 2 on p. 38). Even this was to some
extent a functional term, since a yeoman had to be a fairly
substantial owner (not in strictness a renter) of land which he
had to work himself, for he emphatically did not come under
the idleness rule which defined gentlemanliness. Alternatively,
and here the much greater vagueness of terms for these lower
statuses is already to be seen, such a man might be called a
freeholder, a greater freeholder (much more likely to have the
alternative title yeoman) or a lesser freeholder (probably a
freeholder without the vote, that is with less than 40s. a year
from his own land). Sometimes, during the final generations
of the old order, he might be called a farmer, and this is a
functional name altogether. It has survived as the only term
we now use for those occupied in agriculture.

'Yeoman' then, was the status name of the most successful
of those who worked the land. This was a name which became
sentimentalized very early, whilst the men who had held it
under the old order became farmers under the new. It is
interesting that there was a yeoman status even in the companies of craftsmen in the cities and that it should have come

below the status of master in those associations. The word
yeoman has survived in our vocabulary, whilst the functional
name based upon what we call farming, working the land, the
word 'husbandman', has disappeared. All yeomen were husbandmen, because they worked the land, but not all husbandmen were yeomen by any means, because most of them had
neither the qualifications nor the status. There was a very
special sense in which even a gentleman might sometimes
describe himself, in his letters, shall we say, as a husbandman.
For a gentleman had to direct work on his land, even if he was
not supposed to engage in the labour itself.

Husbandman, then, was an extremely common description
of men in the old world, because it was the description of what
so many of them were engaged in, tending the animals and
tilling the soil. Alongside of husbandmen came all the other
callings, the craftsmen. Husbandmen and craftsmen are given
no titles in our table and were addressed always by simple
name and surname, followed where necessary by their occupational name. The word 'worthy' would sometimes be used as
a sort of prefix to their names, though never in quite the way
in which 'worshipful' was associated with gentry. The prefix
worthy had a feminine form, Goody, a word which has come
down to us as a surname and in the nursery rhyme about
Goody Two Shoes. Yeomen would be called 'worthy' more
readily, and the occasional use of this word emphasizes the
very considerable variation which men called husbandmen or
craftsmen might show in their prosperity and importance.
There was an enormous difference between a draper in the
City of London engaged in large-scale cloth dealings and a
tailor or a blacksmith in a village, even if the draper was not
substantial enough to be regarded as worshipful and gentle.

'Mechanick' was the title often given to the meaner handicrafts: John Bunyan, the tinker, was thought of as a 'mechanick preacher'. The craftsmen in the towns must nearly always
have worked on a larger scale than those in the countryside,
but in town and in country the overriding impression of the
grade of craftsman was of its multifarious variety. Miller,
tailor, ploughwright, weaver, plumber, dyer, bricklayer,
carpenter, mason, tanner, innkeeper, all these are still familiar
words and many of them common surnames. Some of the
occupations of craftsmen which the historian finds have disappeared so completely from our memory that the ordinary

reader does not usually recognize them: there were the fletchers (arrow-makers), badgers (corn-dealers), cordwainers (leather-workers), whittawers (sadlers). How many readers would know that hedge-cutting or hedge-laying was probably what the plasher did, who is listed as living at Clayworth in Nottinghamshire in 1688?

All these men, and the yeomen too, were described simply by their Christian and surnames whenever they were mentioned: plain John Hart, husbandman, or James Buckland, carpenter. It had been many centuries since ordinary Englishmen had lacked surnames, but it can easily be seen how natural it was when surnames came in to call Peter the Smith, Peter Smith. On the continent of Europe the older naming custom survived longer; in Holland for example the common folk did not acquire second names until the time of Napoleon.

There were three further names of common people: 'labourer', 'cottager' and 'pauper'. Only labourer in any sense described status or function. A labourer could be either of the other two, and a man who called himself that could not call himself a husbandman, because he did not work land on his own account. He could have no other calling-name, because he had no specific calling; he just worked for other people. We should think of him now as a person with no other resources than the sale of his labour on the market – neither land, nor equipment, nor specialized skill. This is in general apt enough, for him and those below him, but some labourers did have some land, and some even had servants. Cottager was a description, not of a calling but of a means of livelihood which was not specific. Getting a living where you, you and your whole family, could make one, and wringing all that was possible out of the bit of ground which might be attached to the hovel you lived in. This is an unwieldy description, but it is as short a way as I have found of placing a cottager in the old order. The final term, pauper, speaks for itself.

According to Gregory King (see p. 32), the largest group of families in England was in fact made up of 'Cottagers and Paupers', 400,000 out of 1,350,000. If we regard these as the lowest in the social scale, in spite of the recognition that 'scale' does not strictly apply below the line, the enormous inequality of life in the world we have lost immediately becomes apparent. Not all of these wretched families must be counted as permanently below the level of subsistence, as the early sociologists used to say, or in what was once called primary poverty. But they were for varying periods in poverty of some sort, in need of relief. In fact that whole half and more of the population which Gregory King described as decreasing the wealth of the kingdom may well be supposed to have been living in intermittent poverty in the England of 1688. Indeed it is probably safe to assume that at all times before the beginnings of industrialization a good half of all those living were judged by their contemporaries to be poor, and their standards must have been extremely harsh, even in comparison with those laid down by Victorian poor law authorities.[17]

There is another important characteristic of King's figures which we must not overlook, because it demonstrates a general principle which was a striking feature of social arrangements as they were in his day. The total number of people he gives as five and a half million, of which as we have seen a little over half (2,825,000) were 'decreasing the wealth of the kingdom' and a little under half (2,675,520) were increasing it. But the difference in the number of 'families' (we should now, of course, use the word 'household') between these two halves was very much greater; only 501,000 'families' were in the richer section as against 849,000 'families' in the poorer section. Poor people, therefore, lived in small households, and rich people in big ones, though some members of rich households, the servants, came from poor homes and might themselves die in poverty. The general principle, then, runs as follows: the higher the status of the household or family, the larger it was, and the humbler people were, the smaller were the households they lived in. The majority of households were the small, poorer ones, and the minority the large, richer ones, even though more people in total lived in them than in the smaller ones. Humble families in fact lost some of their members, as servants to richer families. We shall return to the size of the family and household in due course; all we are registering here is its connection with the hierarchy of status.

If the phrase 'middle class' seems to have so many misleading associations when it is used of any part of Stuart society, there was of course a middle range of income and status in the plain numerical sense as there always must be. Indeed the 'middling sort of people' began to enter into social descriptions in Stuart times and it is interesting to find that the term was mostly used of the towns. We must look a little more

closely at the townsfolk and the bourgeoisie in order to decide
the extent to which they can be said to have lived apart from
the rest of the population, even though like everybody else
they found themselves under the domination of the ruling
minority. Can it be said that the 2000 families of 'Eminent
Merchants and Traders by Sea' which Gregory King estimated
as existing in 1688, or 10,000 of them in all if the lesser ones
are included, really formed the bourgeoisie in pre-industrial
England? These estimates were decidedly too small for those
engaged in 'business'. Would it be realistic and useful to call
the whole of Sir Thomas Smith's third sort of men, 'Citizens,
Burgesses and Yeomen' by the title middle class?

Though yeomen and merchants must have come from the
same stock, and though there might seem to be some rough
sort of equivalence in the position of the more modest burgesses with that of the substantial peasantry, Smith is exceptional in linking them together in this way. In the provincial
towns – how insignificant they were will become obvious in the
next chapter – the local grazier who was also a butcher had
already appeared in the sixteenth century and his is a figure
which persisted until the twentieth century. Nevertheless the
towns had a life of their own, small as they were, and any
acquaintance with municipal records will show how intense
such a community feeling could be. It was at the top that the
linkage with society as a whole is to be seen, and it was the
link between the gentry and the merchants which preoccupied
the men of the time.

This is what Harrison says about merchants: 'They often
change estate with gentlemen as gentlemen do with them, by
mutual conversion of one into the other.'[18] William Lambarde,
the first historian of an English county, says very much the
same thing of Kent in Elizabethan times:

> The gentlemen be not here (throughout) of so ancient stocks
> as elsewhere, especially in the parts nearest to London, from
> which city (as it were from a certain rich and wealthy seed-
> plot) courtiers, lawyers and merchants be continuously
> translated and do become new plants among them.[19]

This interchange was by no means confined to Kent, and as
Harrison said it was not simply a flow of merchant families
into the gentry: the gentry became merchants too. Westcote,

the first to write about the broad seafaring county of Devon, with its flourishing ports, says of the merchants: 'Divers of them are esquires and gentlemen's younger sons, who by means of their travel and transmigration are very well qualified, apt and fit to manage great and high offices.'[20]

Some contemporaries, it is true, do give an impression that the merchants were a community of their own: 'These, by reason of the great privileges they enjoy, every city being as it were a Common Wealth by themselves,'[21] wrote one of them in 1600, somewhat obscurely and ungrammatically it must be confessed. There was an interesting and anxious controversy in the seventeenth century about whether a gentleman's son could become an apprentice and still preserve his gentle status, since apprenticeship for a gentleman meant serving in someone else's house and actually undertaking menial tasks for a person ordinarily of lower lineage than his own.[22] But whatever prejudice there might have been, however much snobbery affected our ancestors, there can be no doubt that gentlemen did become apprentices in very considerable numbers to the more profitable trades. There can be no doubt either that the sons of the manor house married the daughters of the city merchants, for as much money in the way of a dowry as they could possibly get, or that the son of a successful goldsmith, merchant, haberdasher or draper, might marry the daughter of a country gentleman.

The gentleman's son who went into the City as an apprentice, and married City money, remained part of the family in the countryside. When the gentry of the county underwent a Visitation from the Heralds, which happened once in a couple of generations, they registered their sons or grandsons, daughters, nephews, living in the City, along with all the others married off to other county gentry. So many gentry got into London in this way that the City of London had its Visitations too. Some London gentry, and many more merchant, families, stayed in the city from generation to generation, as they did in continental cities. But there were English families which maintained a dual allegiance over many generations, dynasties of prosperous London merchants which were also gentry in the countryside, seated most often, as might be expected, in the Home Counties. These were few.[23]

Given that there was no bar to intermarriage, it is extremely difficult to see how any enclave could remain isolated from the rest. The City of London was undoubtedly a community of its own; so extraordinarily rich and powerful did it become in the final generations of the old order that it is understandable that men sometimes described it as a state within a state. We shall shortly see however that it was pretty well alone as an urban community, the only area of the country where rural ways did not penetrate, in the whole of England. Life in London was different from life elsewhere and life in the richest London families very different. But however striking the texture of social life in the *haute bourgeoisie* might turn out to be when it is minutely examined, this does not justify us in calling the city dweller a member of a different class, forming a conscious, permanent community, capable of seeing itself as separate from the ruling segment.

The difference in outlook must presumably have been at its greatest when some city father had risen from truly humble origins, from well beneath the rank of gentleman. Like the rest of those who prospered in the towns, of course, he was called 'master', he was 'worshipful', by virtue of his personal wealth and power over others. We do not yet know how often such a thing came to pass, or how essential it may have been to have come from some gentle or at least yeoman family before such a career of success as a bourgeois became possible in the pre-industrial world. It is clear, however, that social differences of this sort did not outlast more than a generation. A wealthy clothier, or tanner, or victualler, or merchant tailor might, if he lived to see them, feel very different from his grandchildren in the countryside whom he shared with the gentleman whose son had married his daughter. But the grandchildren themselves would not experience any uncertainty of status. Moreover, they might succeed very rapidly to the family fortune because of demographic vagaries.

We have been able in this outline of an argument to refer only very little to other members of the 'middle class', as we understand it today. We now think of professional people such as doctors and lawyers, technicians of every description, teachers, architects, civil servants as the important people of this type. All that can now be said of *professional* people of this sort in the world we have lost is that, just as in Africa now, there were very, very few of them. Those who did exist belonged to the ruling minority by definition. We have seen

William Harrison admitting it and they have been placed accordingly in Table 2 (see p. 38).

Conditions on the continent were often somewhat different from those in England, for nobles were seated in the cities rather than in the countryside, in Italy anyway. The status system differed too, for in some countries the nobility does seem to have been more separate from the rest of the privileged community, and provisions for social descent such as existed in England seem to have been lacking. This is a capital point, which might well have been developed, for the rule of status which laid it down that in England the younger son of a baron was plain 'master', 'Mr', just like a successful merchant, certainly led to an acceptance of social mobility not so apparent elsewhere. In all these directions it may turn out that England was exceptional.

Perhaps the phrase a 'one-class society' would fit no other European country as well as it seems to fit pre-industrial England, even with all the complicated exceptions and reservations which have had to be made in the course of this chapter. This title gives rise to no expectation that the workers of the pre-industrial world can be thought of as a community apart from the rest, which is a further advantage over the usual phraseology. Detailed analysis of the working force, or the labour force as the economists say, cannot be undertaken here. There was a considerable number of wage-earners even before large-scale industry made the wage packet the almost universal form of payment and support. Indeed there is evidence that even in Tudor times well over a half or even two-thirds of all households received some part at least of their income from wages. Nevertheless the paupers, when they were fortunate enough to receive wages, the labourers, the artificers, even the husbandmen and the yeomen who pocketed such payments from their employers, were in a very different position from the worker in the factory, the shop or the office. They did not all share a common work situation by any means, as do the members of the working class in the contemporary industrial world.

A considerable part of the labour force, moreover, cannot have been householders at all. These were the servants living in the households of their masters and the grown and growing children still at home and at work at the bench or in the fields. Some might be solitary householders or even 'inmates',

lodgers. Most of these persons were young, but some of the
servants were as old as the heads of their households, and a
very few even older, unmarried and now largely unmarriable,
as were the elderly solitaries. They were all separated into the
myriad familial cells which went to make up the society. Here
we return once again to the minute scale of life, the small size
of human groups, before the coming of industry. Working
persons were held apart from each other by the social system.
Many or most of them were subsumed, as we have said, within
the personalities of their fathers and masters. If it had not
been for the terminology which was invented for a society like
our own, it would never have occurred to us even to wonder
whether they could be thought of as a community, a class of
their own.

The working families were poor, and we have seen men of
the time openly talking of them as the proletariat. 'Miserable
men,' Westcote calls them, 'in regard of their labour and
poverty.'[24] Everyone was quite well aware throughout the life
of that social order that the poorer peasantry might at any
time break out into violence. Talking about the 'pulling and
contest' after money at a time of deflation, John Locke said
in 1692 that this struggle usually went on between 'the landed
men and the merchant'.

> For the labourer's share, being seldom more than a bare
> subsistence, never allows that body of man time or oppor-
> tunity to raise their thoughts above that, or struggle with
> the richer for theirs (as one common interest), unless when
> some common or great distress, uniting them in one univer-
> sal ferment, makes them forget respect, and emboldens them
> to carve to their wants with armed force, and then some-
> times they break in upon the rich and sweep all like a
> deluge. But this rarely happens but in the mal-administra-
> tion of a neglected or mismanaged government.[25]

Journeymen out of their time, but unable to set up for themselves; small masters miserably dependent on the capital of
rich masters; husbandmen pinched for their rent by avaricious
landlords; these were likewise looked upon as dangerous men
who might sometimes become desperate.

But the head of the poorest family was at least the head of
something. The workers did not form a million *outs* facing a

handful of *ins*. They were not in what we should call a mass situation. They could not be what we should call a class. For this, it has been claimed, if the expression can be used at all, was a one-class society. It must be clear that the question of how the élite, the ruling segment, was related to the rest is not an easy one to answer. A great deal of patient, intricate work of discovery and analysis will have to be undertaken by the historians before they can begin to decide such issues as these. They will have to show an imaginative sensitivity to all those subtle influences which enable a minority to live for all the rest. When they come to do this, it is the symbolic life of our ancestors which will be the most difficult to handle, and especially their symbols of status.

The village community
Chapter 3

The scale of life in cottage, farmstead,
manor house and church

Nothing seems more poignant and appropriate to us than that Falstaff should have died babbling of green fields. Indeed we still think of our English surroundings in this way; lush little meadows and, more commonplace still, the group of thatched cottages, standing in irregular relationship with manor house, inn and church. This is a picture of England which the Englishman goes to make sure about when his holidays come round, and which foreigners see when they look on us from outside, especially from the North American continent.

It is now an entirely false picture, of course, and by this time most of us surely know quite well that it is false. Nevertheless, its persisting attractiveness, the effect it still has on our national image of ourselves is one further example of the influence upon us of the lost world which vanished with the coming of industrial, urban life. In our day, at least four Englishmen out of every ten live in cities. Over half of us live in towns of 50,000 inhabitants and more,[1] some of which are so vast that none of our rural ancestors would recognize his surroundings as human, should he find his way there through some impossible chronological vagary.

London even then was a city on an industrial scale, though industry, as we use the word, did not exist there. The inn in Eastcheap where Falstaff lay plucking at the sheets, his nose sharp as a pen, was quite a long way from green fields, perhaps a mile and a half or two miles, probably as far as it was possible to get. By the end of the pre-industrial era London was undoubtedly the biggest city in Europe and, if men had but known it, with only Tokyo as its rival as the biggest city in the world, it was still smaller than the Rome of the ancients, which was the largest city men then knew about. By the end

of the seventeenth century more than one English person in
every ten lived in London, which had actually topped the
half-million mark.[2] But urban, mass living in an environment
entirely man-made, in no way machine-made, ended at that
point in England. If three-quarters and more of our people
live in cities today, then in Tudor and Stuart times the position was entirely the other way round. When Elizabeth
reigned, Charles and Cromwell fought the Civil War, and
William and Mary came to the throne after the Glorious
Revolution, well over fourth-fifths of the whole people lived
in villages.

These villages were, moreover, small even on the standards
of the villages we still know. It is quite certain that there was
no average size in the sense that most villages could be
expected to contain roughly the same number of people. There
were great villages and little villages, like Great Milton and
Little Milton in Oxfordshire, just as there were large and small
towns and cities. The composition and organization of settlements also varied considerably, from region to region and even
to some degree within the same limited area. But the numerical
mean, that is the number of places divided into the total
population in England and Wales in late Stuart times, was
very probably 300 or smaller. The only example which can yet
be quoted of an appreciable number of places in the same area
yields even smaller figures. This is the Wingham division of
the county of Kent in 1705 where there were forty separately
named places in the collection of lists of inhabitants, with a
total of 6411 people: the size of a settlement was thus 160
people. Much of the Stuart population lived out their lives in
settlements so tiny that in the twentieth century we should
regard them as miniatures, curiosities.

But even in the Wingham area, there was one community
of 1172 people, and 42 per cent of the people lived in settlements larger than 400 people. Like all summary figures, those
we have presented for the whole country, and for this particular area, are deceptive to some degree. Though the figure for
the actual national average, the numerical mean, was so low
a considerable minority (just as in Kent in 1705) presumably
lived in larger places, with perhaps 500 or more inhabitants.[3]
It is possible then, to give a rather different impression for the
country as a whole. Something like two-thirds of the whole
population can be supposed to have dwelt in settlements of

500 or more, and over a tenth of them in a real city on the twentieth-century scale. But when we make the gross comparison with our own day which is the general object of this superficial survey, these different angles of view change the prospect very little. Life in a community of 500 or 600 souls can have been very little different from life in a community of 300 or 400, in contrast with life in a modern industrial centre of 50,000 or more.

The facts of the minuscule scale of living in the world we have lost, therefore, are almost as conspicuous for the size of the communities in which men dwelt as they are for the size of the group in which they lived and worked. England, apart from the phenomenon of London, may have been exceptionally laid out, more blanketed by its fields than many other areas of Europe. It can now be shown that our villages were much smaller than the settlements which their inhabitants established in the New World, for example. But though the details of the distribution of persons between villages, hamlets might be a better word, have still to be worked out, there can be little doubt about urban figures, during the seventeenth century anyway. Excluding London, the centres of over 10,000 (only five in 1600 and seven in 1700) had less than 2 per cent of the population, and when taken together with those of 5000 to 10,000 (fifteen in 1600, twenty-six in 1700) still had less than 5 per cent. So that the total urban population was some 8 per cent of the whole at the beginning and 17 per cent at the end of the century, some two-thirds of it in London in both cases.

Gregory King seems to have been in error over the smaller cities, but he produces some insight into the sizes of centres coming between them and the villages. He worked out a table of some 800 places in the 1690s which would make the mean size of an English local central place only a little over 1000, not much more than one-five-hundredth of the size of London.[4] The height of the step between London and the next level of size is even more surprising. In 1600 the drop was from 200,000 to about 12,500; in 1700 from half a million and more to less than 20,000; in 1750 from nearly 700,000 to getting on for 30,000. The cities at this next much lower level were very few; Norwich, Bristol and Newcastle were consistently present there, but York fell out after 1700, and by 1750 Birmingham, Liverpool and Manchester had risen to this second rank. What

is patently clear from all these estimates, approximate as they
are, is that urbanization was growing very rapidly indeed in
England during these last five generations of pre-industrial
times, faster, so E. A. Wrigley believes, than in any other
European society at any time.

In spite of this highly significant fact, significant because of
what it implies about the growth in the productivity of
agriculture supplying food to the town-dwellers as well as for
'industrial' production, England at this time has to be thought
of in the following way. It was a rural hinterland attached to a
vast metropolis through a network of insignificant local
centres. There was little to correspond with the great provincial towns of France. After the really big cities of Paris, Lyons
and Marseilles, came Rouen, Orleans, Amiens, Bordeaux,
Rheims, Angers, all six of which had between 35,000 and
50,000 people and more.[5] Even Beauvais, a medium-sized
clothing city, had some 15,000 or 20,000, and the relatively
minor provincial capital of Aix-en-Provence numbered 27,500
people in 1695 when a fairly accurate count was made. We
may compare this with an almost contemporary census of
similar reliability, carried out with the knowledge, and perhaps
the co-operation, of King himself, in his own birthplace,
Lichfield in Staffordshire. A cathedral city and a county centre,
it contained 2861 people in the same year, 1695. Chichester
with exactly similar characteristics and functions had about
2500 in 1625.

Our country had no city-states like Italy: no Florence, no
Venice, not even a Frankfurt-am-Main, or a Salzburg. Even
London, for all its fantastic size, could not be called a civic
site: it was then, as it has sadly continued to be, except in
select areas and for a brief period under the Georges, a disorderly sprawl, as much of a haphazard muddle as any English
rural village. But there is one intriguing circumstance which
may make us pause before we set down our English ancestors
as almost entirely provincial, hearing of the great city only at
a distance and with wonderment. 'It is fair to assume,' Wrigley
has rather tentatively declared, that in the early eighteenth
century no less than 'one adult in six in England had had
direct experience of London life.' By living there, that is to
say, for a longer or shorter period.[6]

Gregory King's own writing is proof that the men of the
time were well aware that society did vary between town and

country. His *Observations* are marked throughout by attempts to distinguish rural from urban figures, and he provides tables showing that in London and the towns there were more married couples, more servants, more widows and fewer children than in the country. Our preliminary evidence in some cases contradicts him, in others confirms him. He believed like everyone else that London was a dreadful place, where decent standards were defied. We are certain that he was wrong here in one respect, as to illegitimacy.[7] But we shall not be able to claim that we know enough to pronounce in general on the contrast between town and country.

When we talk of England as being almost entirely a landscape of green meadows and wide-open fields with village communities scattered amongst them, it is a network rather than a scattering which we have in mind. The very large numbers of small settlements in which so much of the population lived were in fact all connected by the local rural centres, as well as through the personal linkages of individuals. They were independent as communities, but their independence implied the existence of communities larger than themselves. Though these larger villages and towns turn out to be so small as compared with the provincial cities of the rest of western Europe, they were nevertheless differently constituted from the others because they were centres of exchange as well as of communication. The countrywide pattern must therefore be thought of as a reticulation rather than as a particulation – a web spread over the whole geography is the metaphor which will come most easily to the mind.

The word 'settlement' is right for the villages and hamlets of our country. They were in fact the knots of households originally set down by the first colonizers of the island, still being inhabited and run by their successors after perhaps a thousand years. Many bore, and still bear, the names which had got stuck when the site was being cleared and the earliest dwellings set up. Such names are Woolpit in Suffolk, for 'wolfpit', or Caldecote, which appears in several counties and means a fold for the sheep from the cold.

Each group of farmsteads was surrounded by the land which had been laid out for it, presumably enough to support the inhabitants. In some areas, therefore, where the soil was rich and even and easy to till, and where the rivers flowed together, settlements came thick and fast. Norfolk has no less than 660 ancient parishes, and in that most prosperous of the shires in earlier times, there were 969 medieval churches; you can sometimes see ten spires or towers from one vantage point. Yet even in Norfolk, on the Breckland, there are miles and miles of desolate landscape where few dwelt and where the settlements are well out of sight of each other. In the highlands of England, the whole area north and west of the famous line drawn from Bristol to the Wash, church was separated from church by five, seven or even ten miles. Yorkshire, which is more than twice as big as Norfolk, had but 459 parishes in Stuart times, Cornwall only 61. In Lancashire, the county where industrial transformation was to be at its most sudden and intense, there were not more than 64.[8]

Parishes are not settlements. There are often several distinct hamlets in one parish, or more than one parish in a village. About three settlements to two parishes is, perhaps, right. These parish figures, therefore, are very rough indications of the variation between size, density and structure of settlements found in various parts of the country, especially between the highland and lowland zones. In the highlands, chapelries had grown up to accommodate the growing population which had often already appeared in response to early industrial activity, especially the making of wool and cloth. Yet, even in these regions parish and settlement were sometimes congruent, or rather the parish covered an area comprising only one hamlet, or two, as in the lowlands. This was so at Widecombe-in-the-Moor, in Devonshire, from whose boundaries Dartmoor still stretches away as far as the eye can see. Life amongst inhabitants of that parish, or of Greystoke in Cumberland, locked in the mountains of the Lake District, was one thing. Life in the large and prosperous village of Colyton on the Devon seaboard, or in the single little bunch of housesteads which went to make up Cogenhoe in Northamptonshire, 200 people on only 800 acres yet with their own church and rector, was another thing again.

The villages of Greystoke, Colyton and Cogenhoe come into the story several times, for they are amongst the fifteen or twenty village communities which have been examined in some detail for the purpose of this essay. But the subtler elements which went to make up the differences between community and community have not yet been reached. It is not yet known how much effect the ethnic origin of the inhabitants

might have had on the way they arranged their community
life, laid out their fields and worked them, or conducted their
religious worship. For the highlanders in Britain, as everyone
remembers, are Celtic by descent, and the lowlanders are
Saxon.[9]

Overlapping the division between highland to the north and
west and lowland to the south and east was that between areas
of predominantly pastoral farming, the rearing of cattle and
sheep, and areas of predominantly arable farming, the growing
of wheat, oats and barley. Most hilly land is suitable only for
grazing, hence the pastoral north and west, but on easier
ground crops can be grown, as well as animals bred and
fattened. Much of England therefore was of a mixed agricultural complexion in spite of the general pastoral/arable divide,
and this, as we shall see, gave our ancestors some protection
against the possibility of the food running out.

Next comes the distinction between nucleated villages,
where the dwellings did in fact cluster round the church and
village green, and where the husbandmen lived along the
village street (often with their holdings stretching out behind
them), and villages of scattered farmsteads where the church
was sometimes in a field, placed there for convenience of access
in every direction. Then there were the woodland parishes and
felden parishes, and finally there were the open and closed
parishes. This last variable was decidedly social though it did
have something to do with geology, altitude or degrees of
afforestation. In the open parishes, which were often woodland
parishes and somewhat more likely to be pastoral than arable,
land was in the hands of many owners, and in small parcels,
whereas the closed parishes were in the grasp of one or a few
owners who controlled ingress and egress as well as economic
and social activity. As might be expected, it was in the open
parishes that handicraft industry tended to take root, where
landless individuals could settle and above all where hand-
industrial families would tend to multiply.

The best-known example of this contrast in England is in
Leicestershire. Here the closed parish of Bottesford belonged
in the eighteenth century almost entirely to the Dukes of
Rutland, and its agrarian character was strictly maintained:
no family here which relied on stocking-weaving, or any other
such activity, only husbandmen and labourers. The open
parish of Shepshed on the other hand where land had been in

the hands of many owners, not sufficiently integrated to control its social life, could be entered by any would-be settler. Shepshed accordingly filled itself up with stocking-weavers, a classic site for the study of what has come to be called proto-industrial activity in England. Its demographic as well as its social composition and its culture were all affected by these differences, as we shall see in Chapter 10.[10] So powerful were these forces that they may have been able to override differences in ethnic origin or tradition, or even the influence of geographical position, and this before ever industrialization of the factory sort made its appearance in the middle of the eighteenth century. Variations in the previous agricultural history of England have tended to take pride of place, however, in the story which historians have had to tell about the contrasts between community and community. The crucial issue has been that of the enclosure of the land of a village.

Did this settlement once work its arable area as open fields, co-operatively, until some grasping or enterprising Tudor landlord managed to bring about enclosure? To enclose a village meant that the inhabitants had to abandon their co-operative customs, and break up their great open fields into little hedged plots, one single piece to each landholder and, of course, the largest by far for the landlord himself. Or was the open-field, co-operative system then still in force there? Or had the land, perhaps, as in Kent or in East Anglia, always been enclosed? These are clearly fundamental questions to ask of any village community in the traditional world, since working the land was the fundamental activity of all its members, and co-operating for the purpose a powerful link between the constituent households. But no very large proportion of the cultivated land had been enclosed by the years 1700–10,[11] which, for our purposes, is the final decade of the old world.

Where enclosure had taken place, moreover, even recently, the differences it had made from the point of view of the life of the community were perhaps less than might be expected. Enclosure might impoverish the smaller landholders, who found themselves disposing of their allocated plots, too small to be viable without the now abolished common rights. Henceforth they would be labourers living by selling their work time on the market. But enclosure could not destroy the distances between the community and its neighbours. Though the detailed arrangements for the working of the land were no longer undertaken at the manor court, and though that court might be dying as an institution, nevertheless the community still had its affairs to run co-operatively.

The church had to be administered, or perhaps two churches in the same village. The poor law had to be carried out; the roads had to be kept up; the constable appointed to maintain the peace. The more important the common responsibilities of any community, presumably, the stronger the association between its members, because each one's interest is engaged. But living together in one township, isolated, spatially, from others of comparable size, of very much the same structure, inevitably means a communal sense and communal activity, even if that activity is trivial and symbolic, as it is in the social club which we treasure so much in our day.

The strength of this sense of community in the English villager can be seen when he removed himself beyond the ocean, and settled again, surrounded by the alien, virgin land, which required new household groupings. In the final years of the traditional order in England, when the British were establishing their townships on the eastern seaboard of the North American continent, the village community at home was of course the model. The men from the ancient enclosed villages of East Anglia and the newly enclosed communities of the Midlands showed no less communal sense, no greater unwillingness to serve the new community, than the men from villages where the immemorial open fields still lay undisturbed under the wide, grey English sky. Open-field villagers would sometimes insist on the open-field system for a new township in Massachusetts. But it is not recorded that those from else-where would welcome this return to the ancient co-operative system.[12]

There is very little reason to believe, therefore, that the husbandry, that is the working landholders, of the English village community who went out to join the Puritan common-wealth which grew up on the rocky soil of New England, were seeking refuge from the enclosing landlord. Nevertheless they were certainly disinclined, in their surroundings, to allow a gentry to grow up amongst them, and quite determined to have no truck with ecclesiastical dignitaries. However, gentle folk were never entirely absent from any part of the American colonies, even from quintessentially Puritan Massachusetts; in the southern areas, as everyone knows, the gentry were much more prominent and even the Anglican hierarchy took root. The plantation-owners of Virginia looked upon themselves from the very beginning as the overseas branches of English county families, and there is evidence that the gentry did indeed take the initiative in opening up the leafy green plain between the Atlantic and the Appalachians, though they had great difficulty in settling it.[13]

It would be easy in our own century to exaggerate the extent to which the new Englishmen of the American continent deliberately rejected the system of status established amongst the old Englishmen of Europe, for we are so apt to seize upon every sign of social resentment or of disaffection. But there can be no doubt that the social hierarchy deeply affected the lives of ordinary people in the Old World. The presence, or absence, of the gentry in an English village made a vital difference. Without the gentry, or any representative of the ruling minority in their midst, the members of an English village community were indeed free to run their own affairs, almost as free, it might seem, as the members of the townships set up in New England. Galby, in Leicestershire, never had a resident squire, and the free villagers have been traced for centuries, running their community as they would.[14] We have seen how important this circumstance might have been in economic development and manufacturing activity. Many such communities must have been present, scattered amongst the villages where the manor house was the largest building, apart from the church, and deference to its occupants the first principle of village life. Perhaps a fifth of all the village communities of England may have been in this gentry-free position.

The surprising thing about this figure, on reflection, is how small it is. The gentry were, at most, a twentieth of the population, yet they managed to spread themselves over two-thirds of the countryside. This is a rough estimate and it would, perhaps, be best if the source of it were given here. In 1680, a survey was published by a map-maker, John Adams, with the following title:[15] *Index Villaris; or, An Alphabetical Table of all the Cities, Market-Towns, Parishes, Villages, and Private Seats in England and Wales.* If the English settlers in America felt that you could not move in the old country without coming up against the honourables and the worshipfuls, this survey shows that they had some justification.

Table 3: *Distribution of aristocratic and gentlemanly seats, England, 1684*

Number of named places	%	Description of titled residents		
13	2·3	Noblemen		
360	64·0	Gentlemen	33 (5·9 %) Baronets 5 (0·9 %) Knights 85 (15·1 %) Two gentlemen or more 174 (30·9 %) One gentleman 63 (11·2 %) Gentlemen, number unspecified	
106	19·0	No titled residents recorded		
83	14·7	Not clear		
562	100·0			

Source: Adams, *Index Villaris.*

It must be used with caution, of course, even if the original information was reliable. Noblemen had more seats than one: the same book names no less than twelve houses for Henry Somerset, Duke of Beaufort, Marquis and Earl of Worcester, Lord Herbert of Chepstow, Raglan and Gower. He had Worcester House in the Strand, in London; Badminton and Wollaston Grange in Gloucestershire; Monmouth Castle, Chepstow Castle, Raglan Castle, Chepstow Grange and Tintern Abbey in Monmouthshire; Crickhowel Castle and Tretower Castle in Brecknockshire and Swansea Castle in Glamorgan. The Duke of Norfolk had ten seats, including one in the very centre of the city of Norwich, castles in four English counties and Norfolk House in London. The town houses, or palaces as they might be called in Italy, are often overlooked. One earl had nine seats, and one baron had eight. No family could possibly occupy so many houses at any one time, and some of the castles were no doubt in ruins. But in the villages where they stood, these baronial mansions spoke eloquently of the power of their owners. If you grew up under the shadow of a castle, or outside the walls of a lordly park, you knew who ruled the country, even if the place was in the hands of tenants.[16] The families of the ruling segment pressed, like the atmosphere, evenly, over the whole face of England. It is time to look at the actual constitution of a village community to see how it felt.

On 7 April 1676, the curate of the parish of Goodnestone-next-Wingham, in Kent, made his reply to the Archbishop of Canterbury, who wanted to know how many people lived under his care, and how many came to communion.[17] He chose to answer in unexpected detail, and presented his list under the following five heads: families of gentlemen, families of yeomen, families of tradesmen, families of labourers and families of poor men. There were 62 households at Goodnestone in that year, and they contained 276 people; the average size of household, therefore, was 4·45, quite a normal figure for pre-industrial England, though below the mean. But the mean is deceptive. Table 4 shows how the households went.

Table 4: *Goodnestone-next-Wingham, Kent, April 1676*

Status of households	No.	Mean size of house-hold	Range of sizes	Numbers of persons	Numbers of children	Numbers of servants	Numbers of resident relatives
Gentry	3	9·0	22, 3, 2	27	7	15	1
Yeomen	26	5·8	12–2	151	64	34	3
Tradesmen	9	3·9	8–1	35	16	2	0
Labourers	12	3·2	6–2	38	15	0	0
Poor Men	12	2·1	6–1	25	11	0	1
Totals	62	4·45	22–1	276	113	51	5

Source: Listing of inhabitants held at the Cambridge Group.

Approaching two-thirds of the people, 178 out of 276, were living in the households of the gentry and the yeomen. Though the tradesmen, the labourers and the poor people made up thirty-three of the households, a clear majority, they contained less than one-third of the inhabitants. In this village the number of children, the number of servants and the number of resident relatives per household went down it will be seen with social standing.

As we have already said, variation of size of household with social status was a universal law of society in the traditional world before the coming of industry. It did not mean that most people were born of rich parents whose families or households were accordingly large, in a society where, as we have seen, social consequence went with size of household. Quite the reverse, for, in the village community of Goodnestone, no less than fifty-one persons, men, women and children, were servants, born in a humbler family, and yet living in another, more substantial one. This is 18·2 per cent of the whole population,[18] an offering, so to speak, of the children of the poor to those above them.

But not always an offering to the ruling minority, to the gentry. In Goodnestone, the three gentle families had fifteen servants between them, certainly a large number but the yeomanry had more; fourteen of the yeomen households had servants, thirty-four in number, and even the tradesmen had two, a girl in one household and a youth in another. More than half of the thirty-three men and boys and eighteen women and girls who were servants in this community were with the yeomenry, and they were serving them in husbandry, on the land and in the land-working households, not as personal menials, not as housemaids or cooks or kitchen helpers. They had left their parents back at home with their younger brothers and sisters, or even alone in the cottages. Five of the twelve labourers' families consisted of man and wife alone, their children gone, or yet to be born: if they had gone, we now know where they were.

Gentlemen, yeomen, tradesmen, labourers and paupers, these were the social orders in the community according to the curate of Goodnestone. They do not quite conform to the titles we have laid down in our last chapter; husbandmen are missing here, included, no doubt, among the yeomen by their curate. Once more, the vagaries of titles might mislead us, if it were not possible to prompt our reading of this revealing document from scores of others like it.[19]

When the priest in charge at Goodnestone looked at the parish under his spiritual care, he saw first and foremost the huge household of twenty-two people living at the manor house. At its head was Edward Hales, Esq., who seems to have been a tenant of the London merchant family of Pennington, owners of the manor of Goodnestone, and, no doubt, of much of the land in the village.[20] Then there were his wife, six children and fourteen servants, eight men and boys, six women and girls. Also in Goodnestone were two smaller households of gentry, whom we may imagine as satellites to the Hales. These brought up the total of people born of gentle blood in this community to twelve. Only these individuals out of the 280 in his parish belonged, like the parson himself, to

the fully literate minority, the people with some knowledge of
the world beyond the parish of Goodnestone and this particular area of the county of Kent.

But the land in the parish was not worked by the family of
Hales, though the eight men and boys in the manor house
must have tilled a good-sized manor farm, with the daily help,
when it was required, of some of the twelve labourers living in
the village. Most of the land was actually run by a dozen
substantial families of yeomen and husbandmen whether or
not it belonged to the squire. There were two families called
Neame, one with fourteen and the other with seven in the
household; three called Wanstall, eight, eight and three;
William Tucker with ten, Richard Fuller and Stephen Church
with nine apiece, and John Pet with eight. These dozen families contained over a hundred people, a quarter of whom were
servants, mostly young men. The squire and the larger yeomanry seem to have dominated the village community of
Goodnestone-next-Wingham in 1676.

But over half its members have yet to be considered. There
were fourteen more families of the smaller yeomen or husbandmen, the nine tradesmen, and a dozen each of labourers and of
paupers. There was, in addition, an institution which we have
not yet mentioned, a hospital for the destitute, with one man
and three women in it, bringing the total population up to 280.
It is not true to say that nobody apart from gentry and yeomanry counted for anything in the village community, though
the pauper families and the hospitallers can be dismissed as
being of no positive account.

Each of the yeomen, the tradesmen and even the labourers
might have had some public life, as we have already seen. The
male head of a labourer's household could occupy office in the
village, and it is possible that by more than the usual back-
breaking, unremitting toil, some cunning and intelligence, and
above all considerable good fortune in the wives he married,
in the relatives who died, a man of the grade of husbandman or
labourer might, in his lifetime, become a substantial yeoman.
We know that this happened, and we know that over the
generations there was an astonishing interchange between the
names of those peasant households which were prospering and
those which were languishing. In Cogenhoe, the one community where we can actually trace the fortunes of each
homestead at six separate points in one decade, the period

between 1618 and 1628, we witness a noticeable change in the size of some of them from year to year. The total population varied too.[21]

The tradesmen added a little variety to village society; there were two families of carpenters at Goodnestone, and one of these had a servant; two of brickmakers; one each headed by a weaver; a shoemaker; a hempster (probably a tailor), and a solitary woman calling herself a grocer. Retailing was a grow-ing occupation in later-seventeenth-century villages and in general this is a normal list of occupations for a rural com-munity, in the old world, if somewhat brief. No smith of any sort is surprising, and it is to be supposed that the specialized agricultural callings like shepherd, or thatcher, or drover, are included here under the 'Labourers'.

There was, evidently, no inn at Goodnestone, and the priest, a curate, seems to have lived outside the village. This, again, was quite an ordinary thing, but a resident married parson with his wife, children and servants, would have had a sub-stantial effect on the little society there, and so might a pros-perous hostelry on a highroad.[22] The most important possible difference would have been the absence of the family of Hales: a decision to live temporarily, or permanently, elsewhere would have considerably altered the social balance, as would the death of the head of the family whilst his son was still a minor. But while the estate continued to be a whole, some tenant would rent the great house, and the man in authority over the estate – the bailiff of husbandry he might still be called – along with those at the head of the table in the twelve substantial yeomen households, ran the village. Nearly three hundred people went to make up the body of the community, but by far the most important member was its head, the squire, and a dozen or fifteen other mature, male heads of household provided all the other working parts.

A different opinion is possible on this point. The walls round the squire's park, the keepers who kept the villagers from his game, the separate pews, high box-pews in the eighteenth century, which he and his household occupied in church, also operated to cut him off from the village com-munity. An absentee, or a minor, a politician on the county or the national level, perpetually preoccupied with business more important than the fixing of the parish poor-rate or the upkeep of the river-bridge, could not be looked upon as the leader, the metaphorical father of village society. Nor could the bailiff. The literature of the Tudor and Stuart age is full of laments about the decay of housekeeping which meant, amongst so many other things, holding open-house for the tenantry. There are endless exhortations to the squires to keep away from the city and the court. There must have been some grounds for the conviction that the country gentry were leaving their own people unsupported, without means of access to that greater world in which the gentry alone could freely move. But no choice between two such different opinions can be made for Edward Hales, Esquire, and the village of Goodnestone; the evidence will not yield it.

Insignificant as it was in the wider political society each village had its own political structure, its own little oligarchy in fact, quite apart from submission to the power of land-owning notables. The offices in that miniature polity, if the Essex village of Terling can be properly taken as typical, were monopolized by those working the larger plots of land and with greater possessions on the modest peasant scale. It was they who were the churchwardens, constables and overseers of the poor; it was they, year after year, son often succeeding father, who sat for their communities as jurymen at the sessions and became vestrymen, when the vestry came into being towards the end of the seventeenth century. The labourers, the cottagers and the poor almost never held these offices. At Terling even the gentry themselves began to play a part in vestry politics as the eighteenth century dawned.[23] It would take a great deal of detailed prose to portray the whole structure and composition even of this tiny society.

Social description, in fact, is a difficult and intricate task, often tedious to the reader. It is necessary to talk in terms of one community, for generalized statements lack the stuff of life, yet no community is entirely typical. We may have spent too much time already on our chosen village, and there are communities now open to examination whose working can be reconstructed in far greater detail. But the shape of society at Goodnestone is particularly well-marked, and it is a convenient model for all the rest. Each of the forty villages in Kent in 1705 whose listings we have referred to before, seems to have been constructed, with variations, very much on this model, and so were villages all over the country.

Lest it should be thought that these large households containing so many working servants, land-working servants, were typical of Kent only, and of the early eighteenth century, they may be compared with the situation at Ealing in 1599.[24] In this still rural village the Goodnestone pattern was quite evident: 404 people in 85 families, an average of 4·75: a gentleman's family of 21, dominating all the rest, and 20 working families of between 7 and 11 apiece. In another village which we have got to know well, Clayworth in Nottinghamshire, the landed gentry had smaller establishments, between 7 and 10 apiece.[25] There were four of them in this village of about 400 people, and some of the yeomen (called 'Freeholders' and 'Farmers' here by the parson who described them) had families of a similar size. But the working families at Clayworth can easily be separated from those whose masters lived without manual exertion, and this distinction is generally obvious from the first glance at a list of members of a village community in pre-industrial England.

The proportion in service varied from place to place for reasons which we think we can now begin to understand. The percentage could be as low as 4 and as high as 25, or even more, which begins to rival the rich London or Norwich parishes of the 1690s where nearly a third of all the people could be servants.[26] In the countryside the members of individual households in the traditional village, man and wife, children and servants, with the help of day-labourers when required, could carry out all the tasks of the agricultural year, except for one, the harvest. From the making of the hay in June until the winning of the corn and pease in late September, every able-bodied person in the place was at work on everyone's land. How much co-operation there was is difficult to say, but when the crisis of the agricultural year came round, right up to the time of mechanized farming, the village acted as a community. After all had been gathered in, there was harvest home.

It is usual, in most places, after they get all the pease pulled or the last grain down, to invite all the workfolks and their wives (that helped them that harvest) to supper, and then they have puddings, bacon, or boiled beef, flesh or apple pies, and then cream brought in platters, and every one a spoon; then after all they have hot cakes and ale; for they bake cakes and send for ale against that time: some will cut their cake and put it into the cream, and this feast is called

cream-pot, or cream-kit; for on the morning that they get
all done the workfolks will ask their dames if they have good
store of cream and say they must have the cream-kit anon.[27]

This was the Yorkshire custom in the 1640s when it was
necessary, at harvest-time, to go even beyond the carpenters,
the wheelwrights and the millers, in order to bring in the
sheaves off the fields. The richer men had to make a home in
the barns during harvest for 'folk', as they were called, sheep-
rearers and cattle-minders who came down from the wild moor-
land. Migration of labour at harvest was common enough in
the eighteenth century, but eating and drinking together was
a universal characteristic of rural life at all times. Whatever
the churchwardens or the overseers of the poor did, when the
church-bell was rung in celebration, or the churchyard mowed,
there was an entry in the ill-written accounts for ale drunk on
the occasion. The meticulous, unpopular rector of Clayworth
in the last quarter of the seventeenth century, entertained the
husbandry of the two settlements in his parish separately to
dinner every year.

When the curate of Goodnestone returned the names of all
his parishioners in April 1676, 'according to their families,
according to their quality and according to their religion', he
did as he was bid and told his lordship, the bishop, how many
of them had been to holy communion that Eastertide. With
only sixteen exceptions every person in the parish known by
their priest to be qualified for the sacrament had actually
taken it at some time during the festival. This fell in that year
between 19 and 26 March and 128 people communicated out
of a population of 281. Even the defaulters promised to make
amends at Whitsuntide, all but the one family in the village
which was nonconformist. But William Wanstall, senior, one
of the absentees, was given no such grace; he had been 'excluded the Holy Sacrament for his notorious drunkenness, but
since hath promised reformation'. Francis Nicholson, the
priest-in-charge, was evidently a devoted pastor, for he could
give an account of each individual absentee. Mrs Elizabeth
Richards, the widowed head of one of the households of gentry,
was excused as 'melancholy', and Barbara Pain as well since
she was 'under a dismal calamity, the unnatural death of her
husband'. He had left her at the head of a yeoman family,
three children and two servants.

This rather exceptional record of communicants draws attention to a feature of the village community and of the whole of the world we have now half-forgotten which has scarcely been mentioned so far. All our ancestors were literal believers, all of the time. Their beliefs were not only religious, of course, since they believed in witchcraft, evil and benign, and gave credence to many propositions and practices condemned by theologians as heathen survivals.[28] But it would be very difficult to maintain that such superstitions ever went to make up a religion which, as a religion, was a rival to Christianity, and the unreflective villager seems not to have noticed any inconsistency within the range of his beliefs and half-beliefs. Christianity had a grasp of their subjective life which is difficult for us to imagine, accustomed as we are to the notion of a really convinced religious person as an individual of a particular kind, a convert, an enthusiast. This was not so in the pre-industrial past.

Not only zealous priests, such as Francis Nicholson, not only serious-minded laymen, but also the intellectuals and the publicly responsible looked on the Christian religion as the explanation of life, and on religious service as its proper end. Not everyone was equally devout, of course, and it would be simple-minded to suppose that none of these villagers ever had their doubts. Much of their devotion must have been formal, and some of it mere conformity. But their world was a Christian world and their religious activity was spontaneous, not forced on them from above. When Francis Nicholson refused the cup to William Wanstall, in March 1676, the scores of other people in the church that morning no doubt approved of what he did, as no doubt Wanstall deserved this very public rebuke. When William Sampson, the formidable rector of Clayworth, did exactly the same thing in April 1679, to Ralph Meers and Anne Fenton 'upon a common fame that they lived and lodged together, not being married', he also had the community behind him. He knew what he was doing too, for Anne Fenton's first baby was christened two months' later, only a week or two, presumably, after she had married Ralph Meers.[29]

It has been shown by historians how it came about that the mass of the English people lost their Christian belief, and how religion came to be a middle-class matter. When the arrival of industry created huge societies of persons in the towns with an

entirely different outlook from these Stuart villagers, practically no one went to church, not if he was working class and
was left untouched by religious emotion.[30] Christianity was no
longer in the social air which everyone breathed together, rich
and poor, gentleman, husbandman, artificer, labourer and
pauper. Perhaps the twelve labourers who lived at Goodnestone in 1676 did not know very clearly what Our Lord's
Supper meant, and the thought of being reported to the church
court by the churchwardens may have influenced them, but
every single one of them took communion. Their descendants
in the slums of London in the 1830s, '40s and '50s did not do
so: they already looked on Christianity as belonging to the
rural world which they had lost. It was something for their
employers, something for the respectable, which, perhaps,
they might go in for if ever they attained respectability and
comfort. This was not true of the hard-working, needy, half-
starved labourers of pre-industrial times.

At Clayworth, at that same Eastertide of 1676, an even
greater proportion of the villagers took the sacrament than at
Goodnestone, 200 out of 401. How powerful the effect of even
formal Christianity could be is shown by an anecdote which
Sampson records of a servant-boy there whose mother died.
The meagre wages of servants, some fifty shillings a year for a
skilled woman and five pounds for a grown man, were subject
to tithe in this village, and the rector was in combat with
masters, maids and men for the money. This poor lad let his
side down by coming and paying 'fully for his wages at one
farthing i' the shilling. The occasion of his mother's death
brought him to an honest mind.' But later in his ministry,
Sampson found that the number of communicants went down
to about 125, though the population did not seem to fall. This
is about the same proportion as at Cogenhoe, in 1612, when
the rector there recorded sixty-three 'Communicants upon
Easter Day', just over half the qualified adults. In judging the
numbers we have cited, it is proper to remember that until
1690, after which religious dissent could be pleaded, the law
of church and state made attendance at service and at
communion compulsory for everyone. But ecclesiastical
punishments were not formidable, and it is known that in
many places numbers were much lower, even before the
1690s.

Every meeting of the village community took place in the

Church, if there was a church or chapel close enough. At Clayworth every Easter Monday, the village community met there and chose the three churchwardens, two for the town, that is Clayworth itself, and one for Wiseton, the separate hamlet within the parish; we have seen that many, perhaps most, parishes were geographically divided like this. Two overseers of the poor were chosen for Clayworth as well as two 'burrough men', who might elsewhere be constables, but in this village they had agricultural duties too.

Here they were, these farming householders, not many of whom could read, sitting in the building put up by their forerunners centuries before, and which they, in their turn, annually repaired and even beautified. In the place where they came so often to Christian service they chose their neighbours for the traditional offices, secular and spiritual.[31] When English villagers found themselves in America, one of the first buildings erected for the new settlement was the Meeting House, for the town meeting had a great deal to decide in starting all anew. The Meeting House was also, of course, the Christian church of the village being born.[32]

The only public appearance of women and children, almost their only expedition outside the circle of the family, as we have said, was at service in church. Wives and maidservants might take and sell their poultry and their eggs to market, or even their apples and cherries, but otherwise they stayed at home. For the menfolk, especially for the substantial ones, there were the occasional meetings of the manor-courts, which still controlled agriculture over most of the countryside. In some places, these meetings were perhaps as important as the Easter Monday gatherings in the Saxon-towered church of St Peter at Clayworth every year.

For the men, too, there were the alehouses, famous in popular history as the poor man's parliament. The single village inn seems in fact to have been rare. Most drinking was done in the cottages of those people in the settlement who had been given permission by the magistrates to keep alehouses, on the strict understanding that there was to be no tippling, and that no liquor was to change hands during time of divine service. Women did go into them; it was not like early twentieth-century Scotland, and courtship sometimes went forward in front of the cottage fire, the public fire. Poor men, and poor women, were often the keepers of alehouses too, though the number of widows in the trade has tended to be overstated. So much was it an expedient for the near-destitute that the poor-law officials sometimes used the granting of a licence as a measure of poor relief.[33]

But the renowned English inn as distinct from the alehouse was not the creation of Samuel Johnson and Charles Dickens, since it was a flourishing institution in the time of Geoffrey Chaucer. Outside London it was the hostelry for travellers, placed on the important roads and common in a country where travel was so painfully slow, but not intended first and foremost for the local people. It could be a large and important institution, on the scale of life which was then the rule, and have an effect on the locality. An alehouse at Harefield in Middlesex in 1699 – it was one of four in this village and not granted the title of inn by the man who made the list of the community[34] – was kept by John and Catherine Baily, and they had in their house the largest family of grown and growing children we have yet traced in pre-industrial England. They had twelve children alive, aged from two to twenty-eight; the two eldest had left home, but of the ten who were left, six were above the age of twelve, all old enough to help run the family establishment, with their aunt, Catherine Baily's sister, who lived there as well. No need of any servants for John Baily, who was also a smith. Meanwhile his potential rival, the New Inn at Harefield, was marked 'Empty not finisht'.

There was plenty of drinking done in the village community, and we shall find ourselves commenting upon it when we come to discuss discipline and survival. Men like Goodman William Wanstall, the excommunicated drunkard of Goodnestone, are met with fairly often. ('Goodman' was used of a substantial householder who was not a 'Mr' and 'Goodwife', or 'Goody', for his partner or his widow.) There is a famous legend from Malmesbury, in Wiltshire, of Sir Thomas Hobbes, the curate of St Mary's about the time of the Spanish Armada and father of Thomas Hobbes, the great philosopher. ('Sir', as Shakespeare used it, could mean a clergyman as well as a knight.) 'Trafells is Troumps', he is supposed to have bawled out to his congregation one Sunday morning, starting suddenly from his slumber in the pulpit, after all Saturday night playing cards with the citizens of that little market town. Trafells was a word for clubs.[35]

These anecdotes from the community life of the world we

have lost convey what we expect, settled, familiar life amongst
a body of men and women who had known one another for a
long time, from birth perhaps; indeed their own family forebears may have known each other too. But this expectation
has turned out to be false; it was overturned by the documents
left behind him by the rector of Clayworth himself. Twelve
years after the list of his parishioners made, like that of
Goodnestone, for the ecclesiastical inquiry of April 1676, he
listed them all again for his own purposes, in May 1688. No
less than 62 per cent of the people living at Clayworth in 1676
were no longer there in 1688, that is 244 out of a population of
401. But there were more people living in the village in 1688,
412: 255 were new, born in the intervening years, or incomers.
Births and deaths were not the important reason for this
astonishing turnover, however, for only ninety-two baptisms
and ninety-two burials were registered in the intervening
period, just over a third of the exits and the entrances.

This then is what could happen to a perfectly ordinary rural
village in twelve years. We can compare it with one other
settlement of its kind, a smaller one, but over ten years rather
than twelve, between 1618 and 1628. This is Cogenhoe in
Northamptonshire, where 86 of 185 people (46 per cent) disappeared in the decade, 16 only dying, and 94 of 180 (52 per
cent) appeared, 29 by being born.[36]

In these two communities people were moving to and fro,
society was changing, whole households were coming and
going, and both villages were in perpetual exchange with their
neighbours. For migration was mainly, but not entirely local.
We know this from the documents which survive for the
intervening period. This was what was said when these still
astonishing facts were first announced in 1963.[37]

In spite of sudden change of this sort, and of the more
gradual change which came about through the succession of
son to father, nephew to uncle, kinsman to kinsman, the
impression of permanence in the constituent households
which composed a Stuart community is easy to understand.
Nearly half of the heads of households at Clayworth had
either died or had left the village by 1688, nevertheless their
successors presided over units of persons which were mostly
recognizably the same. And at Cogenhoe, where eight out of
thirty-three households failed to survive a decade of change,

it is still true that over three-quarters of them did survive, often with different heads, with a membership sometimes extensively revised, but still the same households, inhabiting the same buildings, working the same fields. The system, that familial, patriarchal system which dominated and gave structure to pre-industrial society, had succeeded in maintaining permanence in spite of the shortness of life, the fluctuations of prosperity, the falling in of leases, the wayward habits of young folk in service, and the fickleness of their employers.

The institutions of the old world must be looked upon in this way, as expedients to provide permanence in an environment which was all too impermanent and insecure. The respect due to the old and experienced, the reverence for the Church and its immense, impersonal antiquity, the spontaneous feeling that it was the family which gave a meaning to life because the family could and must endure, all these things helped to reconcile our ancestors with relentless, remorseless mortality and mischance. But they must not deceive the historian into supposing that the fixed and the ancient were the only reality: an unchanging, unchangeable social structure may well be essential to a swiftly changing population.

The historical observer in an inquiry of this sort can only feel himself to be in the position of the scientist in his bathyscope, miles beneath the surface of the sea, concentrating his gaze for a moment or two on the few strange creatures who happen to stray out of the total darkness into his beam of light. Where have they come from, and what will happen to them? he cannot help asking himself. What did happen to poor little Copperwhite Mastin, son of Elizabeth Mastin, spinster, and seven months old in May 1688, the only bastard alive in Clayworth? Or to the Coles household, thirteen strong, which appeared at Cogenhoe in 1623, no doubt as tenants of the leased-out manor, was there in 1624, but had disappeared by 1628? Even more puzzling and challenging is to ask whether these two communities are in fact typical of the whole. On this the historian can only talk as the scientist might. Here are two examples of communities in motion, two tiny globes of light disposed at random a little way down into the great ocean of persons who lived and died in our country before records of persons in general began to be kept. These samples may be ordinary enough, but they may be quite extraordinary. We cannot yet tell: we may never be able to tell.

In the twenty years which have passed since 1963 we have learnt enough to know that neither Clayworth nor Cogenhoe was extraordinary. We have not found similar sets of documents for the study of change and replacement of population, though we have established the fact which such changes must imply, that it was rare, not common, for surnames to persist in a village community over centuries or even scores of years, however.[38] Let us leave the issue of turnover and persistence and turn to Mr Thomas Wawen, called 'lord of the soil' in the 1688 listing of Clayworth.

Like every other landlord, Thomas Wawen was to some degree bound by manorial custom which had the force of local law, and general custom too. These might tie his hands as to the length and conditions of his leases, even the amount of his rents. Custom, what his neighbours, the village generally, thought, as well as universal expectation, would inevitably influence him in making the many other decisions open to him. He had to decide, to begin with, how much of his land he would keep under his own hand, as the saying was, and work from his house with his servants. Then he had to determine how much he would rely on those servants, or how much work he would get done by labourers coming in from the village and working their day's work on his land. Another decision to be made was whether he would feed such day-labourers during their working-time or pay them extra so that they could bring their own food. If he had to 'table' them, then his housekeeping would have to be on a scale to correspond with his obligations. The only way for him to avoid having his workers in his house altogether would be either to let all his land and buy his provisions, a possible but not very easy prospect, or to make arrangements for one or other of the local husbandmen, workers of the land, to come and undertake all the operations on his home farm.[39]

A landlord who lived away from the community in another of his houses, or one who lived in London in hired accommodation and took no responsibility for running any of his land, would of course tend to let as much of his estate as he could. His bailiff or his tenant would, no doubt, also get as much of the work done as possible by putting it out 'to task'. The economically minded amongst the owners of land, more- over, might reckon precisely how much more profitable it would be to make one choice or another amongst those we have listed.

But the social duty of every 'lord of the soil' was made quite plain to him: he was expected to reside in his manor house or at least in one of those he owned. He, or his resident tenant, was also firmly expected to work as much of the home-farm- land as possible, maintain a household-full of servants and keep up a table for the day-labourers. It was not by any means a matter of custom alone. Raising crops and tending stock go on in the night as well as the day, and this gave the household servant system a permanent advantage. Before the coming of the bicycle and the paved highway, there was a fixed distance from the labourer's cottage beyond which a full day's work was out of the question – it took too long to get there and back. These were some of the conditions which made it im- possible for the landowner to act as entrepreneur in the modern fashion, to run their land as our farmers do, using daytime labour alone, hired from outside the house, on the model of the business or the factory.

Even in the twentieth century the limits to economic rationalism in farming are still in evidence, in the socialist perhaps even more than in the capitalist areas of the world. But 300 years ago, this issue could scarcely arise. Working the land, managing, nurturing a 'family' were then one and the same thing, and could no more be 'rationalized' than the cherishing of a wife or the bringing up of children. Even the nobleman with several seats in the countryside, and with a strong preference for living in his London house on his rents, recognized this sometimes irksome fact. Hence the feeling about the 'country' in opposition to the 'town', and hence a great deal of aristocratic guilt and ambivalence. Hence, also the plots of many of our English dramas, of the Elizabethan age, or of the time of the Restoration: and many of the emotional assumptions and overtones of our literature. 'I wish you were married and living in the country,' said Lord Rochester, the rake, to the cur which had bitten him. Even he could find no worse an imprecation.[40] Smaller men, right down to the humblest husbandman, or the labourer on his cottage patch, had no occasion to see any separation whatsoever between keeping house and working the soil, even if it was not his own soil which he had to work to get his living.

The village community was, as we have said, the group of households at the centre of a particular area of cultivated land. It might or might not be a manor, have its own church, or have one owner. If it did have a single owner, he might work it all himself, with one large household, or, at least, as one estate.[41] More probably, he let it out, either in large parcels, or in some large lots and some small (presumably the most usual), or all in small holdings. Apart from the large land-owner or landowners, a village might, and usually did, contain a mixture of freeholders and tenants, again some in a big and some in a small way. There would also be a number of families, often a sizeable minority, with only a scrap of land round a cottage, or no land at all. Proletarian families like this were on the increase as the eighteenth century drew near. Most of the craftsmen lacked land too, the masons and the ploughwrights, the weavers, the tailors, the cobblers, the carpenters and the rest.

But whatever the official description and the distribution of property and the numbers of the callings represented in it, as a community the village consisted of households in association. To the facts of geography, being together in the one place, were added all the bonds which are forged between human beings when they are permanently alongside each other; bonds of intermarriage and of kinship, of common ancestry and common experience and of friendship and co-operation in matters of common concern. To these must be added those created by conditions of living now vanished so entirely that it is no easy matter to imagine what they felt like. The lack of running water in the dwelling brought people, mostly the women of course, into each other's company several times a day at the well, or pool, or brook. The labour of grinding your own corn by hand made frequent visits to the windmill or watermill a convenience for everyone, from the larger houses to the smaller ones. The want of a ready supply of credit at the bank made everyone dependent on his friend, his neighbour or his relative at times when he needed ready money.[42] This is another reason why weight in the community went with wealth; its most evident expression, however, was the size of the agrarian household which a man had to keep in operation.

Households and families, however, are under imperatives

which differ fundamentally from those of locality and of economics, of the turnover of population and the expected manner of carrying on work. They are bound to depend on the chances of birth, of marriage and of death. It is to these that we must now turn our attention.

Misbeliefs about our ancestors
Chapter 4

The absence of child marriage and extended family households from the English past

---

> My child is yet a stranger in the world,
> She hath not seen the change of fourteen years.
> Let two more summers wither in their pride
> Ere we may think her ripe to be a bride.

Capulet says this in the second scene of *Romeo and Juliet*. But whatever he said and whatever he felt, his child Juliet did take Romeo to husband at about her fourteenth birthday. Juliet's mother left her in no doubt of what she thought.

> Well, think on marriage now. Younger than you
> Here in Verona, ladies of esteem,
> Are made already mothers. By my count
> I was your mother much upon these years
> That you are now a maid.

So she had married at twelve, or early thirteen, and all those other ladies of Verona also. Miranda was married in her fifteenth year in the *Tempest*. It all seems clear and consistent enough. The women in Shakespeare's plays, and so presumably the Englishwomen of Shakespeare's day, might marry in their early teens, or even before, and very often did.[1]

Yet this is not true. Every record so far examined, and the number is now considerable, clearly demonstrates that marriage was rare at these early ages in Elizabethan and Jacobean England. Marriage and child-bearing in the late teens were not as common as they are now and at twelve marriage as we understand it was virtually unknown. Girls could be *espoused* then, or even before, but that was a different matter.

Some of the evidence for these blank statements will have to be presented here and we shall have to be clear as to what constituted marriage. Espousals, so common in Shakespearean drama, were not marriages as we think of marriage, but counted as such if the undertaking was made before witnesses in the present tense. They became marriage itself when made in the future tense, if, but only if, sexual intercourse took place. Such espousals *de futuro* will have to concern us again when we come to sexual discipline.[2]

Table 5: *Mean age at first marriage*

	Mean age of bridegrooms	Mean age of brides	Difference
All applicants for licences, Diocese of Canterbury, 1619–60 (1007 bridegrooms, 1007 brides)	26·65	23·58	3·07
Standard deviation	4·61	4·12	
Gentry only amongst Canterbury applicants (118 bridegrooms, 118 brides)	26·18	21·75	4·43
Standard deviation	4·41	3·60	
Marriages of nobles,* from about 1600 to about 1625 (325 brides, 313 bridegrooms)	24·28	19·39	4·89
Marriages of nobles,* from about 1625 to about 1650 (510 brides, 403 bridegrooms)	25·99	20·67	5·32

* Kindly communicated by T. H. Hollingsworth of the University of Glasgow.[3]

People could marry by licence as well as by banns in England then, just as they still can in the Church of England today. They had to apply for the licence to the bishop of the diocese they lived in, and very often they were required to give their ages. The reason was that no one under twenty-one could be married by the church without parental permission: it was a grave sin to do so at an older age without good reason. We have examined 1007 such licences containing the ages of the applicants, issued by the diocese of Canterbury between 1619 and 1660 to people marrying for the first time.[4] Our results are set out in Table 5. The mean age of brides, as will be seen, was over ten years later than Juliet's, about 23½. Bridegrooms were a good three years older, though some of the age gaps recorded were wider. When individual ages are looked at, however, we do find very occasional marriages in the early teens. One girl gave her age as thirteen, none as fourteen, four as fifteen, twelve as sixteen, but all the rest of the brides in the sample, 990 of them, were seventeen or over, and more than four out of five had reached the age of twenty. Only ten of the men were younger than this. The commonest age for women was twenty-two, for men twenty-four; the median – the age below which as many got married as above it – was some 22·75 for women, 25·5 for men.

Put in the familiar form we use in conversation, the average age of this sample of Elizabethan and Jacobean brides was about 23½ and the average age of bridegrooms was about 26½. Our results have been amply confirmed from other sources and from many parts of England and other areas of west and north-west Europe. We shall be quoting more precise figures later in the next chapter showing even higher ages. Surely these facts by themselves ought to be sufficient to dispel the belief that our ancestors married much younger than we do.

But the literary references are so straightforward, and Shakespeare at least so influential that we must go further: there seems to be some desire in our day to believe in this particular mistake. Did the gentry marry early? – after all Romeo and Juliet were not ordinary people.

Table 5 gives an answer to this more difficult question, showing that gentle brides were younger than the others in the middle years of the seventeenth century in the Canterbury diocese, that is eastern Kent. Bridegrooms were of much the same age as the rest of the population. When the first marriage of peers from all over the realm are added, this contrast is made a little sharper, but it cannot be said to be very impressive, and further research has not always confirmed the figures. Later in the century gentry seem to have been a little older at first marriage than craftsmen, and the age at marriage of peers went up. No class of the English population as far as we can see ever seems to have married at anything like the ages suggested by Shakespeare's plays.

The mean age at marriage, all marriages, in our day is twenty-eight or twenty-nine for men and twenty-five or twenty-six for women. When everything now known is added to the evidence presented here the conclusion is inescapable. It is not true to say that in England in earlier times, in the world we have lost as we have called it, people, either ordinary or privileged, married much younger than we marry now. In fact they were markedly older in relation to the number of years for which they lived. Whereas a woman marrying at twenty-five in Elizabethan England would on average live for some thirty-two or thirty-three years, and her husband at say twenty-eight for three or four years less than that, an English-woman of twenty-five in our day has fifty years or more in front of her.

Juliet's mother's statement is a little extraordinary in quite another way, since it is doubtful whether she or her daughter were capable of sexual relations, and above all of procreation, at age thirteen. It has been established that the age of sexual maturity in women has fallen in western Europe in the last century or so, and in all other industrialized areas of the world. In Manchester in 1835 working-class girls could expect their first period at an average of 15·6 years, but middle-class girls at 14·3, a difference to be noted. In 1890 the level seems to have been about the same for the middle class, but the working class showed an average of 15·0 in 1910. Ages could be higher than these in the 1800s: 16·8 in Copenhagen and in Munich in 1820 for poorer people, 15·0 in Norway for the middle class. The fall after 1900 can best be observed in the USA, where the general age was 14·1 in that year, but 12·9 in 1951 and 12·8 today, the current Japanese figure. In southern England it is now about 13·1, but in northern England 13·4 for the middle class, 13·6 for working girls.[5]

This is an intriguing but difficult subject, for it should be evident that age at menarche varies from class to class and area to area as well as from time to time. No single average age at sexual maturity, meaning full physical development and capacity to bear children, can have existed in England in Elizabeth's day, or in pre-industrial Europe generally. But there are fairly persuasive grounds for supposing that the average or mean age cannot have been much lower than sixteen anywhere in Shakespeare's day, or earlier. If both these persons, Juliet and her mother, had been able to behave as the play requires, then both must have been a long way from the average, the average experience of the audience. They would have had to have reached childbearing age well before the young English aristocrat who, as far as we know, produced a baby at the earliest point in the life course, that is Elizabeth

Manners, wife of the second Earl of Exeter. She was brought to bed in 1589 at about fourteen years five months. Even in the 1980s a girl would be hard put to it to deliver a baby much before the age of fourteen, if she matured at the lowest of the average ages set out above.

But such deliveries do occur, since there is always variation about any mean. The extent of this variation has been determined for the present day, and, within limits, for earlier times. There is a fairly remote chance, perhaps one out of every hundred or more, that Juliet would have been capable of accepting Romeo's advances, considering that she was a very exceptional young lady, in her diet and general living standards, even if she could not possibly have borne a child by then. But the chances against *both* Juliet *and* her mother having been able to behave in the way we are asked to suppose have to be reckoned in the thousands. The more the point is laboured, the less credible the view that there was anything realistic whatever in the literary intentions of the play in these respects.[6]

If we ask ourselves what those intentions were, we might suppose that Shakespeare was playing upon the rather hazy information of the bulk of his audience about the maturational differences between aristocrats and the mass of the people, or between Verona a hundred and fifty years earlier and England in their day, or both. He exaggerated, as writers so often do, a difference of considerable interest to everyone. Even this seems to me to ask entirely too much in the way of knowledge and awareness from Elizabethan playgoers and to attribute to Shakespeare an observational percipience only too often bestowed on a great artist in virtue of his imaginative capacity. Much more plausible is the view that he was deliberately writing a play about love and marriage amongst boys and girls without any recognition of the facts about the age of women at their weddings or at sexual maturity. Scholars have discovered that he actually reduced Juliet's age; in the English source containing the plot for the play, Arthur Broke's poem *Romeus and Juliet*, published in 1562, Juliet was sixteen. Four years later another author who told the story, William Painter in his collection of novels *The Palace of Pleasure*, made Juliet eighteen years old. When Shakespeare came to adapt it he may possibly have had to reduce the heroine's age to suit the boy actor who was to play her part. But some of his other heroines seem to be mature enough, Viola in *Twelfth Night* for example. The insistence on Juliet's being a young girl looks quite deliberate.

We have some grounds for supposing that there would have been people present in the theatre who might have noticed Juliet's precocity, and disapproved of it. It would certainly have displeased the testy parish clerk of a church on the other side of London from the Globe in Southwark, St Botolph's Aldgate. This respectable citizen was given to ironical animad-version on the conduct of persons whose actions he was bound to record, but which he thought wrong. On 6 July 1623 he wrote this about the wedding of a threadmaker to the daughter of a porter.

The man was about xvii yeares of Age and ye woman xiiii
A worthie Ancient couple of young Fooles.

Evidently he felt that they were adult, man and woman, at seventeen and fourteen, but far too young for marriage. Very occasional records of such events could be found in most registers at all times. Even people admitted to be children do make a rare appearance in the records.

The 'marriage' of these children, however, was of a kind we should scarcely recognize. One quite exceptional case in the fifteenth century is of a noblewoman being 'married' at a time when she could not have been capable of sexual intercourse. Margaret, Lady Rowecliffe, first had a husband in 1463 at the age of four, but had lost him by the age of twelve, when she was given another one. The bridegroom's father then under-took that 'they should not ligg togeder til she came to the age XVI years', which is the plainest indication I have seen of the time at which an Englishwoman of late medieval times could be expected to be sexually mature. Such early 'marriages' should properly be called espousals *de futuro*, those promises to marry in the future to which we have referred. Life was uncertain amongst commoners as well as amongst aristocrats. The marriage partner to be taken by an heir apparent was always a matter of the first importance where there was an estate and name to be safeguarded.

In 1593, Robert Furse, of Moreshead in Devonshire, for example, a substantial yeoman on his way up in the world and engaged like every other yeoman of ability in building up his family, matched his son at the age of nine years and three months to Susan Alford, an orphan and the ward of a kinsman: the actual marriage was to take place when Robert's son reached the age of fifteen. In this instance either death intervened or one or other of the children exercised their undoubted right not to carry out the bargain made for them by their parents and guardians, for no marriage took place. This was obviously a fairly usual arrangement; the postponement of the actual union must have been usual too.[7]

The records of the diocesan courts, which dealt with disputes over marriage, contain numbers of cases of affianced minors, some of whom, the older ones, did actually live together and were expected to have done so. Frederick Furnivall, that marvellous Victorian literary antiquarian, published in 1897 for his Early English Text Society a volume of extracts from those records with the title *Child Marriages, Divorces and Ratifications, etc.*, which may itself have done much to foster the tradition that the marriage of children was an ordinary occurrence in Tudor times. In the single Diocese of Chester between the years 1561 and 1566 he found documents concerning about thirty couples 'married' young, some of them at a very early age indeed; there were matches between babes-in-arms, matches between teenagers, matches between children entirely unwilling to live with each other. One poor lad of eleven or twelve, according to the testimony of his bride of thirteen or fourteen, was brought to bed with her weeping to go home with his father, 'and lay still till in the morning . . . with his back towards her all night'. 'He never touched her bare skin,' so he himself affirmed.

We could scarcely expect the exuberant Furnivall to put these intriguing facts into any sort of numerical proportion. If we do it for him we can estimate that well over 10,000 weddings must in fact have taken place in the diocese of Chester during the six years in question. These wretched children cannot, therefore, have made up one-half of 1 per cent of all persons marrying in that area in that period. In nearly all the documents which Furnivall prints it is made plain that the settlement of property was at issue. None of the married children mentioned lived together until late in their teens, and it is hinted that some were not fit to do so even then.

Child marriage of this kind may well have been commoner in the sixteenth century than in the seventeenth. But what-

ever their nature and purpose they cannot be called representative of the marriages of the great majority who had no
land, no house and no property worth assuring in this peculiar
fashion. The possibility still remains that it was part of
Shakespeare's dramatic intention to make Romeo and Juliet,
and perhaps some of his other heroes and heroines too, younger
than was usual in his day. If anything, legal and biographical
evidence of the kind presented by Furnivall tends to give
substance to the claim that literary evidence may be system-
atically deceptive in these matters. Like the St Botolph's
parish clerk, some of the witnesses to the Chester cases
remarked in surprise and disapproval at the youth of the
parties concerned; they knew they were talking of extraordinary people. The Elizabethan writers certainly give no
hint that this was what they were doing. But then poets,
dramatists and novelists are seldom commenting on ordinary
people. Even when the effect they strive for is precisely this,
they often succeed in making heroes and heroines completely
out of the ordinary.

It is true, and very important to the social historian, that
the spontaneous assumptions in the literature of any age, the
behaviour of the minor characters, the conventions against
which irony and humour must be understood, reveal with
great precision facts of considerable interest about the structure of society. We shall find ourselves arguing in something
like this way from time to time in this essay. But it is indeed
hazardous to infer an institution or a habit characteristic of a
whole society or a whole era from the central character of a
literary work and its story, from *Pamela*, for example, or from
Elizabeth Bennett in *Pride and Prejudice* just as much as from
Juliet or Viola. The outcome may be to make people believe
that what was the entirely exceptional was in fact the perfectly normal. This certainly seems to have happened with the
Capulet ladies and the Elizabethan age of marriage. It is easy
to see how a very similar distortion might come about if some
future historian used *Lolita* or *Fear of Flying* as a source book
for our own sexual habits, uncorrected by other evidence,
unliterary and statistical.[8] This is a cogent argument in favour
of statistical awareness, and of the sociological imagination, in
studies of this sort. Conventional historical or literary inference is not enough.

All this may seem to be an unnecessary complication of the

task of the historical sociologist at this early stage in his studies, and to have very little to do with an introductory essay of this type. But everything we can get to know about differences between the privileged people and the rest in pre-industrial times is of significance. It is pretty clear from the body of evidence which has been expertly analysed by auxologists, that is students of growth, evidence which ranges over height, weight, breaking of the voice in males, the swelling out of the breasts in girls, and so on, why it is that these things vary from social group to social group and time to time. It is the better health and maintenance, as well as the better feeding, of the middle classes and of those in the more prosperous areas at the present time which are the operative reasons why they mature earlier, put on weight and height more quickly than the working classes. This must mean that everyone, even the most privileged, matured later in pre-industrial times than we all do now. But it also means that differences between classes in these respects may have been greater.

Now if this was indeed true of all privileged people in the world we have lost, of all members of the ruling stratum as we have called it, in relation to the rest, and of the gentry as a society in relation to those below them in the social scale, then it implies a very remarkable contrast between the two sections of the population. The privileged were no doubt taller, heavier and better developed than the rest just as they were in Victorian times. In the Elizabethan age, and in pre-industrial times generally, gentlemen may have had beards and broken voices earlier than the rest of the population, and ladies may have become full women more quickly.

We have spelt out syllable by syllable the analysis of the effect upon us today of this particular fragment of the world we have lost for reasons which go further than those to do with evidence, what shall count and what shall not, and how deceptive things can be. Such a procedure should draw attention to the materials now being used by historical sociologists, and to some of their methods. It shows them in collaboration with literary scholars and even with biologists, though their relationship with other social scientists such as anthropologists, econometricians and psychologists has yet to become evident. But the overriding significance of our chosen example is social structural. The mistake about Juliet's marriage age in its relation to the actual experience of Shakespeare's audience is most decidedly not a trivial one.

For if you are unaware of the conditions imposed on individuals by its marriage rules, you misunderstand English society as a whole, over time and at the present day. Its particular mode of reproducing itself, its means of maintaining a balance with its available subsistence, above all its familial system, all escape you. A case could be made for supposing that unless western Europeans, and especially English people, had been able to ensure that a long stretch of time, longer than any elsewhere, elapsed between menarche and procreation, the social transformation with which we are perpetually concerned in this essay – the coming of industrialization, that is to say – might never have occurred. This is to poise a very heavy weight on one or two social structural facts, and we cannot explicate them to any great extent here. Before we can go any further into such questions, however, we have to confront another historical delusion, that to do with the size and composition of the English family group in the past. And to do with their kin relations too.

As widely held as the assumption about child marriage, and certainly more deeply rooted in belief and in opinion, about the self as well as about society, is the supposition that our ancestors lived in large familial units. Family groups, it seems to be almost universally agreed, ordinarily consisted in the pre-industrial past of grandparents, children, married as well as unmarried, grandchildren and often relatives, all sleeping in the same house, eating together and working together. This was so, it is supposed, because wedded sons and perhaps daughters too, but especially eldest sons, were permitted or even expected to live with their parents. A widowed mother would accordingly stay in the household after her son had taken over, or join him or another of her children in their establishments. If her children were all unmarried and her parents were still alive, she might go to live with them, taking her offspring with her. An unmarried uncle, aunt or cousin might do the same. Married brothers might share households too, perhaps after the death of their father, but under other circumstances, and for working purposes. Given conditions like these, households would have had to be bigger than our households are, and more complicated in their inner relationships as well: extended families is the phrase which is nearly always used.

Now all these statements have been demonstrated to be false, false for traditional England that is to say, as false and as misleading as the statements about age at marriage. It is not true that most of our ancestors lived in extended families. It is not true that industrialization brought the simple nuclear family with it. In England there was actually an increase in the tiny proportion of more complicated households in the period of economic transformation. It is not true that the elderly and the widowed ordinarily had their married children living with them, or that uncles, aunts, nephews and nieces were often to be found as resident relatives. It is not even true that the casualties of earlier, harder times, the victims of age, sickness, bereavement or want, could usually rely on their kin for continuing maintenance even though they did not live with them. Although the average family group was half as large again as it is today, four and three-quarters persons instead of a little over three, the reason for this has almost nothing to do with the extended family. The difference has to be attributed to demography, and to the presence of servants.

We have seen that the huge household run by the Hales at Goodnestone in 1676 with twenty-two persons in it, and the even greater one at Chilvers Coton kept by the Newdigates in 1684 with thirty-seven, contained many more children than we are used to. But it was the servants, fourteen in one and twenty-eight in the other, which made them really large. Since servants, life-cycle servants as we have called them, were transferred children, their presence ensured that the important households should be bigger and the unimportant households smaller. This did not increase the *average* number of persons making up the domestic unit in the traditional world, of course; a simple transfer of persons between them could not have done so. The larger size of the average household then than now must be due to other causes, of which our much reduced fertility is one. The more modest, servant-supplying families of pre-industrial society had fewer births and usually fewer survivors of infancy and childhood than the more substantial, servant-keeping families. This intensified the contrast. But the grand domestic establishments of traditional English society were rarities, numerically, as Gregory King makes clear. They bulk much too large in the view we take of it.

They do so once again for literary reasons, and for touristic

reasons too. Everyone is at home in Olivia's capacious household in *Twelfth Night*. Malvolio, the major-domo; Maria,
Olivia's kinswoman but also her maid; Sir Toby, her resident
uncle; these are all real personalities to us, in our day: we can
identify with them. What is more we can wander through the
great aristocratic houses of the Tudor, Stuart, Georgian and
and early Victorian eras and linger in the servants' quarters.
Hardwick and Audley End, Erddig, Blenheim and Woburn,
the list is endless, and all of them look as if a Malvolio was once
in charge. There is almost nothing to remind us that there
were excessively few Marias or Sir Tobys in that now vanished
social order, and that even stewards of households must have
been limited to the number of great houses. We find it almost
impossible to put ourselves in the position of the single,
toilworn servant who slept in the corner of the 'hall' in the
humble husbandman's house already mentioned. Until very
recently it was not even realized how many such persons there
were in our past, making up most of that whole eighth of the
entire population who were in service at any one time.

The wish to believe in the large, extended, kin-enfolding,
multi-generational, welfare- and support-providing household
in the world we have lost seems to be exceedingly difficult to
expose to critical evaluation. There are a number of reasons
for this. One may be the conviction that those whom we regard
as the casualties of our industrial world, of whom the vast
numbers of our elderly people are conspicuous examples, have
been exiled by history, exiled from the family to which of right
they belong. It is of great importance that we should efface
this impression; the proper understanding of ourselves in time
is what we are charged with as historical sociologists.

But it is also our duty to be just to our English predecessors,
in their terms as well as in our own. If they had an individual-
istic familial system very like the one which we live under, if
they showed forth the principle of neo-localism, as the
anthropologists call it – setting up your own household at
marriage that is to say, and living in it for the rest of your life
– as conspicuously as we do ourselves, they did not lack
familial solidarity outside the compass of the nuclear family.

The claim that few families were multi-generational, the
figure being about one family in twenty, does not mean that
there were no multi-generational families at all. Nor does it
mean that elderly widows, or even widowers, never lived with

their married children, for it was quite common for this to happen. The neo-local rule against living with your parents after marriage does not imply that your parent should not finally come to live with you. Since the widowed elderly were a small proportion of the population, their not infrequent presence in the household did not give rise to as much multi-generationality as might be expected. The neo-local rule itself was sometimes broken, since children did stay at home after marriage occasionally, for a few months or even a year or so until they could move into their own place. Orphans were found familial niches, though these were by no means always with their kinfolk, and the finding, as far as we can see, was not infrequently done by the parish, or other non-familial authority.

The wider kin, as distinct from the immediate, could be of considerable importance on particular occasions in the life of an individual all the same. They frequently appear when it was a question of getting a job, or making a trading connection, raising some capital or migrating for any of these or for other reasons. They come forward at critical junctures in the life course: at the births of children, when illnesses became disabling, at marriages, at deaths, even if they were so seldom sources of permanent support, psychological or financial. But it must be noticed that neighbours and friends are found in those positions too, and in some respects, such as standing surety for debts, were more important than kinsfolk, in the fourteenth century as much as in the eighteenth. It is not without interest that in the language of the time 'friends' covered both kinsfolk and other intimates. Nevertheless, some of the negatives which we have laid down about familial interaction seem to have been absolute. Two brothers living together after marriage and collaborating in the work on the same farm have never made an appearance in the English record.[9] And the famous stem family household, where the heir, the eldest or perhaps the youngest son, stays at home, marries and has children whilst the rest either leave or go unmarried, is conspicuous by its absence too.

Neither the stem family nor the simple or nuclear family is as straightforward as might seem. For the familial group is a process, rather than a state, changing and developing from the time of its formation to the time of its dissolution in a cyclical manner. Its membership at one point in the family cycle cannot be taken as necessarily representing its membership at other points. A stem-family tendency may therefore exist in a society when only a few of its constituent households show forth the stem-family form. There were far too few households in traditional England with this constitution to allow such a thing to be taken as a usual practice, but English family households could change enormously in their membership during the family cycle, a cycle which occurred only once of course in every individual case in the simple family system. Under other systems an individual household could persist while the family within it underwent several cycles.

If the parents, or one parent, of a man or his wife heading a simple family household paid a visit to them, the kin composition of the family household of the younger couple would become complex for that time, and bigger too. Similarly if a brother or sister should dwell with them, or a more distant relative. Most alterations in the family itself changed its size rather than its kinship composition, however, and here the birth, and perhaps the early death, of children, and their leaving home when they were mature, were conspicuous events, and sometimes the death, or remarriage, of one of the spouses. But it was in the membership of the household, rather than in that of the family part of it, that the changeover was most marked, if servants were usually employed. For servants came and went at the end of every servant year, which was in the early or late autumn in most parts of the country, and the numbers which a family employed changed too. A family household could be a very different thing from decade to decade, year to year or even month to month, although it never became complex in its kinship composition.

These circumstances have led to confusion as well as to misunderstanding and disagreement when scholars have tried to compare family systems from region to region and time to time. But we now know enough to state with some confidence that the familial arrangements of northern and western Europe as a whole were like those we have described for traditional England, if not quite to the same extent and not so uniformly over time and from place to place.

We can also show that late marriage and a high proportion of life-cycle servants fitted in to a familial system which distinguished England and the west from much of the rest of the world, even from southern and eastern Europe, and to some

extent from central Europe too. Tables 6 and 7 show some of
the English figures which have convinced us of these points.
They are based on the largest body of such materials which
has yet been assembled for the familial past of any national
society, but the sample is nevertheless woefully restricted.

Table 6: *One hundred English settlements, 1754–1821 –
distribution of households by number of members*

Members	Proportion of households (%)	Proportion of population (%)
1	5·7	1·2
2	14·2	6·0
3	16·5	10·4
4	15·8	13·2
5	14·7	15·4
6	11·8	14·8
7	3·0	11·7
8	5·4	9·0
9	3·1	5·8
10	1·9	4·0
11 and over	3·0	8·5
	100	100

Total population 68,407

Source: HFPT, Table 4.8.

Table 6 brings out the fact that households could be small;
indeed size three was commonest, and nearly two-fifths of the
population lived in those of three, four or five. But over half
were members of groups consisting of six or more, and the
final figure in the second column of the table betrays the
presence of the servant-swollen establishments which we have
discussed, those of substantial yeomanry, the gentlemen, the
knights, the baronets, the bishops and the peers.

The hierarchy of households which we were able to witness
at Goodnestone confirms itself for traditional English society
as a whole in the next set of figures in Table 7. This is a slightly
uncertain conclusion in view of the tiny samples, the numbers
in the column headed N in the table referring to those settlements out of the total of 100 which unequivocally record the
features in question. Still, every further listing of inhabitants
dating from before the nineteenth century which we have
found has tended to confirm the message conveyed by these
numbers, a message on which we have already insisted several
times already.

There is evidence that by the 1850s and 1860s these things had started to change, but in a way very different from what traditional opinion might lead us to expect. It begins to look as if the poor and very poor, especially those long resident in one village and accepted as established members of the community, were more likely to have relatives living with them

Table 7: *One hundred English settlements, 1574–1821 – size of household, size of child group, proportion of households with relatives, proportion of households with servants, by social status of household head*

		Mean size of household		Mean size of child group		Proportion of households with relatives (%)		Proportion of households with servants (%)
	N		N		N		N	
Gentlemen	26	6·63	26	2·94	16	27·6	18	81·1
Clergy	25	5·83	12	3·53	12	25·0	16	81·2
Yeomen	35	5·91	17	2·76	9	17·0	14	71·9
Husbandmen	35	5·09	33	3·10	14	17·3	21	46·8
Tradesmen and craftsmen	40	4·65	42	2·90	18	12·3	25	23·3
Labourers	33	4·51	32	2·70	16	7·9	21	2·2
Paupers	16	3·96	13	2·34	6	7·7	26 ⎫	
Others	39	3·72	37 ⎱ 2·31		18	15·0	26 ⎭	13·9
Not stated	19	4·29						

Note: the proportions in the two right hand columns are means of the percentages in the settlements concerned.

Source: HFPT, Table 4.16.

than anyone else. The hierarchy which puts the élite at the top, with most kin in the households, was being reversed.[10] A possible explanation of this might be that it was pressure on space which compelled these poor people to double up with their relatives. This would scarcely account for the facts. The unsettled, footloose members of the mid-Victorian village examined had fewest relatives alive, and as for the gentlemen and aristocrats, almost universally supposed to be most likely to live in complex family households, they could and did afford houses of any size they pleased.

It seems clear, moreover, that the relative cost of housing in pre-industrial times was less, perhaps considerably less, than it is now. The humblest dwelling of all, a cottage for the labouring poor, could, it seems, be put up new for less than two years of the annual wage of a labourer, and the justices of the peace seem always to be authorizing or ordering such undertakings as if they were a casual matter. Landlords and overseers of the poor would erect them apparently as a matter of course, and one of the persistent, if probably baseless, traditions of the village community was that if a poor man could build himself a cottage on the 'waste', the common grazing land, of a manor overnight, he could occupy it undisturbed. This tradition indicates the restrictions which stood in the way of building. It needed the permission of the justices to divide a cottage between families or to turn a barn or part of a barn into a dwelling. It was easier, and no doubt cheaper, to split up existing structures in such a way as to give something like independent accommodation for different families, though the authorities did not like this either, especially in the towns.[11] Such a propensity makes any argument from housing to household size or structure rather hazardous.

Where lists of the houses in a village have survived, however, some seem always to have been vacant, especially in the later seventeenth century. This is a feature of the Hearth Tax returns of the 1660s, '70s and '80s.[12] Not that homelessness was unknown in those years or at any time in that era of endemic poverty and wretchedness. One Simon Gibbs, writes the clerk to the Justices of Warwickshire in January 1667, 'is destitute of an habitation for his wife and five small children, having long lain out of doors'. A cottage was ordered to be erected on the common of his village.[13]

The last set of facts about households which we can present in tabular form (Table 8) has to do with multi-generationality and with kinship composition. The source from which this table has been borrowed goes on to cite a settlement in seventeenth-century Germany with 17 per cent of three generational households; one in eighteenth-century Italy with 45 per cent of multiple·family households; one in early nineteenth-century Russia, with 73 per cent of multiple households and also with 65 per cent of households containing three generations or more. There is an astonishing contrast with English households with only 5 per cent, especially in the Russian case. It could be said in fact that the illusion about the large-scale, kin-complex household in English society has arisen because the familial past of English-born and

Table 8: *Sixty-four English settlements, 1622–1854 – kinship composition and generational depth of household*

	Proportion of solitaries (%)	Proportion of households with no family (%)	Proportion of simple family households (%)	Proportion of extended family households (%)	Proportion of multiple family households (%)	Proportion of households with:		
						1 generation (%)	2 generations (%)	3 generations (%)
30 most reliably recorded communities	8·5	3·6	72·1	10·9	4·1 ⎫			
35 next most reliably recorded communities	8·7	3·2	71·9	11·9	4.1 ⎭	25·1	69·2	5·7

Note: Simple family households consist of parents (or parent) and child (or children); extended family households, either of these with one or more relatives, these relatives not being married couples; multiple family households, those with two or more married couples related to each other; see *HFPT*, ch. 1 and Table 17, p. 291.

Source: *FLIL*, ch. 1, Table 1.2.

English-speaking peoples has been supposed to be identical with the familial past of those born within the confines of the present day united soviet socialist republics of Russia.

The neo-local rules which have governed the shape of the English family for so long can be written out as follows. Under ordinary circumstances no two married couples could make an appearance in the same co-resident familial group. Even the remnant of a nuclear family, a widowed parent with a child, tended to count as a married couple for this purpose, and servants in the household had also to conform. When a son or daughter took a spouse, therefore, he or she had to leave, even if there was an expectation of taking over the family farm, and a new household had to be established. If this was not possible, then no marriage could take place. Once the wedding was over, the child lost the right of living in the parental family as or when it was convenient, a right which we can observe servants taking advantage of from time to time, returning to live for a while with their own parents when they were 'between places'. The mother and father of a married child were held to the neo-local rule as well. They had no *right* of residence in the family established by a child, even after widowhood, although it is clear that they were often brought in to that household in their final years of dependency. Indeed when it was advantageous for both parties, and for reasons of loyalty and affection, these principles could always be manipulated. The demonstration that the shape of English households has been such as would be brought about by these rules has been fairly straightforward. It was done by applying the classificatory scheme set out in Table 17 (p. 291) to lists of inhabitants like that of Clayworth in 1676. The outcome recorded there shows forth the principles we have been discussing in no uncertain fashion.

The creation of a new familial unit was brought about by the enterprise of the young couple, of both of them. But it usually also required the co-operation of each set of parents, or of those of them who were still alive and accessible. The bride's dowry came from her own family, but to this was added her savings, which were often the wages and the 'vails', that is the tips, which she had hoarded when in service, as well as her experience, her skill and her strength. These were not always and entirely a matter of housewifery, learnt from her mother or in the households where she had served. As we have noted, a few young women had served apprenticeships, and others would even have managed little undertakings of their own, as midwives, perhaps, or as teachers. But spinning or weaving were by far the most important sources of such earnings. If a woman were lacking in these possessions or accomplishments, then she could not get married, though sexual attractiveness would always count, at all times and on all social levels. The conduct of courtship will concern us in due course.

Neither sons nor daughters had to wait upon family inheritance before marriage could take place, except sometimes where land was at issue. For it was not always, or even in most instances, access to land which had to be acquired. Children decidedly did not marry in order of their age, nor is it easy to discern in the records before the nineteenth century any tendency for one or other of them, especially a daughter, to wait behind to look after ageing, widowed or infirm parents. There were other aspects of marriage strategy, for the parents of the parties as well as for the parties themselves. Marriage was a family affair, or rather a two-family affair, affecting the policy of the immediate and sometimes the more distant relatives of both partners.

There was the consolidation or extension of a family's land, which might be secured by the match, amongst those who controlled land. A dowry could consist in broad acres, or the expectation of them, as well as in an assembly of household goods in a chest. There were political alliances to be forged or extended, and these could be in the politics of the vestry and the village pump as well as of the county or the diocese. Parental arrangement of the matches of children was much more likely when the issues were of this kind, much less so with the most numerous of the brides and bridegrooms, where property was small and power unlikely to count for very much. In such cases, especially when a bride or bridegroom was an orphan and distant from home, parental consent could be of little consequence. Nevertheless it was always secured when possible. When, as was so frequently the case, one or both of the parties had been married before, parental consent was not in question, for the spouse was at his 'own dispose' as they put it. For each and every would-be married couple, however, the decision to set up a family for the first time could only be made when there was an opening, an opening in the social fabric so to speak.

For marriage, and particularly first marriage, we must repeat, was an act of profound importance to the social structure. It meant the creation of a new economic unit as well as of a lifelong association of two persons previously separate and caught up in existing families. It gave to the man full membership of the community and to the woman something to run; she became mistress of a household – as the French put it, *maîtresse de la maison*. A cell was added to society, in the town as well as in the country. It is understandable, therefore, that marriage could not come about unless a slot fell vacant and the aspiring couple was able to fill it up. It might be a cottage with its patch of ground and rights annexed to it on the common land, which became available to a manservant and a womanservant, and enabled them to set up as 'cottagers or labouring people'. It might be a bakery, or a joinery, a tailor's, butcher's, wheelwright's, blacksmith's or weaver's shop, each with its 'practice' attached, the body of customers that is to say in the habit of buying what was there turned out. Only for the truly fortunate would it be an assemblage of fields to own, or fields to rent, and this, often but not always, meant inheritance.

For all these slots there was a waiting period. Hence all young people had to wait to marry, and some could not marry at all. Once it is recognized that our English ancestors had the same rule as we have, two married couples not to be together in one family, then size and structure of household, age at marriage and proportions marrying can all be seen to be tied together and to be tied in their turn to the economics of the time as well as to the situation as to births and deaths. How long the waiting period had to be was affected by the numbers of the younger generation in relation to the numbers of the older generation, so that the fertility history of those in possession was at issue as well as their disposition to die. By and large there were bound to be niches for all but a few provided that the population was not increasing so fast that the new generation was greatly in excess of the old, and provided that economic activity increased proportionately. The time taken in actually locating the slots which were vacant, or about to become so, has also to be added to the queuing interval to marriage which society imposed on our ancestors.[14]

No wonder then that they were interested in births, marriages and deaths. No wonder every mother of daughters became

notorious for her curiosity about potential husbands. Since all
these ineluctable circumstances as to succession applied with
peculiar force to the literate and genteel, where finding an
heiress meant heightened wealth and consequence, and failure
to find a slot might mean social descent, it is comprehensible
that so large a part of their lives and their literature was given
up to the marriage market.[15] To understand the demography
of the world we have lost, always in relation to its productive
activities, is therefore to begin to see how its social structure
actually worked over time and at any one time, for rich and
poor, élite and proletariat alike. It happens that it has now
become possible to reconstruct the population history of
England with a completeness and an authenticity which has
surprised even those engaged in its study, and this for 200
years before industrialization began as well as for the industrializing generations themselves.[16] Before we turn our
attention to this astonishing record in the following chapter,
let us look at our ancestors as they were when actually engaged
in marriage as a *rite de passage*, in Yorkshire in the 1630s.

We have learnt to be wary of high literature as a photo-
graphic portrayal, and of what nobles and gentry can be
shown to have done as a guide to what everybody did. The
actors in the following passage must have been genteel too, or
at least of yeoman stock; certainly landed. But the atmosphere
is decidedly different from that of marriage scenes in Shakespeare, or Fielding or even in Defoe.

Concerning our Fashions of our Country Weddings

Usually the young man's father, or he himself, writes to the
father of the maid to know if he shall be welcome to the
house, if he shall have furtherance if he come in such a way
or how he liketh of the notion. Then if he [presumably the
woman's father] pretend any excuse, only thanking him for
his good will, then it is as good as a denial. If the motion be
thought well of, and embraced, then the young man goeth
perhaps twice to see how the maid standeth affected. Then
if he see that he be tractable, and that her inclination is
towards him, then the third time that he visiteth, he perhaps
giveth her a ten-shilling piece of gold, or a ring of that price;
or perhaps a twenty-shilling piece, or a ring of that price,
then 10*s*. the next time, or the next after that, a pair of

gloves of 6s. 8d. a pair; and after that, each other time, some conceited toy or novelty of less value. They visit usually every three weeks or a month, and are usually half a year, or very near, from the first going to the conclusion.

So soon as the young folks are agreed and contracted, then the father of the maid carrieth her over to the young man's house to see how they like of all, and there doth the young man's father meet them to treat of a dower, and likewise of a jointure or feoffment [this was what was settled on her] for the woman. And then do they also appoint and set down the day of the marriage, which may perhaps be about a fortnight or three weeks after, and in that time do they get made the wedding clothes, and make provision against the wedding dinner, which is usually at the maid's father's. Their use is [it is usual] to buy gloves to give to each of their friends a pair on that day; the man should be at the cost for them, but sometimes the man gives the gloves to the men and the woman to the women, or else he to her friends and she to his. They give them that morning when they are almost ready to go to church to be married.

Then so soon as the bride is tired [attired] and that they are ready to go forth, the bridegroom comes, and takes her by the hand, and saith: 'Mistress, I hope you are willing', or else kisseth her before them, and then followeth her father out of the doors. Then one of the bridegroom his men ushereth the bride, and goes foremost, and the rest of the young men usher each of them a maid to church. The bridegroom and the brides brothers or friends tend at dinner: he perhaps fetcheth her home to his house a month after, and the young man comes to fetch away his bride some of his best friends, and young men his neighbours, come along with him, and others perhaps meet them in the way, and then there is the same jollity at his house. For they perhaps have love ? wine [*sic* – as in original] ready to give to the company when they light [alight], then a dinner, supper and breakfast next day.[17]

There are clear signs here of the betrothal which, as we have already seen, was then separate from the later marriage. It is also quite plain that although the parents of the couple were principal actors in the business, everything depended on the consent and the willingness of the young people themselves.

What may be most surprising is that the married pair did not go away together after the feast in the home of the bride, but weeks later. The point which will have to be considered in due course is whether or not sexual intercourse was permissible or condoned, by the church or by the opinion of the village, between the contract and the marriage ceremony, or between the ceremony and the actual departure.

The marriage customs of Stuart Yorkshire may have differed widely from those elsewhere in England and Wales, and a great deal of work would have to be done to discover quite how the mass of the people got married; the really lowly people that is to say, the mere husbandmen, the journeymen, the artificers, the labourers, the paupers. The Ralph Meers, whose marriage in 1679 was mentioned in our last chapter, had been a servant in the house of the Wawens who were 'lords of the soil' at Clayworth, and he became a labourer in the village. He could surely not have afforded the rings, the sovereigns or half-sovereigns to give to Anne Fenton, his bride who had been his fellow servant. There can have been no family portion to speak of for Anne, though she may well have saved her wages, all of them, at 30*s*. or £2 a year against that wonderful day, and no question of a horse for them to alight from at the cottage door.

Anne was already pregnant at the time as we know, and both of them had been in trouble with the parson on that account. Nevertheless, and this is a highly significant fact for the disciplinary system which we are discussing, Ralph Meers became churchwarden within a year or two, and himself took responsibility for reporting on the sexual lives of the parishioners. There are plenty of other signs that the romantic respectability which has now attached itself to marriage and the married state in traditional England may be to some degree misplaced. Many of the brides and bridegrooms had been married before: something like a quarter of them were widowed persons in the seventeenth century, though their numbers were to fall within a generation or two. A far higher proportion had lost their fathers than their mothers, perhaps a third or even as much as a half, depending once more on the prevalent mortality. You could not with confidence expect to see your grandchildren in the world we have lost, not in England anyway.

Amongst the Russian serfs it was different. In their large

households we find more grandchildren of the household head than children: even great-grandchildren make an occasional appearance. This was only possible because marriage took place so early, if not as early as thirteen, then as soon as could be managed after attainment of sexual maturity in both the partners. It is remarkable how much we can teach ourselves about the society of our own ancestors, and of how it compares with other different societies in the past and in the present, by asking whether girls did marry in Elizabethan England at the age when Juliet married Romeo. For Juliet was indeed a child, a child transmogrified by the Shakespearean imagination.

Births, marriages and deaths
Chapter 5

The recovery of the English population record since the close of the Middle Ages

---

During the time when it may be apt to think of it as a world which we have lost, England was a pre-industrial society. In this it resembled the societies which we describe in our day as belonging to the Third World. But it does not follow from this that the incidence of births, marriages and deaths was the same with our country in the past as it is now with them, any more than the age of marriage has been the same.

As we contemplate what has been so recently established about the demography of England since the later Middle Ages, it becomes clearer and clearer how different this has been from that of India, or of Africa, or of South America in recent times. This must imply that the relationship between population and means of subsistence has been different, and we should expect it to have been more favourable in the country which first found it possible to escape from the pressure of numbers on resources. We begin our demographic survey of England before and during industrialization, with the size of the English population in round figures, and its percentage increase or decrease over thirty-year intervals, over the generations in fact (see Table 9).

Growth was rapid in Elizabethan times and up to the end of the reign of James I, very rapid in comparison with other European countries. After that the rate of increase fell quite sharply under Charles I and his successors, until population was actually contracting under James II and William and Mary. But expansion began again under the Georges, and with George III it became as fast as it had ever been before. By the time of Victoria it was at one of the highest levels ever known for a western country. A great deal of the expansion, as we have seen, was in the urban areas, and our record was remark-

Table 9: *Population of England, 1541–1871 (to nearest 1000)*

		% change over previous 30-year period				% change over previous 30-year period
1541	2,774,000	–		1721	5,350,000	8
1571	3,271,000	18		1751	5,722,000	8
1601	4,110,000	25		1781	7,042,000	22
1631	4,893,000	19		1811	9,886,000	40
1661	5,141,000	5		1841	14,970,000	51
1691	4,950,000	−4		1871	21,501,000	44

Source: W and S, Table 7.8.

able indeed for a European society. But even then it was never so fast as that which has been common in the developing world in recent decades.

Populations expand or contract as births, deaths and migration dictate. Our next set of figures, in Table 10, records the birth rate, death rate and migration rate at about the same points in time. The numbers represent averages of the annual rates during the five-year period surrounding the dates themselves. Added to these are more revealing measures of fertility and mortality, the gross reproduction rate and a much better known statistic, expectation of life at birth (e_o). The gross reproduction rate (GRR) is numbers of females, i.e. persons capable of reproduction, per woman, taking no account of mortality.

Figures of this kind, and many more of demographic interest, have been established for every five-year period from 1541 to 1871, but only one in six is presented here. Nevertheless the selection we have made serves to bring out some interesting and surprising things.

First is the fact that the incidence both of births and of deaths was low, certainly low as compared with the developing countries of our own day. There birth and death rates of 35 per 1000 of the population are commonplace, and rates of 40 and over still occur. In our list 40 per 1000 is never attained at all, though the first quinquennium and that around 1811 get quite close in the birth rate. The death rate only once exceeds 30 per 1000, in and around 1721. The full list of 33 half-decades from which the entries are taken shows rates both slightly higher and slightly lower than these. But it confirms the message to which we should attend, that England during

Table 10: *Crude birth rate, gross reproduction rate, crude death rate, period expectation of life at birth and migration rate in England for selected five-year periods*

Five-year period centred on	Birth rate (‰)	GRR	Death rate (‰)	e_o (yrs)	Migration rate (‰)
1541	39·8	2·9	29·4	33·7	1·27
1571	32·8	2·1	29·4	38·2	1·26
1601	33·6	2·3	24·6	38·1	1·73
1631	31·8	2·1	24·1	38·7	1·26
1661	26·8	1·8	26·3	35·7	2·16
1691	31·6	2·1	28·7	34·9	0·79
1721	33·0	2·3	31·4	32·5	1·04
1751	33·8	2·3	26·2	36·6	1·07
1781	35·6	2·5	28·8	34·7	0·48
1811	39·5	2·9	25·6	37·6	0·80
1841	35·9	2·5	22·2	40·3	1·49
1871	33·9	2·5	21·9	41·3	1·12

In 1976 the crude birth rate in Britain was 11·8‰, the crude death rate 15·3‰ for males and 9·2‰ for females, expectation of life at birth 69·7 years for males and 75·8 years for females, and the migration rate 0·72‰.

GRR = gross reproduction rate. e_o = expectation of life at birth.
‰ = rate per 1000.

Sources: W and S, Tables A3.1, 7.11; Government statistical service figures.

the seven or eight generations before industrialization had what is called a low pressure regime in the matter of births and deaths in contrast with most non-industrial societies which have and had high pressure ones. Most of the figures contrast sharply with our own today, as can be seen from the addition at the bottom of the table.

Varying rates of increase in the English population of the past were evidently not brought about by a consistently high mortality hovering in the same region as a consistently high fertility. Nor is a picture of rapid increase occasionally and savagely cut back by crisis mortality the one we should have in mind. In Table 10 above the birth rate never falls below the death rate, though it does so in five half-decades in the full list set out in the original source. These half-decades fell for the most part in the middle or late seventeenth century. It was exactly at this time, it will be noticed, that out-migration was at its highest, removing young and potentially fertile people from the English population, many of them to North America. The English speakers of that continent could perhaps be said to have come from the vitals of the motherland.

But we must not allow this or the many other things which crowd in upon us now that the full record of the population of pre-industrial England is at last before us to distract our attention from a second general point. Here was a society responding to its environment, responding rhythmically.

A vivid illustration of this pattern over time is evident in expectation of life at birth, which can often fall below 30 years, or even below 25, in non-industrial societies, but which varies only between 32·5 and 41·3 in Table 10. High early on, lower in the middle period, higher and higher still in the later period, it does behave rhythmically over time. It is an extraordinary fact nevertheless that its maximum does not lie at the end of the time-span, in high Victorian times, but in the reign of Elizabeth I, during the five years with the year 1581 as their centre. The level was then 41·7 years, a figure which, like all those for expectation of life, especially expectation of life at birth, must be handled very carefully, for they do not always mean what they may seem to mean. Since life expectation has already shown itself to be so crucial to our understanding of how society worked in the world we have lost, and to the personal experience of our ancestors, it is worth while pausing to consider what such a number is intended to convey.

A period life expectation of 41·7 years for the half-decade surrounding the year 1581 asserts that people who spent their whole lifetime under the rates of fertility and mortality prevalent during those five years would live to that age. This does *not* imply that people actually born in that interlude would have had a life expectation of 41·7 years, which would be a different statistic, with the title *cohort* life expectation at birth. Wrigley and Schofield have in fact estimated such figures for most of their quinquennia, and it comes out at 39·7 years for that labelled 1581, two years less, that is to say than the period life expectation.

It is also an error to suppose that if the period life expectation is 35 years, for example, as it was during the 1691 half-decade, someone aged thirty could expect to live for 5 years more, someone aged twenty-five, 10 years more, and so on. Such a misconception leads to much more serious confusion. In fact with an e_0 of 35, a woman of twenty in England before 1871 could expect to live about 36·5 years more; one of twenty-five about 33·5 years; one of thirty, 30·5; one of forty, 24·5. Even at sixty she would have over 12 years to live. To grasp the reason why this is so it is necessary to understand the workings of what the demographers call life tables, and how expectations of life are calculated. But we can go no further here.

These are not trivial points, for they imply that during the long period when expectation of life was consistently modest, for traditional England, between the later seventeenth and the mid-eighteenth century, a marriage might nevertheless last more than thirty years. A family group or enterprise started at first marriage had even better prospects, because it could be continued by remarriage, and remarriage as we have seen was quite frequent before the eighteenth century. The comparison with our day has some little surprises too. In the 1980s when female e_0 is over 75 years, more than double that in the 1690s, a woman aged thirty cannot expect to live twice as long, but only half as much again, 44 years instead of 30. In the higher ranges there is even less proportionate difference. Which goes to show that the demographers' concepts of expectation of life at birth are no guide, and are not intended to be a guide to the ability of those of adult age to live out the human span. The life-span in this sense has not lengthened appreciably since life expectation began its astronomical rise above the levels in our table a hundred years ago. Exactly as the scripture tells us when it talks of three score years and ten, certain people always could and always did reach the maximum length of days, whatever the prevalent mortality.[1]

One of the other traps for the unwary in demographic study is the relationship between expectation of life and proportions of the elderly. For it is not mortality, as expressed in expectation of life or in any other way, but fertility which is the important control on the age composition of a population. This is evident in the next set of figures, in Table 11, which records proportions of young children (those 0–4), proportions of those in active adult life (25–59) and proportions of those over 60 on the same basis as before. Measures of the first importance to the burden of the present chapter are also added, those for proportions of women never marrying. You cannot fail to notice that the percentage of those over 60 years of age was at its highest when Table 10 shows that expectation of life was at its lowest, that is between the 1660s and the 1720s. This was so because fertility was also extremely restricted during these decades. An identical rhythmic or cyclical movement over time reappears in these figures. This is especially true of the estimates for proportions marrying, a highly significant fact in a familial system which we have described as one where marriage could only take place when opportunities for independent living were known to be present, or thought to be so.

Table 11: *Proportions of the English population in various age groups, with proportions of women never marrying, for selected five-year periods*

Five-year period centring on	Proportion aged 0–4 (%)	Proportion aged 25–59 (%)	Proportion aged 60 and over (%)	Proportion of women never marrying* (%)
1541	13·2	39·0	8·5	–
1571	13·3	40·1	7·3	6
1601	12·3	39·4	8·3	24
1631	12·4	41·5	8·3	18
1661	10·9	42·6	9·7	25
1691	12·3	43·2	9·1	13
1721	12·3	40·4	9·5	7
1751	12·6	41·4	8·2	5
1781	13·8	38·9	8.2	7
1811	15·0	36·5	6·9	11
1841	13·9	37·9	6·6	–
1871	14·0	38·3	7·0	–

* By cohort, age 0–4, in period concerned.

Sources: W and S, Tables A3.1, 7.28. Figures not available for half-decades 1541, 1841, 1871.

The value of demographic measures in a general essay of this kind must not be exaggerated, however revealing they can be shown to be, and however important the fact that they now exist in such plenty for the whole of our country for so far back in time. But there are two topics which we should not leave untouched. One is change in age of marriage over time, for this is where we began. The other is infantile and child mortality, a circumstance which seems to exercise all observers so deeply as they contemplate the lives of the often poorly nourished, badly housed, medically ignorant, disease-exposed people which we have reason to believe our ancestors so often were. Here we leave national estimates and have to rely on the results of the lengthy and laborious process called family reconstitution, carried out for a tiny number of individual parishes. These results are undoubtedly more precise than others we have cited but not necessarily representative.

Perhaps the strong stress which has had to be laid on the relative mildness of mortality in pre-industrial England, on the relatively long time which people had to live, on the relatively small number of births and so on, may have clouded the contrast which we wish to draw. Our ancestors certainly lived under a wholly less favourable demographic regime than we do. Still, the numerical discoveries of the last decade or so should teach us to moderate our language when we talk of their disposition to die as babies or as children.

Table 12: *Infantile and child mortality in selected English parishes, with mean age at first marriage*

	Infantile mortality (age 0–1)		Child mortality (age 1–9)		Proportions surviving to age 10		Age at first marriage	
	Male	Female	Male	Female	Male	Female	Male	Female
1550–99	143	127	142	123	778	797	[27·2]	[24·0]
1600–49	162	123	127	118	730	702	28·2	25·9
1650–99	170	133	137	147	736	716	28·0	26·2
1700–49	195	148	143	139	723	690	27·8	26·4
1750–99	165	152	133	117	765	723	26·9	23·3
1800–49	–	–	–	–	–	–	[26·0]	[23·9]

Sources: Mortality, figures in italics, W and S, Table 7.19, other figures in course of publication by them. All rates per 1000 live births. *Age at marriage*, 15 parishes, Laslett, Oosterveen and Smith, Table 1-2. The nature of the data makes the figures bracketed to be biased, upwards (first period), downwards (last period).

Lugubrious statements are all too often made about a half or more of English children dying before the age of ten: we can see from Table 12 that the figure has never risen to much more than a quarter since the sixteenth century. Even direr declarations are to be heard about deaths in the first year of life, and it seems to be widely assumed that this might happen to as much as a third of all the babies born: in Table 12 the proportion never reaches a fifth, 200 per 1000. It was usually nearer 150 per 1000, though it certainly varied by type of settlement, being worse in the towns than the country. These low figures from a small number of places are perhaps a little difficult to accept as indicators of the general position. But when information becomes available from all over the country in the nineteenth century, official information, it tends to confirm them.

None of this must be allowed to obscure the fact that in particular places at particular times mortality could be much, much higher than the figures we have quoted in our tables. Such local mortality crises will concern us in the chapter which follows. People's view of themselves, their fears for themselves, the plans they make for their lives, attach to what might happen, and indeed what they know to have happened to some people, rather than to what may be generally expected. How extreme things could be in a village when times were unfavourable, even if short of critical, can be seen at Clayworth once again. When Parson Sampson listed all his parishioners for the second time in 1688, he did so in great detail. The years since 1676 had been bad years, as will be seen in our tables, years when mortality was consistently high everywhere and the national population was stationary or declining.

The most remarkable effect of high mortality which can be recovered from Sampson's careful recordings in 1688 has to do with the number of times his parishioners found themselves remarrying after the loss of a spouse. He set out the rank order of every marital union in the village. There were seventy-two husbands in Clayworth in 1688, and no less than twenty-one of them were marked as having been married before: thirteen of them had been married twice, one a number of times unspecified, three three times, three four times and one five times. Of the seventy-two wives, nine had been previously married; one of the seven widowers and one of the twenty-one widows are known to have been married more than once. This may owe a lot to chance, but it is spectacular confirmation of the propensity of those who did get married in the English traditional world to go on marrying, at least until later life. At Adel in Yorkshire there was a man who married his sixth wife in 1698 and his seventh in 1702. The law holds for women too, but is weaker in their case, because widows found it somewhat more difficult to get husbands than widowers to get wives. Together with the much marrying majority there was also a smaller and variable community of persons who did not marry at all.

We have given this body of celibates the name nubile unmarried, and it must have consisted for the most part of servants, life-cycle servants in the case of the younger ones,

life-time servants in the case of the older. Nubile unmarried
women, as we have seen, were common generally in Sampson's
day. It would seem that remarriage for companionship in old
age was not a common feature of traditional English life.
There were always widowers as well as widows with children.[2]

The Clayworth documents also contain an affecting example
of how the elderly widowed could be excluded by their own
children from their own home. A little craftman's family of
Bacon dwelt in the village in 1676: Francis Bacon the father,
Joan Bacon his wife, Nicholas, Anne and Francis their children. His occupation was that of cooper, maker of barrels,
which were the only important form of packaging at that time.
By 1688 his elder son Nicholas had succeeded him as the
cooper at Clayworth, since Francis Bacon himself had been
buried on 25 April 1685. The Bacon family now consisted of
Nicholas, his wife Elizabeth, and two of her children, Elizabeth
and Gervas Welter. Nicholas had married Elizabeth Welter as a
widow on 1 June 1686; their own twin children, very probably
conceived before their marriage, had died as babies in 1687.

By the time of the 1688 listing, the younger Francis Bacon,
brother to Nicholas, had left the village. But Nicholas's
mother Joan and his sister Anne were still alive and in Clayworth. Not in the family home however. They were being
supported in the 'Common-Houses on Alms' – paupers in an
institution in fact. In July, 1687 Anne Bacon had a bastard
child by a married man. Little Naphtaly Loversage (the father
was Nicholas Loversage, a shepherd's son) died a six-month-
old baby.

It is true that Nicholas Loversage made an honest woman
of her directly his first wife died, which was very soon after
the rector drew up the list of parishioners in May 1688. But we
do not know whether Loversage gave house-room to his new
wife's mother, and there is nothing to explain the behaviour
of his wife's brother Nicholas. He appears to have turned his
mother and sister out of the family cottage when he himself
got married, leaving them to the mercy of the parish poor-law
overseers and to charitable relief. It may be unfair to condemn
Nicholas Bacon, for the full circumstances never will be
known; indeed it is unusual that so much should have been
discovered about the very private lives of these obscure
villagers who lived so long ago. In the twentieth century it is
tempting to speculate on the emotional effect of this break-up

of marriages and homes on the children, on Nicholas's naughty sister Anne, and on his wife's two orphans. But it may be unwise to go as far as this. The emotional pattern of that society has vanished for ever, and people may then have had quite a different attitude to sudden death, orphanage, widowhood and living with stepparents.[3]

Nevertheless the stepmother and her evil influence is so conspicuous a feature of the fairy tales and of the literature as a whole that it seems to correspond to something important in the lives of those who repeated them. The lonely old widowed woman, witch in possibility and sometimes in her own opinion of herself, is a familiar figure also. It cannot be without significance that 35·5 per cent of all the children alive in Clayworth in May 1688 were orphans in the sense that one parent or other had died whilst they were still dependent. It must be significant too that something like a half of the solitaries were widows. In the face of facts like these, it may become difficult for us to go on being so sorry for ourselves because of the vast numbers of broken homes, and solitary, neglected people, which we think of as characteristic of high industrialism in our day. The society of the pre-industrial world was inured to bereavement, desertion and the shortness of life. It clearly had to be.

We have only to consider what must have happened at that time when a householder died in the prime of life, an event which occurs with us only very rarely. The breaking up of a marriage by the death of the husband threatened an end to the familial undertaking almost as surely as the beginning of a marriage meant its foundation. If a wife died, this result can rarely have followed, though the importance of a capable woman at the head of a farming or even a craftsman's household is easily overlooked. Replacing her with someone approximately suited to her duties with the children and in household management generally must often have been a difficult matter. But should the husband and the father die, everything on which the family depended was put in jeopardy. The effect would vary, of course, with the point of his career when catastrophe came, with the number, age and capacity of his sons, the vigour and determination of his widow as well as with her attractiveness as a possible wife for someone else. An independently minded woman left with security might even prefer not to remarry at all.

But if the land had been leasehold and the lease ended with his life; if there was no son left of the right age, able and willing to carry on, or no daughter ready to be married to a man who could take over; if the undertaking had been a commercial or industrial one, with the proper successor not immediately to hand; under all these circumstances the day of the end of the marriage would also be the day of the end of the family enterprise, or at least the end of a particular regime, of a generation. Even on the land the passing of a generation meant a crisis in each farming household, of a kind which our economic institutions are now much less likely to undergo. This implied a surprisingly high rate of turnover, so to speak, in institutions as well as in persons. How quickly people succeeded one to another in the same small settlement has already been displayed.

The end of a marriage interrupted childbearing, of course, and this was one of the factors in keeping down the number of children in a family. It is not true nevertheless that in pre-industrial England or in France a married woman in her fertile years would have a baby every year while the couple were together. For one thing some were barren and marriage was not confined to the fecund. For another thing childbearing capacity goes down with age, and it declined and came to an end sooner then than now. In the third place the much longer period of suckling babies inhibited conception to a marked degree. It was this more than anything else which ensured that the numbers of children a woman was likely to have was on average only just over seven, even if she married as early as was socially allowable, quite late in her teens, shall we say, and both she and her husband lived together until she reached the end of her childbearing span. Because marriages were often broken by death, and above all because they were usually entered into at later ages, the actual number of children per marriage was considerably under seven, just over four in fact.

An entirely exceptional woman can still bear over twenty children if she does marry early even under the circumstances just described, which is perhaps why it seems sometimes to be believed that this was a normal occurrence – the entirely extraordinary being taken for the ordinary once again. The child-producing record amongst women known to historical demographers is at present shared between the wife of a solicitor of Geneva who had twenty-one births in the late seventeenth century and a girl from Kent, Ann Sackett, who was born in 1779 at Ash in that county. At eighteen she married John Cook, a labourer there. By 1823 they had had twenty-one children at twenty births, and Ann was still alive in 1851.

In the course of his researches in the Genevan records, which can be said to have been the foundation of contemporary scientific historical demography, Louis Henry diagnosed the existence of deliberate limitation of births, taking place as long ago as the later seventeenth century.[4] The demonstration was statistical: the numbers of children being born to wives was shown to vary not exclusively with the age of the mother, as it does under natural fertility, but with the length of the marriage as well. If a woman had married early, and had had all the children she wanted, then her fertility would be less in her later married years than that of a woman of her age who had not been a young bride. Moreover, the overall pattern of birth intervals in Geneva at this time and thereafter already resembled the one shown by birth intervals in our own late twentieth-century society, where contraception is certainly very widespread. It should be noticed that the proof was numerical, and no evidence as to methods of avoiding conception entered into it.

It was surprising to find that the Calvinist citizens of Geneva had adopted this practice so early. Even more surprising, however, was the demonstration by Dr E. A. Wrigley ten years later, in 1966, that the birth schedules of Colyton, an ordinary Devonshire village, also exhibited the tell-tale pattern and at an even earlier period. This result of the first successful process of family reconstitution in our country showed that family limitation seems to have begun in the mid-seventeenth century and to have continued until the early eighteenth century.[5] It raised the possibility that the relationship between numbers and subsistence need not have been maintained solely by the marriage and household formation rules which we have discussed. It could have been done by contraception.

But Wrigley's original suggestion was tentative, and seems to have applied to a part of the population of Colyton only. Without confirmation in other places and on a much wider scale, it was impossible to suppose that contraception could have had an influence on population generally in England at that time. The further work which has now been done on family reconstitution demonstrates that deliberate birth control cannot have been of any importance in the mass behaviour of our English ancestors. Knowledge of it certainly existed, and there can be little doubt that it was used, outside marriage as well as within, the actual method most likely being coitus interruptus. But everything seems to point to the conclusion which we have now drawn from our much, much more abundant evidence, that it was the regularity with which English mothers fed their children at the breast which ensured that the numbers born should be relatively small, and constant over the whole country as well as over time.[6]

Suckling by the baby's mother, in contrast to the use of wet nurses or of the milk of animals and so on, also seems to have been an important reason why infantile mortality was quite markedly low in England as compared with some other countries of Europe. It may be significant that the abandonment of children was never met by institutional provision in our country, or indeed elsewhere amongst the Protestants, on anything like the scale that was usual in Catholic countries. There was only ever one foundling hospital in England, that at London set up by Captain Coram in the 1740s. By the end of the eighteenth century there were over fifty in the cities of France, and they were common in Spain and Italy, where some of them had existed since the Middle Ages. It would not be justifiable to conclude from this fact itself that abandonment of infants was less common in our country than in Latin Europe, for the practice was frequently deplored by English people. But there may well have been a different attitude towards child nurturance, an attitude which accompanied the Protestant temperament, as it has been called, but which perhaps existed in these areas before the Reformation.[7] It has to be remembered that it was in France, in the later eighteenth century, and not in England, that contraception first began to have a controlling effect on a national population. We did not adopt the practice on any scale till the 1880s and '90s.

If children were somewhat fewer in the English family circle, very slightly fewer when differences in infantile mortality are borne in' mind, than in some other European countries in the past, they were certainly fewer than they are in countries struggling to industrialize today. This meant that the dependency ratio, the weight supported by those who earn and produce in maintaining those who do not, was less for us than it is for them, at comparable points in development. It was less because more of our dependents were past work and fewer too young to work, and infants are more of a burden than the old.[8] The facts are set out in Table 11.

Nevertheless we must still imagine our ancestors right up to late Victorian times as in the perpetual presence of their young offspring. A good 70 per cent of all English pre-industrial households contained children – this proportion is remarkably constant from place to place and date to date – and there were between two-and-a-half and three children to every household with them. Sometimes the numbers in those groups of five and above could reach a quarter of the whole number in a village, though most children always lived in groups smaller than this. In the pre-industrial world there were children everywhere; playing in the village street and fields when they were very small, hanging round the farmyards and getting in the way, until they had grown enough to be given child-sized jobs to do; thronging the churches; forever clinging to the skirts of women in the house and wherever they went and above all crowding round the cottage fires, just as they still do in Malawi, say, or in Kenya, or in Pakistan.

The perpetual distraction of childish noise and talk must have affected everyone almost all of the time, except of course the gentleman in his study or the lady in her boudoir; incessant interruptions to answer questions, quieten fears, rescue from danger or make peace between the quarrelling. It cannot be expected that children should have figured very largely in the materials used for traditional historical purposes, the political, administrative, religious, intellectual or even the economic documents. But they do appear in the paintings of the time and in the records of work and of assistance to the poor, as well as in the diaries, the autobiographies and the personal correspondence.

Out of these materials a particular picture of the position of the young and the very young has been built up during the last two decades, in which they appear as young adults, with nothing especially childlike about them, manikins to whom their less than loving parents were largely indifferent, often negligent or even cruel. This was most markedly so, it is claimed, with working people, whose interest in their offspring was largely confined to what they could earn. The high, and exaggerated, rate at which the very young would die has been said to justify this offhand attitude. Who would invest affection in a baby or a toddler so soon to be swept away? After the so-called discovery, or invention, of childhood in the eighteenth century among the upper classes, the twentieth century is congratulated as seeing the establishment throughout the whole society of loving and of caring for the child.

Such an interpretation has now come under fundamental criticism. Not only does it present an account of childhood and child nurture which is unfaithful to such sources as have been uncovered, but it is improbable if not impossible from the psychological point of view. This newer opinion rests on a much deeper acquaintance with the elusive and rather difficult evidence, but it has to be confessed that there is still much research to be done before we can be confident of the facts. Here is a remark by one of the earliest observers of the life of the labourer in Britain writing at the very end of the eighteenth century: 'In the long winter evenings, the husband cobbles shoes, mends the family clothes and attends the children while the wife spins.'[9] That the man should do these domestic tasks so that the woman could earn money at her cottage handicraft is an interesting surprise. Fascinating also is the fact that at this, the most modest social level, fathers did help in the tending of infants and children. Amongst them therefore it was not simply the women and girls, sisters and aunts as well as mothers, who did it all as women's peculiar business. There are indications that child-rearing was a shared activity in the neighbourhoods where children lived, and that attachment to a single mother, or mother figure, was not the universal pattern, at least after early infancy. In the larger family of children covering ten, fifteen or even twenty years from the youngest to the oldest, elder sisters must have been important in the lives of the later born. Perhaps as important as the mother herself. But we have seen that such large groups of siblings were not as frequent as traditionally thought.

We do not know how the instruction of children was divided between the members of the family, though it is natural to suppose that boys at least would learn how men behaved and how they worked the lathe, the plane, the plough, the loom from watching their fathers all and every day. We are even more ignorant of what happened when the children left the house and went out to play; whether it was in family groups, or whether it was neighbourhood gangs, even village gangs, embracing rich and poor, the privileged along with the rest. We do not know very much about what they played, or even about what they were encouraged to play or to do.

We know something about what they were taught when they went to school, which was almost all Christianity and the classics, and about the rigour of their treatment there. But not many of them went to school, and we can only suppose that when they were at home they were as peremptorily treated as they would have been in the classroom. The belief that the most important material object in the world of the child may have been the rod is not as well established as has often been assumed, and these myriads of children have left nothing much material behind them. A cradle or two in most old houses, a hobby horse, a whipping top and one or two other traditional toys, that is all, and most of these once belonged to little gentlemen and gentlewomen, not to the ordinary children, our own ancestors, that is to say.

There is a strict limitation, then, on what we can learn of the attitudes, outlooks, and actual behaviour in the world which we have lost from the numerical facts of births, marriages and deaths. Perhaps we already understand the historical sociology of populations in relation to economy and environment, the nature of that rhythmic fluctuation which the figures we have cited signal with such clarity,[10] than we understand why it was that some Europeans breast-fed their children, as the English did, whilst others did not. Or what it was that made the familial relations of western Europeans, and especially of our own forebears so crucially different from those of the rest of mankind.

Did the peasants really starve?
Chapter 6

Famine and pestilence amongst English
people in the pre-industrial past

'The starving peasantry' is a common phrase, especially in
popular literature. The words bring to mind a picture in simple
black and white of conditions as they were in the bad old days
of the reformer and the good old days of the sentimentalist.
Perhaps 'starving' should not be taken to mean actually
dying of lack of food; rather, badly fed and clothed, wretchedly
housed in hovels, miserable in general. Still, in our own day
the phrase has reverted to its grimmer meaning, reminding us
of the contrast between the rich, industrialized parts of the
world where food is plentiful, and the poorer areas, where
industry has not yet got hold and where literal starvation can
sometimes occur.

It occurs, so some people think, because of the policy and
attitude of the industrial countries as well as because of the
limited resources and primitive technology of the 'undeveloped' area, together with the rapidity of their population
growth. For all these reasons it was of considerable importance
to decide, when this essay was being composed in the 1960s,
how far the developed nations had been themselves at the
mercy in the past of uncertain and exiguous food supply. Did
the peasants really starve, in Hertfordshire and Hampshire, in
Cumberland and Cornwall, just as they sometimes starved in
the area called the Beauvaisis in France, which surrounds and
includes the ancient cathedral city of Beauvais?

The French historian, Pierre Goubert, who had analysed the
evidence in the 1950s, certainly believed that the peasants and
the craftsmen living in this region were liable to starve at
times during the seventeenth and early eighteenth century,
and that starvation also occurred in other parts of France. It
was not quite clear how far these people could be taken as

typical of the whole of that country, and of the whole period before the arrival of industry, all over Europe. The Beauvaisis may have been particularly vulnerable because it was a region gathering only one harvest a year and dependent upon a single crop for food. It was also given over to the production of woollen cloth, heavily industrialized in the old sense. Where the peasants kept cows, starvation was less likely, and this may have been the English case, for all its close resemblance to the situation in the Beauvaisis.[1]

The fund of food was obviously related to age at marriage and to numbers marrying. This was a point fully recognized by Thomas Malthus, the pioneer of studies of this sort in the last years of the eighteenth century. A society conscious that its food resources might be outstripped by the growth of its population will have to control the reproduction rate if starvation is to be avoided, and in the English familial system this means that household formation may have to be postponed or forgone. It also implies that the procreation of children outside marriage will have to be discouraged. This we shall discuss in due course. But the possibility of food running low does not necessarily require the maintenance of a system whereby every marriage leads to the creation of a new household: perhaps rather the reverse. It is certainly possible that living in large, extended and multi-generational households, formed and maintained like those of the Russian serfs in subordination to the owner of the land and to the village community, might have husbanded resources more efficiently.

Since in England and the European west, men and women seem to have been prepared to postpone or to forgo marriage in order to ensure that they lived by themselves, their different familial priorities and values must have been of some importance to them. This importance would be the greater if it could be shown how far there was indeed a risk of the means of livelihood being insufficient unless decisions to marry were appropriate. The possibility of famine, then, was of fundamental importance to the social and familial structure, quite apart from its being crucial to the life chances of every individual.

In this sense it is true to say that each part of our subject is also our whole subject. In such a superficial survey we can only touch on the principles and open up possibilities. The risk of 'starvation', as we have hinted, would not necessarily show itself in conspicuous events, the famines of the history books.

Perpetual undernourishment, or undernourishment lasting for several disastrous harvests, might have been its usual manifestation, which would mean that deaths from simple absence of nourishment would never have occurred on any scale. This itself could be taken as an indication that social mechanisms were in existence to provide against vicissitudes in the food supply caused by weather or by war, or by economic catastrophe. Nevertheless the fear of famine might have been a reality, to citizen and administrator alike.

If it is justifiable to think of the economy of the Beauvaisis in the 1690s as resembling the economy of the whole of Britain at that time, it is relevant to take into account what happened in Scotland in that same decade. There the case for outright starvation seems to be as good as it is for the Beauvaisis and may well have been in the minds of Englishmen when they thought of what might happen to them, amongst the administrators and politicians anyway. The survey of the English evidence should begin, however, by citing an account given by a person of the time, a woman of the people themselves, living in circumstances where the disappearance of food must have been a possibility, if it was ever so in England. Here is a passage from the diary of the great philosopher, John Locke, dated 1 March 1681.

This day I saw one Alice George, a woman as she said of 108 years old at Alhallontide last [1 November 1680]. She lived in St. Giles parish in Oxford and hath lived in and about Oxford since she was a young woman. She was born at Saltwyche [Salwarp] in Worcestershire, her maiden name was Alice Guise. Her father lived to 83, her mother to 96, and her mother's mother to 111. When she was young she was fair-haired and neither fat nor lean, but very slender in the waist, for her size she was to be reckoned rather amongst the tall than short women. Her condition was but mean, and her maintenance her labour, and she said she was able to have reaped as much in a day as any man, and had as much wages. She was married at 30, and had 15 children, viz. 10 sons and 5 daughters baptized, besides 3 miscarriages. She has 3 sons still alive, her eldest John living the next door to her, 77 years old the 25th of this month. She goes upright though with a staff in one hand, but yet I saw her stoop twice without resting upon anything, taking up once a pot and another time her glove from the ground.

Her hearing is very good and her smelling so quick that as soon as she came near me she said I smelt very sweet, I having a pair of new gloves on that were not strong scented. Her eyes she complains of as failing her, since her last sickness, which was an ague that seized her about 2 years since and held her about a year. And yet she made a shift to thread a needle before us, though she seemed not to see the end of the thread very perfectly. She has as comely a face as ever I saw any old woman and age hath neither made her deformed nor decrepit.

The greatest part of her food now is bread and cheese or bread and butter and ale. Sack [sherry] revives her when she can get it. For flesh she cannot now eat, unless it be roasting pig which she loves. She had, she said, in her youth a good stomach [appetite] and ate what came in her way, oftener wanting victuals than a stomach. Her memory and understanding perfectly good and quick, and amongst a great deal of discourse we had with her and stories she told she spoke not one idle or impertinent [irrelevant] word. Before this last ague she used to go to church constantly on Sundays, Wednesdays and Saturdays. Since that she walks not beyond her little garden.

She has been ever since her being married troubled with vapours [either flatulence or depression] and so is still, but never took any physic but once about 40 year since, viz. one pennyworth of Jollop [aperient] which the apothecary out of kindness making a large pennyworth wrought more than sufficiently. She said she was 16 in '88 [1588], and went then to Worcester to see Queen Elizabeth, but came an hour too late, which agrees with her account of her age.[2]

Locke was a practising physician, an exact recorder and very reliable witness, so that we can believe that this is what Goody George did tell him, and that this was her true physical condition. We may, nevertheless, have our reservations about the ages she gives, particularly for herself and for her grandmother, in view of the tendency to exaggerate which has been noticed. If she did have eighteen pregnancies after the age of thirty (this is obviously a round figure in the account and she may have been twenty-nine, twenty-eight or even twenty-seven at marriage) then she was something of a record for English women of her time. But most of her story rings true.

Women did work with men in the field, especially at harvest and could work as labourers all the year. 'The best sort of women-shearers [sickle-wielders]', says the Yorkshire farming-book quoted twice before, should have 'mowers' wages'; 'we should do them an injury if we should take them from their company and not make them equal to those in wages whom they can equalize in work'.[3] Her church attendance is probable enough, as has been seen, though it may come as a surprise to see how often our ancestors held their services. It is not without its interest that she lived alone next door to her son. She was another of the solitary widows we have already referred to, but like so many of the citizens of Bethnal Green today she had managed to get within an easy walk of a member of her family. A superficial survey of a city like Lichfield in 1696 shows that this was common enough then, though perhaps not present to anything like the degree that it has been found in twentieth-century working-class areas: in a street of some sixty-five households, only fifty-two surnames were counted in Lichfield.[4]

Alice George's statements about what she ate, what she liked and how often she had to go without are the most interesting to us at the moment. The whole account reads rather like an explanation of how much she had to do to keep her stomach full. Still, she does not mention 'dearth', the common term in her day for shortage of food. John Graunt, the first man in history to study burial returns, was sceptical about starvation in England in his time. 'Of 229,250 which have died,' he wrote in 1662 referring to burials in London over twenty recent years, 'we find not above fifty-one to have been *starved*, excepting helpless infants at nurse, which being caused rather by carelessness, ignorance, and infirmity of the milch-women, is not properly an effect, or sign of want of food in the country or the means to get it.'[5]

If there was so seldom any lack of food to keep people alive in the huge city of London, surely the possibility of outright starvation for any part of England could be regarded as dubious for the years which Graunt had surveyed. In order to be sure of what it was that the French historians were after in the 1950s and the 1960s when they wrote of crises of subsistence we must be clear as to what exactly they meant by the phrase. Crises of subsistence occurred when the cost of food, that is mainly bread made of wheat, barley or other cereals, rose so much that peasants and craftsmen could no longer afford to buy enough to keep body and soul together, with the result that they died more easily, married less willingly and conceived fewer children. Such crises then could be detected from the analysis of parish registers.

They came at irregular intervals in the city of Beauvais and its surrounding villages; 1625, 1648–53, 1693–4 were some of the dates. The communities affected would show a sudden rise in burials; double or even treble the normal would be entered. Towards the first peak in mortality, marriages would drop and conceptions would go down too. They were reckoned by subtracting nine months from the date of birth, and the year used was the harvest year, from 1 August to 31 July. By the time the second peak in mortality came, for these crises were often though not always double-headed, the poor would be eating grass off the fields and offal from dung-heaps in the streets, dying perhaps more often from the effects of things like this and from the onset of epidemic diseases than from starvation as such. Entries in the registers would occasionally record such causes of death, but other sources would often reveal what was going on. The rich, though they might suffer from the infections spread about in this way, would not be affected by starvation.[6]

Professor Goubert chose this story to show what might happen to one family.

There was a family in Beauvais in the parish of Saint-Etienne in the year 1693 named Cocu: Jean Cocu, weaver of serges, and his wife with three daughters, all four spinning wool for him, since the youngest daughter was already nine years old. The family earned 108 *sols* a week, but they ate 70 pounds of bread between them. With bread up to ½ a *sol* a pound, their livelihood was secure. With bread at 1 *sol* a pound, it began to get difficult. With bread at 2 *sols*, then at 3·2, 3·3 and 3·4 – as it was in 1649, in 1652, in 1662, in 1694, in 1710 – it was misery.

Crisis in agriculture was nearly always intensified by crisis in manufacturing: it certainly was in 1693, so work began to fall off, then income. They went without; perhaps they were able to lay their hands on a coin or two saved up

for a rainy day; they pawned their things; they began to eat
unwholesome food, bran bread, cooked nettles, mouldy
cereals, entrails of animals picked up outside the slaughter-
houses. The 'contagion' manifested itself in various ways;
after hunger came lassitude, starvation, 'pernicious and
mortifying fevers'. The family was registered at the Office
of the Poor in December, 1693. In March, 1694, the youngest
daughter died; in May the eldest daughter and the father.
All that remained of a particularly fortunate family,
fortunate because everyone in it worked, was a widow and
an orphan. Because of the price of bread.

Not all the deaths were from starvation then, but also from
contagion and fevers. There is an echo of some of the details of
this passage in a Scottish state paper of February 1700, referring to the year 1698. The tax collectors themselves were protest-
ing against the claim that the full sums due should have been
exacted, and pleaded that this had not been possible because
of famine, whose presence they proceeded to prove in the
following words: 'Many have died for want of bread, and have
been necessitate to make use of wild-runches draff and the like
for the support of nature, which are kinds of food never before
heard of in this nation.' This nourishment seems to have been
a pottage made of such weeds as charlock. 'When there is not
sufficiency of bread' in one area, and when it cannot be
supplied from other places 'and when for want of bread people
die in the streets and highways in great numbers [this] doth
necessarily conclude an overspreading famine'.[7]

What happened in France and in Scotland in the 1690s fits
well enough into what is known of much better-documented
famines, like that in Bengal in 1943. Not having enough
money to buy food, because it was so expensive, because
incomings were so low, even because taxes had to be paid, was
probably as important as the dearness of provisions itself:
perhaps more so. It was in the localities that we had to seek
for such examples of literal starvation in pre-industrial
England. And it was in other sources than the parish registers,
especially poor-law documents and fiscal records, that we
might find confirmation.

In order to show that local *crises de subsistance* were a
possibility in our country, we should have had to demonstrate
the following circumstances. First that there had been in at

least one parish register a sudden sharp increase in mortality at a time when the price of food was particularly high. Second that there was at the same time a fall in conceptions and in marriages. Third that the stated cause of death of some at least of those buried had been starvation, or diseases known to be due to malnutrition or exacerbated by it. A confirming statement made elsewhere might be taken as almost demonstrating that this must have happened, but an unequivocal phrase in the burial entry would be clearly preferable. There were other features associated with such events which would have had to be looked for as well, such as similar conditions in neighbouring places, the absence of good harvests, or of epidemics, and signs like an increase in infantile mortality and in abortions. But any register showing the three listed features at a time of dearth could be taken as providing incontrovertible proof that in that parish the inhabitants were undergoing a crisis of subsistence as we have defined it.[8]

It must be said at once that only one entirely convincing English instance had been found by 1962. Although very little concerted work had yet been possible on the subject, Graunt appeared to have been right when he claimed that starvation was extremely rare in England as a stated cause of death. But the simplicity of this conclusion was obscured by the exasperating rarity of parish registers which give any indication as to why the person buried died. The third, and most conclusive, of the features listed, therefore, was almost universally absent from the English evidence, and the other two had seldom been found in as extreme a form as they then seemed to have been in France. Nearly all of the English registers which had been studied by the 1960s yielded entirely negative conclusions; they contained almost no example of a harvest year where a conspicuous rise in burials was accompanied by a corresponding fall in conceptions and in marriages. And ancillary evidence from other sources had not been sought out.

The possibility was therefore that our country in the seventeenth century or even earlier was already immune from these periodical disasters, whereas France and Scotland were not. Perhaps the English peasantry were justified rather later on in despising the French for eating black bread and wearing wooden shoes. Nevertheless approaches to the *crise de subsistance* were discoverable. The wool-weaving parish of Ashton-under-Lyne in Lancashire could be taken as an

instance of an incomplete crisis of subsistence, occurring during
the harvest year 1623–4. Its incompleteness, its difference,
that is to say, from the original French model, consisted first
in the fact that the evidence was imperfect, owing to gaps in
the register and its reticence about cause of death, and second
in that not all the symptoms were present in a very clear or
pronounced form.

The harvest year 1623–4 was one of bad crops and high
prices all over the country: the weather was very nasty. The
textile industry was in the depth of depression, just as it was
in Beauvais during 1693 and 1694. There had been a sudden
rise in burials at Ashton two years before 1620–1, but after
this they returned to their average over the previous twenty
years of about seventy-five a year. In the harvest year 1623–4,
184 people were buried, over two-and-a-half times the normal,
and 'conceptions' fell from an average of about 105 to 60.

Unfortunately causes of death were not given and the words
'famine', 'starvation' etc. did not appear, either in the
register or in any source known to us which might confirm
such possibilities. These events might nevertheless provisionally be classed as an English crisis of subsistence, if not a
severe one, taking place at Ashton. Confirmation of a somewhat unexpected kind could be seen in the recordings of
abortions in the register, a rare circumstance in our country.
These reached nearly 7 per cent of baptisms in 1623, their
highest level. Meanwhile it was known that twenty-five miles
to the north, in the neighbouring part of Yorkshire, 1623 stood
out as the worst for burials for some fifty years or more, with
the town of Halifax in trouble.[9]

Even further north, at Greystoke, six or seven miles west of
Penrith in the Cumberland hills, it was at last established that
every one of the conditions just laid down for a crisis of subsistence could be shown to have been present during that same
year 1623 and continuing into 1624. There had been 474
baptisms there during the decade 1610–19, with extremes of
40 and 58, 368 burials (20 and 61) and 96 marriages (6 and 15).
The expected average then must have been about 47 baptisms,
37 burials and 10 marriages every year. Even here, alas, there
was a chasm in the record from 1 December 1620 to 16 June
1622 so that the full story of the crisis could not quite be told.

In the calendar year 1623 no less than 161 people were
buried in the churchyard at Greystoke, over four times the

expected number. Only twenty babies were baptized, almost down to half the average, and marriages fell about as much, to six. In the worst period for burials, which was September to November 1623, there were only three conceptions, one marriage and sixty-two registered deaths. We know that some of these deaths were due to starvation, for the entries actually confessed this melancholy fact.

Extracts from the Register of Greystoke 1623
[Johnby is a hamlet forming another settlement in the parish of Greystoke]

29 January: 'A poor fellow destitute of succour and was brought out of the street in Johnby into the house of Anthony Clemmerson, constable there, where he died.'

27 March: 'A poor hungerstarved beggar child, Dorothy, daughter of Henry Patterson, Miller.'

28 March: 'Thomas Simpson a poor, hungerstarved beggar boy and son of one Richard Simpson of Brough by Mandgyes house in Thorp.'

19 May: 'At night James Irwin, a poor beggar stripling born upon the borders of England. He died in Johnby in great misery.'

[In the same month 'a poor man destitute of means to live']

12 July: 'Thomas, child of Richard Bell, a poor man, which child died for very want of food and maintenance to live.'

11 September: 'Leonard, son of Anthony Cowlman, of Johnby, late deceased, which child died for want of food and maintenance to live.'

12 September: 'Jaine, wife of Anthony Cowlman, late deceased, which woman died in Edward Dawson's barn of Greystoke for want of maintenance.'

27 September: 'John, son of John Lancaster, late of Greystoke, a waller by trade, which child died for want of food and means.'

[The register tells us that he was baptized on 17 October 1619, so he was four years old.]

4 October: 'Agnes, wife of John Lancaster, late of Greystoke, a waller by his trade, which woman died for want of means to live.'

27 October: 'William child of Lancelot Brown, which Lancelot went forth of the country [the district] for want of means.'

The fells of Cumberland, with their scattered flocks of sheep and their thin crops of cereals, were very different from the sad Beauvais plain, though they may have suffered as badly from too great a press of people dependent upon a textile industry stricken with depression. 'The smallness, barrenness, and the multitude of inhabitants in the habitable places of this country is . . . far incomparable to the other counties of the kingdom,' declared the justices of the neighbouring county of Westmorland in the year 1622, then already attempting to make some headway against the conditions which were to have such a tragic effect at Greystoke.[10] The deaths which took place there were not, as was usual in France, predominantly of children, in spite of the impression which may be created by the extracts we have printed here.

If these dismal details were to be made the most of, the fact that there were two cases of a mother and child both dying of famine at almost the same time could be pointed to, and the fact that one of these destitute families was without a shelter. Wandering beggars, like the miserable James Irwin, were, as we have already said, a feature of the countryside at all times, though most noticeable under the Tudors. They may perhaps have attracted more attention than is numerically justified, for it will be seen that Gregory King's table provides for only 30,000 of them in the whole population in 1688. A significant thing for the study of men's attitude to the means of keeping themselves and their families alive was the action of Lancelot Brown, named in the last entry. He appears to have left the starveling hillsides of Cumberland to try to find subsistence in some more fortunate part of England; maybe he became a beggar too.

His child died in any case, and perhaps it was the loss of the bread-winner, rather than exhaustion of the food supply, which had been the immediate, if not the final cause of death. We could not tell, any more than we could say in the 1960s whether or not the wandering father would have found much more favourable conditions anywhere in the highland zone of England in the dreadful season 1623–4. Other parish registers showed a pattern similar to that at Ashton-under-Lyne, and some of those which ran unbroken through the troubled years 1640 to 1660 revealed what could have turned out to be a terrible climacteric about 1645, just as the war between King and Parliament was reaching its crisis. At Colyton in Devonshire it was reckoned that something like a quarter of the thousand and more inhabitants were buried during the calendar year 1645; but there the words 'great sickness' appear in the register, and that might have meant the plague.

It was not possible to say a great deal about the relationship between famine and nutrition, though common sense suggested that they must have been connected and might be difficult to distinguish as causes of death. But when entries like those from Greystoke were found, or when the clerk of the rich metropolitan parliamentary parish of St Margaret's, Westminster, recorded the causes of death during the summer months of the year 1557 and ascribed 15 out of some 200 to 'famine', we could be fairly certain that individuals were dying of lack of food. This must have been true at Wednesbury in Staffordshire in 1674, where the register reads under 22 November: 'John Russel being famished through want of food (Josiah Freeman being overseer), was buried with the solemnity of many tears.' Food prices may have been high in the area at about that time, though the mid-1670s certainly did not resemble the early 1620s in Cumberland and Westmorland. But poor John Russel's fate was obviously thought by his indignant neighbours to have been due to the neglect of the overseer of the poor.[11]

In the extreme conditions which wrecked the family of Cocu in Beauvais it seemed probable that no system of poor relief could have been effective, and the arrangements in that city were apparently exceptionally good. If this was so, transfer payments, as the economists call them, between the prosperous and the dependent could never have prevented crises of subsistence of the kind found by the French historical demographers. There was simply not enough food to go round at such times, and poor people were inevitably in danger from high prices. More efficient means of distribution between country and country, region and region, even perhaps village and village, might nevertheless have mitigated the crises, and a really effective policy of buying and storing corn could have gone far towards eliminating them. In spite of relief arrangements within the city of Beauvais everything in the French evidence as to famine points to the absence of adequate stocks and of the means of distributing them when they were wanted. It would have been necessary to have had an accurate idea of the numbers of people to be fed in order to make quite certain that food would never run out, and there are indications that counts of the population were in fact carried out for the purpose in some cities: at Ypres in the fifteenth century, for example, and at Coventry in the year 1520. The story of what Joseph did in preparation for the Seven Lean Years in Egypt might well have been written for the administrators of the pre-industrial world.

Once we became alive to the real possibility of famine the perpetual preoccupation of the authorities of that era, governmental and municipal, with the supply of food for the poor took on a new significance. The insistence on fair prices for all victuals and especially for bread was a reminder that people might starve even where supplies were available, if they had exhausted their savings and lost their employment, and if taxation had pressed them too hard as well. Hence the strict control of all dealings in breadstuffs and all handlers of them, especially buyers and sellers of wheat. The stocks of corn so conspicuous in the records of Tudor and Stuart London were examples of a policy which had to be pursued all the time and in deadly earnest. It was indeed a matter of life and death and felt to be so by King, Council, justice of the peace, mayor and overseer of the poor alike. Right up to the time of the French Revolution and beyond, in Europe the threat of high prices for food was the commonest and most potent cause of public disorder.[12] It was dangerous when overseers were as neglectful as Josiah Freeman of Wednesbury, and during the years of scarcity in the early 1620s corn was stored locally. The harvest year 1623–4 was in many places the worst of a succession of bad harvest years, and in this it is typical of the crises detected in France. It might also have been typical of these black periods that this one should have ended in an outbreak of plague.

At this point we found ourselves faced with the most difficult of the many questions which will have to be settled before we can make up our minds about the issue which confronts us. We had to decide whether liability to starvation, extinction owing to an insufficient supply of food, must be taken as a defining characteristic of the world we have lost, and fear of such catastrophe an attribute which all our ancestors shared, but which we no longer experience, at least not in respect of ourselves. Were many of the deaths which had been put down by historical writers to the plague, pestilence, endemic diseases, in fact to be attributed to lack of food? If not always to a famine, to a sudden visitation of the sort so far discussed, then more often to months and months, or even years, of under-nourishment?

Twenty years of search has failed to add another Greystoke to our knowledge. But much work on epidemics, infection and crisis mortality, above all the establishment of the demographic history of our country, enable us to answer some of the questions posed in the early 1960s. Deaths by inanition due to want of food were certainly a rarity, probably an extreme rarity. England may have been free of local crises of subsistence to a greater extent than France or even Scotland. However, the theory of the *crise de subsistance* has itself come under criticism, especially in the country of its origin, for inexactitude and, among other things, for failure to take account of coincidence. Some French scholars now reject it altogether.

It is not necessary that every change of births and marriages at a time of heightened mortality should be due to famine. Scarcity of food decidedly did not always lead to excessive mortality and crisis due to illness also led to falls in conception. What is more, deaths demonstrably and entirely due to outright want of bread turn out to have been very, very uncommon in France as well as England. Indeed we have had to recognize how exceedingly difficult it is to decide when people genuinely perish for lack of nourishment, and for that cause alone, anywhere and at any time.

As to starvation in our second sense, chronic undernourishment and general wretchedness, precarious health and high susceptibility to disease associated with a failure in the means of livelihood, these things certainly existed amongst the poor and poorest. Though uncommon in England, they evidently did send down marriages and births as well as sending up mortality. They could assail a fair number of communities and they could extend over several years.

At a particularly unfavourable time in an especially vulnerable region a much wider area might be affected, and on one known occasion a whole British province suffered starvation in this second sense (famine or near-famine would be better descriptions) whilst an individual settlement in that province did experience actual starvation in our first sense at the same time. The occasion was the year 1623–4; the province was the north-west, extending upwards into the Scottish Lowlands and downwards into the west Midlands, and the individual settlement was Greystoke itself. What happened there and then could also have happened in other places, in other regions and at other times, although we have no indication that it did do so after the mid-sixteenth century outside this particular arena. It remains an open question, therefore, how far fear of starving was present as a possibility in the minds of the whole of our population in pre-industrial times.

In his admirable study of *Famine in Tudor and Stuart England* (1978) the late Andrew Appleby established the fact that a similar condition of famine or near famine had existed twice before in this same Cumbrian area, in 1587–8 and 1597–8. Distress seems to have been even acuter in these earlier occasions though deaths by outright starvation have not so far been found in the records. The more closely the matter is examined, however, the less appropriate this somewhat sensational and rather clumsy criterion turns out to be. It is a little like judging the low morale of a population from its suicide rate.

The whole set of questions, and the many possible inter-relationships between births, marriages, deaths, wages and prices, together with epidemics and infection, are analysed in detail by Wrigley and Schofield in *The Population History of England* (1981).* Apart from national emergencies in mortality, large numbers of local mortality crises are identified and the demanding questions of causes extensively discussed.[13] The issues readily become complex and the arguments difficult to follow. In attempting to unravel them we shall keep our eyes steadily fixed on the scene which came into view when the world we have lost was first surveyed, that of the Cumberland hills in 1622–5.

The principled investigation of these things shows how easy it is to get an inaccurate impression from the dramatic circumstances which were discovered there. Exact methods of measuring and comparing must be worked out and consistently applied if misinformation is to be avoided. The calculation of a trend, at a certain point above which a critical position is reached, is the nub of the problem, but it transpires that to

* In the rest of this chapter figures in square brackets indicate the page numbers of this book, and the definition of crisis is that set out there on p. 647.

fix a normal level is no simple matter of averages of previous years or decades. Apart from rises or falls in the total population during the relevant year, internal structure in the series of figures has to be reckoned in, such as variation by season, and it is essential that allowance be made for community size. A small percentage increase in the burials in a city may be more serious than a doubling or trebling in a rural parish of average dimensions [646–9]. Our earlier statements about Greystoke have been checked so as to make sure that they are significant, but few of the figures cited here from other authors can be so treated. These may seem to be refined points in the present context, but if such things are not appreciated, it is difficult to provide against exaggeration to the point of distorting the everyday experience of our ancestors.

So important is it to get the record straight in such a serious matter that it is worth our while to glance at an example of such exaggeration.

> Barely half the country dwellers and hardly any inhabitants of the towns could hope to live out their lives in a community which did not experience at least one of these psychologically devastating events, during which anything between a third and a half of the population would disappear in a matter of months.

Such are the terms in which Lawrence Stone appends the demographic uncertainties of the years before the Civil War to his list of causes of what is conventionally called the English Revolution. Now our present information goes to show that the death of one-third of the population in a matter of months from any cause, pestilence, famine or war, was unknown in any English community, in city, town or country during the parish register era [687].

Indeed it would require an increase in the number of burials by a factor of twelve over a whole year, or by a factor of forty-eight for three months. At Greystoke, we have seen, the rise was four times in one year, not twelve, and for the worst three months it was seven times, not forty-eight. The average (median) local crisis implied the death of 1·5 per cent of the population concerned, not 33·3 per cent and 1·5 per cent represents just over half of the proportion who would ordinarily die in the course of one year. The period before the Civil

War was indeed one when crises were still relatively frequent and sometimes grave, on the realistic scale the numerical data require us to adopt. But they were present in well under one-tenth of the places we know about in any one year. They were certainly fairly frequent, since in any given parish a crisis could be expected once every twenty years or so. But they usually lasted only a month or two, and were not very often linked with food shortages [686].

In 1623 Greystoke was one of some 60 parishes affected out of the 372 under observation. We have seen that a forty-year-old inhabitant who had lived all his life there would, as it happened, have had a similar experience of dire food emergency twice before, in the 1580s and 1590s. But then Greystoke was one of the most crisis-prone communities in the most crisis-ridden region of the country at the time to which Stone refers, and was especially subject to failure in subsistence. Nevertheless nothing is known ever to have happened in this village which approaches what he describes as normal for everyone everywhere.[14]

It is to be hoped that the coming of age of historical sociology since the statements we have quoted were made in the early 1970s will persuade historians to proceed with due respect to the principles of numerical analysis in subjects of this kind, and to weigh with great exactness possible discontinuities in the social structure. Our interest in Greystoke and its region has to be exemplary only. The reader with an interest in the extent, frequency and character of such mortalities must be referred to the works we have cited for greater detail about them, especially those due to epidemics, and particularly outbreaks of the plague. How widespread these visitations were, what diseases in addition to the plague could have been responsible, the regional distribution of such events, and the changes which occurred in these directions over time, subjects like these are now fairly accurately known about. But there are still topics of great significance, as we shall see, which are marked by uncertainty.

'*Hoc anno multi fame periere:* many perished (or must perish) this year by famine.' That year was 1625 again. So runs a comment in the register of the parish of Bainton in Yorkshire and comes closest to the entries in those of Greystoke, Wednesbury and St Margaret's, Westminster, which we noticed earlier. It is not however a statement made at the graveside declaring the cause of death of a named person, and further clear examples of this have yet to be discovered.[15] The excessive rarity of such statements and the infrequency of disasters like that of Greystoke may be taken to establish one vital point for England. What Malthus called the preventive check in his famous essay of 1798 had been in operation for at least the preceding eight generations of its long career as what we call an undeveloped country. Dearth when it came had led to births not happening, to marriages being postponed or forgone altogether. But the positive check of Malthusian theory, population control by extinction due to failure in fundamental resources, was never near the surface.[16]

Dearth might indeed be regarded as a recognized element in the fabric of society. Its perpetual possibility seems always to have been in the minds of the people in authority and of the people most likely to suffer. These made their exasperation plain, should their governors falter in their vigilance, by their actions as well as by their words. Such is the message of a justly famous study by Edward Thompson, *The Moral Economy of the Crowd in the 18th Century*, published in 1971. The disorder which might break out if food shortage threatened the poor was a signal to the authorities to intervene in the operations of the market in grain, symbolic rather than substantive violence. Those likely to suffer expected action, and they usually got it.

In spite of the impassioned and exaggerated statements which were made on such occasions, it is not easy to believe that the possibility of actually dying was often in the minds of the participants. However, the persisting connection of the price of food with the death rate has been made apparent from the demographic series. Although a rise in corn prices certainly did not always correspond with a rise in deaths, searching analysis shows them to be associated with each other in a statistically highly significant fashion. Nevertheless 'most variations in scarcity or plenty merely altered by a couple of years the timing of deaths which would in any case have soon occurred' [399]. What is more, except when conditions were extreme, the effect of high prices was delayed.

The impact of the price of food on deaths is measured in the study we are citing by reckoning what happened to mortality when wheat prices doubled, in the year itself and in each of the four subsequent years. A rise of 5 per cent in the same year after such a doubling was followed by one of 9 per cent in the second year and by a further rise in the third year. This last however was more than cancelled out by a subsequent echo effect, as it is called, when mortality actually went down [372]. The explanatory value of prices in relation to mortality, that is the proportion of the whole variation in the incidence of death associated with prices alone, was only about 16 per cent [375]. This was because fluctuations in the propensity to die were overwhelmingly affected not by variations in the availability of food but by variations in the prevalence of disease.

We have to reckon at this point with an arresting recent development in the theory of famine in respect of developing countries today. The supply of food is no longer regarded as the single and sufficient cause, and even its price may not rise at times when people are dying for want of nourishment.[17] This may modify the view we take of our own nutritional history. It is notable too that our evidence indicates that neither a succession of poor harvests nor a sustained high level of prices was associated with extra difference in deaths.

The strongest link between the current price of food and demographic behaviour was with marriages. This is just what we should expect if the decision when or whether to marry was the key to the regulative mechanism. 'A doubling of prices in one year would lead to an apparently permanent loss of 22 per cent of the normal number of marriages' [369], for here there was little in the way of a rebound. The impact came immediately and was strongest in the year of price rise. As for explanatory value, about two-fifths, 41 per cent, of variation in the marriage rate can be associated with variation in mortality and prices combined.

The indications that marriage failed to make up such losses is rather disconcerting, especially since there seems to be little room for mortality having created slots, as we have called them in Chapter 4, slots to be filled up by newly marrying couples. But we should bear in mind that at times of food shortage, those dying may leave precious little behind them to be taken up by their successors. When it comes to fertility, straitened conditions have considerable explanatory value, since 64 per cent of changes in births were associated with prices and deaths taken together. But the actual impact of the cost of food on fertility was markedly less than on marriage. Over five years a doubling of prices led to a loss of no more than 14 per cent of births to married women. Strict analysis like this requires us to revise the assumption that births after nine months fully represent conceptions, for some of the loss must be put down to foetal mortality, spontaneous abortions, rather than to the inhibition of the capacity to conceive which might go with malnutrition. This quite apart from loss of sexual appetite under such conditions, in the men or in the women.[18]

The effects we have described are national effects, made up of course of the assembled histories of all the communities in our national sample. Fluctuations in births, marriages and deaths could be much more extreme in the localities, and it is the conspicuousness of sudden peaks in the number of burials in particular places which has attracted most attention. A village population, however, is much less stable than a national one, and it may be wrong to assume that the resources on which it subsists are internal, as they are for all practical purposes with the nation itself. Extreme variability in individual places certainly played a part in the ups and downs of the national figures but these ups and downs were not the most important element in the schedule of death. The evening out of the jagged variations in the national record of burials in the middle of the seventeenth century did not lead to a lower level, for as we have seen mortality in general was higher thereafter.

However, years when expectation of life in England fell abruptly certainly tended to be years of an increase in the proportion of parishes observed being gripped by crisis. Nevertheless even at the very worst points in our mortality history only a minority of parishes were so affected. It is a characteristic of mortality crises in our country in fact that there were always 2 or 3 per cent of places in that unpleasant position at quite normal times, and that these conditions could be very local indeed. You could apparently step over a parish boundary and leave the crisis atmosphere behind you [656].[19]

Up to the middle of the seventeenth century it would often have been plague which held a particular settlement in its grip without affecting its neighbours. We do not know why epidemics of infection by the rat-borne micro-organism *pasturella pestis*, as this disease is properly called, disappeared in England after the 1660s. Plague is one of the most unpleasant and dangerous of all infections and its quiescence in our country for the two-and-a-half centuries before a scientific remedy was found in the 1930s must be counted as a great good fortune. Enough has been found out, however, to identify many of the mortalities which it caused and to distinguish them from other epidemics. Thus plague can be exculpated at Greystoke in 1623 and it acted independently of the level of nourishment, as did others of the diseases known to be prevalent. Most local crises had these infections behind them, as indeed did a great deal of mortality as a whole both in England and in France. Therefore they did not have a necessary connection either with the supply of bread or with its price.[20]

There can be no confidence in fact that all, many, or more than a very small proportion of the people who died at Greystoke in 1623 had been suffering from malnutrition alone. Here we reach the obscurest passageway in our progress towards a decision as to whether the English peasants really starved. Not only is the surviving evidence resistant to interpretation, but the medical testimony is confusing. There is certainly much in favour of the commonsense expectation that although the casualties in our village did not all die of shortage of food, a large proportion of them would have stayed alive if food had not been short. Most persuasive perhaps is the fact that even in the two most famous famines in our history, famines which occurred not to ourselves but to populations for which the British were politically responsible, starvation was a minor and not a major stated cause of death.

These were the great Irish famine of 1845 and 1846, and the Bengal famine of 1943. The official Irish record attributes some 20,000 deaths to starvation but 193,000 to fever, 125,000 to dysentery and diarrhoea and 22,000 to dropsy. The medical expert who examined these statistics and the circumstances decided that all 360,000 deaths were the outcome of famine conditions, while in Bengal 'famine' deaths appear in the most recent study under dysentery and diarrhoea. These made up only 5 per cent of excess mortality, about the same as those put down to famine in the Irish figures. The rest were due for the most part to an enormous increase in mortality of the usual kind: 'the Bengal famine killed mainly by magnifying the forces of death present in the pre-famine period'. There is little to confirm that this has been true of other episodes in other countries and much to suggest that the famine in question was a law unto itself, and perhaps other famines too.[21]

For these and other reasons we should be careful in supposing that food shortage was behind many or most of the local mortality crises observable from our parish registers. We should be cautious in inferring from our fragmentary evidence that mixed crises, where starvation and disease were both at work, have been a common reason for an upwelling of recorded deaths. This in spite of the fact that some medical opinion favours such a supposition. 'Infectious diseases', it is authoritatively stated, 'nearly always make co-existing malnutrition worse and the consequences of infection are likely to be more serious in a malnourished host than in a wellnourished one.' This self-intensifying process is given the name synergistic, the opposite of antagonistic. The interplay between the two elements, however, is no simple matter. The outcome of a lack of food exacerbating the seriousness of a disease, for example, differs with the disease in question, and this is especially true of the worst outcome of all, that is to say the death of the victim. Even if complications of this character could be allowed for, issues of coincidence, and of identifying which events were connected with subsistence and which were not, would still remain.[22]

Let us now turn to our specific instance and make a diagnosis, remembering that certainty is at present not within our reach. The manifestations with which we are concerned in Cumbria in 1623 were undoubtedly widespread and perhaps exceptional for that reason alone. Whilst one or two persons were actually being buried as victims of starvation in Greystoke and similar conditions were present elsewhere in Cumbria, indices of death in the Scottish regions to the north were the highest ever recorded, between 375 and 432, where 100 is the average overall. This compares with less than 250 in the bad years of the 1690s.

At Kelso, Dunfermline and Dumfries conditions were decidedly worse than at Greystoke. To the south and east, in those areas of Yorkshire which have been examined, deaths were at unprecedented levels, marriages and baptisms the lowest for at least a decade. In Lancashire to the south and west, the only entire county for which our knowledge of baptisms, marriages and burials is virtually complete during any period of dearth, burials doubled, baptisms fell by two-thirds and marriages by one-fifth. These effects were not equally serious in all the parishes in the county, but particularly so in those high on the hills, like their Cumbrian counterparts. Meanwhile the English crude death rate leapt from $21\cdot3\%_0$ to $33\%_0$ between 1622 and 1623, the birth rate sank from $32\cdot3\%_0$ to $27\cdot9\%_0$ and the marriage rate declined from $6\cdot7\%_0$ to $6\cdot2\%_0$.

These are unrefined statistics and the impact on marriages is not pronounced. A great deal more would have to be known, and a considerable effort of analysis and elimination made, elimination of food-independent diseases, before we could say with unshakeable confidence that the whole set of circumstances constituted a crisis of subsistence. But I believe that it is useful, and correct, to call it a crisis of subsistence all the same.

Probably the class of part-time students who assembled the Lancashire figures went too far when they concluded as follows, without any knowledge of food prices in the area: 'The prime cause of the 1623 population crisis in Lancashire was almost certainly famine, associated with subsidiary famine fevers.' They did so when they were in no position to exclude diseases independent of food as a cause of death. It was even riskier for them to have seized upon famine amenorrhea, that is cessation of menstruation and of the capacity to conceive, as the cause of the collapse of fertility, when disease might have been the agency here as well. Famine amenorrhea is a condition described by the famous French historian Emmanuel le Roy Ladurie for the famishing populations of Europe during the last two great wars and applied by him to seventeenth-century France. It is seen by an American biologist as part of a general system linking nutrition, body weight and body fat to the whole set of issues about procreation and bodily development.[23]

We do not yet know whether such theories will simplify and perhaps finally solve the problem which weighs upon us. But there seems to be no good reason to abandon altogether the crisis of subsistence as a model of what happened when the food ran out. For we must, I think, be prepared to accept the probability that many poor people in many, though by no means all, of the communities in Cumberland, Westmorland and Yorkshire, in Lancashire, in Dumfriesshire and in Roxburghshire, even perhaps in Staffordshire and Derbyshire, were exposed in 1623 to starvation in our second sense. They were under such anxiety about the future; required to sacrifice

so much of their comfort, convenience and well-being just to
stay alive; they were forced to endure faintness, loss of energy,
of the power and will to beget children, even in some cases loss
of shelter because of abandonment of their homes, on such a
scale that they can be said to have experienced famine.

Only a very small number indeed can have died of want of
means to live, though more must have seen the bodies or
witnessed the burials of those who did. In fact quite a large
proportion of the affected population may have feared that
they might die in such a fashion. For how were they to know
that the dearth would cease? How could they be confident that
those in authority would supply, and go on supplying, what
was required to meet the shortfall between their reduced or
vanishing incomes and the costs of the wherewithal to stay
alive? After all the magistrates and the poor-law officials were
all members of that securer part of the population which
might even add to their wealth because of the increased value
of their crops in time of scarcity. People prepared to benefit
from those with not enough food were always present. They
are found in Africa, India and Pakistan today in times of
shortage.

These are circumstances replete with conflicting interests
and with politics. It is with politics that we shall end this
hurried survey, the politics of the public supply of necessities
in dire emergency. But we must run our fingers over some of
the rest of the large body of new knowledge which bears on
the events at Greystoke, whose symbolic significance we have
so strongly stressed. Not all of it confirms what was suggested
originally, and we shall find ourselves surprised by the relative
unimportance of near famine in the north-west in the early
1620s, rather than by its relative importance.

The weather is of obvious relevance to the harvests which
were gathered and to the well-being of the harvesters. Here
our information is entirely novel, of the first interest to a study
of the lost world of our ancestors and invites a much longer
discussion. Unfortunately our accurate knowledge does not
begin quite early enough for our present purposes, though it
is suspected that the weather may have been unfavourable in
the north-west for the whole period from the 1580s to the
1620s. From the 1660s onwards, we are told, mortality in the
country as a whole was increased by cold temperatures in the
months from December to May and by hot in June to November

[398–401]. A one-degree-centigrade rise in the first period of the year combined with a one-degree fall in the second would increase the period expectation of life at birth by two full years. In bad years then it was appropriate to look up reproachfully at the unyielding sky, as we still do today, even though 'annual rainfall was not associated with mortality' [398] as our ancestors seem to have supposed. They could scarcely have suspected that too hot a summer might be dangerous because it multiplied the flies which spread disease, especially those borne from the filth in the dwellings and in the streets to children and to infants.

It seems entirely unlikely nevertheless that crisis mortality in the north-west in 1623 was worsened by a heatwave. Much has been poised on the wording of the Greystoke register, and it should now be obvious that that of Wednesbury in 1674 is critical in another way, because it testifies to breakdown in public support leading to someone dying. We now know that the year in question was not a crisis year nationally, not one of a fall in real wages, or of local emergencies. This must modify our original statements about Wednesbury, but it emphasizes the incident itself, since it happened by neglect at a time of relative plenty. How restricted the area of crisis conditions could be is illustrated by their gravity in the Forest of Arden at about the time of Shakespeare's death in Stratford-on-Avon in that district. An informative account of demographic crisis there between 1613 and 1619 explores its different effects on the landholders and the others, the rich and the poor, and associates it with what some historians have called the general European crisis of the seventeenth century. Yet we are now aware that these years, like 1674, were insignificant in the national story of subsistence and mortality.[24]

We cannot say with quite complete confidence, moreover, that the deaths marked 'famine' in St Margaret's, Westminster, in the summer and autumn of 1557 were as likely to have been due to starvation as those at Greystoke in 1623. This in spite of the fact that they took place in a year and in particular months marked by critical mortality in Westminster and in areas bordering London, which could have been associated with earlier bad harvests [338–671]. But 1557 itself was a bumper year, and other diseases were present which were not necessarily related to famine. The notorious searchers who inspected London corpses must have known what to look for in respect of starvation, but even they may have got it wrong. In the metropolitan case of course the likelihood of some people starving at all times, whatever was going on elsewhere, and in spite of what Graunt maintained, makes judgement more difficult.[25]

We are pretty certain, however, that plague did break out at Colyton in 1645–6, as was hinted earlier on, and that as a consequence of one of the most skilful analyses which has ever been made of parish register evidence (see note 20 of this chapter). But nothing confirms the suggestion that malnutrition can have caused the subsequent plague nor even have exacerbated it. It was not justifiable, moreover, to think of the 1640s as unique in being a terrible climacteric, even though it was at this time that the hazard due to war and the movement of troops, a prime cause of mortalities under the *ancien régime* on the continent, was of some importance in England [680–1]. The direst interludes were in the 1550s and the 1720s. The 1620s come after that in order of severity, equalled however by the 1540s. Even then the evidence goes to show that it was not 1623–4, but the year following, when crisis mortality was at its greatest. What is more, the infective agents at large in 1625 and later do not seem as likely to have been associated with food failure, and very few of the settlements we have been lamenting over are known to have been involved in this subsequent, more formidable emergency [675–6].

In addition to all this, and here at last we reach the end of the inferences which can be made from measures of prices, baptisms, marriages and deaths, the 1620s in the north-west most likely saw the final occasion when the inhabitants of English villages underwent this particular diffuse and elongated crisis of subsistence. After that time it was not the distant, upland, 'undeveloped' areas which suffered, or continued to suffer, sudden mortalities to the greatest extent. It was the centres of wealth and activity, which were also the centres of infection, whose vulnerability remained, though less and less it would appear, vulnerability to dearth or to dearth-associated onslaughts [688–9].

Accordingly, the further a place was from a market town and the greater its altitude, the less, not the more, was it likely to suffer mortality crises. But such events were becoming rarer and rarer after the earlier seventeenth century, and mortality

due to them progressively less significant. Up to the time of the
Greystoke incidents then, there were two Englands. The one
where the village and its region lay, was pastoral, hilly, remote,
subject to harvest failure. The other, arable, developed in its
communications, economically integrated, suffered inter-
mittently from disastrous epidemics [677–8].[26] Neither region,
we can now perceive, was quite like the Beauvaisis and we have
yet to consider why it was that the pattern of events which we
have been studying seems to have vanished not at the point
of industrialization but some five generations earlier.

We may begin with some further extracts from an English
parish register very close in their wording to those we have
been trying to interpret.

The place is Brewood in Staffordshire

5 Mar 1618 A certain poor man dying in the cross.
30 Sep 1618 Yevan, a poor wandering boy.
23 Mar 1619 Margaret, a poor wandering wench dying in
the cross.
11 Aug 1621 Edward Smith, a poor child, dying in the
church porch.
22 May 1623 A certain poor child dying in the church porch.
19 Oct 1623 A poor man dying in Thomas Johnson his barn,
whose name we know not.
27 Sep 1624 A poor wandering boy, whose name is unknown,
dying at Sommerford.
26 Jun 1625 Thomas Pooler, a poor wandering boy.
26 Sep 1625 A poor wandering man.
23 Oct 1625 A poor wandering woman.
23 Nov 1625 A poor wandering man, name unknown.[27]

The striking resemblance between the list of names from
Brewood and from Greystoke is in how many of the dead had
been wandering. They had taken to the road away from the
home village and from home, and often at the very last had
sought refuge in the church porch, that half sheltered space so
salient in parish life, where marriages had once been performed
and where unwanted babies so often were abandoned. But the
church porch was also the place where the overseers of the
poor of the parish usually met, churchwardens as they so often
were. The Rev. David Davies, vicar of Barkham in Berkshire,
whose *Case of the labourers* published in 1795 has been cited as

to the care which labouring fathers took of their children, had this to say of the matter: 'It is manifest that our laws consider all the inhabitants of a parish as forming one large family, the higher and richer part of which is bound to provide employment and assistance for the lower and labouring part.'

Poor relief, then, was a Christian duty as well as a legal obligation, and responsibility for the poor meant making sure that everyone in the village was able to live. The overseers had to see to it that money was collected from those able to spare it to give to those who could not, and who must suffer, perhaps might even die, if they were not so relieved. Payments from the poor rate were actually called alms sometimes and in some parishes, and their recipients almsmen and almswomen. Thus the obligation to secure the livelihood of the unfortunate was far older than the famous Elizabethan poor law Act of 1601, which codified the duties of overseers. That law reads harshly to us in our very different circumstances, as do the later enactments which proscribed vagrancy and aimed to prevent possessionless immigrants entering the parish, whose presence might burden its resources even further. If we find it difficult to accept such legislation, it was even more difficult for the villagers themselves to forgive their own officers should they falter in their duty of provision, or should they fail to prevent the unscrupulous from making money out of scarcity.

Difficulty in supply was no excuse: if grain was short it was the duty of the national authorities to acquire supplies and of the local authorities to distribute them. People seem to have believed that there would be a sufficiency of food for every single person if what was available was justly distributed, and if everyone was ensured the means to buy his share or hers. Such a guarantee was a right under the traditional social order, as much of a right as the right to welfare nowadays, under what we are pleased to call the welfare state. 'Bread riots', 'grain riots' and such disturbances, nearly always marked by the seizure of foodstuffs and the selling of them at a price the poor could afford, were regarded by the women and the men who took part in them as an exercise of that right. The rough or natural justice of their cause was widely acknowledged even by the authorities. The compulsory sale of food to the needy at a lower price was precisely what they did themselves at a time when famine threatened.

The assumption that resources could never run out entirely,

and prices always be controlled, is easy to ridicule, and during the eighteenth century the secure and the respectable did not miss their opportunities. It behoves us to remember however that between 1940 and 1946 the food supply of the English people was perpetually diminishing and in danger of failing to be adequate. Yet it is said that the population as a whole has never been better fed because of the efficiency of political arrangements to ensure that each single individual had an entitlement to acquire enough to eat.

In his castigation of the way in which the government of India handled the Bengal famine of 1943, Amartya Sen maintains that it made the mistake of concentrating perpetually on prices, supply and transport, and not on the extraordinary failure of effective purchasing power which he demonstrates occurred to the labourers and handicraft workers of that area at that time. One of the reasons, he claims, why these exceedingly poor people could not buy the rice they needed was that the high wages paid by the government to numbers of their luckier companions for work on war installations enabled them to buy as much rice as they wanted to. The famine was a political failure, a failure in the distribution of purchasing power, and so for the lamentable events of the 1970s in Pakistan and the Sahel.

There is ample evidence, as we have seen, of the activity of the authorities in traditional England in keeping a close watch on the supply of grain, on the price of food and on market-rigging of all kinds. Reserves were maintained both in the town and in the country, to be made available to the needy when required. 'Forestalling', buying up before the market opened, and 'regrating', selling again at a higher price in a neighbouring market, are expressions we often recall. These were punished right up to the eighteenth century. There are indications that stocks were carefully counted and the probable shortfall of corn calculated when famine threatened, even down to the piles of wheat, barley, oats and rye in the granaries of the smallest hamlets.[28] But they went further than the policy which Sen declared was so ineffective in Bengal.

We have seen in an earlier chapter that transfer incomes from those who had to those who had not may have been no inconsiderable part of all English goods and services and the authorities in question administered a great proportion of them. That they nearly always succeeded in underwriting the entitlement of the poor to food is the inference we must draw from the local character, the relative rarity, of near famine, and from the virtual absence of outright starvation in the English record. When they blundered in respect of an individual, men like John Russel of Wednesbury died. When their policy was ineffective, or the problem was too difficult, situations like those of 1586–7, 1596–7 and 1623–4 came about in areas like that of the English north-west. When they failed, it was an administrative and political failure, as well as, perhaps rather than, an inevitable outcome of the weather, or warfare, or uncontrollable economic vicissitude.

The peasants ceased to starve in England, starve in the special sense we have adopted, because of the expansion of resources, because of economic integration, because of improved communication. But it could not have happened without the greater efficiency with which entitlements to a share in these more favourable conditions were distributed. We may end this consideration of the fundamental facts about the livelihoods of our ancestors by repeating the following phrases of what was first printed in 1965.

> Why is it that we know so much about the building of the British Empire, the growth of Parliament, and its practices, the public and private lives of English kings, statesmen, generals, writers, thinkers and yet do not know whether all our ancestors had enough to eat? Our genealogical knowledge of how Englishmen and their distant kinsmen overseas are related to the Englishmen of the pre-industrial world is truly enormous, and is growing all the time. Why has almost nothing been done to discover how long those earlier Englishmen lived and how confident most of them could be of having any posterity at all? Not only do we not know the answers to these questions, until now we never seem to have bothered to ask them.

Not one of these plaintive queries is as appropriate now in 1983, and some, that to do with length of life for example, are entirely inappropriate. It might still be justifiable to hint, however, that the historians of our decade are more interested in the riot and revolt which sometimes broke out when food supply was threatened, than they are in the extent to which that threat menaced the life chances of the people who rose up.

Once having begun to respond to them, we are only just beginning to recognize the implications of such queries for human association altogether, and that not only of the English people in their pre-industrial past.

Personal discipline
and social survival
Chapter 7

With notes on the history of bastardy and
of sexual nonconformism in England

Prone as we are to be sentimental about our ancestors, we seem quite prepared to believe that they were often wicked people, at least on the standards which they set for themselves. When bastardy comes into the conversation it is sometimes said that country people, and our forefathers in general, were more likely than we are to bring illegitimate children into the world, and more tolerant of bastardy as a condition. It is widely supposed too that no shrewd, hard-working peasant or craftsman, to whom strong, hard-working sons and daughters were a tangible asset, would ever undertake to marry a girl unless he knew from his own sexual experience that she was capable of bearing children. If she did prove barren (this implies) no marriage would take place, and the poor girl would live out her life as a reject.

This element of suspicion in our attitude to the world we have lost is probably complicated in its origins. So sudden and complete has been the desertion of the countryside for the cities in our recent history, that it was perhaps natural for people to assume that those who remained behind were, and are, the inferior people – in aptitude and intelligence, and presumably therefore in what has been called moral calibre. Such an unsympathetic attitude could perhaps be supposed to have had something in the way of justification from surveys of the condition of rural communities in recent times.[1] It has been shown, moreover, that the English village has been rather more likely to be marked by the presence of illegitimates than the town.

In the 1950s a French scholar went so far as to put forward the view that the crises which concerned us in our last chapter were also interludes of moral collapse. At these times, so the suggestion went, the peasantry broke free to some extent from the strict rule of sexual continence outside marriage which the church universal and established opinion prescribed for everybody at all times. Hence a dangerously large number of children with no hope of survival, leading to infanticide as well as to a sudden growth in numbers of children not within the familial system.[2]

In the 1980s it is far more difficult to think of those who live in the countryside as a backward remnant, sunk in the rural idiocy of early Marxist dogma. For one thing a proportion of the well-provided-for, commuting professional and businessmen, and above all the retired, have begun to move back into the villages, which are tending to become *embourgeoisifiés*, as the French would say, at least in certain areas. Furthermore the moralistic attitude to such things as illegitimacy has at last begun to fade, especially among those professionally concerned with them, and amongst young people, whose procreative habits are markedly different from those· of their forebears. The publication of the first attempt at a comparative history of sexual nonconformism* in 1980 marked the recognition that rules of respectability – officially the rules of the dominant élite and later of the middle class, though certainly not entirely consistently observed by their members – had never been universally established in western Christian society, especially among working people and least of all in England. 'Christianity was never, anywhere, a full description of what people did' [xiv].

What is more the famous *principle of legitimacy* has begun to lose the status as 'a universal sociological law', claimed for it in the 1930s by Malinowski, the best-known anthropologist of his day. In traditional English society it seems to have been unnecessary to ensure social survival that each and every child should have a man, and one man at that, in the role of father, of unique, mature, masculine, protector [5]. The engendering of children on a scale which might threaten the social structure was never, or almost never, a present possibility. It has become obvious from our English evidence that

---

* *Bastardy and its Comparative History: Studies in the History of Illegitimacy and Sexual Nonconformism in Britain, France, Germany, Sweden, North America, Jamaica and Japan*, ed. by Peter Laslett, Karla Oosterveen and Richard M. Smith, Cambridge, 1980. References in square brackets in the text are to page numbers in the book.

neither rapid urbanization nor industrialization were necessarily linked to the production of illegitimate children. This
makes it doubtful whether these processes did always lead to
a breach of Malinowski's principle, or indeed of familial control. It certainly makes it difficult to look on the bastardy rate
as an indicator of anomie, of social structural breakdown so
often considered to be inevitable in really large areas where
the traditional social structure ceased to be sovereign, in the
great cities that is to say.

Paris has always stood at the head of all France in its
bastardy level. But up to the 1910s London had one of the
lowest levels in the whole of England [63–4]. This is one of the
circumstances which makes local influences on the illegitimacy
rate a matter of intriguing interest, as we shall see. There have
been further assaults on the long-established assumption that
sexual nonconformism is to be taken as a symptom of social
discontinuity as well as of personal irresponsibility. For there
is some evidence that there may have existed bands of people
in English communities who held to rather different rules as to
marriage and procreation from those proclaimed as imperative
by the respectable and obeyed by the majority. These have
been provisionally entitled bastardy-prone sub-societies,
whose members seem to have been related to each other by
kinship, at any one time and over time. Their outstanding
further characteristic for us, whose power of observation is
limited for the most part to the names and dates in parish
register recordings, is that their members tended to have more
than one bastard apiece, and that the numbers of illegitimates
which they contributed was proportionately greater when
illegitimate, and general, fertility were high than when these
were low. Nothing which they did, nor any other circumstance,
could be used to confirm an association between peaks of
illegitimate births and crises of subsistence, and their activities
must not be permitted to contradict the impression that bastardy
was generally uncommon in England, certainly as compared
with Iceland, or Austria, or Portugal, or even Scotland
[217–46, 40–8].

The peasants and the craftsmen of Tudor and Stuart times
seem on the whole to have been cautious about the procreation
of children and the formation of families. Testing a woman's
fertility before deciding to marry her cannot be confirmed
amongst our ancestors. For one thing there were far too many

marriages where no births at all were ever recorded. All the facts we have surveyed about the late age of marriage amongst them, and the circumstances which surrounded every decision to set up a new household, seem to imply that they were well enough aware that the fund of food and conveniences of life were strictly limited even if starvation did not ordinarily have to be reckoned as a possibility. Their marked success in finding themselves new partners when they were widowed is another sign of their recognition that the position of a child was precarious indeed without a father's support, or a mother's care.

Norms of sexual conduct were enforced by the established church, though enjoined might be a better word. The church had its spiritual courts, its executive officials called apparitors and its humiliating and very public punishments. Anyone who committed or tried to commit a sexual act with someone other than his spouse, whether or not conception took place, ran the risk of a summons to the archdeacons' court – the lowest in the hierarchy of spiritual courts – of a fine, and then of penance in church at service time, or in the market place. It seems to have been accepted that this was much less likely to happen when the couple concerned were in courtship, but no one was at liberty to live a life of sexual freedom. If a person about whom a *fame of incontinency* had got abroad (that is a suspicion of a sexual escapade) ignored the summons or refused the punishment, then excommunication followed. This meant exile from the most important of all social activities, isolation within the community. The bastardy-prone must have been to some degree outcasts.

So notorious was the archdeacons' court for its preoccupation with sexual misdemeanours that it had a folk title, the 'Bawdy Court'. Its jurisdiction went back to the Middle Ages and extended to many other things. But the church was not alone in the supervision of sexual and marital conduct. Really grave offences, especially those judged likely to breach the peace or to burden the community financially, were dealt with by the justices of the peace. 'Things fearful to name', like homosexuality or intercourse with animals, were referred to high judicial authority, for they were capital crimes, punishable by death.

It would seem, however, as if the awfulness of the penalty, and a desire not to take notice that such outrages were actually being committed, had the effect of ensuring that there were very few prosecutions for them, and even a degree of tolerance. There was certainly a community of sodomites, male prostitutes and their customers for the most part, in the city of London in the eighteenth century, whose existence was revealed by the prosecuting zeal of associations set up to counteract such laxity, the Societies for the Reformation of Manners. This community shows a surprising resemblance to its counterparts in our own day. We have no reason to be confident, however, that homosexuality, commercially organized or between consenting individuals of either sex, was confined to that city, or absent from the countryside where most people lived. Men were fairly often court-martialled for buggery in the armed forces during the eighteenth and early nineteenth centuries, especially in the Royal Navy, and the proportion put to death was surprisingly high.

We know from the manuals used by the justices of the peace that buggery was a transgression which they might possibly encounter. It was specified as all offences 'against the order of nature committed by mankind with mankind, or beasts, or by women willingly with beasts'. The implication here that lesbianism might be overlooked seems to be borne out by such other indications as we have on the subject, but it was evidently supposed that a woman might be forced by an animal. The Christian west may have had a greater horror of buggery as defined in the phrase we have cited than is to be found anywhere else. There was undoubtedly a belief that an animal/human monster could be engendered from bestiality, and the deep disquiet about the possible conjunction of the genes of the two in our time by genetic engineering may re-echo this dread felt by our forebears. When the convicted offender was executed the cow, sheep or pig with which the act had been committed was put to death as well.[3]

It seems likely from our knowledge of what goes on today that only very little of what went on ever reached the authorities, especially as to homosexuality. Otherwise the number of cases would surely have been unmanageable. Plenty of people got away with ignoring the church courts and, if they were unfortunate enough to get convicted, with laughing at its penalties. But there can be no doubt that much reporting, summoning and writ-executing was always in progress. You could not let fornication take place in your house, or allow a bastard to be born there, or as much as offer a job to an excommunicant without running these risks. It was not wise, if you had become notorious in the village where you lived, to rely on the silence of your neighbours.

This was because notice was taken of the conduct of those who were felt to be a threat to decency and order, so that the courts could be said to have upheld what was thought to be right. Sexual irregularities going beyond what was tolerated in courting couples, and what everyone knew perfectly well had to be winked at, were certainly disliked. They were regarded as breaches of the peace by ordinary people. It is only necessary to read what was said by witnesses in the spiritual courts to recognize these facts. And Keith Thomas insists that the Act of the Cromwellian Parliament of 1650 which made incest and adultery felonies, carrying sentence of death as buggery did, represents a fairly general view that the community needed protection from such actions rather than an expression of puritan authoritarianism in sexual matters. The Act was ineffective nevertheless, and lapsed in 1660.[4]

Some of the more light-hearted beliefs which have been held about this subject seem to have little justification. No confirmation is to be found in parish register evidence for the view that the Elizabethan peasantry disported themselves in the hay and along the hedgerows in the leafy month of June as Shakespeare's *Midsummer Night's Dream* might lead us to suppose. Such goings on would have led to a peak of irregular conceptions at this season, which close analysis shows not to have been present. Even the heady weeks of the early summer of 1660, when the rule of the Puritans was cracking and the permissive reign of Old Rowley, Charles II the merry monarch, had its beginnings, did not leave a perceptible mark in the baptismal recordings nine months later, for illegitimates or for legitimates either.[5] Nothing whatever in the demographic record indicates a change in sexual habits to correspond with the period of licence and licentiousness which has always been associated with the Restoration, unless it was a trivial and temporary rise in the consistently low level of aristocratic illegitimacy.

This is quite evident from the figures for bastardy in England between the middle of the sixteenth and the middle of the nineteenth centuries which are set out in Table 13. They represent percentages of all births (baptisms until the 1840s) marked 'illegitimate' in the registers.

Table 13: *Illegitimacy ratios in England, 1540s–1840s* (%)

1540–4	[4·4]	1700–4	1·8
1545–9	[3·0]	1705–9	1·8
1550–4	[2·4]	1710–14	2·0
1555–9	[1·9]	1715–19	2·2
1560–4	[2·0]	1720–4	2·1
1565–9	[1·3]	1725–9	2·4
1570–4	1·9	1730–4	2·7
1575–9	2·5	1735–9	2·7
1580–4	2·8	1740–4	2·9
1585–9	2·9	1745–9	2·8
1590–4	3·1	1750–4	3·1
1595–9	3·1	1755–9	3·5
1600–4	3·4	1760–4	4·0
1605–9	3·0	1765–9	4·3
1610–14	2·8	1770–4	4·3
1615–19	2·5	1775–9	4·6
1620–4	2·5	1780–4	4·9
1625–9	2·6	1785–9	5·1
1630–4	2·2	1790–4	5·1
1635–9	2·0	1795–9	5·0
1640–4	1·8	1800–4	5·3
1645–9	1·5	1805–9	5·3
1650–4	1·0	1810–14	5·0
1655–9	0·9	1815–19	4·6
1660–4	1·5	1820–4	5·4
1665–9	1·4	1825–9	4·6
1670–4	1·4	1830–4	4·2
1675–9	1·2	1835–9	[5·8]
1680–4	1·5	1840–4	not available
1685–9	1·5	[1842	8·0]
1690–4	1·6	1845–9	6·7
1695–9	2·0		

Source: Bastardy, Tables 1.1a–1.1c, sample of 98 parishes: figures in
brackets unreliable because too few of the parishes were in observation.

The sharp-eyed reader will immediately recognize in this
table the same rhythmic pattern which was observed when we
were discussing births, marriages and deaths. Indeed if you
draw a graph of these values over time and one for the values
of the gross reproduction rate contained in Table 10 on p. 108
above, as has been done in Figure 1, you are astonished by
what you see. Illegitimacy pursues almost precisely the same
path as general fertility; high but falling in late Tudor times
just as fertility was; continuing its descent to a conspicuously
low point under the Puritans and Cromwell in the middle of
the seventeenth century, like fertility again, but with a rising

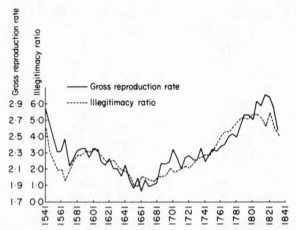

Figure 1: *Relationship between the gross reproduction rate and the illegitimacy ratio in England, 1541–1838*

(*Source: Local Population Studies*, Spring 1980, no. 24)

tendency for the hundred years which follow, neither curve attained the level recorded under Queen Elizabeth I until the 1750s. After that both statistics rise to a new high, a peak which was succeeded after an intermediate drop by an all-time maximum in the early years of Queen Victoria, not illustrated here. You cannot but believe that bastardy and general fertility were in some way connected with each other.

But illegitimacy was somewhat steadier in its progress over time: it changed more deliberately than fertility as a whole. With these intertwining filaments in front of us, stretching as they do over so lengthy a period, it is exceedingly difficult to suppose that anything like a sexual revolution ever took place in England. Such a catastrophic change has been read into the briefer and often less satisfactory series of illegitimacy figures from other European countries, some of which rise much more abruptly and to greater heights in the last decades of the eighteenth century at about the time when political revolution began its heady career in France and in Europe generally [26–9]. Before we infer that our country escaped this sudden dislocation of its marital institutions at that time, just as it escaped from constitutional disruption, we have to bear in mind that the notion as well as the factual occurrence of a sexual revolution have been hotly disputed.[6] The really interesting peculiarity of the English experience lies elsewhere.

Ages at marriage for both sexes were rising, not falling, in the earlier seventeenth century as illegitimacy went down, and proportions marrying were falling too. When men and women began to marry earlier in the later eighteenth century and fewer of them remained unmarried, illegitimacy went up.

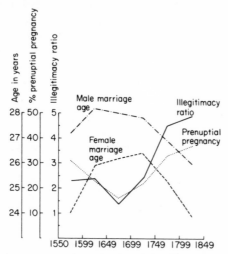

Figure 2: *Age at marriage in England for both sexes: illegitimacy ratio and rate of prenuptial pregnancy, by 50-year periods, 1550–1845*

(*Source: Bastardy*, Tables 1–3; based on the figures for 17 parishes)

Marriages postponed or marriages forgone therefore were associated with fewer bastardies, not larger numbers of them as might be expected.

The same thing can be said of prenuptial pregnancy, the disposition to give birth to a child less than nine months after marriage, a disposition which can also be measured by the analysis of parish registers. Figure 2 plots three graphs: marriage age of women, marriage age of men, illegitimacy and prenuptial pregnancy, in sixteen English parishes where family reconstitution has been carried out. Schematic as this figure has to be, it suffices to show that bastardy and prenuptial pregnancy varied together over time, and that they did so in inverse relationship to marriage age and so to proportions marrying [19–24].

Deprivation of marriage therefore did not lead to a greater propensity towards sexual adventures, not to those which gave rise to pregnancy, whatever may have happened to sexual activity of other kinds. We can observe strict and efficient social control in operation here, a discipline which did serve to ensure social survival even if it worked in entirely unexpected ways. This should not surprise us if we recognize, as Wrigley has repeatedly advised us to do, that a force which is capable of keeping people from marrying at all must also be capable of preventing them from procreating outside marriage. When therefore we observe that bastardy grew less in England from the 1600s to the 1640s whilst the doctrine of the Puritans was gaining influence, and fell to its lowest point in the 1650s when they were in undisputed control, we need not suppose that it was Puritanism itself which brought these things about. Other and more efficient means of regulation seem to have been at work, the same it would seem as those which reduced fertility generally during these years.

Keith Wrightson has demonstrated in fact [176–9] that the Puritans were never in a position to effect such a result even if their activities did have some impact on what happened. He makes the pertinent suggestion that the disturbances which they had caused may have affected the registration of illegitimacy in the 1640s and '50s in such a way as to create an illusory impression of a nadir. There are difficulties even with this explanation, however, and the vagaries of registration could not possibly account for the general shape of the English illegitimacy curve [48–53]. Whatever were the pressures from the environment, economic as well as ideological, which kept illegitimate in line with legitimate fertility, it certainly respected one feature of the social structure. This was the influence of localism [31–43]. The persistence of illegitimacy by locality is perhaps more noteworthy in its way than its association with prenuptial pregnancy and with general fertility, or than its inverse relationship with age at marriage and proportions marrying.

Let us turn for a moment from these more abstract issues and observe what actually went on in the disciplinary courts, spiritual and lay. The presentments made by the church-wardens of each parish tend to give the impression of wide-spread immorality, as the respectable have insistently called sexual nonconforming behaviour, an impression which those writing about the subject have done little to play down. But it is impossible to gain any sort of numerical impression from evidence of this kind [78–9]. We have only to imagine the result of an attempt at estimating the extent of extramarital intercourse from the records of our own divorce courts to recognize this fact. Even the proportion of baptisms marked *illegitimate* in the parish registers is an exceedingly uncertain indicator of the extent of sexual irregularity.

Numbers of baptized bastards may well have to be multiplied fifty, seventy, or even a hundred times and more[7] in order to guess at the number of sexual lapses which lay behind them. What is worse, this large but indefinite multiplier may be expected to have varied with the length of cohabitation. It may have varied also from time to time, place to place, and perhaps social class to social class, both of man and of woman. By sexual lapses responsible for such illegitimacy as can be observed, acts of fornication only are at issue for we know nothing numerical whatever about acts of adultery in past time, almost nothing about them in our own time. The two twentieth-century figures for adulterine bastards, that is birth to married women of children procreated by men not their husbands at the time, suggest that these numbers may not have been negligible.[8]

If the records of the church courts are filled with notices of sexual incontinence, those of the magistrates courts are studded with measures taken in punishment of unmarried mothers, and sometimes of unmarried fathers too, with provision for the upkeep of the child.

> Jane Sotworth of Wrightington, spinster, swears that Richard Garstange of Fazarkerley, husbandman, is the father of Alice, her bastard daughter. She is to have charge of the child for two years, provided she does not beg, and Richard is then to take charge until it is twelve years old. He shall give Jane a cow and 6s. in money. Both he and she shall this day be whipped in Ormeskirke.

So ordered the Lancashire justices at the Ormskirk Sessions on Monday, 27 April 1601, though the language they used was Latin and lengthier. At Manchester, in 1604, they went so far as to require that Thomas Byrom, gentleman, should maintain a bastard he had begotten on a widow, and be whipped as well. On 10 October 1604 he was whipped, in Manchester market-place.[9]

Not many 'gentlemen' can ever have suffered this indignity.

But we must again insist that the frequency of these cases in the records, even the number of times behaviour of this character has appeared in the present essay, must not be allowed to create the impression that illegitimacy was commonplace, or that every instance was so punished. Nor can we suppose that such punishments served to keep down the number of base births. When the spiritual authorities relaxed and finally ceased their activities against fornication in later Stuart and Hanoverian times, the figures in the records of baptisms marked 'illeg.', 'base', 'spur', or plain 'b' for bastard did not increase. As Table 13 has demonstrated, they remained low throughout the decades of the early eighteenth century when the English church is said to have fallen asleep and the magistrates to have become progressively less effective.

This in itself speaks to the lack of co-ordination between what the powers were trying to do and what was really going forward. We cannot be surprised that the end of the church's attempt to control sexual behaviour made no observable difference to the illegitimacy ratio. But it would certainly be wrong to dismiss the change as trivial. Sexual behaviour then ceased forever to be a matter of legitimate neighbourly concern, affecting the church, the parish and even the magistrate, and became that supremely private affair which we now assume that it has to be, subject occasionally to censorious gossip, but to gossip alone.

How public sexual irregularity might become in Somersetshire in early Stuart times can be judged by what follows:

Upon Sunday the 18th and 25th days of this instant month of July, Thomas Odam with a white sheet upon his uppermost garment, and a white wand in his hand, shall come into the parish church at Charlton at the beginning of the forenoon service and stand forth in the middle space before the pulpit during the whole time of divine service, and a sermon then and there to be preached against the crime of fornication and incest, and immediately after the sermon shall with an audible voice make this humble acknowledgement, repeating the same after the minister namely

'I, Thomas Odam, do here before God acknowledge and confess that I have grievously offended the divine majesty of almighty God in living incestuously with my wife's daughter'.

Odam had to repeat this public act of shame on the third Sunday, the first of August, in the loveliest of all English cathedrals, 'the church of St Andrew in Wells', 'wearing in his wand a piece of paper spread abroad containing in great text [very large letters] these words':

CHARLTON

THOMAS ODAM, FOR INCEST WITH

AUCHARETT WHITE HIS WIVES

DAUGHTER

Only tiny numbers of sexual infringements were publicly punished with such marvellous, symbolic, cathartic effectiveness. Incest was and still is a more serious infringement of the code than fornication, adultery or bastardy, and it is probably correct to suppose that Thomas Odam and his vicious behaviour were deeply offensive to the neighbourhood. Still G. R. Quaife, who cites the case tells us that 'incest did not cause the horror that it did in later centuries'. Most incest seems to have taken place between stepfather and stepdaughter, as with Thomas Odam, or between a man and his sister-in-law. But there were instances of its occurrence between brother and sister and even an attempt by a cobbler of Glastonbury on his own fourteen-year-old daughter.

The occurrence of all these misdemeanours in one county, which happened also to be the diocese of Wells, in the years between 1600 and 1660 gives us a clear enough notion of what was possible, even if it tells us nothing about the frequency with which such things occurred. In the year 1700 a man with a phenomenal memory noted down all that he knew had happened to the people of a Shropshire village, and he also recalled a father committing incest with his daughter, a bastard daughter on this occasion who had a child as a result [231]. But the William Tyler of Myddle stated to have been guilty of this peculiar outrage seems to have been quite exceptional in his villainies, an ogre hero almost, whose actions are portrayed as so extreme that we begin to suspect exaggeration. Such a recital might leave us with the impression that the traditional English village was peopled by a laughterless body of men and women, chaste by compulsion nearly all of the time, and when they did transgress, given to joyless lust.

But this is not at all the atmosphere conveyed by the

testimony which has come down to us, even though it is in the
formal prose of court officials. The language of the passages
which follow would have been ungrateful to the Victorian ear
and is not entirely acceptable even today. We should as we
read them remember how apt people are, and presumably
always have been, to give themselves over to fantasies about
their sexual lives and sexual prowess. Here is the clergyman's
wife who

> saw a young man try to put his hand up her daughter's
> dress as they sat at table, and there was recrimination. The
> young man boasted: 'I'll fuck thee and they daughter
> before I go home ... I have fucked ten old women of this
> parish.' To which the vicar's wife replied: 'Tell me one of
> them for I will not believe you.' 'I have fucked Kent's wife,
> the miller, to flitters.'

And here is the loose woman from the village of Cutcombe who

> most shamefully wrestled with John Snow and threw him
> on his back and took out his privy member and said unto
> the rest of the women there present: 'His name shall be no
> more called John Snow but I will christen his name John
> Toggerpin.'[10]

The only likely place where the woman from Cutcombe
could have put on such a performance was in an alehouse.
They were probably all far gone in drink at the time and the
clergy never ceased to complain about drunkenness, which
was also subject to church court discipline. Something like
alcoholism is to be seen in the records, and in discussing the
village community we found it hinted at even in the accounts
of the churchwardens and of the overseers. Brandy might even
be provided for a pauper on her deathbed. Booze crops up
continually among the families of Myddle, with the women as
well as the men. It could ruin them.[11]

The living representatives of law and order, of high social
life as well as the ideals of religion, were decidedly not absent
from the scenes we have described. The sexual lives of the
English élite between the sixteenth and the nineteenth
centuries have recently been investigated so thoroughly that
we can have no doubt that fornicating, adulterous, whore-

mongering males like Samuel Pepys, James Boswell and William Byrd, the Virginia planter at large in London, were by no means isolated figures amongst the aristocracy and gentry of England and her colonies, though we certainly must not think of them as representative. There was a streak of libertinism in 'good society', and there is a fascinating possibility that those inclined to literature amongst them, such as the Hobbes, Byrons, Rochesters and, more surprising, the Darwins and Wordsworths,[12] displayed this trait the most conspicuously.

As for the parsons and their much recorded libidinousness, they face us with a paradox well known to the student of normative behaviour.[13] Those who are entrusted with enforcing the regulations and who expound their rationale cannot be supposed always to obey them themselves, any more than all our policemen always obey the law of the land. The priest who molested the women under his spiritual care had been a familiar figure since the Middle Ages, along with the others who took part in that highly interesting type of contact between classes, a man of education and position consorting with harlots from the lowest social level [226–8]. But here the tendency to exaggerate and to fantasize is so serious that it may never be certain whether the priest who withheld the communion cup from a parishioner upon a fame of incontinence was not himself occasionally or consistently incontinent. What we can say is that in taking advantage of their superior position and masculinity the delinquent parsons of the world we have lost demonstrated what we must expect, a marked inequality in sexual matters between men and women.

Bastardy ratios and rates of prenuptial pregnancy tell us little of such subjects as these. There is one form of analysis, however, which does help us to make a judgment about how persistent sexual nonconformism was. When used with other evidence, locality persistence can be made to yield something like a general hypothesis as to the way in which sexual behaviour was related to procreation and to the means of subsistence in England.

If our counties are ranked in order of illegitimacy level at successive dates, they are found to retain their relative positions to a significant extent, and this over half-centuries and even centuries. The county of Shropshire for example, where Myddle is situated, belonged to that western area which had high ratios as early as Elizabeth I and throughout the parish register era. Shropshire was the third county for bastardy in England in 1842, second in 1870–2 and second or third at every ten-year ordering until 1900–2 [30, 34–5]. Unlike Bedfordshire or Hertfordshire, Shropshire was never what we call a 'rogue' county, that is to say it never shifted numbers of places in the rank order quite suddenly as they and a few other counties did [39]. As far as we can see these movements in the bastardy level did not accompany developments in the economic, social or religious life of the areas concerned. Counties underwent sudden industrialization and urbanization without their relative positions changing much, and they might, like Lancashire, grow less prone to illegitimacy as factory production came to dominate them. Already present, as far as we can see, when our evidence begins, the national ordering of areas by illegitimacy certainly persisted until well into the twentieth century. It has been demonstrated quite independently for the year 1911. The image must be of superimposed geological strata, all rising and falling together over this long period of time, with an occasional, at present inexplicable, breaking of rank by certain counties.[14]

The phenomenon of locality persistence is not confined to English records, and has been found in Scottish, Irish, French, German, Swedish and even Russian figures, in the last case before and after the revolution of 1917. It is well marked in France in the nineteenth century [278–83] and in that country it has been recently shown that marriage rituals and conjugal relations also differed between region and region, even between district and district.[15] This might explain something of local variation in illegitimacy and in prenuptial pregnancy as well. Since it is usually, though not always correctly, assumed that local custom is perduring, originating at a point no longer known and continuing as long as the social structure continues, courtship practices might possibly be connected with locality persistence, and with its relative immunity to economic and to other change.

Societies of the bastardy-prone may have been characteristic of some areas and not of others too, and their existence has also been demonstrated outside Britain, in a Norman village and in another in the Italian alps. Unfortunately our information is still exasperatingly vague on all these points even for our own country. Still courtship and the point at which the risk of conception was permitted are known to have been to some extent specific to certain places or areas in England. This is evident from the following report of the proceedings in the Registry of the Archdeaconry at Leicester, the case in question dating from July 1598.

> The common use and custom within the county of Leicester, specially in and about the town before mentioned (Hoby and Waltham) and in other places thereunto adjoining for the space of 10, 20, 30 or 40 years past hath been and is that any man being a suitor to a woman in the way of marriage is upon the day appointed to make a final conclusion of the marriage before treated of. If the said marriage be concluded and contracted then the man doth most commonly remain in the house where the woman doth abide the night the next following after such contract, otherwise he doth depart without staying the night.[16]

No ceremony in church can have been in question here although it would certainly have been planned when the marriage was 'finally concluded'. What had taken place was an espousal, a troth plight, a hand fasting before witnesses, of the kind which we found ourselves discussing in relation to *Romeo and Juliet*. It seems correct to infer then that when he did leave the morning afterwards, the man was already married, in the eyes of both church and state, at least as things were until the year 1754. When they arrived at the church for their weddings, brides in this part of Leicestershire must frequently have been in the early and sometimes in the late stages of pregnancy. We may recall the uncertainty about this point in the account of the Yorkshire country wedding of the 1640s which was cited earlier.

There is an intriguing hint in the wording of this passage that procedures may even have varied from time to time, as well as from place to place. We know that clandestine marriages, where the couples never got to church at all, though a parson may have gone through a ceremony, were particularly widespread in the late seventeenth century and then ceased to be so. But clandestine should not be taken to mean private, without witnesses. A Mary Gillot testified as follows to her marriage-in-progress at the Oxfordshire archdeacon's court in 1598.

She doth and hath used the company of William Whit, who is contracted to her before witnesses and meaneth to marry her soon as he is out of service.

Living together before the church ceremony, as would seem evident, they were apparently confident that having been contracted before witnesses was a defence against any charge of immorality. Sixty years earlier, in the diocese of Ely, Joan Wigg was careful not to commit herself before witnesses, though she admitted she had privately promised to marry John Newman of Royston, Hertfordshire. When he brought such witnesses to hear her testify to her undertaking she burst out:

John Newman, I marvel what you mean. You follow some evil counsel. I cannot deny but I have made a promise to you to my husband; but shall we need to marry so soon? It were better for us to forbear and [have] some household stuff to begin withal.

This was about 1535; Joan Wigg was clearly a prudent girl.

A special study would be necessary in order to decide how widespread was the customary assumption that espousals permitted cohabitation and to estimate their consequent effect on vital statistics. It is suggested that their persistence in England has given rise to the misplaced belief in the existence of trial marriage. Contracts of this sort were abolished in the Catholic world by the papal bull confirming the decree of the Council of Trent in 1564, making privy contracts null and void and directing that all marriages should be performed by a priest in the church of the parish where one of the parties dwelt. Though by then very little used, at least formally, espousals were not officially abolished here until the Act of 1753, usually called Hardwicke's Marriage Act. The assumption that an agreement to marry meant freedom to copulate clearly persisted up to that time in spite of the fact that 'prenuptial fornication' was an offence punishable in the archdeacons' court. This body proceeded against pregnant brides even in the eighteenth century.

There is some doubt as to what authority in church law was at issue in this matter, and even more so in Scotland, where the ferociousness of the kirk sessions at this late date in dealing with parents who brought babies to be baptized within nine months of marriage makes melancholy reading. Folk opinion at this time in a remote Cumbrian parish was evidently in no doubt of what was permissible, if we can trust a passage in the guide to one of the churches:

> The Kirk of Ulpha to the pilgrim's eye
> Is welcome as a star.

A story told by the old folks, relates how a certain parson, before the days when marriage must necessarily be held in church, gathered together those living together and not yet legally united, and performed the wedding ceremony over seventeen such couples who assembled at Frith Hall on one day in the year 1730 for that purpose.[17]

Frith Hall was a large house in that scattered hamlet on the Duddon and it is unclear why the parson did not do the job in the chapel of ease, which was certainly available for use in the place.

In spite of local variations in the words used and the actions taken, it is possible to make the following tentative generalizations about espousals or contracts in England in relation to marriage. A contract publicly entered into before witnesses and marked by two overt actions, the kissing of the woman by the man and the presentation of gifts – often a gold ring, or, oddly enough, half a gold ring – constituted a binding marriage, provided only that the couple then proceeded to sexual intercourse. In the Roman Church after 1564 such an action between an affianced couple was a grave sin. In the English church it was a much less serious matter. If the two people concerned underwent a church ceremony sometime later, this was indeed the celebration of a *fait accompli*.

In extreme Protestant practice, amongst the sects in America as well as here, the whole issue was different. For the nonconformists marriage consisted simply of a promise followed by consummation: church ceremony was irrelevant. Since in our day Puritanism is closely associated with sexual authoritarianism perhaps an example ought to be cited from the works of an English Puritan divine on this interesting point. William Gouge had this to say in 1622:

I would advise all Christians that desire a blessing and good success on their marriage to be contracted before they are married. Contracted persons are in a middle degree betwixt single persons and married persons: they are neither simply single, nor actually married. Many make it a very marriage, and thereupon have a greater solemnity at their contract than at their marriage: yea many take liberty after a con-tract to know their spouse, as if they were married: an unwarrantable and dishonest practice. The laudable custom of our and other churches showeth, that at least three weeks must pass betwixt contract and marriage. For the contract is to be three times published, and that but once a week before the wedding is celebrated.

Gouge's advice in favour of a definite contract confirms what is known from other literary and legal evidence, that the formal practice was on the way out in his time. The informal act of affiancing no doubt continued without document or sworn witnesses, but marked by social celebration and having the same effect on the behaviour of the parties. The really significant revelation in this passage is in the words about sexual intercourse during the period of the contract, whilst the banns were being called and the actual marriage ceremony prepared. Though ascribed to the temptation of Satan, though 'unwarrantable and dishonest', such an action was not described as sinful.

No hard-headed peasant would have let his daughter get to the point of espousal until a firm agreement had been made between the two families. Still, some risk remained that the banns might be forbidden from the body of the congregation on one or other of those three successive Sunday mornings. William Perkins was a better-known spokesman of the Puritans in the years of their rise to power in the seventeenth century, and he also skirts round the awful word 'sin' when he reaches this point, though he used it freely enough else-where. He talked in frowning disapproval of affianced couples 'seeking to satisfy their own fleshly desires, after the manner of brute beasts' but he goes no further than that.

Towards the end of the seventeenth century the non-conformist view of marriage as a personal matter, not a sacrament of the church at all, evidently grew much more influential in our country, which may do something to explain why clandestine marriages rose in popularity. In 1680 William

Lawrence, a Scottish Presbyterian, published a long treatise insisting that all ecclesiastical matrimony was unnatural outrage, and that indissoluble partnership between man and woman began whenever the first sexual union took place, needing neither witness, nor confirmation, nor any public celebration. It is true that his highly unconventional book ends on page 242 with the confession 'By the interruption of the Press I am compelled to break off this book abruptly.' In registering his protest against what might be called the authoritarian orthodoxy being established in his time, he cannot be said to have been expressing anything like relaxation of moral discipline or anomie in English or in Scottish society. He was, after all, merely giving early expression to attitudes which were to become standard in the American colonies. By the nineteenth century it could be said of the marriage practices of the state of New York that the children born of such unions and legitimate there 'are counted bastards by every nation of Europe' [11].[18]

Although illegitimacy and prenuptial pregnancy have been widely supposed by sociologists since the time of Emile Durkheim to indicate social breakdown, and still seem to be accepted as such by many historians, suicide has been regarded as a much more telling symptom. 'Self murder' as Hamlet calls it could certainly be described as the extreme act of personal indiscipline. We can tell a little about this even obscurer subject, and even get a hint or two about its prevalence. There are two further aspects of marital and procreative behaviour which we should glance at, however. One is the prevalence of infanticide and the other of the much less melancholy, even to some slightly comical custom of the sale of wives, said, and perhaps correctly said, to be a uniquely British trait.

> Oct. 29, Samuel Balls sold his wife to Abraham Rade in the parish of Blythburgh in this county for 1ˢ. A halter was put round her neck and she was resigned up to this Abraham Rade.

So runs a notice in the *Ipswich Journal* in 1789 and if we take it seriously – which it would seem we probably have to do – we are bound to think the worse of the attitudes of our ancestors towards marriage and towards women than we would like to do. Sensitive and humane people do not traffic in each other, least of all in their spouses. They do not put a halter round the neck of anyone in a public place, nor do they insist on the woman whom they take to wife coming to the church clad only in a smock in order to relieve the husband of responsibility for her debts. They certainly could not accept even in jest jumping over a broom as a public demonstration of the forming of a marital union. Yet all of these practices have been shown to have existed among our British ancestry. Wife-selling and wife-buying can be faintly defended as a form of divorce, unavailable in the world we have lost except to the very rich and powerful. Or it might be claimed in condescension that only the dregs of society would do such things. Against this there is an insistent report that so vain and successful a social climber as Sir Godfrey Kneller bought the wife of a Quaker.[19]

Wife-selling, however, like child marriage, is a topic which attracts the sensational writer, and a great deal of notice may have been given by the men of the past to a minute, a minuscule number of events. There are references to the practice in church court records, as for example to the doings of a Thomas Heath of Chinner in Oxfordshire in 1696, but most of the evidence comes from early newspapers and tracts in the late eighteenth and nineteenth centuries. As an element in the personal discipline, or the neglect of it, characteristic of our ancestors, the sale of wives must be pronounced as inconsequential, though accounts of it reveal something of the slightly quizzical attitude of ordinary people to the official marital code. It is good to say that chaffering in wives was infamous, and is often so described by witnesses to the marketplace auctions or by the journalists themselves. But it was nothing like as serious an outrage as infanticide and this was extremely uncommon as well.

In the 1610s the criminal courts of London dealt with less than three indictments for infanticide in a year, an annual incidence which has been reckoned at 1·35 per 100,000 people. For the county of Essex at the same time the estimate is 1·44. No threat to social survival can possibly be descried here, though these figures are so uncertain as indicators of the true occurrence of the offence that it is rather hazardous to cite them at all.[20] Keith Wrightson has guessed that they have to be multiplied two-and-a-half times to represent reality. It would still leave them entirely negligible as compared with those for a country like Japan, where the killing of new-born babies has claims to an important place in the maintenance of a balance between population and subsistence.

Nevertheless an Act of Parliament was passed in 1624 reaffirming that the killing of new-born babies was murder. After that time it has been noticed that there was an increasing tendency for women slaying illegitimate rather than legitimate children to be convicted and to be executed. Most mothers, however, in English traditional society seem to have accepted their infants, whatever the difficulties of the position they found themselves in, accepted them and reared them through infancy, and that slightly more successfully than their sisters in France.

If the disposal of the new-born can be counted out in considering the relationship between personal discipline and social survival, so also can suicide. This dreadful act did not seem to be entirely without defence in the opinion of the writers of the time; John Donne, the poet, was one defender. But it was punished by the one sanction available, by the denial of Christian burial to the body. Instances of people doing away with themselves are of great rarity. But they are found nevertheless in the parish records from time to time, along with references to the custom of burying the offending corpse at the crossroads, which was not abolished until 1823. At Ashton-under-Lyne there seems to have been a more humane attitude. On 11 June 1683, for example, the following entry appears in the register.

> Roger Peake of Treehouse Bank, who hanged himself in his own barn the 9th day and was stolen into the churchyard and buried on the north side about one of the clock in the morning.

In hugger-mugger they had to inter him, just as they did Ophelia.

The parson must have connived at this neighbourly defiance of the church's rules, since the register is so frank about it. Suicides appear with what looks like fair regularity in the Ashton parish register throughout the seventeenth century. Most decades passed with only one suicide or none at all, but in the 1610s and the 1680s there were two, whilst in the 1620s there were four. Nothing like a suicide rate can be guessed at from figures of this isolated character, but it is at least worth remembering that the 1620s were times of depression in the textile trade, and of dearth; the crisis of subsistence in the area and at Ashton itself in 1623 and 1624 has already been discussed. The actual years in which suicides occurred there, however, were spread evenly out over the decade; 1623, 1625, 1626 and 1628.

Suicide in this one settlement, then, could have been associated with demographic crisis, though it is perhaps more plausibly connected with economic fluctuation. In his classic work on the subject, Durkheim noticed that suicide increased at times of economic depression, but he also related it to many other social phenomena which are often thought of as leading to disintegration of social life. Urbanization is one of them, and it so happens that a little can be said about suicide and the life of cities in Stuart England because Graunt's study of the bills of mortality can be made to yield a suicide rate of sorts for London during the middle decades of the seventeenth century, and the bills themselves could be used to continue the series up till the end of the eighteenth century.

Taking the population as 400,000, a working minimum, something like 2·5 people per hundred thousand 'Hanged and made away with themselves' during the twenty years preceding 1660 for which Graunt prepared figures. This is a low rate as compared with those which obtain today, when a figure of 10 per 100,000 inhabitants is regarded as favourable, and when in a city like San Francisco the rate can rise as high as 25·9, as it did in 1950. It is probable, however, that many or even all of the people classified in the bills of mortality as lunatic at death were in fact suicides, and if this was so the suicide rate might well have been as high as 4 or 5 per hundred thousand in London in Graunt's day.[21]

Though we have no means of comparing these very vague estimates with suicide rates in rural England at that time, these first, preliminary figures do make two things clear. One is that suicide was a known and even a familiar phenomenon in traditional society and is not a peculiarity of our own highly urban, industrialized era. The literature of our ancestors could be used to confirm this essential fact, but it is very important that such evidence should now be related to actual happenings. The second point is that the enormous growth of London in Stuart times with all the disorganization of the pattern of people's lives which it must have brought with it does not on the face of it seem to have been accompanied by a suicide rate which was high on our own standards. Further work might establish some correlation between urbanization and anomie in pre-industrial England, but unfortunately so few parish registers record suicides that a credible rate for rural areas may never be a possibility. It is perhaps worth mentioning that suicide rates in London varied from year to year and decade to decade as they did at Ashton-under-Lyne. The years 1648, 1657 and 1660 seem to have been the bad ones in the seventeenth century. In the eighteenth century suicide in the city was consistently higher than in the seventeenth, and from about 1735 it shows a steady tendency to rise.

Perhaps too much attention has been given to these particularly sketchy and unconvincing figures, especially since it seems so unlikely that we shall ever be able to follow Durkheim into those subtleties of social analysis of the incidence of suicide which would so illuminate the society of our ancestors. It will be obvious that sexual and marital nonconformism is much more likely to open an avenue into their experience, personal experience, as it was subjected to modulation from social influences. Let us lay out the plan of the tentative explanatory hypothesis to which we have already referred [53–9].

We have given it the title *the courtship-intensity hypothesis*. It is assumed to begin with that not all eligible but spouseless persons – the nubile unmarrieds of an earlier discussion – were perpetually engaged in spouse-seeking. Courtship only took place when the individuals concerned had reached what has been termed the age of onset of procreative union[22], and this varied with individual circumstances, and with general conditions, especially economic prospects. When these prospects were favourable, or judged to be so by young men and women whose final object was matrimony, more and more of them began to engage in courtship, so that the age of marriage tended to fall and the proportions marrying tended to rise. Since courtship so often meant risking conception, though to an extent which varied from area to area, it follows that at times of increasing courtship intensity both prenuptial pregnancy and illegitimacy should also become commoner. This is the suggested reason for the inverse relationship between marriage age and levels of illegitimacy and prenuptial pregnancy in England.

The association between servants and bastardy is quite understandable from such circumstances. 'Servants were in a sense all waiting to marry each other,' but they were in courtship only when the time was right. The 'cost' of such a system of family formation has to be reckoned in terms of the rate of first conceptions taking place before and so outside marriage. This rate is a combination of prenuptial pregnancy with the proportion of first births which were bastard births. The level varied from time to time and place to place but could be surprisingly high. The lower bound, it has been claimed, was 'some 10 per cent, the higher bound about 50–55 per cent, with most of the distribution between 20 and 40 per cent'[55]. How naive to expect the wedding night always to have been what tradition requires that it should have been!

All of which implies, and evidence which has been gathered supports it, that most illegitimacies arose in circumstances very similar to first births within marriage. They were certainly not a teenage affair. Bastards tended to be born of persons of an age and condition to marry each other, who often, even usually, intended to marry each other, but who were prevented by circumstances. Analytically then prenuptial pregnancy and illegitimacy were very closely associated indeed.

If a woman had had a bastard by a man this would not have made her ineligible for another husband. It was even possible that a girl might take her chance of conceiving with one or two possible partners before she accepted the man who became her husband. It goes without saying that the men took even greater liberties with the women, though mostly within the conventions of courtship accepted in their locality. To describe a high proportion of all apparently nonconforming behaviour as arising in this way still leaves a considerable number of illegitimacies which were not at all of this character. Such are those which came from rape, a man overpowering a girl who might even be a stranger to him, or from the sexual exploitation of women servants by their masters, or by their masters' sons, or from the exploits of disorderly women and of the whores, mostly members of the society of the bastardy-prone, the whores belonging by definition.

These were the cases which were apt to get into the records because they had a higher probability of being presented to the courts by the churchwardens. Hence perhaps the impression of rather more exploitation and brutality than in fact took place. It is no part of my purpose to play down the cruelty which could be shown to pregnant single women, or the harsh fate of anyone judged to be sexually delinquent, especially if he or she was a defenceless pauper, as was so often the case. The outstanding features of the courtship-intensity hypothesis are that it supposes courtship to have been not a constant but an occasional feature of the lives of the nubile unmarrieds, amongst the poorer and of course the largest part of the population and that it varies accordingly in its relevance between social classes. We should think of the girls in the manor houses and the houses of the substantial bourgeoisie as perpetually in courtship after they had 'come out' but as never, never being allowed to risk conception until the union had been signed, sealed and delivered in the approved public place, in church, at the wedding. Only thus were family succession and family property to be secured.

We can see here why the subject matter of the plays, the poems and the treatises written by the élite for the élite were as we have known them to have been. The protective father is perpetually doing his best to make sure that his mate-attracting daughter should not behave as girls of the populace might do when they finally were in a position to engage in courtship. How misleading it is then to interpret the behaviour of literary heroines as if it represented the behaviour of women at large! We cannot suppose that patterns of courtship either in the mass or in the élite were uniform from area to area, and even the inverse relationship between age at marriage and illegitimacy level could apparently vary between countries generally obeying the west European familial rules. Though this relationship can be found in nineteenth-century France, more strongly marked in some places than in others [273], it was scarcely evident in the preceding century. Indeed traces of the pattern which we have rejected as inapplicable to England are to be found at that time in France, and French women did show some tendency to produce more bastard children when marriage was late than when it was early.[23] We have to be cautious therefore about the appropriateness of the courtship-intensity hypothesis, about personal discipline and social survival in general in the world we have lost. We may linger a little longer before we take our leave of this topic by dwelling on a question which has come up almost incidentally, the question of sexual privacy.

Much has been made of the growth of privacy as marking the greatest of all differences between family life in the world we have lost and in the social world we now inhabit. It has been seen as a cardinal contrast between bourgeois domesticity and that of the peasantry and proletariat.[24] The extent to which acts of intercourse were undertaken when couples from these two social orders were alone, secure from being seen or heard, is a topic on which, as might be expected, little information is available. The crowded conditions under which everyone lived and, in the cold climate of northern and western Europe, the necessity of gathering round fires and sharing beds, make it obvious that the privacy now regarded as indispensable, almost as a human right, cannot always have been available to everyone. Those with experience of living within severe spatial restrictions, however, such as a man who served as I happen to have done in a grossly overmanned naval vessel, will know that physical privacy is not entirely a physical affair. A socially maintained barrier around the inviolable space reserved to one individual can keep him from intrusion from sight and from sound. It seems likely that our predecessors in their hutments, shacks and divided dwellings maintained such social walls. They have left statements which show that they did strongly prefer making love entirely alone nevertheless. There is a famous New England law case of the seventeenth century in which the accused asked his companion to leave the room because he wished to swive Susan.

If the extent to which we now have greater sexual privacy in the physical sense is somewhat uncertain, there is no doubt about it in the psychological sense. We have seen that the regime of public humiliation for sexual frailty came to an end in our country towards the middle of the eighteenth century, when industry had scarcely begun to transform society, when the scale of life was virtually unchanged. That regime had depended on everyone accepting the fact that his or her sexual affairs were rightfully open to surveillance by the neighbours, and that their sexual affairs in turn were also open in this way. The sanction of such regulation was public as well as private, public shame and public punishment too. Since that system disappeared, shame and shame alone sanctions sexual practices apart from gossip, and this shame is entirely subjective, the private conscience working within the personality.

Sexual anxiety, it might well be, has been the outcome of this privatization of our sexual lives. This has given psychoanalysis and analysts themselves their opportunity. It may have transformed our personalities, in so far as they are related to our sexual proclivities.

Social change
and revolution
in the traditional world
Chapter 8

With an attempt to expunge the phrase 'the English Revolution'

In spite of the smallness of its scale and the simplicity of its economics, the society we have been describing was a highly complex arrangement of persons. Moreover, the whole structure was subject to conflict and change. Up to the end of the feudal era proper, civil strife was commonplace all over Europe. Shakespeare still preserves for us the interminable quarrels of the fifteenth century, during which time the houses of York and Lancaster embroiled baronage, knighthood, church, citizens and people in a dreary contest for dynastic power, only occasionally a matter of open fighting and never as dramatic as Shakespeare had to make it out to be.

But the contest which sticks in the imagination and which the whole world immediately associates with civil war and revolution in our country is the last such conflict which ever occurred, that between Roundhead and Cavalier, when Charles I was defeated and beheaded. The years between 1640 and 1660, when desultory fighting turned into desperately serious campaigns, and constitutional crisis led to usurpation and to an irregular regime, is now conventionally called the Puritan Revolution. After the much less romantic imbroglio of 1688–9, vitally important constitutionally all the same, the whole English Revolution had run its irregular course, in the conventional account. This English Revolution needless to say, along with the French, American and Russian Revolutions, is one of the great historical realities in accepted parlance. The implication of these expressions has to be that one such event, or set of events, and one only, should be expected to occur in the life of a nation.

We shall not attempt to deal in this preliminary essay with

the course of the secular, overall change which brought about the contrast between our world and the world we have lost. Our subject is rather the comparison of the two, and all that we shall need to do is to dwell briefly on the England of the early twentieth century in order to point the contrast as sharply as we can. The task of the present chapter will have to be entirely analytical, therefore, and at a rather more academic level than the rest of the book. The reader who wishes simply to get to know some of the facts about the comparison as such may safely pass it by.

In this interlude between our discussion of the personal, everyday life of the traditional world and the brief description we shall attempt to give of its political workings, it is necessary to analyse the reasons for internal conflict and the Civil War. The question to be asked is whether the word 'revolution' can justifiably be used of seventeenth-century England, if anything of social revolution is intended.

The term 'social revolution' in the question we have put to ourselves is taken here to mean an irreversible displacement of the social structure as a whole, occurring abruptly and by violence in a manner not to be described as evolutionary. Progressive social change of an even character, however final or fundamental, cannot in this view be called revolutionary. Social revolution, then, is held to be distinct from political revolution. This last is change of government or regime, or of the membership of a political élite, or of the relationship between a political élite as an institution and society at large. Shifts of this kind also have to happen swiftly and sometimes violently in order to be called revolutionary, and may involve rebellion and widespread fighting. Such vicissitudes were common in our country during this period and historians seem to feel free to decide for themselves what particular sets of events they wish called revolutions, political revolutions.

On this view social revolution is almost inevitably accompanied by political revolution, but political revolution most decidedly does not necessarily imply social revolution. Since it is the term 'the English Revolution' which interests us most, we shall have to glance at the possibility of any or all of the happenings in question having had nation-building attributes, which might justify the national adjective in the title.

The American nation can be said to have been created to

some extent by the experience of the American Revolution in the eighteenth century, and so for a number of nations brought into being during the nineteenth and twentieth centuries. There are other issues to which we can do little more than refer, whether for example the people of the time ever thought of their revolution as a thing in itself, a continuing reality to be defended by its supporters and betrayed by those who had lost faith in it. Betraying a revolution is a common phrase in the political lives of many twentieth-century national societies. Finally there is the issue of movements of quite different kinds to which the description revolution has been accorded, as for example the Scientific Revolution of the seventeenth century. The challenge here, and it is a very difficult challenge too, is to discover how these things were connected with each other, and how far they can be brought together as parts of 'the English Revolution'.

Our concern with revolution and revolutions does not arise from our subject itself, which is the analysis of traditional English society in the final periods of its existence, so much as from the persistent preoccupations of historians and from their responsibilities to the political beliefs and to the social controversies of their own day. The possibility of what is termed present-mindedness, or judging from hindsight, is quite evident, but this request to the historical sociologist is useful nevertheless. It is always interesting and important to know the circumstances under which a society will be at war with itself, even though social description can be undertaken without going into particulars of any given crisis, however fundamental it is felt to have been, or however pregnant with possibilities of what was to come. There can be no doubt that dwelling on the differences over which men fought at Naseby in 1645 and at Sedgemoor forty years later, has helped to distort the shape which traditional English society has taken up in the minds of the people of our time. But since the following question is so often put to the evidence by historians and learners alike – for the elementary teaching of the subject has led to much of the foreshortening and misleading description and phraseology – 'What was it in Stuart society which led to political disaster and fighting?' – it can scarcely be evaded here.

As the twentieth century wears on towards its end, the issue becomes more, not less important, and that to an increasing number of people throughout the world. Now that the revolutionist ideology predominates in so large a part of the globe, and every nation, to be a nation, has to have had its revolution, it is a necessity, an urgent necessity, to decide whether the first revolution of them all did take place in our own country in the seventeenth century. It could be argued that to have had the first social revolution to which the name of a nation could be joined is as significant as to have had the first industrial revolution. Taken together these are the reasons why something of English history, and of the general lineaments of what we have called the world we have lost, has to be known to everybody everywhere.

In 1949, at a time when authoritarian socialist regimes were becoming established in central and eastern Europe and when their exportation to Asia and other underdeveloped parts of the world was just beginning, an admirably bold and simple statement was made on the topic. 'Our subject here,' said Christopher Hill, already becoming the best-known and most influential historian of the English Revolution (and since that time Master of Balliol College, Oxford), 'is how one social class was driven from power by another.' He was referring to the events of 1640–9 in England and was writing, in collaboration with a future Labour minister, a book entitled *The Good Old Cause*.[1] Their judgement has had an enormous impact. Whatever may be urged against the proposition which they put forward, it has an obvious advantage.

It provides a clear definition of what a national social revolution has to be, a contest between classes, a class in possession and a class wanting possession, where the prize is political supremacy. Success is essential to the concept: an abortive attempt at changing the ruling class is no social revolution. In the English case a capitalist or bourgeois class has to be seen to have won a struggle against the so-far dominant aristocratic or landowning class, to have ousted that class from power and to have gained political control of the country, in perpetuity. This is the form which the English Revolution must be known to have taken if we are to be satisfied that our own ancestors really did undergo the first national revolution in the history of the world.

For that is what revolutionism assumes demonstrably did happen in France after 1789 during the great French Revolution, and there the contesting classes were the same as in

England. In Russia in 1917, in central and eastern Europe, and in China, during the 1940s to the 1960s, at the beginning of their present regimes, the victorious revolutionary class was no longer the already possessing bourgeoisie, but the third member of the Marxist trio, the working class, the proletariat. Elsewhere the class enemy was simultaneously an occupying foreign power, as it was in North America when the American Revolution took place. Important as this element of national liberation has become in the revolutionism of our own time, in Africa, Asia and Latin America especially, it was not a factor in England in the seventeenth century.

It is true that academic writers who have expounded the revolutionist doctrine since the 1940s have done so with an ever increasing subtlety and much more tentatively. All traces of the salient position which was originally occupied in respect of social classes fighting for political power had disappeared when *The Good Old Cause* was reissued by Christopher Hill in 1969. It is now usual to declare that such simplistic statements as those of the 1940s belong to something which has the title 'vulgar Marxism', to which no scholar will confess adherence. But a great deal of the analysis of social change in Britain still proceeds on the assumption that a national bourgeois revolution did occur in England in the seventeenth century, although definitions of what exactly such a process would look like are very seldom found. And when people from other countries make use of the English precedent for comparative purposes, they also wish to appeal to statements of this kind. In 1974, for example, when there was a debate amongst French Marxists under the obviously ironic title 'La revolution Française a t'elle eu lieu?' – Did the French revolution happen? – it was a clinching argument that there had undoubtedly been an irreversible national, bourgeois, social revolution a century before, in England.

A crucial characteristic of the English events, if they are to be used in this way, is that the combative, rising class which reaped the benefit from social and civil strife, must itself have been actually engaged, have fought for its objectives. It will not do for the revolutionist historical doctrine to retreat to the position which the former master of Balliol has adopted in what appears to be the latest of his many subsequent declarations on the topic, a declaration made in 1980. There he submits that in Marxist usage a bourgeois revolution 'does not

mean a revolution made or consciously willed by the bourgeoisie'. Therefore, he goes on to argue, it simply does not
matter to the reality of the English bourgeois revolution of the
seventeenth century that the bourgeoisie cannot be shown to
have engaged themselves in the conflict, individually or
collectively. All that matters is that the capitalists and their
classmates finally benefited from the outcome.

Here is a retreat indeed. It would follow from Hill's statement that any set of events, violent or non-violent, fast-paced
or slow-paced, evolutionary or precipitous, could be taken to
constitute a revolution. The heady experience of participation
in violent actions felt in Paris as recently as 1968 would cease
to be of any significance whatever, for the aims of the revolutionaries themselves become irrelevant. It would even be
possible for some series of occurrences, quite a lengthy series
since time no longer matters – shall we say the Reform Bills
which extended the English franchise in the nineteenth and
twentieth centuries – to be both a bourgeois and a proletarian
revolution at one and the same time. This would be so because
bourgeoisie and proletariat could colourably be shown to have
benefited from them.

This is to lose all the advantages of class revolution, indeed
of social revolution itself, as terms in historical sociology.
Such words cease to indicate events of any particular type, or
their duration, or their tendency as to success or failure. The
possible analogy between bourgeois and proletarian revolutions is so attenuated that they become quite different types
of thing. Under these circumstances it is difficult to see the
point of retaining the term 'the English Revolution' as a
phrase to denote certain occurrences between 1600 and 1700,
at least on the part of those who define social revolution in
terms of class conflict leading to change in the politically
dominant group. But an enormous variety of views of what
social revolutions can be, or have been, are now in use, and
the habit of using the term 'the English Revolution' certainly
persists. Indeed it seems to grow. We are not relieved from
trying to answer the question we have set ourselves, as to what
it was which led to violence in Stuart society.

Historians, as we shall see in our final chapter, are something of a nuisance to the sociological enquirer just because it
is their habit to ask questions of this blank and simple sort.
What is more, they expect to get swift and straightforward

answers to them. In the present case, because of the form
which an answer is expected to take, the question is not simple
at all. Along with a request for the social origins of a particular
political crisis, there goes a demand for a descriptive response
of a kind which would relate the English revolution with the
long-term social transformation which finally gave rise to the
modern, industrialized world, 'capitalist' on the one hand and
'socialist' on the other. Can any connection be traced, it is
required to know, between Cromwell and his Roundheads and
the social forces which led to the dethronement of the patriarchal family in economic organization? Or between the
Glorious Revolution of 1688 and the coming of the factories?
This is what must now engage our attention.

We may notice at the outset a curious uncertainty as to the
most conspicuous feature of all in the industrialized world –
the factory, that instrument of mechanical and mass production. No one seems quite to know exactly when the factory
appeared. Final origins of things like this are in fact much
more difficult to arrive at than might be supposed. Like the
source of a river, as you trace the institutional story back, it
first branches into numbers of streams of similar size, so that
it is difficult to say which is the one you should follow, and
then finally disperses into the runlets and the raindrops of the
distant and misty heights of time.

The ergasterion, or work-centre for slaves, where these
human chattels were congregated for collective work in the
ancient world is one such tributary. Another, in the analysis
laid out by the great sociologist Max Weber, is the *fabrica* or
cellar-den, found in the medieval town as the collective
property of a group of masters, or deep in the countryside as
part of the lord's property in a manor.[2] Though Weber and the
more learned and cautious of the other writers express surprise
at the absence of evidence for factories in earlier times, when
they get to Tudor England they feel at last that they are on
firm ground. Listen to this:

Within one room being large and long
There stood two hundred looms full strong
Two hundred men, the truth is so,
Wrought in these looms all in a row.
But every one a pretty boy
Sat making quils with mickle joy.

And in another place hard by
An hundred women merrily,
Were carding hard with joyful cheer
Who singing sat with voices clear.
And in a chamber close beside
Two hundred maidens did abide.

And so on; 'quils' were needed by the men for the loom-work, as was the carded or combed twine, and the maidens did the spinning. Here was a building large enough for two hundred looms, with two hundred men, a hundred women, two hundred boys and two hundred girls, all employed by Jack of Newbury, the famous clothier of England. The poem comes from the novel of Thomas Deloney, published in 1619 and dedicated to the Clothworkers Company of London.[3] Jack's great establishment, Deloney tells us, became so famous that it was actually visited by the reigning King and Queen, Henry VIII and Katherine.

But the fact seems to be that this Jack of Newbury was as much of a myth as Jack and the Beanstalk, and the 'factory' he is supposed to have set up as deceptive as Juliet's marriage, if it is used as a guide to the actual institutions and real behaviour of our ancestors. Throughout Deloney's ribald and formless work, the manufactory is referred to as a 'household': he tells us at one point that 'This great household and family had its own butcher, who killed ten oxen a week for its members to eat.' It soon becomes plain that Deloney was engaged in making up a story about a fabulous clothier's household for the diversion of the London clothworkers; his subject was a Panurge among craftsmen, not perhaps capable of drowning a whole city when he made water as Rabelais's character could do, but certainly recognizable in the master-baker with whom this book began, built on Gargantuan lines, with his household enlarged to impossible size. This fragment from that fascinating half-world between literature and folklore does not show after all that factories existed in Tudor times. What it does show is that the successful clothier could be idealized as a hero and his household poetically exaggerated. But it was a household still.

This may set us on our guard once more against literary evidence as a literal guide to the social structure of the past. It would be impossible to prove that factories were entirely absent in the world we have lost, but we can say with confidence that large-scale undertakings for the purpose of manufacturing goods are conspicuously lacking in all descriptions of life in England before the late eighteenth century. Approaches to that peculiarly industrial form of social and economic organization certainly existed before the great industrial revolution, and some of them were listed in the first chapter. Mining, building, shipyards, saltworks and a whole list of other forms of manufacture certainly brought together dozens and sometimes scores of workers and placed them under some sort of discipline. Contracting for military and naval operations, turning out tapestries and other articles of refined manufacture needed for monarchical and aristocratic purposes led to the establishment of royal workshops all over Europe, and in England to such institutions as the Mineral and Battery Works set up by Queen Elizabeth.

But a complicated system of definitions has to be adopted before it can be decided how far such institutions could be called factories, and the part which all of them put together had to play in the whole economy of the country was exceedingly small. Interestingly enough the closest approximation is to be found in the municipal workhouses, established under a succession of Acts of Parliament and as part of various bursts of energy on the part of municipalities to 'set the poor on work'. In its prehistory the factory was associated with poverty and destitution, just as manufacture generally was regarded by the commentators of that time first and foremost as a means of keeping people occupied who would otherwise be idle, perhaps even keeping them alive when otherwise they might die.

In recent years attention has been drawn to a somewhat different transitional form between the handicrafting family group of a family-based society, and the factory of our own social order. This is the proto-industrial household, to which reference has been made several times already, and which had become so widespread by the end of the eighteenth century, especially in England, that a German work of considerable importance which describes this organization and its social position bears the title *Industrialiesierung vor der Industrialiesierung*, industrialization before industrialization.[4]

Here a whole household, sometimes with its own servants and apprentices, was set on work from outside, by a capitalist entrepreneur, who supplied the materials, bought the products and might even own the looms and spinning wheels, which he hired to the workers. Since an individual capitalist might employ, partially if not wholly, several domestic units, dozens or even scores, and since he organized them in a sense for collective production, such a man can be said to have been an industrialist. But the outstanding characteristics of the system from our point of view is precisely that the familial form and scale of production was retained in this traditional organization. The proto-industrial household survived into the industrial age as an alternative to the factory, as well as a complement to it for some purposes. It cannot be regarded simply as an intermediate productive form, leading to modern industrial organization.

There can be no doubt, nevertheless, that the spread of such arrangements could have modified social structure, especially in the great wool- and cloth-producing areas so conspicuous in earlier English history. Proto-industrial households were in a position markedly different from that of the village craftsman supplying local needs, if only because their products were sold in distant markets and on a very large scale. This put them at the mercy of international market fluctuations as well as of the self-seeking policy of capitalist entrepreneurs. Much research, and speculation, has gone on in trying to find out how this organization affected the demography, the work relations, the role structure as sociologists would say, of the family units caught up in the process, including the division of labour between the sexes, even sexual attitudes and procreative practices.

It would seem logical that each household would have a collective interest in assembling the largest number of pairs of hands to do the work. Hence fertility would go up, age at marriage would go down, children would stay with their parents longer, the size of family and household would grow, and the co-residence of relatives might become commoner. Since the parents, and the elder generation generally, no longer controlled access to the means of livelihood as land-working parents did, their authority would be eroded, authority over marriage as well as other things, so that bastardy, perhaps repetitive bastardy, would become prevalent. In so far as they were exclusively dependent on their pooled labour-power for subsistence, proto-industrial households would be proletarian.

Here we find ourselves back with rules of household composition and of courtship and marriage practices. We cannot
pursue these interesting and important possibilities much
further here, but it can be stated that none of these developments necessarily accompanied proto-industrialization in our
country and that surprisingly few of them ran across what was
already established as part of the social structure. Numbers of
children in the domestic groups wholly caught up in hand
manufacture certainly tended to be high, usually higher than
in labouring households, which were often entirely proletarian.
But the suggestions as to fertility, age at marriage, extended
households and pauperization are more dubious, the one to do
with extension very dubious indeed. In England, moreover, in
spite of the enormous numbers of such households, only a
proportion were wholly devoted to activities so organized. For
many of them production for a capitalist selling on the international market was a bye-employment.

These investigations have been accompanied by a growing
recognition that, quite apart from proto-industry, not all
production did in fact go on in individual households under the
old order. In England from the high Middle Ages onwards only
a minority of households were work groups, agricultural or
handicraft. Indeed it has to be acknowledged that the men of
the time tended to use familial and patriarchal terms for work
groups which were not in fact confined to houses or households. The ideology of the organization of work did not exactly
correspond to the actuality, and that ideology varied from
area to area in Europe. In England the familial, patriarchal
image of work groups of all kinds seems to have been particularly strong.[5]

Proto-industrial households, then, could be, but they certainly did not have to be, as poverty-stricken as the groups of
paupers put to work on the wool, the flax and the withys,
supplied by the parish overseers to the poorhouse, or the
workhouse as it was significantly called. A great deal of
historical experience had to go by before the factory could
take its place as a social organization in its own right, still
perhaps the typical institution of the industrialized world,
though said by some to be at the end of its career in that
position. When at last a document appears which belonged to
an organization justly described as the first English factory
the emphasis on poverty and remedies against it are a conspicuous feature.

Winlaton iron mill at Swalwell in the county of Durham, where ironmaster Ambrose Crowley began work in about 1691, turned out metal for the navy in William III's war with the French. Within a few years Crowley was literally employing workmen by the hundred. The 'Law Book' which he left behind makes it evident also that many of those workers were banded together in one building; certainly they were treated by him as a single labour force, a platoon in an industrial army.[6] The provisions against poverty were many and various and there was a Clerk of the Poor who also ministered at a chapel for the workpeople and kept school for their children. Something of the atmosphere of the factory as it was deliberately established in the close-knit, patriarchal society of Japan under the Meiji emperors in the 1890s is already present here.

Once again, however, the point which impresses the late-twentieth-century reader in this lengthy and complicated document is the extraordinary mixture in its provisions of elements of the old order with those of the new, the family workshop with the communal workroom. Much of the actual production for Ambrose Crowley was obviously still being done in the homes of the workmen under conditions which had prevailed since the beginnings of history. In the present state of the evidence the arrival of the factory in the earliest country to become industrialized must be firmly placed in the middle and late eighteenth century and it is exceedingly difficult to imagine the discovery of documents in such quantities as to make it necessary to revise this conclusion.

Those changes of scale, that sense of alienation of the worker from his work, that breach in the continuity of emotional experience in which we have sought for the trauma inflicted at the passing of the traditional world, cannot be referred to Tudor or to Stuart England. Capital and capitalism were already very common as we have seen, but industrial capitalism, our sort of industrial capitalism, was absent. When factory life did at last become the dominant feature of industrial activity it condemned the worker, as we can now see, to the fate previously reserved for the pauper.

It is still possible, however, that the changes in scale which went forward five or six generations before large-scale industrial organization began may have had some part to play in the political malaise which then prevailed. An exhaustive understanding of politics and social change in the world we

have lost ought presumably to take every little influence into
account which might have made more difficult the preserva-
tion of political stability. Perhaps the intensification of trade
and commerce could be called divisive, because of the differing
relationships it presumably brought with it, and because of the
operation at long last of an institution entirely alien to the
traditional structure, the joint-stock company. This new
principle of economic organization was present before 1700;
the East India Company and the Bank of England had
already set up the model for those institutional instruments
which were to bring into being 'business' as we know it. The
impact they can have had before the early eighteenth century
was infinitesimal in relation to the whole of commercial and
industrial activity. Still, in the vocabulary of current expressions favoured by historians 'the commercial revolution
of the sixteenth and seventeenth centuries' is a recent but
fairly respectable phrase: if there was such a thing, it must
supposedly have had some effect on politics.

It could be shown, however, that enormous commercial
expansion and contraction was possible under the old order
without a change in the scale of institutions or even of undertakings, and that the major social outcome of growth of this
sort was in the geographical mobility which it gave rise to,
especially the amazing growth of the city of London. The same
can be said of manufacturing activity and wealth, as it is
known to have developed in Tudor and Stuart times, even
though mining was growing so fast and other industries too.
There was another area of social relationships which can be
thought of in the same way, though it may turn out that here
expansion in size was in fact accompanied by a change in
structure of much greater strategic significance. This was
governmental administration. Samuel Pepys of the Navy
Office may prove to have a claim to be a forerunner of industrial and capitalist England as important as that of
Samuel Smiles.

If, as we shall try to show, social mobility was a constant
feature of traditional society, then neither commerce, industry,
the growth of urban life nor bureaucracy need be thought of
as always disruptive because of their expansive tendencies.
But there was one current in economic development which
affected many more people than all these put together, in ways
which clearly led to unrest. Although we were disposed to

minimize the enclosure movement as a solvent of the village community, there can be no doubt of the social displacement which it caused, even though only a small proportion of villages was concerned. Changes in access to land, particularly increase in landlessness, were critically important, especially when they were linked with that breakneck growth in population which has been shown to have been going on continuously throughout the late sixteenth and early seventeenth centuries.

We have seen that the polarization of village society between the haves and have-nots was proceeding from the time of Elizabeth. By the end of the eighteenth century, after industrialization had made its appearance, these things were to culminate in a manner which has been called tragic, and the tragedy can be seen as a theme in the poetry of George Crabbe, the poetry and prose of John Clare, the paintings of George Morland and the descriptions of the labouring poor made by the clergyman David Davies.

But this act of the drama was four generations in the future at the time of the Civil War. The secular fall in real wages which came to an end in the 1620s, and the descent of the growth rate of the population which took place some thirty years later, did represent social adjustments which affected the fundament of the social structure. These developments were European ones, and there has been, as we have seen, discussion of a general crisis over the whole continent at this time, even though the influences in question were diffuse and gradual rather than concentrated and precipitate. Crisis on this scale lacks persuasiveness as a precipitant of revolution, and even when all these influences are added together indiscriminately, as they too often are, it seems entirely unlikely that a social revolution on a national scale could be brought about by them. Discussion in such terms as these of the reasons why civil war should supervene in England lacks conviction. And this if only because so many of the subtler aspects of social change, its pace and extent, are at present beyond the resources of historical sociology.

The claim is often made that the pace of that change was faster in the century before the Civil War than ever it had been before. The implication seems to be that this helps to explain the catastrophe. But in the absence of any estimates of the relative rates of social change at different periods it is difficult to know what to make of such an assertion. And when it comes to revolution itself, it has to be considered how far alteration has to go before the elasticity of the social structure is exhausted and breakdown can be expected. The immemorial social order we have been describing must be supposed to have had considerable tolerances or it would not have been immemorial. It should surely be an accepted principle of such discussion that 'revolution' is a term which is to be reserved for the change which goes on over and above what is to be expected as an unceasing process of routine social evolution, going forward in all societies and at all times.

If a rather different period were taken for the study of social change in England, that of the so-called Century of Revolution between 1603 and 1714, the opposite claim could be made with equal dogmatic conviction. The impression left by an attempt to survey the fundamental framework over these years is of how little, not of how much, alteration seems to have taken place. There is no indication that what are thought of as the revolutionary years in the middle of the century were those when change was speeded up, nor could there be, once again, in the absence of comparative measurements. Nothing in economic organization or in social arrangements seems to have come about which could be supposed to exhaust the capacity to compromise and so perhaps to have led to the political catastrophe. The changes which did occur seem to have been gradual rather than sudden.

The proving of a negative is exceedingly difficult historically, especially when uncertainty is as great as this. This opinion of the pace of evolution during the interludes in question may be shown to be misplaced, but it is at least more modest than those which have often been advanced about crucial shifts which then have to be recognized as 'revolutionary'. The vagaries in the fortunes of the nobility, for instance, or the success of a particular textile innovation, or the possibility of marked progress in literacy and education will tend to be made into that one crucial social change which explains everything else. But once it is recognized that the rise-of-a-capitalist-class interpretation can be misleading as well as informative, and that social mobility was present in the traditional world, then the idea of a social revolution however occasioned becomes an embarrassment rather than a help towards understanding political breakdown.

It might be very different, if for example the facts so far discovered did indicate the possibility of fundamental change in the size, structure and function of the family and household over this period. Or if the growth of town life had looked as though it must have led to social dislocation on an impressive scale. Or if there were unmistakable evidence of class-consciousness and collective resentment building up over the generation in question amongst a group of persons increasing in power, number and organization, though always frustrated in their expressed aims.

None of these things seems to have happened. There were changes in all these respects, perhaps some overall changes in the atmosphere of family life. The movement of population and the transformation of environment associated with the enormous growth of London must surely have led to discontinuity of experience even if it did not give rise to anomie. But these long-term, gradual tendencies cannot in principle have been the cause of political upheaval in the middle of the seventeenth century. The famous ructions which led to the execution of Charles I and the exile of James II, the two outstanding episodes in 'the English Revolution', seem therefore to have little relevance to the passing of the world we have lost, to that contrast between our world and the world of our ancestors which is the subject of this essay.

Nevertheless it is understandable that historians should always strive to relate political frictions to what is called 'underlying social change'. If this is to be done, great care must be taken to avoid the pitfalls which words like 'underlying' or even words like 'reflecting' or 'expressing' carry with them when society as a structure is contrasted with its political and intellectual life. Religious and political beliefs have tended to be looked upon as displaced symptoms of something in the material structure of society, manifesting itself in what is called ideological terms. It will be a long time, so it seems, before historians recognize that no simple, powerful, universally adaptable mechanism capable of bringing about such effects ever existed in any society.

If we are to understand how violence and military contest did fit in with social arrangements we may be able to learn from the attitude which professional sociologists are now developing towards social conflict. After long years of insisting that stability was the normal state of human society, and that integration was the function of every distinguishable element in the social structure, they are now prepared frankly to accept the existence of conflict as a permanent and even a necessary element in every social system. Some emphasize the social purposes of conflict to such an extent that conflict itself appears to be functional: 'where there is no conflict, there is no change, no progress', is the point they make. Others feel that this is unnecessary, and suppose that in all societies at all times there are disintegrative tendencies, some of which have the final effect of furthering social purposes and others which do not. If the problem of relating political crisis in Stuart England with long-term, overall change is approached along the lines of this second attitude, these seem to be the conclusions which may be reached.[7]

In the first place the tendencies to disruption and disintegration which were obviously at work at that time need no longer be regarded as abnormal, in the unexpected sense. The unruliness of the Puritan clergy and gentry, the obstinacy of the common lawyers, the arrogance of the parliamentarians in the early 1600s, cease to be things which have to be explained because they existed at all. Historians need no longer go on looking at all contradictions as peculiarly significant, on all conflict as the exception to what is to be expected, and on anything which could be described as 'revolutionary' as very special indeed, requiring the most determined effort of understanding. Once it is realized that all societies, including those as stable as the England which was described in our first chapter, are liable to divisive conflict, sometimes armed, it becomes possible to look at political violence with a cooler eye. This can be done not only in our country in the 1640s, but in France in the 1790s, and in Russia in the years after 1917. In Paris in the 1960s or Belfast in the 1970s for that matter – surely this point does not have to be laboured in a generation so plagued with political violence as our own.

Conflict, as has been said elsewhere, is a common enough form of social interaction.[8] Since nearly everybody has an obvious interest in preventing differences from becoming collisions all parties will take strenuous avoiding action when collisions threaten. But collisions sometimes take place in social and political life, just as car collisions do, and there is a logical resemblance. When accidents happen on the roads, it makes sense to look for long-term, even 'deep-seated' causes, as well as for the errors of the drivers concerned; the continued growth of traffic, the increase in its speed, the progressive inadequacy of the roads may all have to be analysed. It does not follow that the more dramatic the crash and important its consequences the more profound its causes must be and the more likely to be the climax of some perennial 'process'.

Now it is natural, though it may not be justifiable, to suppose that great events have great causes. The Civil War and the Puritan Revolution, together with the Glorious Revolution of 1688, are so conspicuous, so interesting, so momentous in their consequences and so fraught with the origins of our liberties and of our political values, ours and those of the rest of the English-speaking world, that they have inevitably been looked upon as cataclysmic, the apex of some mountain-building movement in historical evolution. And this from the very time of their occurrence. 'If in time as in place,' said the acutest of all contemporary observers, Thomas Hobbes, 'there were degrees of high and low, I verily believe that the highest of time, would be that which passed between 1640 and 1660.'[9] The parliamentary struggle and the bloodshed on the battlefields must have been the final outcome of a process going deep down the social fabric, and extending over many generations, backwards and forwards in time. This assumption comes the more easily to the English because we pride ourselves on the continuity of our political life, and believe it to be unbroken except for these particular events. What could be more understandable than that historians should have set aside the whole century, from 1540–1640, for the causes of the Civil War, and the whole period 1640–88, or even 1625–1714, for the English Revolution?

But what is true may also be trivial, which is perhaps why the discussion of this portentous question has become by now so tedious. Nothing beyond a fuller demonstration that conflict was everywhere necessarily follows from showing that the causes of war between Roundhead and Cavalier can be infinitely extended into areas 'social', 'economic' or even 'social structural', for every event that ever happened can be treated in this way, and be made to appear culminatory.[10] But the most constrictive effect of the conventional assumption about the relation of the struggle in Stuart England to social structure and change has yet to be mentioned; it leads us on to the second lesson we can learn from the sociology of conflict.

The habit of expecting to discover that 'revolution' was a geological catastrophe, when a situation of ever-increasing instability suddenly gave way to a situation of rock-like permanence, obscures the possibility that society at that time had what might be called a conflict-mechanism built into it. This oversight is the more extraordinary since the supreme achievement of the whole epoch was the adaptation of a medieval institution into a classic conflict-defining, conflict-restricting and conflict-resolving social instrument, that is to say the Houses of Parliament with their Oppositions, their motions of censure, their parties and their unending, superbly conventionalized political battle.

Once the imagination is set free, there are many possible comparisons in social organization which spring to mind for Stuart England. There are, for example, the segmented societies described by anthropologists. The late Max Gluckman's examination of African communities shows how a fight over the dynastic succession is a permanent feature of political life. Far from weakening or destroying the whole, conflict actually confirms its solidarity. This fits some of the features of political life in England aptly enough, from Tudor to Stuart, to Hanoverian and even to Victorian times.[11] The segmented characteristics of the political community of our country in pre-industrial times, its division into a network of small county communities which were also conflict arenas, will concern us in our next chapter.

The picture of political institutions and political life which might finally be adopted is one where the stream of variation was wide enough to include the 'despotism of Charles I' as one extreme, and the rule of the parliamentary army as the other. Both were unlikely to be permanent, but both nevertheless belonged within the definition; each was possible, though not as much to be expected as the traditional King-in-Parliament arrangement. But the most useful concept to be borrowed from the sociological study of conflict in industrial, as opposed to pre-industrial, society does not concern itself with extreme situations as such but with the reasons why they alternated with each other. 'Revolution' as meaning a resolution of unendurable social tension by reshaping society as a whole has been rejected here as impossible in seventeenth-century England. But what Ralf Dahrendorf has to say about the process which occasionally brings it about in the twentieth

century has its value in understanding irreconcilable conflict
as it happened in England three centuries ago.[12]

Political breakdown is only likely to come about when it
happens that several sources of conflict become *superimposed*
– Dahrendorf's word. To the permanent divisive influences in
the society are added specific issues about which the men of
the time care so passionately that they are prepared to fight
about them. The particular reason why political agreement
becomes impossible is often that forces of conflict which at
other times tend to modify each other, even to cancel each
other out, all conspire together to make compromise impossible. This is not a very novel nor perhaps a very subtle way
of looking at things, but its important virtue is that each
individual conflict, each pair of antagonistic forces, is regarded
as for the most part an independent variable. None of them is
taken as an 'expression of' another, nor as necessarily 'underlying' one or all of the others.

In the particular case we are examining it could be said that
the crisis which led to the Civil War happened when a desperately acute religious controversy was superimposed upon a
fierce dispute over political organization, and upon much more
than that. A number of other sources of conflict were polarized
at the same time, and complete knowledge would presumably
show that some of them were what we should call conflicts of
economic interest; many of them might well deserve the title
of challenges by capitalist organization and the values of a
market economy to traditional organization and assumptions.
But the discontinuities which had arisen to commercial,
industrial and administrative life which were referred to above
were decidedly not all of this character, and can only, as we
have said, have had additive effect of problematic and perhaps
negligible importance. When after a year or two of Civil War
the Levellers raised their platform and the Diggers added a
tiny scrap of plain communist protest over the distribution of
property, then it could be said that something like a conflict
over membership of the ruling élite became involved. To this
limited degree the description 'conflict over a class differential'
might be applied to part of the general disagreement.

Using a word like superimposition for all these elements of
conflict emphatically does not imply that one underlay all the
others, or was expressive of it, or that overt aggressiveness was
the displaced symptom of something else. A general release of

suppressed resentment was quite apparent in the events of the 1640s nevertheless and there is truth in the claim that, like other movements of political disruption, the whole episode had a certain dynamic of its own. Contemporaries at the time and the observers of our day have reason, moreover, to believe that as the struggle intensified, social structural friction became more apparent. When the Clubmen appeared in Dorset, that latent fear of the *jacquerie*, that betrayal by those in superior positions that they were well aware of the resentment of those beneath them, had something tangible to fasten upon. But not all the sources of stress were at play in the struggle, and it is quite unjustifiable to exaggerate their breakdown into a general social structural cleavage. Of this, let it be repeated, there is no indication, and the notion of a social revolution is not permissible.

So much for the relationship of political violence in the seventeenth century to the structure of society in the world we have lost, and to the overall transformation which at the time of the military battles and the constitutional crises was still well in the future. Before we inquire why it was that our ancestors endured the supremacy of the very few, we ought perhaps to complete the story of what happened in seventeenth-century history in a very summary form. We shall have to anticipate what will be said in our next chapter about the county community of country gentry, but the suggested mechanics of constitutional crisis under the Stuarts can be understood in a formal way without knowledge of the nature of political associations as it then existed. We shall be quoting once again from the context in which the comparison of political breakdown with accidents on the roads was first suggested.

The political stability of England in Stuart times depended on two things, on the maintenance of ordered responsibility within each county community of politically active gentry, and on the interplay between those county communities and the central organization, that is the Crown and its institutions. The occasional meetings of Parliament were opportunities for local and national political awareness to be merged for short periods; the politics of Parliament when it was in session were national politics, the stuff of constitutional development. Far greater in extent and absolutely unbroken were the politics played within each county community. It was there, for

example, that the collective memory of Parliament was to be
found between its sessions.

Though many of its members had presumably met and discussed parliamentary affairs before, and though the London
season had probably brought a good number together for very
different purposes, the reason why a new House of Commons
was able to take up just where its predecessors had left off,
perhaps as much as a decade or more before, must be sought
away from the centre of the country. It was at their meetings
as justices of the peace, at the quarter sessions in the country
towns, at petty sessions in the smaller places, over their
morning draughts, as they called them, when the militia was
exercised or sporting engagements took place, that the gentry
of England talked parliamentary affairs. The truly political
among them, of course, must have met for the purpose in their
own manor houses. But however its continuity was maintained
the memory of Parliament was dispersed during the periods
when no sessions took place and only became collective again
when the MPs, new and old, appeared at Westminster with the
years and years of conversation with their neighbours, friends
and rivals in the shires reverberating in their minds.

In the county community of gentry, Court-patronage was
angled for, local offices were intrigued over, parliamentary
seats were lost and handed down from generation to generation, changing their objects of competition and their ideological content with the times. Continuity was kept up over
the whole area of national politics and within each county
because differences were resolved by argument and compromise, by the victory in the political struggle of one official, or
of one man over others, or of one family or faction over others.

This is only the beginning of an anatomy of political consciousness at that time, and we shall have to go into it a little
more closely in our next chapter. For the moment let us turn
our attention to what happened to this complex of relationships in the year before the Civil War.

As the Tudors gave way to the Stuarts, politics, national
and local, began increasingly to include the politics of intellectual difference, of argument about theory or something
approaching it. This may be recognized as the beginnings of
constitutionalism, told however without supposing that the
occasional and intermittent life of the House of Commons was
the whole political life of the English gentry. In the counties

from day to day, as well as in the Palace of Westminster once
every three, five or seven years, men differed volubly over
issues which were brought up for discussion, as well as com-
bating each other over matters of prestige and office, matters
of economic interest and policy, matters above all of family
aggrandizement. The overriding issue which was tearing them
apart during the early Stuart reign was of course religion.
Differences over the content of the faith and the proper
organization of the Christian church set man against man and
family against family. Some of them wrote about these bitter
controversies, some published what they had written and
others even preached about them, so little did the clergy retain
their monopoly as the official intelligentsia.

Naturally only a small minority within every community
took to argumentation in this way, but politics are always a
matter of the articulate, vigorous, able few at work amongst
an inert majority. The questions which the vocal ones chose to
raise and to become indignant about may not all have been
those which most of their companions would have thought the
most important. But anyone who resented the activities of the
proselytizing Puritan gentleman, or of the fanatical defender
of the ancient constitution, or of the grim-faced lecturer
expounding the necessity of restoring the constitution of the
primitive church, found himself drawn into argumentation
too. Under such circumstances each county community, and
the ruling segment as a whole, found it increasingly difficult
to maintain political continuity, to contain their frictions.
Even the men who sincerely wanted to be loyal and to maintain traditional arrangements, which for the most part everyone protested he wished to do, became exceedingly difficult to
manage. Even if they agreed on fundamentals, as they all
perpetually claimed they did, what now interested them were
their differences, and there were always arguers on hand to
exacerbate them.

As disaster and ineptitude succeeded each other in Charles
I's conduct of affairs, the royal task of maintaining assent to
policy became hazardous. In the crisis of the 1640s, after long
years of difficulty over the national finances, this task became
at last impossible. What wonder that the Stuarts wished to
dispense with Parliament, and so added to the turbulence by
giving the gentry reason to believe that their liberties were
indeed in jeopardy.

This analysis might perhaps look like one further attempt to assign a new meaning to that controversial yet appealing phrase, 'the rise of the gentry'. Certainly the appreciation of political and constitutional issues in something like intellectual terms by the communities of gentry in the counties may turn out to be a crucial development for the conduct of political life in late Tudor and early Stuart times. The communities of gentry themselves had an origin and a history, and it might perhaps be possible to reserve the expression to the story of that particular process. But the associations of the phrase with the pattern of interpretation which has become misleading seem too strong for it to be worth while to keep it at all. It would, if it were possible, be far better to lay 'the rise of the gentry' carefully alongside 'the rise of the middle classes', and to place them reverently together in the great and growing collection of outmoded historians' idiom. There they might long exercise the ingenuity and delight the hearts of the historians of historiography.

Once the limitations of the revolutionist way of thinking about the last generations of the traditional world have been recognized, a different view will have to be taken of its other attributes, some of them even more important to us in the twentieth century. This was after all the 'century of genius' for Englishmen, and the social structure which we have been discussing formed the surroundings of Shakespeare, Milton, Locke and Donne as well as those of Cromwell and Charles I. Even more significant for the world as it has developed since their time are the names of Bacon, Boyle, Harvey and Newton, since this was the era when the new 'natural philosophy', natural science, came into being. In so far as historians generally, and historians of science in particular, have thought of the final cause for this astonishing departure in human activity, they have tended to suppose that it all was in some sense an expression of the rise of the bourgeoisie, just as the rise of the gentry is supposed to have been by historians of the Marxist persuasion.

Only the most ingenious manipulation of the theory of ideology could possibly make such a final explanation sound at all convincing. But though it seems to be unwarrantable to suppose that any overall evolution like 'the rise of the bourgeoisie' was in fact characteristic of England at that time, which means that the new natural philosophy cannot be thought of in any convincing sense as its ideological expression, this does not settle the question of the relation between science and social arrangements. Scientific activity, as has been said elsewhere, during the heroic generations when Englishmen were so prominent in it, was heterogeneous, so various that it can scarcely be called an activity in itself.[13] It has to be sought in the tiny interstices, the nooks and crannies of the social structural whole, since the number of people able to contribute to it was tiny even on the scale of their own small society and they were socially remote from each other. The study of an activity of this sort is a study of what might be called residues, minutiae, not of a general preoccupation which can be easily associated with the trend of overall, widespread social change.

In the 1980s further subjects have become manifest as appropriate candidates for the respectful embalmment hesitantly recommended in the 1960s for the rise of the gentry. 'The English Revolution' is the most conspicuous. Its meanings have become so multiple, its associations so various and uncontrollable, that the words obscure more than they reveal. If it is an open question whether the phrase 'the French Revolution' is appropriate in view of the fact that the French have revolutions every two or three generations, with us it is open to fundamental doubt whether the English Revolution ever happened at all. There is no agreement as to what it consisted in or even as to when it came about, who caused it, or what its effects can have been.[14]

For these reasons, and above all because it invites comparison with other 'national revolutions', 'the English Revolution' ought to be entombed. It is a term made out of our own social and political discourse, in which a revolution can indeed signify national liberation, from felt social and political oppression. The phrase belongs therefore with the nineteenth century, and especially with the twentieth century, when disciplined and conscious social revolutionaries of the Leninist mould do in fact exist, and act, and bring about social transformations. A national, social revolution has no place in the analysis of an earlier English polity.

Along with the English Revolution might have to go the Bourgeois Revolution of the seventeenth century, even such old friends as the Puritan Revolution and the Scientific Revolution, or lesser used but influential combinations like the

Educational Revolution, the Protestant Revolution, the Revolution in Government, the Revolution of the Saints, the Financial Revolution – the list is endless.

In their places differing expressions would have to be invented and used, phrases which did not imply that a widespread rebellion precipitated by a minority of religious ideologues is the same sort of thing as a violent episode of social conflict leading to the wholesale dispossession of a ruling class, or the same sort of thing as an epidemic of discoveries about the physical world taking place amongst a scattered handful of intellectuals. If the character and connections of these various types of movement are to begin to be understood, they have to be shaken apart from the social whole, disentangled and held up to the light for inspection, discussion and analysis. To attach to them all the same ill-defined, over-emphatic word, suggestive of rebellion, violence, reversal, culmination, liberation, is obfuscatory. It gets in the way of enquiry and understanding, if only because it requires that change of all these differing types goes forward at the same pace, the political pace.

The structural interrelationships between these various forms of change was a historical reality, a subtle intriguing subject of reflection and research. No progress can be made by bundling all or any of these things together under so clumsy and crass a heading as 'The English Revolution'. We need an extension, a reformulation, of our vocabulary for development and change. If the word 'revolution' is to be retained at all, it might well have to be restored to its original context and time scale. Even to allow one usage of the term, for the Industrial Revolution itself, may turn out to be ill-advised, though it does serve to concentrate attention on that supremely important set of transformatory changes.

Revolution was a seventeenth century English coinage. It denoted the political vicissitudes so woefully familiar to the people of the time, when those vicissitudes did indeed take the form of bewildering reversals, particularly when the players on the field were replaced, partially or wholly. This was especially so when the rules of the political game, the 'constitution' so beloved of historians of earlier generations, were themselves subjected to change, sometimes to transformation. In this sense there were revolutions in the 1600s in England; in 1642, in 1646–9, in 1660, in 1668–90, and on other occasions as well, enough perhaps to justify the title 'the Century of Revolutions'. But the word would have to be used in the plural, not the singular, and a query placed against any interpretation which would see them as teleological in their tendency. Uncertainty would remain as well on the question of whether rebellions, rebellions which were put down, ought to be covered by the term.

Hints of revolutionist ideology were certainly evident in that time of enormous intellectual outpourings on almost every topic of speculation and enquiry. Revolutionist notions were often associated with rebelliousness and with gyrations in the political and constitutional sphere, though they consisted much more of millenarian religious ideals and elements of social perfectionism than of political programmes. Perhaps it may be justifiable to look upon small, self-conscious groups like the Levellers and the Diggers as the first to hold a Utopian political ideology and to act on it in a way which casts its very distant shadow forward to the politics of mass publics in our time. But this limited activity does nothing to justify the belief that something which could be described as the English Revolution was going forward in their day. They never talked of an entity which could be betrayed, and the disposition to invoke *The Good Old Cause* belongs to later generations.

The distinction between a national social revolution, not in question in the seventeenth century, and political revolutions, of which there were many, cannot be a final one of course. A violent *coup d'état* taking place within a governing military élite and other events of that kind certainly have little in the way of social aim or social meaning. Nevertheless each and every one of them is socially suffused to some degree, because political is always also social activity.

It is for decision which of the politically revolutionary episodes of seventeenth-century England was more socially suffused than the rest, and how far all, or many of them differed in this respect from other revolutions, in other political societies, in other periods. It will be concluded no doubt that certain of these happenings, especially the symbolically charged occurrences like the trial and execution of the monarch, had long-term effects on our national political consciousness, even on our sense of national identity. There would be little point, however, in constraining the term we are excoriating, into an overall description of such things as these.

There never was such a set of events as the English Revolution. But this does not mean that we English have lived, and now live, independently of the political experiences of the Englishmen whose lives went forward in the world we have lost. It is to that political inheritance that we now turn our attention.

The pattern of authority
and our
political heritage
Chapter 9

Social deference, political obedience
and the county community of gentry

Hatfield House at Hatfield in Hertfordshire, seat of the
Marquises of Salisbury, stands as the embodiment of the importance to our political history of the famous house of Cecil.
A reward from the Crown for services rendered, it is a symbol
and has been an instrument of the enormous political effectiveness of the members of that family line. In recent years,
however, Hatfield House has been open to the public and
overtly anxious for paying visitors, with the National Collection of Model Soldiers as a special attraction.

There are two English marquises bearing the name of Cecil,
because the eldest heir to the original William Cecil, Minister
to Queen Elizabeth I, still lives at Burghley House near
Stamford, enjoying the title of Marquis of Exeter. It was the
younger son of the first founder of the family's greatness who
became minister to her successor, James I, and built Hatfield
House. The Cecil clan, derived from these two so far unbroken
lines of descent, gave rise to an enormous political network,
between the early 1600s and early 1900s. The members of that
network were relatives, by blood or by marriage, and clients,
associates, dependants among the gentry of the counties concerned, sidekicks some of them would be called in the American
journalistic argot.

Twenty miles to the south-west of Hatfield, in the neighbouring county of Middlesex, lies Syon House on the River
Thames. This is the southern residence of a much older English
aristocratic name, originally Norman, that of the Percys,
Dukes of Northumberland. Their seat is at Alnwick in
Northumberland itself, on the Scottish border, where they
have belonged for six or seven hundred years. Syon House,

like Burghley and Alnwick too, also plies for the tourist trade
and is open every day of the year except at Christmas. If you
look closely at the genealogy of the Duke of Northumberland,
you will find, however, that it is only by express decision of the
sovereign made in 1766 that the present family bears the name
of Percy.

The male line of the Percys of Alnwick, that to which Harry
Hotspur belonged, had been extinct for many years by then
and the Northumberland title was renewed for the person and
the descendants of a successor to their estates through a
female Percy. The family name of this successor was Smithson,
as would be that of the present Duke of Northumberland if the
crown had not decided otherwise. It is one of the quirks of
national and genealogical history that a wealthy bastard of the
Smithson family, himself a scientist, should have founded,
funded and conferred the name Smithson on the Smithsonian
Institution in Washington, USA. We shall have to return to
the prerogative of the Crown in prompting genealogy in this
way. Patriline repair is what we shall call it.

In spite of the persisting splendour of Syon House, Hatfield,
Burghley, and such monuments as Blenheim, seat of the
Churchills, Dukes of Marlborough, everyone knows that the
great English houses are an anachronism. Nevertheless the
political life and the pattern of political consciousness, which
made of the county community of gentry its local instrument,
faintly affects our life and conduct even now. This pattern did
not vanish at once before the advance of the factories, firms,
railways, schools and building estates of industrialized society,
and has put up a little resistance even to the motorways. For
the political system which the Cecils, the Percys, the Churchills, the Pitts and the Walpoles worked in and through became
after all one of the most efficient, formidable and humane that
the world has ever known.

Nevertheless the political machine of the landed families
was bedded into a social landscape fundamentally different
from our own. It could only work at full power when men's
assumptions about political organization were of a kind which
now we can only imagine. This was the time when the great
house in the park was the sole centre of political authority
away from the royal court; when its size and magnificence were
the one means of expressing political influence and achievement in monumental form. The influence and achievement in

question here attached to the resident family and its reigning head.

'Family' here has a dual meaning; the actual group of persons living in a mansion, along with the retinue of servants, and the complex of blood relations of the same lineage scattered across the face of the county, or of several counties, and inhabiting many seats. It was not true, as we have seen, that the individual English household in the traditional order was ordinarily an extended group of kin living together even in the great noble household. But it was true that political relationship went to some degree with kinship. How important this could be in the upper reaches of society may be illustrated by an incident from the court history of Queen Anne.

In self-defence against the bullying of Sarah Churchill, born in some obscurity as Sarah Jennings, but known to posterity as the wife of the famous soldier John Churchill, Duke of Marlborough, Queen Anne finally took into her favour one of her dressers, Abigail Hill. A dresser's duties were to do such things as to lie on the royal bedroom floor at night and to empty the royal chamber-pot. Abigail had been given this humble post by Sarah herself, because the duchess had been told that one of her large band of relatives was living in complete penury. Abigail and Sarah were in fact first cousins.[1]

This was in the early 1700s. No sooner had the high-church chambermaid whom Sarah had raised 'from a broom', begun to share the royal confidence, than Sarah's political rival, Robert Harley, master as he was of political intrigue, discovered a blood relationship with the new favourite. His actual connection with Abigail has never been worked out. He schemed so effectively through her, and in other ways of course, that the final fall from favour of the Churchills was brought about, and also the Treaty of Utrecht in 1713. The French dramatist Scribe once wrote a play about the negotiations for this treaty, which he made out to have been held up because of a cup of coffee being spilt down the dress of Abigail, by now Lady Masham. Sarah Churchill went on, however, to build Blenheim Palace in Oxfordshire as a memorial to her husband.

It was here, after another conspicuous royal act of patriline repair had taken place, that the most famous of the English politicians we shall name, Sir Winston Churchill, came into the world. Once more female succession had been 'converted' by a change of surname. If it is demographically correct to think of the Duke of Northumberland as a Smithson, not a Percy, it is also demographically correct to think of Sir Winston Churchill as a Spencer, not a Churchill, as much a Spencer as Lady Diana before her marriage to the Prince of Wales. In the middle of the sixteenth century, we may notice, when the Percys were of great importance in royal and national politics and the first of the Cecils was about to get into the royal favour, the Spencers of Leicestershire were still rich, successful, sheep-farming yeomen. They were not to step into the peerage for two more generations.

Though it underlines the intimacy of kinship and politics, the story of Anne, Sarah and Abigail is scarcely typical of the workings of court patronage. Moreover, as we have already seen, the enormous household of the possessing minority is a deceptive guide to the family in general. What goes for their household arrangements may go for their kinship connections. A person of quality, especially a politically active person of quality, had very important reasons to know who his kinsfolk were, the influential ones anyway, and to make use of a relationship if he could. A yeoman, a husbandman or a labourer had no political motive of this kind, although his kin might be useful to him in other ways. We have already assigned to the varying sizes of household within each community a function in maintaining social authority, in keeping the hierarchy in being and ensuring the deference of lesser land-holders, so often tenants of the gentry, of the tradesmen and craftsmen, and of the landworkers. This is of obvious import-ance when we approach once more the question of the reasons for political obedience.

This final chapter on the nature of the traditional world and the contrast it presents with the world we now experience concerns itself with that unquestioning subordination which marked relationships then, and which marks them no longer. From a short survey of the political education of our ancestors, the conditioning process as we might say, we shall proceed to a brief exploration of the actual mechanics of political life.

A beginning may be made with a statement about the pre-dominant tone of social and political life at that time, and of almost the whole of political literature. In this society, social subordination and political obedience were founded on tradition. Therefore critical examination of the reasons why some were better placed than others was unlikely to come about. This submissive cast of mind is almost universal in the statements made by individuals about themselves. 'There is degree above degree. As reason is . . .' 'Take but degree away, Untune that string, And hark what discord follows.' It would seem that once someone in the traditional world got into a position where he or she could catch a glimpse of society as a whole, he or she immediately felt that degree, order, was its essential feature. Without degree, unquestioning subordination, and some persons being privileged over all others, anarchy and destruction were inevitable. Any threat to the established order was a danger to everyone's personality.

It is true, and it is a great disadvantage to the enquirer, that statements of this kind tend to come from the ruling segment itself, whose members had every reason to complain that anything which endangered existent social arrangements menaced all and everyone. But it would not in itself be surprising that the threat should be felt to be real by those who were oppressed by the arrangements as well as by those who profited from them. Deference as a set, customary outlook works in this way. Not everyone below the gentry was subservient of course and attachment to the system of subordination decidedly differed between those above and those beneath.

There is no clearer manifestation of what might be called social opacity, the blank inability to realize the situation of the other individual, than that which is shown forth by masters and mistresses in respect of their servants, owners of property in respect of their tenants, employers in respect of their employees, slave-owners in respect of their slaves. So little are they aware that their superiority might seem to its subjects not to be of necessity, and could be disliked, that when insubordination shows or hostile actions occur, they are almost always amazed, puzzled, hurt. The submissive individual may likewise also be unaware to some extent of his or her position whilst subordination goes unqualified. But she or he has a motive to dissemble, to conceal resentment, to exaggerate or to feign affection and respect. What is more, the means of publishing expressed dissent are usually not to hand. When they become available, as they did to a certain degree in England during the stirring decade of the 1640s, the recognition of social suppression can be expected to become apparent.

Even then the self-appointed spokesmen of those in subjection tend themselves to be members of the ruling segment.

There are several reasons why it is to be expected that deference should mark the attitudes of those not in élite positions.[2] In the first place nearly all superiors held their places by ascription, rather than by achievement and desert. They had been born great. In the second place the set of standards used to make judgments about society and varying positions within it stayed constant for almost all people at all times. Put into more technical language, it must be presumed that neither yeoman, husbandman, pauper nor craftsman, nor even a gentleman, in the pre-industrial world would be likely to change his reference group in such a way as to feel aware of what is called relative deprivation.*

Directly this assumption is recorded, it raises questions about those occasions on which change of reference group did come about in seventeenth-century English society. Those who moved upwards in the way we shall describe, though very few of them achieved greatness as the Duke of Marlborough did, certainly might have greatness thrust upon them. It could be argued, furthermore, that the disturbances caused by the Civil War, especially those connected with the recruitment and activities of the parliamentary armies, brought humble people into contact for the first time with those who were better off and had a more aspiring outlook. The very fact of sharing a common, vital purpose for months and years together might be expected to have some crystallizing effect on their attitudes to their social position and their political rights. In another of the cant expressions of the 1980s, Cromwell's soldiers had become politicized.

If the literature of the Levellers of Cromwell's army and of the city of London could be shown to have arisen to any extent from such circumstances as these, it would provide a fascinating parallel with events in our own century. National war, conscription and disbandment are now commonly assumed to be associated with intense feelings of relative deprivation and revolutionism. Social mobility in industrial society is also known to have the expected effect on reference groups. Once

* The developing theory of relative deprivation and reference groups is admirably described by W.G. Runciman in his book *Relative Deprivation and Social Justice*, 1966, where English social history since 1918 is analysed in these terms.

the opportunity of rising in society is envisaged, and once its actual fulfilment begins to look possible, then men do become aware that they are being deprived of what their superiors enjoy, and may well begin to question the rationale of the established social order. Those who study relative deprivation suggest that this questioning arises most often when expected social promotion does not take place.

Interesting as these possibilities are, it is not yet known how important they were at any time, in the 1640s or any other decade. A further reason why the society we are so hastily describing must be presumed to have been acquiescent in its usual tendency is that the phrase stable poverty does on the whole seem to be a fair description of most of its area. It is a commonplace of observation that stable poverty means resignation to the situation as it is. Such an impression seems the only possible one to gather from Gregory King's table, in spite of the political, military, even commercial and industrial energy which was displayed by the England of his generation and its immediate forerunner. It seems entirely unlikely that anything resembling a revolution of rising expectations could have been contemplated by the ordinary people of our country in Stuart times. Further information and more determined analysis may modify this claim, but an acceptance of unvarying, even poverty affecting most people seems to be as much a characteristic of those local village communities we have yet been able to examine as it seems to be of King's description of the whole nation.

Nevertheless it is generally supposed that such a situation will have its share of desperate men, and that the downtrodden pauper if ever he does find an opportunity will express his resentment of the hardships he is forced to suffer. We have mentioned that men were aware how the deprived might take to violence, able-bodied men in civil disorder and neglected, elderly women perhaps in witchcraft.[3] Quite apart from those in extreme situations, some rationale must have been present to settle the doubts of those who were disposed for any reason to question the rightness of arrangements as they were and the duty of submission and obedience. Social superiority and political authority did to some small extent depend for their maintenance on outside sanctions.

The outside support for authority in the traditional work was religious, though 'outside' scarcely expresses its relationship with the social system. We can gain a little somewhat unexpected insight into the way in which attitudes of obedience were inculcated into every personality in the formative years.[4] The stated duty of each parish priest was to teach the children and young persons in his flock the catechism, a straightforward statement of the Christian doctrine as taught by the church. After morning prayers on Sundays in every one of the 10,000 parishes of England there gathered, or should have gathered, the group of adolescents from the houses of the gentry and the yeomen, the husbandmen, the tradesmen, the labourers and even the paupers, to learn from the priest what it meant to be a Christian. This is what they all had to repeat after him: every single one of them had to get to know it by heart:

> My duty towards my neighbour is to love him as myself, and to do to all men as I would they should do unto me: to love, honour, and succour my father and mother: to submit myself to all my governors, teachers, spiritual pastors and masters; to order myself lowly and reverently to all my betters; to hurt nobody by word nor deed; to be true and just in all my dealings; to bear no malice nor hatred in my heart: to keep my hands from picking and stealing, and my tongue from evil-speaking, lying and slandering: to keep my body in temperance, soberness and chastity: not to covet nor desire other men's goods: but to learn and labour truly to get my own living, and to do my duty in that state of life unto which it shall please God to call me.

These words may be familiar and evocative to the reader because they come from the catechism of the Church of England, originally composed in 1549 and still officially in use, in the language of the 1660s. Some effort of the historical imagination has to be made to recognize how important they were at the time when practically every living person in England was both a believing, fearing Christian and also by compulsion a member of the national church. 'We hold', said Richard Hooker, the official spokesman of the established order, 'that there is not any man of the Church of England but the same man is also a member of the Commonwealth. Nor any man a member of the Commonwealth which is not a member of the Church of England.' We must not forget that everyone was compelled by legal regulation to become a member of that church.

The only thing that young people were ever told about obedience, authority and the social and political order was contained in the catechism. Many or most of these youths and maidens, moreover, had no means of confirming or revising what the grave minister had to tell them, for they could not read. He had to teach them by word of mouth what they would have to say before the formidable figure of the Lord Bishop when it came to their service of Confirmation.

Lest it should be thought that only the orthodox had this formal lesson so firmly impressed upon them, here are the words adopted for the *Shorter Catechism* in the year 1644, when the Puritan clergy were taking control of the Church of England at the height of the war between King and Parliament.

> Question 64: What is required in the fifth commandment?
> Answer: The fifth commandment requireth the preserving the honour and performing the duties, belonging to every one in their several places and relations, as Superiors, Inferiors or Equals.
> Question 65: What is forbidden in the fifth commandment?
> Answer: The fifth commandment forbiddeth the neglecting of or doing anything against the duty which belongeth to every one in their several places and relations.

In this case the English Presbyterians were overtly stating the position universally adopted in the traditional interpretation of the Bible, by separatists and sectarians as well as by the hierarchies, that the duty of Christian obedience rested on the commandment 'Honour thy Father and thy Mother'. The Puritan preachers urged 'fathers and masters of families' to catechize their children and servants at home, and it was a dissenting preacher who based landlordly rights on the fifth commandment (see p. 20). What more familiar sentiment for the beneficed rector, the itinerant preacher or the conscientious householder to appeal to when children were being instructed in their Christian duties? Submission to the powers that be went very well with the habit of obedience to the head of the patriarchal family, and it had the extremely effective sanction of the universal fear of damnation to the defiant.

'Short life', so the doctrine went, 'was the punishment of disobedient children.'[5]

All the same, the effect of this clerical conditioning must not be exaggerated. We have seen that church commandments were not necessarily respected when it came to sexual conduct. The tenant obeyed his landlord for what may be thought were much more compelling reasons than his early training and his care for the salvation of his soul. He might be evicted if he showed insufficient respect, especially in what was his clear political duty when, providing that he had got a vote, he came to exercise the franchise. His landlord might also be a justice of the peace, and would in any case have all the forces of the established order on his side. As for those below the land-holders, there was the relationship of menial service, past, present and to come, which was described when we talked of the village community. Many a labourer, a cottager or even a husbandman had been a servant in one of the larger houses in the locality, and his sons and daughters might well have to look to those same substantial householders for a day's work for the rest of their lives.

There is no need to labour the point about the familial basis of society and submissiveness further than this. It may begin to look odd that any one was ever bold enough to escape at all, impossible that ideas of individual rights, of the account-ability of superiors, of contract as the basis of government could ever have occurred to the men of seventeenth-century England.

This is one more of the paradoxes which urgently await systematic study by the historical sociologist. If we are to begin to understand why it was that a society so static and authoritarian in its attitude to discipline, and so strict in maintaining it, could be at the same time so free and inventive in the political ideas and institutions which some members of it brought forth, we must turn our attention to the actual mechanism of political life. There can be no doubt of the contrast between what some men sometimes said about the rights of individuals and what those rights actually were.

All and every particular and individual man and woman, that ever breathed in the world, are by nature all equal and alike in their power, dignity, authority and majesty, none of them having (by nature) any authority, dominion or magisterial power one over or above another.[6]

This is a famous statement made by John Lilburne, gentleman, the Leveller leader in 1646, and it reads rather strangely in view of all that has been stated here about universal subordination and inequality. These bold phrases should warn us against being misled by official declarations like those in the catechism. They may blind us to the existence of an entirely different story in the social attitudes and mental life of the people we are studying. Deference may have had another face behind what it was necessary to dissemble, a face turned towards the oral culture of the people at large. This expression, we may believe, conveyed the resentment of authority, the assertion of the independence and of the right to subsistence of everyone, an attitude which showed through so vividly when the womenfolk proclaimed their right to buy bread at a just price. Leveller notions must have come from somewhere.

Nevertheless the Levellers were an extraordinary phenomenon in every way. Their appearance in the parliamentary army and in London during the later years of the Civil War and the earlier years of unkingly government certainly provides the most revealing evidence we have or ever shall have of life below the level of the élite. Here, if anywhere, we must look for those sentiments which did take all the people into account and were not distorted by supposing that the claims made for the few need never be supposed to apply to the many. There are grave difficulties in deciding exactly how many Levellers there were and how they were placed in society; whether they really were confined to London, the army and a few of the home counties, or whether every intelligent villager with a smattering of education would have supported them if he had been given the opportunity. Perhaps some sort of half-collective life, quasi-political life, of this kind was present well before the Civil War, and maintained itself all the way through the centuries until the Chartists brought Leveller demands again into the public arena, and there finally developed into an attitude which is supported by at least half of those with political personality in our country today.

If anything of this last statement could be shown to have been true, a quite different strand of interconnection between the political outlook of the old world and our own might come into view, this time not confined to the fully literate minority and not providing reasons why we should respect and obey our traditional leadership, but grounds for criticizing and replacing it.[7]

But in the world we have lost a critic of political arrangements might well give expression to statements which seemed to affect every living individual without his actually contemplating more than a small proportion of them. Political humanity to John Lilburne presumably meant far more people than it did to John Locke thirty years later, when he wrote a declaration with a marked resemblance to that of Lilburne, but in the measured tones which were to make it the classic text for the liberties enjoyed by the gentlemen of eighteenth-century England and the citizens of eighteenth-century America.

> To understand political power aright, and derive it from its original, we must consider what state all men are naturally in, and that is, a state of perfect freedom to order their actions, and dispose of their possessions, and persons as they think fit, within the bounds of the law of nature, without asking leave, or depending upon the will of any other man. A state also of equality, wherein all the power and jurisdiction is reciprocal, no one having more than another.

Though the cautious Locke omits women, and later excepts children from natural equality, he sounds as if he meant literally all humanity in this statement. Indeed he may well have supposed that he did mean such a thing, provided only that the ordinary assumptions of his day about who was in fact concerned in political matters were maintained by his reader. In fact almost everyone did stay within these limits at that time, even Lilburne himself. Very, very few ever found themselves wondering whether a government literally having consent from every breathing, responsible human could or should exist, so far were the assumptions of twentieth-century democracy from their minds. One of Locke's associates, James Tyrrell, did get into a position where this possibility crossed his path, but it will be seen how peremptorily he dismissed it.

> There never was any government where all the promiscuous rabble of women and children had votes, as not being capable of it, yet it does not for all that prove that all legal

civil government does not owe its original to the consent of
the people, since the fathers of families, or freemen at their
own dispose, were really and indeed are all the people that
needed to have votes. . . . Children in their fathers' families
being under the notion of servants, and without any property in goods or land, have no reason to have votes in the
institution of government.[8]

Locke and Tyrrell were both answering Sir Robert Filmer,
the Kentish squire and apologist for the Crown, who wrote
out his defence of absolute monarchy before ever the Civil War
came about and called it *Patriarcha, or the Natural Power of
Kings*. This document, a codification of unconscious prejudice,
as it has been called, was addressed to his neighbours, to his
contemporaries amongst the Kentish community of county
gentry, and not to the intellectuals of a later generation who
made of it the most refuted theory on the history of English
politics. Locke, Tyrrell and even Lilburne were as much
gentlemen of England as the Filmers of East Sutton Park,
though neither Locke nor Lilburne was the scion of an established landed family. Filmer's patriarchalism, for all its
oddities and its entirely uncritical acceptance of the Scripture
– he really believed that Charles Stuart was the literal heir of
Adam among the English and so entitled to exercise upon
them all the prerogatives conferred on the first father of
mankind – provided a reason for the duty of everyone to obey,
whilst his critics could justify the right of only a minority to
resist. There is however no need to suppose that Filmer took
any more account of the really humble mass of the people than
his opponents did. Nobody took much notice of them when
politics were in question.

Perhaps Colonel Rainborough came nearest when he made
his oft-quoted statement to the victorious parliamentary
soldiery at Putney in 1647, debating the future of English
state and society: 'For I really think that the poorest he that
is in England hath a life to live as the greatest he.' The response of the weighty champions of authority was just what
we might expect: they invoked the fifth commandment:
'Honour thy father and thy mother', said Ireton, Cromwell's
son-in-law, 'and that law doth extend to all that are our
governors.'[9]

Rainborough's response was nothing like as confident as the

emphatic challenge with which he had begun. He was not prepared to contradict the catechism. What is more we can be fairly certain that Rainborough himself, not exactly a man of the masses since his father had been a naval commander, did not really mean all the poor people of the country.

Like the rest of the Levellers he presumably excluded both servants and paupers from the franchise. When women are excluded, and it is clearly implied by Rainborough's phraseology that they have to be, only a tiny fraction of the adult population remains. But like everyone else at the time he seems to have had no very clear picture of what the *whole* people of England, every single one of them, can have looked like. Even in 1647 the facts of political life and the workings of the political machine were against it. This was nowhere more evident than in the local, as opposed to the national, polital arena.

In the analysis of the political breakdowns which occurred in Stuart times, something has already been said about the local instrument of political awareness which was characteristic of pre-industrial England and whose lingering survival into our own time has also been remarked upon. This was the county community, in which full membership was so much the preserve of the gentry that the word 'county' survives in the snob language of the present day, as an indication of upper-classness. The function of these political organisms in maintaining subordination is quite evident.

But the county community did not consist exclusively of the gentry, nor was the governance of the country as a whole a federation of county communities. The position was more complex and subtle, as it always turns out to be when such relationships are examined for the local texture of any large, national, political entity. We shall have to go a little way into these intricacies if we are to understand what it was that the traditional English political system handed down to its successor.

When the county community was discussed from the point of view of the pattern of authority and our political heritage for the very first time 35 years ago a phrase was quoted from a petition drawn up by a grand jury of gentlemen in the name of a particular English shire. The date was July 1642, an electric moment in national affairs. 'The Gentry and Commonalty of the County of Kent' were the words used.[10]

The Kentish gentry, then, knew well enough that the clerics of their county were distinct from themselves, and that the ordinary people were as well. How was it, it was asked in 1948, that they acted then and on all similar occasions as if they included all the inhabitants of that ancient shire, possibly the most unified and homogeneous region in the country? It was concluded 'that it is difficult to see how any other grouping could have made much of a contribution to political consciousness' and here continuing, permanent political participation must be intended.

The ministers of the county certainly belonged to an institution which had something of its own political and intellectual life and outlook. They were a small body of men however and we now know that the doctrine they inculcated was legitimatory of the social and political order then in being. Amongst the 'Commonalty' the more substantial citizens of Maidstone, Chatham and the other towns might have been capable of a quasi-independent attitude. But examination has shown that as an interacting body they were scarcely distinct from the gentry themselves. The yeomanry, those who were not illiterate, must have had some political knowledge and occasionally their own distinct political purposes; but they acted as individuals rather than as a collection of individuals. In so far as they participated then, these other sets of persons did so through their connections with the gentry, whose right to talk for the whole county was unlikely to be questioned, and as far as I know never was so in Kent or any other county.

These facts must certainly not be taken to mean that the politically prominent felt themselves to be at liberty to ignore the interests, opinions and aims of these other persons living in 'their' county. They could scarcely afford to do so. Recent work on voters and voting – for parliamentary elections were quite often held and electoral campaigns had to be mounted – has gone to show that ordinary voters were of increasing importance after the later years of Queen Elizabeth, more important in the seventeenth century perhaps than they were to be again until after the Great Reform Bill of 1832. Keith Wrightson has read these developments as constituting the emergence of 'the people' occurring by the time of the troubles in the middle of the seventeenth century. He insists, as many others have done, that what happened then was not an affair confined to the aristocracy, the greater gentry and their retainers, but included also the aspirations and the willing participation of thousands of their immediate social inferiors, among the minor 'parochial' gentry and the 'middling sort' of town and country.[11]

The gentry politicians, therefore, had to keep their fences mended with the voters. They were the forty-shilling freeholders, yeomen for the most part, in the countryside and urban householders, with qualifications varying considerably from town to town. Getting out the vote meant making your own tenants do their duty and 'persuading' others to do so too. If the politically active gentry had to behave like this in respect of those who mattered electorally, they also had to be sensitive to what was happening to poorer people; artificers, labourers, cottagers and so on, the great mass of the lower orders who had to be kept in tranquillity even though they had no vote. The county politicians and the gentry at large were well aware that should they fail in these ways there might be resistance: their county might become ungovernable. They were therefore in a dual position, of feeling themselves to *be* the county and yet knowing that they were *governors* of the county, a paradox familiar to the political sociologist.

There were other obliquities in their situation. The gentry of a county, the gentlemen, the esquires, the knights, the baronets and the lords, ruled that county in two capacities, as those uppermost in the whole population living there, and as representatives of the Crown, the central, national authority. The notables amongst them moved both in the national, and in the local sphere; in the court and in Parliament at Westminster, and in the assizes and quarter sessions in the county. Moreover the lesser men, those with little court connection and few London associations, were grouped round these notabilities as their clients, whilst many of the great men themselves had a clientage of this kind in several county communities to which they belonged because they had houses and land in each of them. There was still another set of men in authority in the localities, if only occasionally. These were the royal judges visiting as professional servants of the Crown to declare the royal will and to execute the royal justice. Such officers were not often members of the county communities, as residents, or property owners within their boundaries. A complex system, as has been said, even in this simplified description, but no more so than in other territorial political societies.

It has been necessary to touch on these complications because of a tendency to misunderstand the character of the county community and to exaggerate the extent of local autonomy which is sometimes found in the numbers of interesting and impressive descriptions of county communities in the early seventeenth century which have appeared since the 1960s. This is understandable since the outstanding fact was that each and every one of these communities could sustain its own governance if the central authority no longer operated in its area. Thus it came to be that county committees made their appearance to take over the running of local affairs during the Civil War, and the running of the Civil War itself to some extent.

But this must not be taken to mean that the conflicts in question were fights for local sovereignty, least of all that the realm of England was wholly composed of county communities conjoined together. Even though Professor Everitt informs us that the people of Kent at that time of trouble actually put up fortifications along the ancient boundaries of their one-time Anglo-Saxon kingdom, and even though the refusal of one county community to help another during the campaigns was quite frequent, no one in Kent or any other county wanted independence from England, and every participant on each side of the quarrels wanted the English nation to persist as an undivided polity. The county community was a mediatory instrument, not an instrument of separation.

Nevertheless the county community in that past political order could have singular characteristics. The original description of Kent in 1640 from which we have been quoting lays it down that the gentry there formed an intellectual society of their own. This was why an author like Filmer wrote out his theory of politics for his companions in the manor houses, rather than for publication in the capital. Certain of the Kentish gentry maintained something like a dispersed university, where research went forward not simply on the materials in their libraries of classical and scriptural authorities but also on their own boxes of title deeds.

The account of 1948 continues thus:

There are two characteristics of English society at that time which may prove more important to the world than the tensions which ended in fighting. One is that persistent preoccupation with political speculation which was a dominant trait of intellectual life in England in 1640 and for two generations thereafter. This finally gave us the theoretical presuppositions which now underlie our institutions and those of the whole English-speaking world. The other is that urge to create new societies in its own image, or in the image of its ideal self, which appeared in the self-confident years of Queen Elizabeth, though its first momentous consequences became apparent by about 1640 – when the Colony of Virginia was beginning to show the characteristics of American society in infancy.

Many of the Virginian planters were the younger sons of Kentish manor houses, and a Filmer was amongst them. In the years which have passed since these words were written the shape of political society in the country as a whole in 1640 seems to have turned out to be much as might have been expected from the rough model worked out in Kent. Though emigration was a special feature of certain maritime shires, and though intellectual interchange may not have been as common between country seats in other counties, political England does appear to have been a reticulation of such familial networks as the one in which Sir Robert Filmer lived his life.

If we had time we could fill out the details here, beginning with the life of the village community which was earlier described and which was politically isolated save for those at the head of the community. The squire and sometimes the parson were the links between the village élite and the county community, though villages had internal politics of their own which had to be taken into account. More important to the present purpose is the manner in which the political game was played between the houses of the squires and the lordly seats: how even a minor gentleman in a new family might win one of the political prizes if he had the skill; how even an ancient lineage and a baronial estate could not help a lordling with the wrong opinions, or lacking a head for management, intrigue and plain political aggrandizement. Not many of the gentle families were of great political importance at any one time, we may notice, and very few from any one county counted nationally: like other political societies, most of the units were inactive, in reserve for a new occasion, another generation. But virtually every genteel establishment always possessed political potential, and, when crisis came, support or resistance could be expected from almost every cell in the battery.

For all their weight and their political effectiveness, therefore, the great houses and the familial dynasties could not have ruled over English society by themselves. They acted as the agents, even as the representatives of the bands of their supporters in the counties, as well as manipulators and controllers. Only thus could the rule of a landed minority be maintained and be kept in concert with what was going on at the centre of society. If we are to understand more fully how it was that minority rule was accepted for so long as inevitable, and how it gradually gave way to representative, finally to democratic institutions, there are two topics with which we shall have to have some familiarity. One is the extent of literacy in the society, and the other the amount and nature of social mobility.

The politics of exclusion and the rule of an élite
Chapter 10

Literacy and social mobility in the traditional social structure

The study of literacy in the past is a responsibility of historical sociology and here there is a substantial achievement to record. Only the fully literate, we shall claim, were likely to be actively or potentially engaged in political activity in the traditional social structure. By full literacy is meant being able to read and to write and being in the habit of doing both in the course of daily life, using written, even printed records and owning books. We now know the largest possible size of that minority of the population which was fully literate in this sense from dates as early as the outset of the seventeenth century.

From the researches of Roger Schofield and David Cressy, using the literacy file of the Cambridge Group and other sources, it can be confidently stated that less than one-third of Englishmen could sign their names at that period.[1] The conclusion must follow that at least two-thirds of all mature males, and certainly a larger but not easily calculated proportion, were disabled from sharing to any great extent in the political upheavals of the seventeenth century with which we have been so much concerned. They could make their presence felt on the national scene, especially at times of trouble, by the pressure they could exercise in their localities on the politically important. In Elizabethan times as we shall see an exceptional man who was unable to write might with difficulty occupy offices in a little town. But by and large political life passed them by.

The numbers of those made politically marginal on these grounds fluctuated: there was a sharp reduction in the later sixteenth and again in the eighteenth century. But when industrialization began, those unable to write still made up a large minority of the whole population, and the effect of industrialization itself in its early stages seems to have been to increase rather than to decrease this proportion. The principle at issue is fundamental to our subject. Politics, administration and governance in general were carried on in writing by the fully literate using manuscript and printed materials. No one else could have much more than an occasional or an incidental part in the political process.

Let us look at a few of the figures as to the ability to sign set out in Table 14.

Table 14: *Ability of men to sign the Protestation Returns, 1641–4*

25–9 %	Berks, Bucks, Cornwall, Derbyshire, Durham, Herts, Lincs, Norfolk, Notts (24 %), Sussex, Yorks
30–4 %	Hunts, Dorset, Oxon, Shropshire, Surrey
35–9 %	Essex, Middlesex, Somerset, Staffs
	48 % Chester city, 55 % Suffolk, 78 % London
	Overall (unweighted) mean 30 % n = 29,000.

Source: Adapted from David Cressy, *Literacy and the Social Order: Reading and Writing in Tudor and Stuart England*, Cambridge, 1980, p. 73.

These returns were made out in every village in England, where each male parishioner was required to affirm his declaration of loyalty to Parliament in writing, although only certain sets of documents survive. Evidently writing skills varied from area to area in a manner not easily accounted for by the geographical and developmental divisions of the country, between lowland and highland for example. But superiority of urban over rural shows itself, and that of London over the whole. If we ask how signing varied between sex and sex, status and status, the answers Cressy has to give us can be found in Table 15.

That the level of signing ability should be higher among the men analysed there than in the Protestation Returns is understandable because those who took part in the church court proceedings were unrepresentative of the population as a whole. Far too few of the poor and poorest appeared in them. The lack of labourers and servants is quite evident in the figures, and there were only about a quarter of the women that there would have been if both sexes had had equal chances of being counted. Nevertheless these figures demonstrate in no uncertain fashion how name-signing grew less common as social status descended: comparison with the hierarchy set out for size of household, proportion of households with servants and so on in an earlier chapter (see p. 96) shows a striking correspondence. The steep reduction between yeomen and husbandmen is particularly interesting, as Cressy insists, because of the uncertainty of the social distinction between them in other respects.

Table 15: *Ability of individuals to sign their names in the ecclesiastical court records during the sixteenth and seventeenth centuries* (%)

	Diocese of Norwich 1580–1726		Diocese of Exeter 1576–1688		Diocese of Durham 1561–1631		Diocese of London and Middlesex 1580–1700	
Clergy and professions	100	(332)	100	(101)	[98]	(5)	100	(168)
Gentry	98	(450)	97	(263)	79	(53)	98	(240)
Yeomen	65	(944)	73	(367)	27	(1326)	70	(121)
Tradesmen and craftsmen	56	(1838)	53	(889)	35	(727)	72	(391)
Husbandmen	21	(1198)	21	(598)	9	(379)	11	(132)
Servants	[18]	(28)	[50]	(8)	[22]	(18)	*69	(134)
Labourers	15	(25)	[0]	(1)	2	(176)	[22]	(27)
Women	11	(1024)	16	(512)	2	(706)	24	(1794)

Sizes of samples in round brackets; proportions based on less than 10 % of the total in the column concerned are placed within square brackets.
* There were also 33 apprentices of whom [82 %] signed.

Source: Adapted from David Cressy, *Literacy and the Social Order: Reading and Writing in Tudor and Stuart England*, Cambridge, 1980, pp. 119–21.

No great surprise here perhaps, since the low educational standard of our ancestors is fairly familiar to us. We should not be led to suppose, however, that the literary disabilities of common people and of women were due entirely to traditional attitudes and to the enormous difficulty of providing instruction for the whole population. In Sweden, a poorer country and not to industrialize until much later than England, the whole population could sign their names by the early eighteenth century. Those who have studied the matter in England report a repeated fear that educating the masses on too large a scale might be a threat to social stability, that is to the supremacy of the political élite. Something like this may have applied to the second, the subjugated sex. In the 1720s Richard Brinsley Sheridan's mother, who herself became an author, would have been prevented by her father, a well-placed clergyman, from learning to read and write, had it not been for the surreptitious assistance of her brothers.

Table 16: *Proportions of bridegrooms able to sign the marriage register after 1753* (%)

	1754–84		1785–1814		1815–44	
Gentry and professional	100	(68)	99	(170)	97	(204)
Officials etc.	100	(20)	[95]	(43)	98	(94)
Retail	[95]	(19)	90	(94)	95	(150)
Wood	84	(187)	83	(361)	89	(448)
Estate	83	(29)	82	(66)	70	(87)
Yeoman and farmers	81	(97)	82	(262)	83	(315)
Food and drink	81	(57)	82	(189)	82	(277)
Textile	[80]	(20)	61	(83)	[84]	(38)
Metal	78	(60)	71	(170)	81	(301)
Dealer	77	(78)	70	(232)	78	(320)
Miscellaneous	70	(81)	68	(129)	75	(130)
Transport	69	(154)	62	(462)	70	(549)
Clothing	65	(63)	79	(112)	86	(135)
Armed forces (non-officers)	59	(100)	49	(773)	68	(122)
Husbandmen	54	(665)	44	(560)	48	(123)
Construction and mining	49	(146)	53	(352)	62	(499)
Labourers and servants	41	(192)	35	(596)	34	(1632)
Unknown	76	(37)	75	(130)	[74]	(19)
All	64	(2126)	61	(4784)	65	(5443)

Source: 23 parishes specifying occupations in marriage register. Adapted from Schofield in Graff, 1981, p. 211.

The Marriage Act of 1753, usually called the Hardwick Marriage Act, marks an important stage in the study of literacy because it required both bride and bridegroom to sign the marriage register, by writing his or her name, or by making a distinctive mark. In some places occupations were also entered, which permits an analysis of the relationship between what people did for a living and their writing accomplishments. The outcomes of such a study undertaken by Roger Schofield are set out in Table 16.

The dip in the level as economic change began to accelerate is noticeable enough. Schofield concludes from the most reliable body of evidence of all – proportion of signatures in a random sample of all 10,000 English parishes in the years after 1753 – that a little over 60 per cent of males were able to sign in the later eighteenth century. After some vicissitudes this proportion grew to 66 per cent by the third year of Queen Victoria, in 1840. Meanwhile the proportion of women was 40 per cent in the 1750s, improving to a little over 50 per cent in 1840.

These results consort uneasily with the ones we have cited for the preceding period and remind us that even this topic in historical sociology is still at a preliminary stage. The evidence shows that clergymen and professionals were more universally literate than gentry, and that gentlemen could sometimes fall well below the level which we might expect was necessary for full political participation, as for example in the diocese of Durham before the Civil War. Clearly the identification of full literacy with political effectiveness was not absolute. But although our present interest is in political participation, we have to recognize that the issue of literate as opposed to oral communication is of very much wider significance and goes to the very roots of the contrast between our own society and that of our predecessors in the world we have lost.

The discovery of how great a proportion of the population could read and write at any point in time is one of the most urgent of the tasks which faces the historian of social structure who is committed to the use of numerical methods. The challenge is not simply to find the evidence and to devise ways of making it yield reliable answers. It is a challenge to the historical and literary imagination.

What we have to recall, to reconstruct, to make a present reality to ourselves is a time when most men and many more women could only think, and talk, and sing, and play, and till the soil, and tend the beasts, and nurture children, and keep house, and make things, like skeins of wool or barrels or ploughs or windmills, whilst only some could also read and write, and record, and refer again, and criticize, and tell others what was the truth of the matter and what should be done about it. Until recently history has indeed been literally history, the record of men who have been able to leave written records behind them. What has now to be done is to recognize what it means to observe only the literate activity of a society most of whose life was oral, above all to try to get the feel of how the attitude of the illiterate mass, female as well as male, affected the literate few, and so was allowed for, taken into account, in the social process and particularly in the process of politics.

Here we must look for the most important reason why the great majority of the population of one village tended to be politically separated from that of other villages, and why the fully literate few could feel that they were thinking for the whole mass. Without access to books, without usually being able to write as much as their own names, how could the husbandmen of a village where the politically active gentlemen lived be expected to develop and defend a political opinion? And if so many of the landholders were in this mute, if not unreflecting situation, what about the labourers and the artificers, the millers, the wheelwrights, the weavers, shepherds, drovers, masons, shoemakers? What about the paupers?

More than political communications is at issue here. Inability to read and write amongst ordinary folk makes it quite possible to suppose that the kinship network now studied by sociologists of the family may have been more restricted amongst people living, as we have seen so very many of them did, in the tiny communities of the countryside than it is today among the masses who inhabit our huge urban centres. An illiterate maidservant whose place was five or ten miles from home was cut off from her parents and her brothers and sisters far more effectively than a computer puncher in Woking, shall we say, is separated today from her father and mother in Glasgow. She usually has a telephone and sometimes a motor car, quite apart from the railway, and above all she can write letters for immediate and certain delivery. A maidservant could only record her message if someone would write a letter for her; only send it home if someone happened to be travelling that way; in fact could only communicate effectively by walking home one day, staying the night, and walking back the next, if her master would let her. It must be assumed that most kin-connected households lived more closely to each other in terms of miles than they do today. But keeping up with your relatives may have been more difficult nevertheless.[2]

If someone was unlikely to possess what might be called a political personality unless he were fully literate, even a nonwriter could take part in governance at one remove. The first English Poll Tax in the 1660s, for example, was framed in such a way that a written statement had to be drawn up for every household in the country. We have made it clear that these documents could certainly not have all been supplied by heads of households themselves. This draws attention to the fact that there existed a whole system of instruments, enabling individuals, if, unlike the humble maidservant, they had the necessary means, to make such returns, or to send letters, or to make applications and declarations such as wills, even though they themselves were unable to write. Indeed there was a profession, or 'mystery' of scriveners for the purposes, paid writers whose services were supplemented by neighbourly assistance.

These circumstances ensured that the roads and streets of our ancestors should assume an appearance very different from our own, for every building had to have a sign in order that people unable to read words or even figures could locate it. In the case of shops the sign was often an implement used in the trade concerned, and some of the sign language was conventionalized, as is well known in the case of haircuts and of alcoholic beverages. If you wanted a drink, all you had to look for was a bush above the door; if a shave, it was the stripey barber's pole. The most important messages for the society, of course, were religious, and in medieval Christianity the pictures in the windows and on the walls of the churches told with wearisome repetitiveness the story which everyone had to know for the sake of his or her salvation.

We can understand why the Protestants, and especially the Puritans, were so anxious to get people to learn at least to read. They had no use whatever for stained glass, or pictures, or statues, and did their very best to destroy them. There are those who believe that it was the Puritan religiosity of the original colonists which ensured that early Americans should have rapidly become more literate than their English parents and contemporaries. Doubt has been cast on this, just as it has been doubted whether the ability to read, or to read and write, was necessarily an advantage to the careers of ordinary people in the world we have lost, or the wider dispersion of such accomplishments a condition of economic progress.

Transmission of literacy – measured again by signing ability – from parents to children was by no means assured, especially within the poorer families. In the only sample so far surveyed, by David Levine, and a small sample it had to be, many children who could sign the marriage register had parents who could not, but many parents who had themselves signed had children unable to do so. It does not seem after all as if the mother's influence was the key to the children's progress with letters, since more children with illiterate mothers could sign if their fathers were literate, than those with illiterate fathers but literate mothers. It is quite evident that a name-signing bridegroom was indifferent as to whether or not his bride could sign her name along with his, and so for brides in respect of bridegrooms.[3]

It has several times been hinted that full literacy means much more than being able to write out your name and surname when required, and that functional literacy – reading, writing and the use of books and papers in everyday affairs – would be required for full and continuous participation in political life, certainly in national political life. We are fairly confident that writing implied being able to read, but we are far less clear as to how many of those who could sign were also book-users, document-keepers and dependent on these things for their livelihood. Men in the clergy or the professions and the 'businessmen', that is the merchants and the craftsmen in a big way, especially in the towns and above all in the capital, had to be in this position, but how many of the gentry is not so easy to say. A careful examination of the tradesfolk of the Kentish towns between the 1560s and the 1630s has been carried out, using inventories of their goods made after their decease. There is a steady increase from a fifth or less leaving books to nearly a quarter, though we have to remember that only the more prosperous were likely to have their goods listed in this way.[4]

In Leicestershire in the 1620s to the 1640s, 17 per cent of all will-makers left books, and 50 per cent of the gentry. This again suggests that full literacy, literacy for political purposes, was by no means general even in the manor houses. That even modest craftsmen could and did own serious and difficult works has recently been demonstrated in the area of Glasgow in Scotland in the 1750s. There farmers, shoemakers, and even coal-hewers, but especially textile workers and above all weavers, are known to have paid good money in order to buy, and presumably to read, serious works of theology.[5]

Where there were schools undertaking the instruction of a good proportion of the community, male and female, then perhaps we can assume that the monopoly of literate communications held by the ruling minority was broken into, especially in the eighteenth century. But the attempt to pin this accomplishment down by studying book-owning has proved to be frustrating: too few books were listed at death in most collections of inventories to be entirely credible. Contemporary statements and the rapid growth of schools in Tudor and early Stuart times have recently been used to make out the case for yet another revolutionary process in England over these years, an educational revolution between 1550 and 1640 which made English society into the best instructed of all societies up to that time. The whole movement has been linked with changes in higher education over the same period of time. These statements seem exaggerated to me in the present state of our knowledge.

Nevertheless there can be no doubt of the development in higher education, the education of the gentry, the clergy and the others. We have already referred to the growth of an intellectual interest in political matters amongst the gentry of England in the early seventeenth century, and the story of the universities over the relevant period is now well known. Interesting evidence is beginning to come to light which links educational change of this kind with social mobility downwards. It would seem that in the largely illiterate society of England in early Stuart times there may have been for a generation or so too many highly educated people for the needs of the society, and in particular too many university-trained clergymen for the number of livings available to support them adequately.

This paradox has its parallel in Africa and India in the 1980s, where there is also a surplus of highly educated people although the general educational level is extremely low. 'Alienated intellectuals' is the phrase which has been applied to the unwanted graduate priests of Charles I's reign, but in assessing their possible significance we must once again bear in mind the fact that such a surplus is exactly what might be expected to appear from time to time. There was no necessary connection between the presence of highly educated men without a proper livelihood and a general raising of educational standards, except in so far as they took to teaching the poor their letters as a means of keeping alive. In order to make a perceptible impression on social and political life, furthermore, they would have had to have brought about in large numbers of communities a substantial increase in the numbers of reading, writing, book-owning households.

If such a hypothetical argument as this is to be pursued, it might be said that in the eighteenth though not in the seventeenth century, there may turn out to have been just such a development. The freeholders of the county of Middlesex, already to some extent a suburban county, who repeatedly defied their traditional political rulers and managers in the 1760s to elect the incredible John Wilkes as their member of Parliament, were beginning to dissolve the immemorial pattern. Wilkite radicalism may therefore rightly be heralded as a sign of an altered relationship between the common man and his gentleman superior, in which quiescent political ignorance had begun to give way to demands for a share in the national political life. If we go back to the technical language, it could perhaps be rightly said of them that they showed signs of relative deprivation of political power, taking as their reference group the members of the ruling minority rather than their own companions. If this is what took place, it seems extremely likely that they were better informed than their ancestors, less completely lost in a world where inability to share in literate life cut most men off from even contemplating a share in political power.

Political power, we have agreed, resided in the self-conscious stratum of gentry with their professional and merchant allies in the one class to which political history was for the most part confined. But – and this is the last of the topics we can survey from the world we have lost – it is not correct to suppose that the one class was impermeable, that mobility was absent at this, the social level, where its existence was of such significance to the general political and social life of the time. The fundamental fact about an élite consisting in descent lines is that it is extremely unlikely to be self-sufficient over time. There will always be movement across the dividing line from the rest of society, and that in both directions. In the phraseology of a former generation of English historians there will always be a rise of, or rather into, the gentry and there will always be a greater fall of the gentry, or out of it.

The reasons for this are both demographic and social structural. They are complex and lengthy to describe, and so will have to be very sketchily considered here.

Everyone who is at all familiar with aristocratic families and their lines of succession will know that the Percys and Churchills are not exceptional in having been unable to maintain unbroken series of male heirs, as had to be admitted in Chapter 9. If we take a sample, rather than a few cases, we can examine the capacity of the family lines to survive amongst the baronetcies, an honorific order created by James I in 1611. It has been established that of the 204 families on which he conferred this hereditary distinction, transmitted through 'heirs male of the body', 116 were extinct by 1769, that is some 60 per cent in 150 years. We also know that in Japan the élite order of *samurai* lost patrilines at about the same rate.[6]

It is possible that some extinctions may have been due to kinship ignorance, a man not knowing he had become entitled to a baronetcy. But estimates have been made of how many fathers could expect to have a male heir under the demographic conditions which obtained in England between these two dates. It turns out that if the demographic rates are held constant at levels which keep the population constant too, under a wide range of possible demographic conditions only three married men in every five could count on having a male heir amongst his own children. One in five could expect to have a female but no male heir, and a further one in five no heir at all.

No less than 40 per cent of all families, therefore, would have to go outside the immediate group to ensure the succession of the name and of the title if there was one. These circumstances are consistent with our evidence on the baronetcies: almost one-eighth of an established body of patrilines will die out in the male line at every succession, even though cousins or more distant heirs male of the body of the founder of the line are allowed to succeed.

The royal prerogative of patriline repair can be seen therefore as a necessary expedient enabling a select body of patrilines, in this case the noble élite within the élite as a whole, to preserve the appearance of a demographic or biological continuity over time which could not be maintained in fact. Amongst the gentry at large, that is amongst the élite in general, the same thing happened informally. Bridegrooms of girls who were the final representatives of family lines were required to assume the name of the failing family. When no suitable successor whatever was to be found, relatives were in effect adopted, even quite distant relatives, and offered the house and property on condition of taking the name; all this in spite of the fact that adoption was unknown in English law before the twentieth century.

There is a highly conspicuous example in our literary history. Miss Jane Austen's younger brother, Mr Edward Austen, was 'adopted' by a Thomas Knight, Esq., in order to continue the Knight patriline which had no heir. In fact Thomas Knight's own father had himself been 'adopted' to save the Knight patriline from extinction in the preceding generation. Thus it was that Miss Jane Austen's brother, Edward Knight, Esq., had come to own the great house and most of the village of Chawton in Hampshire, where the cottage in which she wrote many of her novels was part of the Knight estate. It is the relationship between the two patrilines which is the most striking: Edward, born Austen, was Thomas Knight's paternal grandmother's brother's great grandchild. Evidently kinship ignorance was not in question here.

If the monarch decided not to repair a noble patriline, and if there was a want of peers, then suitable families could be ennobled; social promotion from below in order to make up for a demographic failure and to fulfil a social need. At the level of the gentry it was possible to move sideways within the élite without royal intervention, as Edward Austen did, so as to fill up a slot being vacated by a patriline: upward or downward movement would not necessarily have to take place. Both would be likely to occur, however, if the market in slots, in patrilines, in heiresses and unbeneficed sons wanting to marry them was to any degree imperfect. By this is meant that patrilines needing heirs would be unable to find them, in spite of the fact that gentlemen and gentlewomen seeking mates able to keep them from descending, were being disappointed. To the extent that the market was imperfect in this way, and also to the extent that the élite was increasing or decreasing faster than the rest of society, there would have to be movement to and fro across the dividing line.

The importance of information, the information of the births and deaths columns, of the peerage books and so on, is very evident. Although infantile mortality was high amongst the privileged, because of their habit of putting their children out to nurse, and in spite furthermore of some disposition towards contraception and remaining unmarried, in general there seems to have been a demographic surplus in the élite, because of their entirely superior living conditions. The general tendency would be for a greater downward mobility both for demographic and for market reasons, than upward mobility. Such is the framework into which to fit the familiar stories in the history books about humbly born merchants whose children lived as gentry or even as aristocrats, and about the nobly or gently born who had descended. Social descent is much less conspicuous in this literature than social promotion and it is indeed much more difficult to discern in the records. Nevertheless demotion from the élite was something like an institution of the traditional order in England.

This may have distinguished our country from the rest of Europe. The complaint that the social system played cuckoo to the superfluous children in a privileged family is often met with in the perennial form of the younger brother's lament. Here is one from 1600, written by Thomas Wilson.

> I cannot speak of the [number] of younger brothers, albeit I be one of the number myself, but for their estate there is no man hath better cause to know it, nor less cause to praise it. Such a fever hectic hath custom brought in and inured amongst fathers, and such fond desires they have to leave a great show of the stock of their house, though the branches be withered, that my elder brother forsooth must be my master. He must have all, and all the rest that which the cat left on the maltheap, perhaps some small annuity during his life or what pleases our elder brothers worship to bestow upon us if we please him, and my mistress his wife. This I must confess doth us good some ways, for it makes us industrious to apply ourselves to letters or to arms, whereby many times we become my master elder brother's masters, or at least their betters in honour and reputation, while he lives at home like a mome [a buffoon might be our word for this] and knows the sound of no bell but his own.[7]

The industrious younger sons of the manor houses of Kent were those who went and carved out careers for themselves and a new future for their family names in the southern colonies of North America. In departing for the colonies they were certainly not abandoning all hope of finally succeeding to the manor houses in which they had been born. They could not tell what the vagaries of birth, marriage and death might bring, nor how far their own efforts might provide them with the means to found their own 'county' families, either in the enormously different atmosphere of a country being settled or even back at home. They regarded themselves, we may imagine, as being relegated to a holding position in respect of the ruling élite, and so for all those without the prospect of a slot to occupy, and all women without husbands. It seems possible that this penumbra, as it has been entitled, to the ruling segment may have been larger than the élite itself. But we have as yet no probable estimates of the numbers it contained at any time or over time. They must have varied.

A man lucky enough to find himself at the head of an established family might have many sons whom he could, if he wished, either set up in the city, the army or elsewhere, reasonably cheaply, or else, if they would stand for it, quietly neglect. On the other hand, he might be affectionate and indulgent, unwilling to allow dependants to fall into penury, or unable to prevent them from insisting on a maintenance. In the first case the family fortune would be handed down intact, provided always that he had been a good manager, and in the second it might be dispersed. If daughters predominated amongst his children, inroads into capital would be more difficult to resist, because without dowries daughters of the gentry could not be married at all. Being idle by compulsion they were in no position to earn towards their own dowries as the daughters of the common people often did. Many a bearded patriarch besides King Lear was ruined by his daughters.

This is only the beginning of what went on, and it must be noticed how much difference numbers of births and expectation of life made in any such situation. Economic historians have studied the market in dowries and jointures (these were the amounts which had to be settled on a son's bride to maintain her if he should die) and have shown how the price of a good match for a child varied over time. Naturally the situation would be very different for a family where there was only one child, and a male at that; or where a great deal was unexpectedly inherited from the early death of the wife's father and only brother; or where the wife died early, and a new marriage brought in a rich heiress; or where a ne'er-do-well cadet suddenly returned from the Indies with a fortune and added it to the main stock. In the eighteenth century this went on offstage in India perhaps or in the navy, and during Victorian times in New Zealand, or in South America. This is the stuff out of which the plots of novels and plays were woven; in the end they mostly consist of a study in the ups and downs of the fortunes of a family line. The perpetual presence in these stock situations of impoverished relatives now begins to look significant. Not all of the grandchildren, not to speak of nephews and nieces, could possibly expect the golden prospects of the hero and heroine when finally they settled down to live happily ever after.

That interchange took place across the crucial social boundary was certainly noticed by contemporaries. An example may be taken from a book published in 1656, *The Vale Royal of England, or the County Palatine of Chester*.

> In no country of England, the gentlemen are more ancient and of longer continuance than in this country. I have thought good to set down all such arms, as I find them to bear, or to have borne. And not by order or in degree, but after the manner of the alphabet. It goeth with such matters in this country as in other countrys of England. For riches maketh a gentleman throughout the realm, which is contrary to the manner of some countries beyond the seas. So you shall have in this country, six men of one surname (and peradventure of one house) whereof the first shall be called a Knight, the second an Esquire, the third a Gentleman, the fourth a Freeholder, the fifth a Yeoman, and the sixth a husbandman.

So convinced was this urbane author of his main point that he put in the margin against this passage: 'Riches maketh Gentlemen in all countries of England.'

'Country' we must notice here means the county, the county he was writing about and other English shires, perhaps even similar areas abroad. The truth of his observation that the names of gentle families in the neighbourhood were often the same as those of much humbler families can be confirmed from lists of inhabitants. But a man might attain the status of gentry only for the middle of his career, just as he might rise from complete obscurity to enormous reputation and distinguished position in one lifetime. The most conspicuous examples come from the intellectual world.

William Shakespeare and Isaac Newton were perhaps the

most important persons ever to be born in England in the pre-industrial era. Of the poet's family and upbringing it has been established that 'the sons and daughters of John and Mary Shakespeare were brought up in an illiterate household; neither parent witnessed except with a mark'. Yet in the year 1569, when young Will was five, his father John Shakespeare was bailiff, that is mayor, of the little town of Stratford-on-Avon, and he occupied other municipal offices as well, even as President of the Court of Record and justice of the peace.[8] Although he came to grief towards the end of his life, his career reminds us once again that in strictly local matters illiteracy could be effectively compensated for, even if it was an obstacle to full political activity in the sense we have defined.

The manor house at Woolsthorpe in Lincolnshire is virtually bookless at this day, save for one copy of *Principia Mathematica* lighted up in a corner of the bedroom where Isaac, son of Isaac Newton, yeoman, was born in 1642. This is appropriate enough in view of the fact that Isaac, the father, who died before his only child was born, was as much an illiterate as John and Mary Shakespeare. Hannah, the mother, married a fully literate man on the second occasion when, after three years as a widow, she became the wife of a local rector. She left her little son, so Newton himself has recorded, to live at Woolsthorpe, 'with his two grandmothers', thus forming a household composed as no other I have ever seen in English records.

We are compelled to suppose therefore that a man born into a bookless home could die world-famous as a writer of momentous books. In our own generation we are accustomed to assume that to be brought up in such a home would be an insurmountable barrier to intellectual success of such a kind. It would seem that the fully literate amongst our ancestors, and those who could only read, would live together with the wholly illiterate in a way which we can no longer imagine. When John Locke died in 1704 he left a small sum to all the servants in the house of Sir Francis Masham, where he lived, and whose daughter-in-law was to be Abigail Masham herself. Only two of these servants were able to sign their names for their legacies: the rest made marks. The great philosopher, whom Newton used to visit in that house, must have been surrounded by a bevy of men and women entirely incapable of comprehending what Locke and Newton were about.

But it will not do to bid farewell to the world we have lost in the study of a great intellectual. Here is a document quoted in the magnificent account of *The Making of the English Working-Class*, by Edward Thompson (1963, p. 526). The words were originally scrawled on a piece of paper by a Luddite and sent to a clothier in Gloucester in 1803. 'Wee Hear InFormed that you got shear in mee sheens [shearing machines] and if you Dont Pull them Down in a Forght Nights Time Wee will pull them Down for you Wee will you Damd infernold dog.'

Behold a barely literate man, the lilt of his ordinary speech showing through his attempt to make himself understood in writing, struggling and just succeeding in expressing his passionate resentment. We can look on it as a sign of the terror which the coming of the factories and the machines struck into the hearts of ordinary people, those village labourers and craftsmen who have occupied us so much. We can also look upon it as a token of what it meant to live an entirely oral life in a world which was dominated by those able to read, to write, to record and to consult. Surely this is the most compelling of all the contrasts between our world and the world we have lost.

After the transformation
Chapter 11

English society in the early twentieth century

The working class since 1901

> Rattle his bones, over the stones
> He's only a pauper whom nobody owns

When Queen Victoria died at the very outset of the twentieth century one Londoner in five could expect to come to this, a solitary burial from the workhouse, the poor-law hospital, the lunatic asylum. On the whole the second year of our century, 1901, was a prosperous time for the English, one of the twenty good years not marked by depression or by war to the death which they were to have in the fifty which followed. The Marquis of Salisbury was still Prime Minister, and had been on and off since 1885. There was a war going on, it is true, the South African War, which, if men had but known it, was the beginning of the end of the English as a people of commanding world-wide power, but its social effects at the time did not go very deep. The huge coalfields of Yorkshire and Lancashire, the great shipbuilding towns, the acres and acres of factory floor given over to textiles, were made busier by the demand for armaments and uniforms and machinery. Nevertheless something like a quarter of the whole population was in poverty.

Poverty, we must notice, was no vague condition then, nothing like as uncertain as the state of 'decreasing the wealth of the kingdom' has to be for the historian looking back to England in 1688 through the eyes of Gregory King. Families were in poverty 'whose total earnings are insufficient to obtain the minimum necessaries for the maintenance of merely physical efficiency'.

Those precise syllables come from Seebohm Rowntree's book called *Poverty* which appeared in 1901 and which published the sombre results of a house-to-house survey carried out with monumental thoroughness in his native city of York,

a railway centre, where the family firm of Rowntree manufactured chocolates. Confectionery is perhaps as representative
a light industry of the twentieth-century type, as railways
were of the heavy industry of the nineteenth century, which
had given England and especially the north of England her
world-wide manufacturing supremacy. Young Mr Rowntree
had done his work in order to find out whether a reasonably
typical provincial city was like London. He had discovered
that 27·84 per cent of the citizens of York were living in
poverty according to his definition. In London 30·7 per cent
of the people were in poverty as his predecessor and mentor,
Charles Booth, had already shown, London which was the
richest city in the world and a fifth of the whole kingdom.

Englishmen in 1901 had to face the disconcerting fact that
destitution was still an outstanding feature of fully industrial
society, a working class perpetually liable to social and
material degradation. More than half of all the children of
working men were in this dreadful condition, which meant
40 per cent of all the children in the country.

These were the scrawny, dirty, hungry, ragged, verminous
boys and girls who were to grow up into the working class of
twentieth-century England. This was the generation which
was to man the armies of the First World War, although they
were inches shorter and pounds lighter than they would have
been if they had been properly fed and cared for. Those who
were left of them became the fathers and mothers of the working people who endured the Depression of the 1920s and the
Great Depression of the 1930s, and who saw at last the squalid
streets in which they made their homes luridly lighted up by
Hitler's bombs. They were also the men and women who
nurtured the Labour Party, the working man's party, and
brought it to maturity in the 1920s, and to overwhelming
victory in 1945, stable political power for a few years after
1964. They are, it could be claimed, the most easily neglected
element in English political and historical consciousness even
today.

We might take a very well-known example to demonstrate
this fact, though the tenacious memory of Labour politicians
and Labour voters for the terrible days of not so long ago
might seem to prove it straightaway. Young Beatrice Potter
was an assistant in Booth's survey, as gifted and extraordinary a member of the governing minority as ever took to

'Social Reform', as the Edwardians called it. But she did not stop after a year or two with the Charity Organization Society, and marry one of her own set, compounding for a series of subscriptions to worthy causes as so many of her fellows seem to have done. She became the wife of Mr Sidney Webb, of the London County Council and the Fabian Society, and the two of them founded the London School of Economics as well as the *New Statesman*. As Lord Passfield and Mrs Webb – for the aristocratic Beatrice would have nothing to do with Sidney's silly title – they visited Russia in the early 1930s. Hence the title of their final book, the last of a long series, *Soviet Communism, a New Civilisation*. Irreducible poverty, that of London in the 1890s and of all the English unemployed forty years later, had helped to turn them from liberal socialism and a successful movement of gradual reform, into prophets of communism.

In this final mood, and perhaps only then, they ceased to be typical of the attitude taken up by their countrymen to what was ordinarily known in their youth as the 'condition of England question', one question amongst the many others which eminent English political leaders had to deal with. The exact percentages in Booth's and Rowntree's figures make uneasy reading in our generation, when statistics are so much more cautiously handled that two places of decimals almost never appear in sociological percentages. An attempt at a scientific, a physiological definition of poverty, one graduated in terms of the biological needs of an ordinary man in performing his day's physical work, would never be attempted today. It will, therefore, perhaps be doubted whether the shift from 1688 to 1901, from counts of parishioners and Gregory King, to house-to-house surveys, Mr Booth and Mr Rowntree, makes much difference as to reliability. Can we really be so certain that the problem of poverty was still so urgent after a century and more of miraculous economic growth and change? Our traditional picture of England in 1901, the first year of the golden Edwardian age, is altogether lighter than this.

What about the countryside, and the country towns? What about the really prosperous manufacturing areas, which were to make the England of Edward VII more expansive economically than it ever was to be again until George VI was on the throne and Mr Attlee became his Prime Minister? The actual condition of the population as a whole of course will

never be known, though in the succeeding two generations
many cities were submitted to the treatment given to London
and York, using an ever more realistic criterion of prosperity
and poverty. But Rowntree had thought of agricultural
England.

Some years were to pass before his analysis of agriculture
was to be completed, but in his book on York he pointed out
that in 1899 over three-quarters of the population of England
lived in 'urban areas'. The time in fact had already almost
arrived which we talked of when discussing the village community of the traditional world, when the balance between
town and country would be completely reversed, and the
typical Englishman would be brought up amongst concrete,
bricks and mortar, and only the exceptional amongst trees and
fields. Moreover Rowntree was probably right to assume that
those who had remained in the country after three or four
generations of steady emigration from it lived rather below
the standards endured by their grandchildren, great-nephews
and cousins in the city streets.

In 1903 the little village of Ridgmont in Bedfordshire, over
the wall from the great park at Woburn, the seat of the Duke
of Bedford, was investigated according to the principles of
Booth and Rowntree. The Dukes of Bedford were doing very
well in that year, with income tax at elevenpence in the pound
and death duties at a maximum of 11 per cent. Like most
noble families they had urban as well as rural property, industrial and commercial wealth as well as landed. In fact the
Fabian Society alleged that the Bedford Estate was receiving
£15,000 a year from Covent Garden at the time that Professor
Higgins met Eliza Doolittle outside the Royal Opera House.
Still the estate was managed in an exemplary way and Ridgmont was being rebuilt cottage by cottage; the tall red-brick
roofs of that time of shapely, if cumbersome, domestic archi-
tecture are still to be seen in the village. Yet the investigator
found that 41 per cent of the population living there were in
poverty, the sort of poverty which left biological need
unsatisfied.

We cannot linger long in Ridgmont, though the facts about
countryside and town, about inequality in income and about
the persistence of the country house as the political instrument
of a very different society are all very important to our subject.
In October 1900, the Marquis of Salisbury submitted the

name of the Duke of Bedford to Queen Victoria when he was
reconstructing the Cabinet, and his Grace declined because of
his interest in estate-management: Woburn remained a centre
of political power nevertheless. Perhaps the annual income of
this great noble family was some £100,000 and it must have
ranked with the largest in the country, even with the huge
industrial and commercial fortunes, though an English duke
might already find it advantageous to marry an American
heiress, as the Duke of Marlborough had done in 1895. Here
is a splendid contrast with the income of about £50 which was
earned by a farm labourer in Ridgmont. This disproportion is
even larger than that between a duke (with, shall we say,
twice the average noble income) and a labourer in the time of
Gregory King.

But though agricultural labour was still the biggest occupation in England in the early 1900s, it cannot have been any
longer true that the country could be divided, as King divided
it, into two almost equal parts, with the smaller consisting of
families receiving on average no less than six times the
income of the families in the larger part. We cannot tell how
the £6 10s. a year which King reckoned to be the resources per
family of that quarter of the people in his day whom he called
cottagers and paupers compared with Rowntree's £100 a year,
or rather less, which he reckoned as what a family needed to
be above the poverty line in 1899. Still it is clear that the
traditional, agricultural society as it had survived in Ridgmont was not more prosperous than the commercial and
manufacturing society of the city of York. Nothing went on
in this part of Bedfordshire except the tilling of the soil and
the keeping of beasts; rural industry was already almost
entirely dead. A few cottagers still plaited straw, but lace-
making had disappeared completely. The making of hats had
gone off to the factories of Bedford and Luton. Not so much as
a loaf of bread was baked in the village; it all came in horse
vans from the towns. And every single village child was living
in poverty.

To the historian of an earlier England it is a gross and telling contrast that Ridgmont should have belonged in 1901 to
a residual area of rural society within an expanding industrial
whole, an agricultural remnant which was already not much
more than a fifth and still getting smaller. This made English
society different in order from anything which had ever gone

before, in Europe or in the whole world. It means that the process of social and economic transformation which we call 'Industrial Revolution' was already virtually complete in our country. This distinguishes the society of England as it now is, very sharply from other societies. English social experience since the death of Victoria is the only lengthy experience any country has ever had of really mature industrialization.

It has been in fact experience not of a state of things exactly, but of a perpetual tendency towards continuous change. For industrialization is not a once-for-all process and it is an English error to suppose that it is. Since 1901 our country has tended to fall progressively behind others in the race to re-industrialize with every new technique, but our history since 1901 has been a history of successive transformation all the same. The question of importance for the contrast we are trying to draw in this essay is the question of welfare. In so far as the industrializing process is to be described above all as a change in the scale of living, such as we dwelt on in our first chapter, only in England does it seem to have been virtually complete by 1901. What has happened since then has been a matter of the levelling up of standards, the lengthening of life, the diminution of poverty, the universalization of education. This may not have been the result of what became so suddenly and shockingly apparent after Booth and Rowntree had done their work. But since that time, intentionally or not, the spread of the benefits has gone on both by political compulsion and perhaps also of itself.

This may seem an easy and too comforting generalization, since the contemporary world is even now discovering that in rich societies great hidden areas of poverty go on persisting. The conclusion that we shall reach about the welfare state which arose in England out of the attitude which Rowntree represents will not be that it was completely successful in abolishing want in an industrial society, rather perhaps that it was just the last and most effective way of convincing the conscientious that it had been abolished. But when all this has been said there is a difference between the revelations which shocked the 1960s about the condition of the old in Britain and of the coloured in the United States. It is difficult for us now to realize what it meant in 1901 for England to have to recognize that after a century of leading the world in economic matters, when Britain was still undoubtedly the world's greatest political and military power, still in many ways the world's wealthiest power, a quarter of the English population was living in poverty, in something like destitution.

If King's figures are comparable with Rowntree's, and if both are somewhere near the truth, then the growth of wealth brought by industry did succeed in reducing dependency and destitution by more than half in two hundred years, from the 1690s to the 1900s. If this was so, then it accomplished a great deal, especially when we remember how little sign has ever been found that progress of this sort was ever possible in the world we have lost, where the text 'the poor ye shall always have with you' was a truth not worth the disputing. But the difference in standard between these two observers, the Stuart pursuivant-at-arms and the Edwardian industrialist with a conscience, is so enormous that this most challenging and difficult of questions must be left on one side for the present as unanswerable.

Unfortunately the same objection, that of a difference in standard, can be urged against the known facts about the subsequent history of poverty in the England of the twentieth century. The truly remarkable thing about Seebohm Rowntree was that he lived long enough to satisfy himself by personal investigation that poverty of the hopeless sort had virtually disappeared. In 1936, thirty-seven years after his first survey of York, he examined the city again. This time he used a much more sophisticated method of survey, impelled as he was by the disaster of unemployment which made him expect rather less of a reduction of poverty by 1936 than he had hoped for. Things were even worse than he feared, for on his new and more realistic standard 31 per cent of the working class of York were still in poverty in the late 1930s, as against 43 per cent in 1899, on the cruder standard he was then using.

But there were other differences between the two years. The greatest individual cause of poverty in 1899 had been insufficient wages, and no more telling indictment of industrialism could be imagined: but by far and away the greatest cause of poverty in York in 1936 was unemployment. When he was eighty years old in 1961, Rowntree was able to publish his last, and, it must be said, his least satisfactory, survey of poverty in the city. Using a new and still more sophisticated poverty line, he found that only 3 per cent of the population were in destitution, and that the great cause of poverty was old age. From being a predominant feature of our social life, poverty, so Rowntree tended to think at the very last, had been reduced to insignificance.

We must notice that the abolition of poverty, if abolition it was, came about not gradually over the years, but suddenly, between the late 1930s and the late 1940s, as part of the foundation and functioning of the welfare state. Within half a generation of that time, in spite of the warnings of Rowntree's successors as investigators of poverty in our country, some people began to think of the problem of industrial society as a problem of affluence, of having too much leisure and too many goods.

This attitude did not survive for long. There are signs that the remainder of the twentieth century may also interpret its social mission as the equalization of wealth between every citizen, whatever his colour and his history. This time the redistribution will have to go on not only within so-called 'rich' societies, but between 'rich' and 'poor' areas of the globe as a whole. But gross and familiar contrasts between our country as it was in 1901 and as it is now are quite immediate nevertheless. If any such superficial attempt as this one to describe the twentieth-century English working class is to be successful it must rely for the most part on the reader to make the comparisons from his own experience. Here is some of the obvious material.

In 1901 people in the upper class could expect to live for nearly sixty years, but those at the very lowest level for only thirty: paupers in fact had a life expectation lower than that of the whole population in Stuart times. In 1901 you could tell at sight whether a man belonged to the upper or the working classes – bearing, dress and speech, size, attitude and manner were noticeably different. Some are still alive who remember seeing the Victorian farm labourer in his smock. School teachers then had an average of seventy children in every class. Only two-fifths of the population had the vote, and no women at all. Shop assistants worked an average of eighty hours in every seven days, and many of them lived in dormitories above their work, compulsorily unmarried. Since those who had no separate room were excluded from the franchise, a shop assistant living in voted only if the partitions between the beds in the dormitory reached the ceiling. So conscious indeed was this earlier

England of social class that the bath-houses of London displayed the following notice:

Baths for working people, 2*d*. hot and 1*d*. cold.
Baths for any higher classes, 3*d*. cold and 6*d*. hot.

Of course such a crude method as this cannot convey anything like an accurate idea of what we are trying to show and the choice of poverty as a starting point for our survey has grave disadvantages. It distorts our picture of the working people because it leaves out prosperous workers. A wrong twist may have been given to the evidence a little while ago. It was not those who were sunk in hopeless misery who founded and ran the trade unions, who organized the Labour Party. The submerged tenth, as they were sometimes and too hopefully called, were not pre-eminently the people who created and transmitted the traditional culture of the working men which interests our own generation.

We must never forget that well over half of the workers were above the poverty line at any one time, though we are at the great disadvantage of knowing very little from first hand evidence of how they lived. Poverty was on the consciences of our fathers and grandfathers and it was poverty which they described for us. The working-class family, said Rowntree, pursing up his lips, spent 6*s*. a week on beer, a whole sixth of their income – hence a very great deal of secondary poverty, which the people could have avoided, and which less sympathetic people blamed them for. Now for 6*s*. you could get thirty-one pints of beer in 1901, and a working family in the clear can get a great deal of fun out of thirty-one pints of beer, even if it did sometimes finally lead to the workhouse.

Nevertheless, as has been said, the most important cause of poverty at the turn of the century was low wages. 'The wages paid for unskilled labour in York,' Rowntree concluded, 'are insufficient to provide food, clothing and shelter adequate to maintain a family of moderate size in a state of bare physical efficiency.' Here, then, was the proletariat of Marxian theory and the Marxian law of increasing misery under capitalism seemingly demonstrated for all to see, in the only mature industrial society then known.

The great puzzle about the English working class may therefore seem to be why it was that the active, intelligent and well paid amongst them did not all draw the correct Marxian inference, why it is that there has been no violent social revolution in England in the twentieth century. It cannot be said that geographical and personal propinquity has been lacking in anything like the way that it was lacking amongst their ancestors in the Stuart countryside. Working-classness has existed since well before 1901. It should become clear as we go on that the issue of revolutionary action was never quite as simple as this might make it seem, and that critical social change has in fact occurred without it. But though revolution in this latter sense is the subject of the last section of this chapter, the problem of the acquiescent attitude of English workers in the twentieth century goes beyond the limits of this essay. Let us turn our attention to the cyclical character of poverty in recent times, not so much the alternation of periods of prosperity and depression as the succession of events in the lifetime of an individual working man. This is one of the interesting points of resemblance between his situation and that of his predecessors in traditional society.

> A labourer [Rowntree tells us] is in poverty and therefore underfed:
> In childhood, when his constitution is being built up.
> In his early and his middle life, when he should be in his prime.
> In old age.
> And
> The women are in poverty for the greater part of the time when they are bearing children.

This is how the life cycle of working people went. Very few manual labourers in York in 1899 could have been without neighbours, friends, relatives struggling for subsistence. Infantile mortality was 94 in a thousand in the middle class, but no less than 247 amongst those in poverty. Again the resemblance with Clayworth in the 1670s comes to mind. One baby in every six died in the working class generally – the small coffin on one of the family beds, or on the table, or under the table when the family had a meal. This was a sight every working man must have seen and every working woman grieved for.

The discovery of the cyclic descent into the area of poverty was the most interesting sociological discovery which Seebohm Rowntree ever made, and has too often been forgotten. It meant that everyone in the working class had at some time in his life had personal experience of people living below the poverty level even if he himself had never been so unfortunate. It meant in fact that the fear of poverty, the insecurity which that fear brought with it and the resentment against the system, all these things went deep down into the character of the English working man. It is not entirely fanciful to think of them as an inheritance from the traditional world of peasant, craftsman and pauper.

Those amongst us who now talk of the bourgeoisification – the horrid word they use – of the working class should take due note of this. Those who look for a centre for the sense of community in the working class should note it as well, the sense of community which is forever being stressed as the heart and soul of the Labour movement. The positive urge to remake the world in a way which would abolish poverty has its spring in a negative attitude, the fear which dominated the lives of grandfathers, fathers, uncles, aunts and cousins. To call the prosperous working family of the later twentieth century simply bourgeois or middle class is a superficial historical misconception. It is rather the working family of the 1900s, of the 1920s or the 1930s with something of the horror of poverty removed. 'Working-classness' in the social development of England in the twentieth century has, therefore, an obvious justification in attitude, in instinctive response, though of course it has many other defining characteristics. It has an immemorial history too.

So much for the English working class since 1901. For all the over-simplification which is inevitable when complicated description has to be done by allusion, it must be obvious that no such phenomenon could ever have existed in the world before the coming of industry. The probable resemblances and direct descents are fascinating to contemplate nevertheless.

The solid middle class

The solid middle class is a very familiar expression. It is surrounded by a cluster of clichés which reappear when the English think of themselves as a society, and look back on

their history, particularly their recent history – the backbone
of the nation, even the salt of the earth. These commonplace
sentiments are less acceptable in the 1980s, but the idea of a
middle class which was the anchor of a community's stability
goes a long way back. Aristotle first suggested the notion and
it has been applied to almost every political system and
situation known to the historian. We have seen how commonly
the expression has been used of England before 1700. But
Victorian and Edwardian England is usually looked upon as
the outstanding example of apotheosis of the middle class as a
community and a culture. The decline of that solid middle
class has sometimes been made into an account of the social
development which has gone on in England since the twentieth
century began. Meanwhile the working class has also been
supposed to have begun to become like the solid middle class,
to be taking on its attitudes and values.

We have glanced at the notion of the working people of
Britain becoming middle-classified and when the evidence is
closely scanned it turns out to be somewhat misleading to
think of a solid middle-class community as existing in England
in 1901. It is even more misleading to suppose that social
development since that time has been the story of its decline.
The word 'community' is the important word here. There most
certainly was a lump of persons in English society in the age
of Arnold Bennett and Thomas Hardy and George Meredith,
to which they applied the phrase 'the solid middle class'. The
question is whether it can ever have been so nationwide a
community.

The very fact that the phrase has been in perpetual use
gives the solid middle class an independent existence of sorts.
The people we shall be examining were, at least as individuals,
solid in the substantial sense of the word. They were substantial because they were rich and had big establishments, and
because they bulked very large in all the affairs of the nation.
What we shall find is that the notion of a community at one
level, more or less homogeneous in its consistency and composed of fairly equal units, is a very questionable one. The
twentieth-century working class which has just been discussed
has these two characteristics, although it is much less usually
referred to as solid. But the facts about the middle class are
rather different. Fortunately these facts are no longer entirely
guesswork and riskily made inference as they had to be when

we were talking of the seventeenth century. By and large the
evidence is reasonably well known.

Arnold Bennett recognized something of the truth in the
suggestive and inexact way which is typical of the literary
artist and which we have had to become so wary of. In
February 1909, this highly representative author wrote one of
his many essays speculating about who bought and read his
books:

'When my morbid curiosity is upon me,' Bennett says, 'I
stroll into Mudies or the Times Book Club, or I hover round
Smith's bookstall in the Strand. The crowd at these places is
the prosperous crowd, the crowd which pays income tax and
grumbles at it.' In February, 1909, we may notice, income
tax stood at 5 per cent of earnings. 'Three hundred and
seventy-five thousand persons paid income tax last year,' he
continues, 'paid it under protest. They stand for perhaps a
million souls, and this million is a handful floating more or less
easily on the surface of the forty millions of the population.'

We ought perhaps to underline Bennett's words about
income-tax payers being only a handful of the population:
'floating on the surface' is very significant too. His description
continues thus:

> Their assured, curt voices, their carriage, their clothes, the
> similarity of their manners, all show that they belong to a
> caste, and that the caste has been successful in the struggle
> for life. It has been called the middle class, but it ought to be
> called the upper class, for nearly everything is below it. I go
> to the stores, to Harrods, to Rumpelmeyer's, to the Royal
> Academy, and to a dozen clubs in Albemarle Street and
> Dover Street, and I see again just the same crowd, well-fed,
> well-dressed, completely free from the cares which beset at
> least five-sixths of the English race. I do not belong to this
> class by birth. I was born slightly beneath it. But by the
> help of God and strict attention to business I have gained
> the right of entrance to it.

In one nostalgic Edwardian image after another Bennett
goes on to list the notorious characteristics of the solid middle
class. He talks of its sincere, religious worship of money and
success – the world, he says, is a steamer in which the middle
class is travelling saloon. He talks of its barbarism, the bar-

barism which toasts the architect *and the contractor*, and might
as well toast the poet *and the printer*. He talks of the dullness,
the humourlessness, the unresponsiveness of that 'great, solid,
comfortable class which forms the backbone of the novel-
reading public'. How appropriate Rumpelmeyer's is, that
Mayfair shop which catered only for the carriage trade, and
which has not survived to share in our day the fate of the
other exclusive Edwardian emporia.

Here, then, is the solid middle class of Edwardian times as
a contemporary saw it. Here too we may notice a distant
reminder of the shadow of poverty which we have just considered, that other community within the nation which had
not been so successful in the struggle for food, housing, clothes
and freedom from perpetual insecurity. Bennett's openness in
telling his readers that he had not been born into the solid
middle class is interesting, but should not be counted as all
that revealing; although a solicitor by his best description, his
father had kept a pawnbroker's shop at one time, at Hanley
in the Potteries. His other uncertainties and inconsistencies
are interesting too, for rather a different reason.

He talks sometimes of the 'upper' class, as if that were the
better term, of a 'caste' rather than a 'class'. Yet he is prepared to believe that a million people belonged to it, as if the
crowd of faces which he saw so often at Rumpelmeyer's or the
clubs could possibly belong to as many as a million people. He
was wrong about the figures, as will appear in a moment, but
his instinct in thinking of the income tax in order to calculate
the size of his potential readership was apt enough. If Bennett
had been taken more seriously, if his hint about consulting the
income tax returns had been acted upon and the figures they
contained had been prominently displayed, then perhaps the
numerical fallacy, as it might be called, about the solid middle
class would never have come into currency. The other part of
this particular illusion, that of a community on one level,
might have been avoided too.

By the numerical fallacy about the solid middle class of
Bennett's time is meant the uncritical supposition that the
middle class can then have contained a sizeable section of the
English population, an eighth, shall we say, perhaps even a
fifth or a quarter, or a third of the whole population. It did
not. It consisted at most of about a seventeenth. If we rely on
the income tax figures by themselves it was even smaller. Only

one person in twenty-five was rich enough in England, in 1909, when Arnold Bennett wrote his essay, to enjoy the famous middle-class standard of living. The resemblance to the figures we have quoted for the privileged minority in the pre-industrial world may simply be a coincidence, but a very interesting coincidence it is.

Income is not the only way to measure such things as class membership, and these few numerical facts do not prove that only this tiny minority regarded themselves as belonging to the middle classes. Quite the reverse. The truth seems to be that for the whole of this century some millions of people have been aspiring to live as only a few hundred thousand of people could in fact afford to live. The secret of the historian's stereotype about the solid middle class is imitation, what might be called in Arnold Toynbee's expression 'mimesis'. Only if imitation, mimesis, is taken to constitute 'solidity' can the phrase 'the solid middle class' be made to apply to any substantial part of the population, not only in Arnold Bennett's day but for most of the time since.

Decline of the middle class, which is how some historians have tended to look on social history since that time, could unfortunately mean many things. It is as elusive a phrase as 'the rise of the gentry'. But if its possible qualitative meaning is disregarded and its numerical meaning only is retained, then it is completely untrue of England in the earlier twentieth century. There has been a completely uninterrupted growth in the numbers of those who could be called middle class in the economic sense since the year 1901. This growth was slowed down but not interrupted by successive depressions, and it has never been more rapid than it has been since 1945.

The numerical fallacy about the solid middle class, then, is very easy to see and to dispose of. More difficult is the fact that historians have allowed it to persist, as have some of the social scientists in spite of their repudiations. To see why the facts have been difficult to appreciate, we must glance at the figures of middle-class occupations as well as of middle-class persons.

It is difficult to decide how much money was needed to maintain the suburban villa which we associate with the solid middle class of Bennett's time, to pay the servants, to educate the children – five or six of them – to run the carriage, and to pay for Bennett's books. Seven hundred or a thousand golden sovereigns a year, shall we say, together with the expectation that the value of money would never go down. Though the precise numbers of tax-payers is not known for that period, it is known that there were about 280,000 households in England and Wales in 1909 with £700 a year or more. That is to say there were less than 300,000 families out of a total of 7,000,000 which reached the level necessary for comfortable middle-class living. Not that there was a plateau at this level, or at any level in British incomes over the century. Indeed, the variation above our chosen point was enormous, with gaps yawning far more widely than the gap between those who had enough to live adequately in the middle class and those who did not.

There were in Edwardian times 120,000 'capitalists' who were reckoned to own two-thirds of the wealth and they obviously constituted a large proportion of those with seven hundred or a thousand a year and above. There were something like 40,000 landowners who owned twenty-seven out of the thirty-four million acres in the country. Some of these of course were aristocrats and perhaps a case might be made out to show that there was a useful sense in which these people were upper class, not middle class. We have already seen that the very rich and powerful played a distinctive role especially in politics even after the transformation. In this arena, in the relationship between the country house and the suburban dwelling, there was a cleavage between the bourgeoisie and the landed families.

But Bennett's typical hesitation between upper and middle class shows how difficult the distinction was even in his day. In fact in the twentieth century the upper class has been a nullity, just as the second class was for so long on our railways. The only sensible course for the historian is to put the people at the very top in with the rest of the successful, and face the fact that this makes the whole an extremely various group of persons. We can now recognize the second misconception in the historian's stereotype of the solid middle class, that of homogeneity, in income, and in occupation. However vivid the impression which these privileged people give in the *sameness* of their attitudes and tastes, nevertheless their surroundings, their experience, their wealth and its sources were all very various indeed – these lawyers, clerics, imperial officials, businessmen, doctors, professors and plain receivers of dividends and rents.

The confusion over class distinctions and their relation to political and other forms of power led to the appearance in English of a word which began its career as such words often do as a piece of slang, a smart expression for journalists and satirists. This word is the 'Establishment'. Vague as its meaning is, if it yet has a settled meaning at all, this term seems to express what Bennett was trying to say rather better than anything else we have to hand. What he had in mind turns out to be very much more like an Establishment than it is like that class community which we found amongst the workers and the poor. Instead of a solid middle class, with an upper class above it, we should rather think of a minority of some 300,000 families which several million families were busy imitating, and imitating rather unsuccessfully because they had not enough money to do it well. The figure of 300,000 belongs to the 1900s; it is a much bigger number of families now and it is growing rapidly. It is still a small minority, to some extent an isolated minority, but nevertheless the goal of social aspiration.

The resemblances between this situation and that which we have tried to describe for the traditional world are coming into view, together again with the very important differences. Mimesis, social imitation, did not first appear in England in late Victorian times. The perennial complaint against citizens and citizens' wives from the Middle Ages onwards was that they imitated their betters, the aristocracy. This was resented for more reasons than one, although the most important was no doubt ordinary snobbery and the contempt of those who could afford to live well for those who could only pretend to. There was also the knowledge that some at least of the imitators could in fact afford more than those whom they imitated, and would be in their places before long. In a society where downward mobility was, as we have seen, probably greater than upward, and where status was regarded as a fixture, part of an unchanging universe, this led to legislation as well as to satire. In high industrial times such an attitude has become impossible and movement in every direction is undoubtedly much easier. The perpetual growth of the privileged section of society has become a possibility, even a reality, both because the whole population has been growing and because ever expanding wealth has made for an increase in the proportion of the rich to the whole.

There is a feature which the two systems manifestly shared, the presence of a large marginal area between upper and lower, a penumbra, we might call it, to the privileged minority. This interesting region can only be very roughly sketched in the case of pre-industrial society, but by Arnold Bennett's time its outlines have become fairly clear. In 1909 income tax began at £3 a week, and the figures show that there were 800,000 incomes between this, the lowest level, and the level where we believe true 'solid middle class' living was possible, that is at £700 per year. This was the area of the imitators, the people in between the working-class community below them and the privileged above them. To make it manifestly clear who these people were, let it be repeated that they were placed below those who could objectively afford a 'middle-class' standard of living, and above those who were by universal agreement working class, manual workers, men and women living under the threat of poverty.

These in-between families with £150–£700 a year were the chief of the aspirers, the Mr Pooters of the Edwardian world. They were the people whom Arnold Bennett missed out when he walked round London looking for his readers, and from whom he himself had his own origin. There can be little doubt that *Clayhanger* might well have been found on the mantel-piece of Mr Pooter's sitting-room, if it had been written in 1895, rather than in 1909. It would have found a place along with the rest of the bric-à-brac, not quite as appropriate as the two stone lions which, as Mr Pooter tells us, graced the flight of steps leading up to his front door, but a likely book for his rebellious son Lupin to be reading. George and Weedon Grossmith who contributed their pieces on Mr Pooter to *Punch* in the 1890s were as shrewd in their observation of English life as Bennett, Wells or even Shaw.

There were nearly three times as many people of this type as there were with an adequate middle-class income. Some of them could justly be called more than aspirers, for even with four, three, or two hundred a year a man could do very well in 1909, especially if he belonged to a respected occupation like that of the clergy. He could often afford a servant, and sometimes had expectations of succeeding Mama and Papa in their genuine establishment. Or he might resolve to make his own way up to solidity; opportunities were not wanting to the really vigorous and enterprising, especially to those willing to go abroad.

Even if all the families of the imitators are added together only about a million at the very most, a seventh of the whole number in the country, can be made out to be middle class. Considering how this seventh now appears to be composed it would seem to be extraordinary to think of this section of society as a 'solid' community or even a community at all. Moreover it cannot have been true that the whole remaining part of the population was embraced within the working-class community, over 85 per cent of the whole country. There is yet another intermediate area, an area considerably larger than the one we have classified as the area of aspiration, which has to be traversed before we reach the working class proper. In order to observe the people living there it is necessary to go below the £3 level, beyond the realm of a somewhat uncertain light given out by the income-tax figures. Only if large numbers of people from this region of society are admitted into the middle-class could it ever become a fifth, a quarter or a third of the population.

Some of these people certainly had a claim to middle-classness. At least they felt themselves to belong to the professions, the lettered and liberal occupations, rather than with the manual workers. From the little which is objectively known about their way of life it seems that, although aspiration was out of the question for them, they also were subject to mimesis. Deliberately rejecting the artisans outlook, what else could they do but model themselves upon their betters? But if for that reason we include them with the middle class, perhaps now dropping the adjective 'solid' as conceivably intended in some vague way to qualify one part of the middle class but not the whole, this is what we find in terms of income. 'Elementary schoolteachers' were a large component of this type, and three-quarters of them in 1909 were women, whose average income was £75 a year. The same sort of thing is true for office workers, in business and in government, especially local government, who made up most of the rest of the people in this category. White-collar workers they are called now, but it is worth mentioning that in the 1900s they did not contain many women. It seems quite out of the question to try to classify them on the conventional three-layer scale, especially if one layer is null. We need a wholly more realistic vocabulary.

This subject like all social description becomes tedious if it is pressed beyond a certain point. All that the reader is required to acknowledge is that the 'solid middle class' of the incautious historian and social commentator turns out on closer inspection about earlier twentieth-century society in Britain to be to a large extent bogus. Bogus is used here in its original technical sense, meaning blank types put in to fill out space. Perhaps it may be doubted, whether these claims have ever been seriously made about the middle class in our country over recent generations, and a reference or two is required here.

The late Sir Arthur Bowley was a distinguished statistician and social historian of the first half of this century. By reckoning in the white-collar workers generally and insisting that everyone who was not working class must belong to it, Sir Arthur fixed the middle class at 23 per cent of occupied men in 1901, 25 per cent in 1911 and 26 per cent in 1931, growing steadily as we have already noticed but checked by the blight of the Depression. Mr Bonham in his very interesting study of the middle class vote decided that it comprised 30·1 per cent of the electorate in 1951 and was again growing rapidly. No less an authority than the late G. D. H. Cole willingly accepted this figure for the class as a whole in the 1950s, though he admitted the difficulties about defining the middle class.

Perhaps all that it has been possible to do in this section is to convict them of the rather cumbersome and misleading use of an obsolete terminology. There are other ways of describing the 'middle class', and Seebohm Rowntree suggested and consistently used the expression 'the servant-keeping class' for his purpose, which was to find a way of putting on one side all those who were neither in poverty, nor ever likely to be so. It has none of the political and other overtones of 'the Establishment'. For that reason, because it lays the emphasis on the fact of social superiority alone, this is the phrase we shall have in mind as we turn to the issue about revolution in England since 1901.

The social transformation of our time

When we discussed social change in England 300 years ago, at a time of military violence over civil issues, it was concluded that to talk of social revolution was inappropriate. Though there were breaches in the political fabric and constitutional changes which were so abrupt and sudden that the most extreme descriptions have always been applied to them, the notion that the social structure itself was violently and radically changed had to be rejected. The third and last of the issues which has to be considered in this swift survey of English society in the earlier twentieth century is whether something which might well be called social revolution in accepted parlance has been happening in our time, although neither civil conflict nor, as yet, any sharp constitutional conflict has taken place.

The discussion has to go on in recognition that the general contrast between seventeenth- and twentieth-century English society is the one which seems to us now considerably more important than any other known to English history. If by the exercise of historical ingenuity it could be attached to a particular set of events, there can be no doubt that it would have been called revolution, *the* revolution in fact. This being so, any change confined to the period since 1901 could only appear as incidental. There is a further complication too. No one in the later twentieth century whatever his definitions could possibly decide whether a social revolution occurred earlier in the century, because everyone is still caught up in the process under description. Only the decision to defy convention and to choose deliberately to write history from the present backwards puts us in the uncomfortable situation of having to raise such a question at all. We must return to this crux in our final chapter.

Meanwhile we can address ourselves to the following possibility. Even in the light of the overall change which can be observed between the older, traditional social world and the industrial one which has succeeded it, a change of shape in the social structure of our country (which might turn out to be a critical one) does seem to have taken place since 1901. The argument will be that some sort of crystallization may have been taking place, with its apogee between the years 1940 and 1947. The result was a reduction in the social height, to pursue the spatial metaphor about social relationships: to go even further with the image, from a pyramid, lofty and slender, English society began at that date to look something more like a pear, tending to become an apple. Because it has an altered shape in fact, people have tended to change their image of

English society, if only by very little. Englishmen, perhaps even more Englishwomen, have ceased to look upwards as much as they had always done; outward-looking has begun to compete with upward-looking.

These newer metaphors, directly they are written out on paper, begin to look even more gawky and inadequate than the older ones. Let it be clear before any attempt to justify them has been made, how modest is the claim being put forward. It is no cataclysm of the Eastern European type which is here at issue, and not therefore a revolution on the definition we have suggested in an earlier chapter on that theme. The society described for the Jugoslavia of the 1950s by Djilas, for example, obviously differs from Jugoslavia as it was in 1939 by a great deal more than our England differs from the England of Mr Neville Chamberlain, even of Mr Lloyd George.

The fact that productive capacity has stayed to such an extent in private hands clearly distinguishes the nature of the social change in the two countries. The change in Jugoslavia and in other countries has also been a change towards greater industrialization, a very rapid advance indeed towards a society dominated by the factory and the office. This has not been open to the English in the twentieth century to anything like the same extent because we have been highly industrialized all the time. Moreover the system of social status in our country is still officially much as it always has been, even if in fact it has been considerably less definite, whilst in the communist countries status has been completely transformed. If the height of the social ladder in England is now much less, the number of rungs is somewhat the same.

The inappropriateness of 'revolution' to describe these changes is obvious when their nature is considered. It is a fact for example that in 1898 no less than 13,000 people in England and Wales died of the measles, and there are no doubt plenty of people still alive who can remember the terror which these infectious diseases caused, especially amongst families with children. By 1948 this number had dropped to about three hundred, and the other infectious diseases show the same amazing decrease in their incidence and in their power to kill. Deaths from diphtheria dropped from 7500 to 150 over the same period, and deaths from scarlet fever show a hundredfold decrease.

Changes like these can only be counted as marking a deliberate transformation consciously contrived. The tendency is to call these things 'revolution', yet this merely makes us think of them in terms of a conflict, a turning point and final victory which is almost physical. And this is a nuisance.

There was, nevertheless, a critical point in these medical advances, when mortality really began to go down sharply. This point also came in the early 1940s, or somewhere near that time, for it was in 1937 that the effect of the sulphona-mide drugs first began to be felt, and in 1945 that penicillin went into general action. But the experts count the new drugs as only one amongst a whole list of other changes, much more general and long-term, such as better sanitation, better hous-ing, cleaner bodies and so on. All these tendencies combined then to produce this triumphant result in our country, though we must remember that they are features of contemporary western industrial society as a whole. We may notice that this achievement marks the early twentieth century as a time of progress far more rapid and intense than any process of this kind which took place in the nineteenth century. Yet it was the nineteenth century which called itself the century of progress and which historians have always thought of under this title.

Perhaps it may seem surprising that the point at which the shape of English society can be seen to have changed came during the last war. For this was when our country was in greater military danger than it has ever been, and under a government, the Churchill coalition, which certainly did not take office to bring about reform, least of all of the social structure.

But the sociologists have recognized for a long time that national warfare, especially warfare which requires a high proportion of citizens to participate, tends to produce changes of social attitude and policy, in the 'reformist' direction. There was such a tendency during and after the war of 1914–18 all over Europe. The programme of the Levellers in the late 1640s has already tentatively been brought under the same heading. Universal military conscription is one of the charac-teristics which distinguishes twentieth-century societies from their predecessors and in Britain in the early 1940s participa-tion in the national war effort was at a level rarely equalled anywhere at any time. Not only were able-bodied men conscribed to fight but all mature men were required to work. Not only were women enrolled voluntarily to help in a womanly way but all women were directed to some task useful to the war effort. Factories, institutions, communities, everything British was made to play its part with an efficiency and a success which is a high tribute to British administrative skill, whatever its record since that time.

The impression should not be that under these quite unique circumstances the people of this country, or a particular number of them having support from many others, deliberately decided to introduce something like a new social order in the early 1940s. They had some success, even though it looked at the time to be much greater than it really was. The overall changes we are discussing were not exclusively a matter of the social results of medical advances, of changes in mortality, of a rise in real wages and alterations in the distribution of income. Such advances might conceivably have come about without any governmental or political policy being at play, as they did to a large extent in the USA over the same period. Deliberate shaping of social change did go on at the same time, however, in England. But before anything more is said about the causes of the transformation, a little more must be added about fertility, mortality and the family.

We have talked at some length about the number of children born to peasant women 300 years ago, and made some reference to changes at age of marriage of women and numbers of children born to a marriage. These varied in ways which may turn out to be of great interest for the study of social and economic history and of social structure. The nobility and gentry showed similar fluctuations in these respects, but with them the process is clearer. It seems more obviously a question of deliberate policy in reaction to the changing situation. Over the last half-century and more there has been a very remarkable deliberate change in England of this kind, affecting now every level of society, almost every married couple.

In the later years of the nineteenth century over four children were still being born to every marriage. Though, as we have seen, average household size in England remained the same from the seventeenth to twentieth centuries, by the 1950s it had fallen by a quarter. This was due, among other things, to the fact that the figure of births per marriage had fallen to two and a half per family, a decline of over one-third in less than two generations. Although the family means something very different in the industrial world from what it meant in the pre-industrial world, this phenomenal fall in the numbers of children has meant an enormous change in the position and outlook of women. Together with the lengthening of their expectation of life, this change, in Professor Titmuss's authoritative opinion, has brought about something like a total transformation.

'At the beginning of this century,' he wrote some years ago, 'the expectation of life of a woman aged twenty was forty-six years.' Approximately one-third of this forty-six years, Titmuss continues, about fifteen years, that is to say, was to be devoted to child-bearing. At the time when Titmuss was writing, the expectation of life of a woman aged twenty was fifty-five years and of this only four years, about a fifteenth, was spent in child-bearing: the contrast with Edwardian England is now even more pronounced. He also tells us that about half of all working-class wives had borne between seven and fifteen children by the time they had reached the age of forty, in the early twentieth century, that is to say. All this is entirely different today.

One is tempted to say that a society which has changed so far and so fast in such a fundamental particular is quite simply a new society. The emancipation of women, beginning with the right to vote, has meant the addition of a new and a different half to public society. Though the direct political effects have not yet been as dramatic as such language as this might lead one to expect, the final outcome is not yet apparent. For it has all happened very recently, within the twentieth century. Once again, the rate of transformation in Victorian times begins to look modest in comparison.

The change in the size of the family was undoubtedly deliberate, as deliberate as that which came about amongst the bourgeoisie of the city of Geneva in the early years of the eighteenth century, for it was likewise due to the use of contraceptives. It cannot however, be dated to the 1940s, like so many of the other changes we have discussed. The lowest point reached by the biological family in England occurred during the Great Depression of the 1930s. Not until the later 1970s were the demographically inevitable consequences unmistakably evident in the change in the age balance of the population. In a study with the title *Britain, be your age,* I hope to demonstrate that it is this which must be called the social transformation of our time, of the last quarter of the twentieth century.

Moreover, bursts of welfare legislation have undoubtedly led to the intensification of the rate of social change, in education, and in the social services generally as well as in the maintenance of minimum standards of living. It seems just to say that the series of measures passed in the late 1940s were the most conspicuous and the most effective. Under Churchill's coalition government a series of reports and of individual Acts began which continued almost without interruption into the years of Labour rule from 1945–51. The Butler Act of 1944 was looked upon for nearly twenty years as the charter of educational opportunity for our generation, for it instituted the principle that a secondary education, free of charge, was the right of every English citizen who could pass the proper examination, the notorious 11 plus.

We have already outgrown this very moderate educational ambition, just as the classic of the British welfare state, the Beveridge Report, published in that year now seems more than a little antiquated. 'Full employment in a free society' as Lord Beveridge's remarkable document was called, was a world best-seller in its time, as much read in the western hemisphere as in Britain. No one anywhere in the west can read it in the 1980s without a sense of unreality and of wistfulness. Its great principle was that everyone in Britain from the Queen to the pauper child should be insured against financial misfortune, against the economic effects of loss of work, health and youth. Most of its provisions were enacted by the Attlee governments. The National Health Service, like all the other enactments of those reformist years, codified and made into a culmination all the earlier legislation of that kind. Then came the new towns, the nationalization of industries, the final democratization of the parliamentary system, and many other things – all of them having their origins in plans which were laid down before even the war was won in 1945. In the 1980s this whole structure is in the course of slimming down and of dismantlement, though other, richer, more expansive countries, which have built for themselves more elaborate and efficient versions of the welfare state, still sometimes look to Britain as the creator of the original model. The downgrading of these institutions in our country does not of itself imply that their foundation should be denied the title of fundamental social change.

The actual shift of opinion in favour of radical reform seems to have taken place about 1943. From that point on it might be said that 'ideological politics' became at last the accepted pattern in England. This seems to be the decisive argument in favour of the later 1940s as a time of critical social change and we must pursue it a little further.

The Labour Party began in 1901 as a practical political proposition, and its success was rapid for the first twenty-five years. This was not surprising since what we should quite spontaneously call the natural support of the Labour Party, that is to say the working people, constituted then and has ever since at least two-thirds and probably more like three-quarters of the whole population. With the great extensions of the franchise in 1919 and in 1929, the eclipse of the Liberal Party in favour of the Labour Party, and a situation where Conservative and Labour governments alternated, were to be expected.

But though the Labour Party did head minority governments in 1924 and in 1930–1, which were both in their own way political disasters, this did not occur. Nor did the Liberals take a final quietus. If we take a great gulp at a huge pudding of a historian's problem we might claim that what happened was this. The society of England was unwilling to accept ideological politics where there are two possible governments, one of the economically privileged and the other of the economically dissatisfied. Not until 1943. In that year apparently it did accept the prospect of Labour rule and of nationalization, the very distant possibility of socialism. In the 1960s it began to be thought that ideological politics of this kind were a little out of date. In the 1980s of course the attitude is very different. Nevertheless the effect of the great change we are describing was to bring together the two opposed attitudes to some extent. But when every qualification is made, this shift still looks as if it was decisive, although Labour governments have not lasted long, and although fears of socialism as others understand it have turned out to be baseless in our country.

So much for an attempt to make the social history of England in high industrial times a history of critical social change, in particular a reduction of the social height, if that patient metaphor will stand. If the exact meaning to give that phrase is still in doubt, we may pick out one last little strand from the bewildering tangle of social developments in twentieth-century England which may make it a little clearer. In 1901 personal domestic service was the major occupation of all the employed women of the country, a million and a half servants there were amongst the four million women at work. It was the largest occupational group for men or for women, larger than mining, engineering or agriculture. By the end of the First World War the numbers had fallen so far and so fast that there was an official inquiry. But even during the 1920s and 1930s when everyone, men or women, one might think, would have been glad of a job and when the demand was as great or greater, domestic servants continued to get fewer. By the 1930s they were down to half, though still a considerably sized occupation. By 1951 the female domestic servant had practically disappeared – all 'servants', men and women, in institutions and in houses numbered only about 175,000; in the same year the numbers of women in offices reached exactly the number of domestic servants in 1900. The price of domestic help has risen in the last forty years more than almost any other item of household expenditure, but servants are still not to be had. Englishwomen simply will no longer do the personal work for other Englishwomen, whoever they are asked to serve. The social height is too low.

Understanding ourselves in time
Chapter 12

It is very easy to show how important contrast is to understanding. The architect in his drawing and the painter in his picture both casually introduce some human figure, to give the onlooker a proper sense of scale and an opportunity to contrast the scene with himself. When the astronomer sets out to show us what our earth is like, he finds it important to talk about other planets, other sunlike stars, other solar systems. When he tells us that its diameter is 8000 miles, he also tells us that the diameter of Jupiter is 86,800 miles, and this adds to our understanding. In fact we feel we can understand fully only when we can confidently say 'It might have been otherwise', and give the details – what it would be like if the earth were hundreds of times as big, and five and a half times as far from the sun; how heavy things would be, how long the day, how cold the night.

The astronomer is genuinely interested in Jupiter for Jupiter's sake, quite apart from the comparison which that planet and all the others offer to him with our earth. In the same way the marine biologist is interested in the plankton of the sea and the geneticist in the varying types of drosophila fly, interested in them dispassionately and not simply for what they can tell us about our own environment and about how to devise ways in which we can control it. We call this attitude scientific, and a scientist will often insist that he has no other reason for this interest in what he works on.

We may look a little quizzically at a man who says this to us, but we must freely admit that men do not find out about their world exclusively with themselves in view. Or rather, for the point raises philosophical questions, the sense in which all human knowledge is knowledge for human purposes can be very general indeed and can be virtually ignored in such activities as pure mathematics and general scientific theory at large.

But it is true nevertheless that all human knowledge gets caught up into the overriding interest which we take in ourselves and in our doings. Even the pure mathematician, if asked what he is doing with himself, will talk in this way. The sort of scientific endeavour which everyone is disposed to call really important brings the two elements clearly into view. The theory of continuous creation of matter, for example, very much of the mid-twentieth century, was extraordinarily satisfying simply in the scientific sense of adding to knowledge. But the other interest it aroused, its possible effects on ourselves and our own experience, was even greater. If the theory was true, then the world had no beginning and would have no end, just as the universe had no boundary. Neither the time sequence nor the space continuum in which men live had any sort of boundary or limit. This was knowledge about ourselves and it fascinated us. Even now, when the theory seems likely to be abandoned as a part of 'scientific' explanation, something in the change which it made in our view of ourselves will remain for ever.

We may now turn with these very general considerations in our mind to the activity of the historians. Since we can only properly understand ourselves and our world, here and now, if we have something to contrast it with, the historians must provide that something. It is true that people and nations and cultures vary in the extent to which they wish to understand themselves in time in this way, but to claim that there has ever been a generation anywhere with no sense of history is to go too far. From this point of view therefore all historical knowledge is knowledge with a view to ourselves as we are here and now. But, and here is our second consideration, historical knowledge is also interesting in itself, objectively, 'scientifically' once more. It is in fact almost always of greater intrinsic interest than Jupiter's moons, or the wingspan of fly populations, because it is knowledge about people with whom we can identify ourselves.

Historical knowledge then, and the activity of the historian, need no apology. Without such knowledge we could not understand ourselves in contrast with our ancestors, and possessing it we also satisfy a spontaneous interest in the world around us and in the people who have been within it. Taken together, though with the emphasis on the first source of our interest, history often provides useful knowledge which we could not have in any other way. In order to know how to change and improve the National Health Service in our country, for example, it is necessary to know what it actually consists of and knowing that almost always means getting to know its history. So it is that politicians and administrators find themselves going through the story in chronological order; how before 1911 everyone in England had to pay for medical attention, although in New Zealand and in Germany health insurance was already in force; how in 1911 Mr Lloyd George got the first National Health Insurance act passed and how various acts succeeded it as the century went on, until in 1948 Mr Bevan and the Attlee government . . . and so on, and so on. The same sort of chronological explanation is necessary, along with some considerations about geography and economics of course, to understand why Poland will not fit into the Communist Bloc, or why it is that the Elgin marbles are in the British Museum and no longer on the site of the Parthenon.

Historical knowledge for use might perhaps be regarded as distinct from historical knowledge acquired to understand ourselves in time and to satisfy our curiosity about our past. But these distinctions need be pressed no further for our present purposes, and we must recognize that the functions of the historian which are implied by these elementary considerations scarcely make it likely that this subject will be a progressive one. If this is what the historian has to do, it is not to be expected that what he is doing in England today should be very different from what he has always been doing, here and elsewhere. There cannot be a 'new history' in quite the sense that Einstein founded a 'new physics' nor indeed a new branch of historical study of quite the type of radio astronomy, which is a new and very recent branch of physics as a whole in virtue of its subject matter. Nevertheless the shift of interest towards inquiries of the sort which are reported with such brevity and sketchiness in this book, ought perhaps to be called a new branch of history.

The phrase 'sociological history' has been occasionally used here as its title, but it might almost be better to use 'social structural history' instead. This new title is required first and foremost to register a distinction in subject matter, for confessedly historical writing has not previously concerned itself with births, marriages and deaths as such, nor has it dwelt so exclusively on the shape and development of social structure. But the outlook is novel as well as the material, at least in its emphasis. Perhaps the distinctive feature of the attitude is the frank acceptance of the truth that all historical knowledge, from one point of view, and that an important and legitimate one, is knowledge about ourselves, and the insistence on understanding by contrast.

From this flows an irreverent impatience with established conventions of the subject as it has been traditionally studied in our country. The search for contrasts in social arrangements leads one to demand that English society shall not be seen for itself alone, but alongside French, German, Spanish, Dutch, Italian, Scandinavian society, as one variation on the western European pattern. But even this cannot be wide enough. Russian and eastern European societies, Asian, African and Latin American societies too, are relevant to the study of our own, if contrast is what we are in need of. The object of the English historian of his own country may remain to get to know his own society, but now as one amongst others.

The search for contrast does not end even here. It is not simply geographical. We all know (and an exasperatingly imprecise thing it is to know) that in England and in western Europe we live in an 'advanced' industrial society, to be further described as a 'capitalist' as opposed to a 'socialist' industrial society. There are in the contemporary world societies which are not industrial at all in the sense given to the word here. These are the primitive societies, as we somewhat patronizingly call them, of Africa, Asia, Australia, South America and Oceania. But what is 'industrialization', what are 'socialist' and 'capitalist' economies, what indeed is 'society' and what is objectively known and knowable about the constitution of societies and the ways in which they cohere, change, evolve, solve their conflicts and fight them out?

These are questions which have had to concern us in this essay, but they cannot be called exclusively or even predominantly historical questions at all, even if the historian has his responsibilities in helping to answer them. They are to some extent economists' questions, and so fall within the province of the most exact and advanced of the social sciences. For this we should be grateful. But too great a reliance on exclusively economic analysis has led in the past to all the sterilities of the economic interpretation of history. The complete description of questions of this sort is sociological as well as economic, and one of the important discoveries of the contemporary historian has been that he has carried on as if this were not the case.

History, we now begin to recognize with some dismay, has been written as if questions about social structure and types of society, questions about causation too, were fairly straightforward and answerable by common sense and a little economics, the more the better, but always fairly elementary. Historians have in fact tended up till now to look upon that area of inquiry which we have called social structural as if they knew it all already. This unfortunate tendency might be called 'naïf sociologism'.

We must not, after all, exaggerate the importance of the differences between the new historical criticism and the old; no doubt the distinction between naïf and sophisticated sociologism, if that is what should now replace it, will look very uncertain to those who come after us. But the somewhat sudden recognition that historians have habitually attempted to solve complicated problems of social structure and social causation by guessing a little, with the help of a few insignificant statistics, has undoubtedly had a disconcerting effect. We have glanced back over our history books and found them full of the crudest sociological generalization, of highly unconvincing speculation on the nature of social development. This has led to scepticism, and it was inevitable that the new historical criticism should have begun by being negative. But we have chosen not to confine this essay merely to critical analysis, and to make an attempt at something more positive by the use of the method of overall contrast.

Some of the difficulties of deciding to compare rather than to recount, as historians ordinarily do, must have been evident throughout this essay, especially in the last chapter. So deeply embedded in the whole tradition of writing history is the feeling for development, process, evolution, for the necessity of knowing everything that happened in between, that the whole enterprise may seem wrong-headed, especially to those whose interests lie in the interval missed out here, the eighteenth and nineteenth centuries that is to say. To many it may seem unhistorical in the final sense, since it abandons the method of explanation by telling the story. Even the sympathetic critic may feel that it could only succeed at the very superficial and introductory level; directly there is time and available information to go at all deeply beneath the surface any impression that there could be two constants capable of entering into an intelligible contrast must soon disappear.

Perhaps this objection should be discussed a little further, for it is justified to a large extent. England in 1700 cannot be at all adequately described as wholly pre-industrial nor England in 1901 as wholly industrialized. A claim of this kind would have to assume in the first place that the expressions themselves have agreed and constant meanings, which they do not. Industrialization has been defined in almost as many ways as there have been historians and economists who have studied that elusive process. It assumes in the second place that the entity England was in fact without industry at the first chosen point and wholly industrialized at the second. There are many historians who could maintain that both these claims are quite without foundation, that the eighteenth century saw not the only but simply a particularly conspicuous 'industrial revolution', one of a series which goes far back beyond 1600 and still continues. Nothing can have been more obvious from the brief discussion of English society in recent times than that it has been in intensifying flux rather than in constant 'post-industrial' condition, and that many of the points of contrast with the world we have lost have made their appearance only very recently indeed.

It may be simple-minded or even rather worse than that, to respond by appealing again to the reader's ordinary familiarity with his own surroundings, especially in respect of the scale of life. Still it was not found necessary to insist that the working man since 1901 has ceased to do his daily work in the circle of his family and has become almost entirely subject to the discipline of the factory and the office, to the necessity of going there and back to work every day, to all the experience known as mass living. Surely we know all this in a much more straightforward way than the historian seems to think that he knows how society works at any time he chooses to study it. Of course if this leads people to suppose that because we all know that economic organization is no longer almost entirely a familial matter, that therefore the family no longer plays any part in economic life then it does become deceptive. Yet the self-evident importance of the overall comparison does justify its being drawn in heavy outline, and only a direct confrontation between our society before and after whatever it was that went on between 1700 and 1900 gives it sufficient emphasis. It does enable us to understand ourselves by saying with conviction: 'It might have been otherwise.'

The same point could be made for the other two heads which were chosen for twentieth-century England, though here the issues are more complex. When talking of the middle class in the twentieth century it was not necessary to compare directly the general similarities and differences between the ruling segment of the older world and the social and political establishment of the newer world, though some remarks had to be made about the pattern of social mobility. But surely it does not have to be elaborately reasoned that an élite minority cannot nowadays live the whole political, intellectual and social life of a whole country. We all know this already, in a way. We know that representative chambers, parties, elections in our system, the whole machinery of totalitarian politics elsewhere, have had to come into being because élitist politics cannot work in our world in the easy, spontaneous way described earlier on. When it comes to authority in contemporary politics and to the possibility of revolution, we may perhaps hesitate somewhat. But we recognize easily enough the profound difference in these crucial respects which has come with two very obvious and evident changes. These are the departure of a common religious belief shared by everyone, and the arrival of universal literacy and with it universal access to the public, political world. These must have much to do with the fact that revolutionism is now a credible political belief and actual social revolution a possible tactic. We all know also that the disappearance of servants means more than an inconvenience to the rich.

Historical contrast if too blankly presented may obliterate the subtler forms of change and survival. This was perhaps apparent in what was said about the country house in the politics of the old world and of the new, a topic which along with the many others urgently requires a defter and more informed analysis. Authoritarianism arising directly out of the patriarchal family in the manor house may have departed from the scene. But allegiance and submission to the father figure continue to play their parts in the psychology of politics, even if actual fathers now push prams and have thrown the rod away. The Pope, as was said elsewhere in trying to make old Sir Robert Filmer possible to believe in, is still Papa, and Stalin died Little Father to the Russian people.

Contrast over time, furthermore, might conceivably be allowed to divert attention from contrast over space, or rather cross-cultural comparison as the anthropologist might put it; understanding ourselves in time is after all understanding ourselves in one dimension only. It might be thought that it would be so much more illuminating to draw the comparison with the Trobriand Islanders, or the Nuer, or the Ainu of the Northern Island of Japan, vanishing survivals of societies wholly pre-industrial in everybody's sense and offering a much profounder depth of possible distinction. Only a glance or two has been made in this direction and the thorny problem of how to combine the different types of comparison, cultural and chronological, has been left on one side. Obviously there is much more to be said, and the beginnings of work on the feudal era in Europe as compared with contemporary African society may yet yield a great deal.

But it is an impressive fact that Louis Henry, when he made the first move towards a really scientific historical demography, the earliest element to appear in a properly sociological historical method, deliberately rejected contemporary under-developed societies in favour of the societies of our pre-decessors in western Europe. He wanted to get to know what 'natural fertility' was and he decided that he would be more likely to find out from the village of Crulai in Normandy over the seventeenth and eighteenth centuries than from any twentieth-century primitive society, however benevolently administered and however carefully counted and registered. His reasons were entirely statistical nevertheless; no extra-European unindustrialized society yet keeps its *état civil*, as the French say, its births, marriages, deaths and so on, with the accuracy of the parish priests and parish clerks even of Stuart England. This being so, quantitative comparison may perhaps not turn out to be as efficient for cross-cultural as it already is for chronological contrast.

Figures are not everything, even in our present mood of preferring any set of facts which can be counted over all those which arise from impressions, literary, legal and otherwise. The justification of the method chosen for understanding ourselves in time may seem to need sharper illustration. We may take it from the size, structure and function of the family and household.

The evidence about the household as it was in England before the industrial process began has been referred to on various occasions throughout this essay, though not presented in a systematic way. It seems to make impossible any belief that the independent, nuclear family-household of man, wife and children is an exclusive characteristic of industrialized society. When all allowance has been made for the very different assumptions about the English household which then obtained, and the very different kinship relationships too, it remains the case that there ordinarily slept together under each roof in 1600 only the nuclear family, with the addition of servants when necessary. Therefore in that respect our ancestors were not different from ourselves. They were the same.

The assumption seems to have been that the contrary was true, an assumption made not so much by historians, too preoccupied with traditional activities, but by the sociologists themselves. Much of the alienation discussion of our time seems to suppose that the horror of industrialization was in part the result of separating the nuclear family from the kin group and the kin group was usually conceived of in terms of joint or extended households.

There is more to this than a faulty account of how things have changed. Our whole view of ourselves is altered if we cease to believe that we have lost some more humane, much more *natural* pattern of relationships than industrial society can offer. When we inquire, for example, what we are trying to do for the lonely old people who are becoming so lamentably common as the twentieth-century decades go by, we find ourselves assuming that they must be restored to the family, where they belong. Perhaps none of those who write so urgently about these problems have a very clear notion of the situation which they are trying to restore. But few of them can have realized how inappropriate it is to think of restoration at all, in the sense of returning to the historical past. We have already talked of the identical error in relation to broken homes and the criminal tendency of our young people and shown that the problem of our ancestors in this regard may well have been worse, not better, than our own.

In fact, in tending to look backwards in this way, in diagnosing the difficulties as the outcome of something which has indeed been lost to our society, those concerned with social welfare are suffering from a false understanding of ourselves in time. Not completely false, of course; if that were so it would make nonsense of our general title. We have seen that in the traditional world the family did fulfil many functions which are left to very different institutions in our day, or which are not fulfilled at all.

But was it more 'natural' that this should have been so? Was *The World We Have Lost* a more appropriate one for human beings to dwell in? These are very vague and general questions, unlikely to be worth trying to answer in this book. But the point of importance to our argument is to have got into a position where such questions must arise. To recognize their urgency is also to begin to take a different view of our own place in time, and more than this. It may, perhaps ought, to change our view of what we should be trying to do. We can only begin to get into this position if we admit that historical knowledge is knowledge to do with ourselves, now.

Answering these questions does also yield objective knowledge about the past. The demonstration that the society of pre-industrial England maintained the principle that each marriage meant a new household, and that the whole social structure can be ranged round that one critical feature, could justifiably be claimed as an addition to 'scientific' knowledge, much of it very remote indeed from simply knowledge with a view to ourselves now. It may make a great deal of difference to the work of the anthropologist, the sociologist and the social sciences generally as well as to social history. The conviction that this piece of information belongs to a type of historical criticism previously little practised is suggested by the fact that the evidence on which it was based was not new, but always available in very obvious places.

This somewhat arrogant claim can perhaps be made most convincingly in respect of the liability of the peasants to starve, not exactly a part of the principle of the one-marriage household but closely connected with it. Hundreds of parish registers have been published in England, more than in any other country. This has meant that millions and millions of entries from obscurely written, badly preserved documents have been painfully transferred into print at considerable expense for the use of thousands of persons bent on tracing their ancestry. Apart from the biographers, no other users have ordinarily been found for them, and as we have seen it has occurred to no historian before the 1960s to try to see if the registers could tell us whether our ancestors did in fact sometimes die of starvation. Only in the last year or two have they realized that they could be used for the purpose of family reconstitution, and then only as a consequence of the pioneering work done in France.

A romantic might say that this looks like a breach of faith with the Cowlmans and the Lancasters who, it will be remembered, were two of the tiny group of families so far known to have starved in England, in the year 1623 at Greystoke. Perhaps this infidelity is merely a part of the inevitable tendency to look on past individuals as important and worth investigating only if they show forth some political, economic, social or intellectual trend which the historian is concerning himself with. The indifference to questions such as these looks peculiarly inhumane, a failing which comes from too much concern with abstractions. Still it is not for any generation of historians to condemn its predecessors too easily, for who can tell what blindness our successors will detect in us? The additions to the historical record which the close study of the contents of the humble parish registers will bring, may conceivably turn out to have their biological importance.

In order to undertake genetic analysis, it is necessary to be able to study a community of specimens over a number of generations, the more the better. The great disadvantage of human beings for genetic study is that the generation is so long. With drosophila it is possible to observe the passage of ten generations in a matter of days. With humans ten generations would take some 300 years to observe. Now 300 years happens to be within the period during which the registration of births, marriages and deaths can be studied from this evidence, and in England we can go back two or three generations further.

It is difficult as yet to see how this opportunity might be used. If we refer to the example of the age at sexual maturity which has been discussed in the text, we can see how vague and confusing the evidence is likely to be, even on a point which in principle might be examined from the bare facts appearing in the parish registers and on the forms used for the reconstitution of families. No one would yet venture to suppose that the problem of distinguishing a possible genetic element in the fall of the age at menarche from the effect of improved diet and living conditions can be solved. Nevertheless the evidence exists to make some initial study of recent human biological history. It is necessary for biology even more than for sociology to understand its subject matter in time, over the generations.

The historian cannot hope to make his contribution to studies of this sort unless he is rather differently equipped than he has previously been. He must obviously be something of a statistician; at least he must have that statistical expectation and caution which so clearly distinguishes the inquirer after truth from the creator of impressions. He must have some economics, some sociology, even conceivably some genetics, as well as anthropology. But it would be wrong to think of the historian of the newer sort solemnly sitting down to acquire this extra-historical knowledge before he even begins to examine the evidence or to write about it. What must come into being is a working community where the historian is in the confidence of the economists, the statisticians and the others. Nevertheless the responsibility for enabling us all to understand ourselves in time must still rest where it has always rested, on the historian as an individual.

It is sometimes said that Clio the Muse is dead and that history is no longer written as literature. Perhaps the difficult situation we have been trying to explain is to some extent responsible. Once the historian brings himself to recognize anew that what he knows he knows with a view to himself as well as with a view to the past, this situation may change again. Herodotus had no doubt that what he wrote was for his contemporaries, relevant above all to his own generation. Neither had Lord Clarendon, nor Lord Macaulay. Macaulay indeed, and this is why he is now criticized, was perfectly aware that England under Victoria was the culmination of the story he was telling, and that the past had to be appreciated where it anticipated that splendid era, recounted as leading up to and evolving into it. Though we must be suspicious of the evolutionary, culminatory element in this attitude we must envy him the frankness with which he came out with the story as it looked to him. He might find it difficult to understand why we, his successors, are so much less attracted to the task of making literature out of how the past looks to us.

Certainly the imaginative reconstruction of a former society can only foster an interest in its people as people. The shortcomings we have mentioned have been called failures in sympathy as well as of method, and if the future is to see the historian in partnership with the other social scientists, it is important that he should never lose sight of his humanity. Naïf sociologism may indeed have come into existence because of an unwilling and largely unaware subservience of the historical imagination to the dogmatic social principles of an earlier generation. These principles dealt exclusively with those rise-of-a-class interpretations which have been criticized here, together with their wearisome insistence on cataclysm, crisis and revolution.

There has been a tendency in fact for English historians to give currency to certain features of Marxian historical sociology, which they have made no conspicuous effort to understand, perhaps because its political associations have been so inimical to them. Advantage was not taken in creating from it historical hypotheses at a time when it really was a novel and developing system. At the present time this half-recognized attachment stands in the way of a confessedly sociological historical criticism of the type we have tried to recommend. In such a new historical criticism the Marxian element in sociological thought because of its explanatory power will play a formidable part.

Perhaps too much fuss has been made here of what in the end will turn out to be just another swirl of opinion which is not simply historical. It could easily be shown that the interest historians are beginning to take in the contrast between English and European society before and after industrialization is also an interest recently acquired by politicians and economists, though their eyes are turned on 'underdeveloped countries' in the present world for the most part. Nevertheless I have no doubt myself that the sort of questions which arise out of an attempt to explore our own, contemporary, late twentieth-century relationship with what we have called the world we have lost could have arisen from no previously established form of historical inquiry. History, I believe, is about to claim a new and more important place in the sum total of human knowledge.

General note

Progress in the publication of research results has made referencing considerably easier than it was in earlier printings of the book. The five most quoted volumes have been given abbreviated titles:

HFPT   *Household and Family in Past Time: Comparative Studies in the Size and Structure of the Domestic Group Over the Last Three Centuries*, edited by Peter Laslett with the assistance of Richard Wall, Cambridge, 1972.

FLIL   *Family Life and Illicit Love in Earlier Generations*, by Peter Laslett, Cambridge, 1977.

Bastardy   *Bastardy and its Comparative History: Studies in the History of Illegitimacy in Britain, France, Germany, Sweden, North America, Jamaica and Japan*, edited by Peter Laslett, Karla Oosterveen and Richard Smith, 1980.

W and S   *The Population History of England, 1540–1870: A reconstruction*, by E. A. Wrigley and R. S. Schofield, 1981.

Famforms   *Family Forms in Historic Europe*, by Richard Wall with J. Robin and Peter Laslett, Cambridge, 1983.

Sources for Demographic and Social Structural History being assembled and analysed by the Cambridge Group for the History of Population and Social Structure.

The specific source in unpublished documents for the first edition of *The World We Have Lost* was the embryo of the collection of listings of inhabitants of English communities before 1801, which has now become one of the files (File 3 in the succeeding notes) of the Cambridge Group for the History of Population and Social Structure. This file remains the most important for the development of the studies described in an introductory way in the present work, but all the other files of the Group are relevant to them, and have been used. The present research objectives and procedures of the Group are described by Roger Schofield, the executive director, in the *SSRC Newsletter*, 44,

November 1981, under the title 'Group for the history of
population and social structure'.

A current bibliography of the publications issued or in
preparation by the Cambridge Group for the History of
Population and Social Structure, a Unit of the Social
Science Research Council, may be obtained from its
Cambridge address, 27 Trumpington Street, Cambridge,
CB2 1QA.

FILE 1 – *Reconstitution*

Select English parishes, at present 30 in all: Southill plus
Campton-with-Shefford, Bedfordshire; Willingham,
Cambridgeshire; Eccleshall, Cheshire; Bridford, Colyton,
Dawlish, Hartland, Ipplepen, Kenton, Moreton Hampstead
and Thurleston, Devonshire; Terling and Great Oakley,
Essex; Aldenham, Hertfordshire; Ash-next-Sandwich,
Kent; Hawkeshead, Lancashire; Ashby-de-la-Zouch,
Bottesford and Shepshed, Leicestershire; Gainsborough,
Lincolnshire; Hartley and Seaton within Earsdon parish,
Whickham, Northumberland; Gedling, Nottinghamshire;
Banbury, Oxfordshire; Odiham, Staffordshire; Alcester and
Austrey, Warwickshire; Easingwold and Great Ayton,
Yorkshire (North Riding); Birstall and Methley, Yorkshire
(West Riding).

The process of family reconstitution has been or is being
carried out on these select parishes, and the operations
themselves are being computerized. The derivation of
demographic statistics from the reconstituted family forms
(FRFs) is now done entirely by machine. The methods of
family reconstitution are described by E. A. Wrigley, in
Wrigley (ed.), *An Introduction to English Historical
Demography*, 1966. In his article in the *Transactions of the
Royal Historical Society*, 1971, Schofield gives the briefest and
perhaps the most useful description of the technique with an
indication of its usefulness to historians, demographic, social,
social structural. From family reconstitution it is possible to
recover quite exact information on such matters as age-
specific birth rates and death rates together with age and
order within family at marriage, for a series of overlapping
samples of the inhabitants of parishes concerned alongside
of less complete evidence on expectation of life, prenuptial
pregnancy and infantile mortality. The development of back

projection (see File 2) has reduced the importance of family reconstitution to some degree.

FILE 2 – *Aggregative analyses*

Returns from about 750 English parish registers, being monthly totals of baptisms, marriages and burials from 1538 (the beginning of ecclesiastical registration in England) until 1837 (the final year before civil registration began). These parishes are mostly fairly large (with a population of 1000 or above in 1801), are rural rather than urban, and were selected with a view to the requirements of reconstitution rather than from the point of view of typicality. No London parish is present. The collection, then, which is still growing through the activities of volunteers who do the extraction of figures locally for the Group, is by no means a random sample of all 10,000 English parishes, and the geographical spread is uneven. Nevertheless, the collection as a whole represents a twentieth of all parishes and perhaps a tenth, an eighth or even more of all such recordings that were ever made before 1838. The file already constitutes the largest body of historical demographic data ever assembled for any country. W and S is a presentation of the results of analysing the statistics of 404 of these sets of returns, weighted and modified in such a way as to represent the whole population of the country. Many of these outcomes were derived by means of a technique developed out of a model due to Ronald Lee of the University of California, Berkeley, and called *Back Projection*. This technique allows for the establishment of such measures as expectation of life at birth, crude demographic rates (birth rates, marriage rates, death rates), more sophisticated ones (e.g. gross reproductive rates), age composition, and proportions emigrating, to be calculated for the whole English population at five-year intervals between 1561 and 1871 as well as totals of population.

FILE 3 – *Listings*

Photographs of lists of inhabitants dating from before the English Census (1801) with some up to 1841, after which the Census began the satisfactory recording of relationships within households. This file lies behind much of the text of the present book, but it must be said that only a few of the

workings for individual settlements are cited and that
research has proceeded much further than the discussion
here implies. There are some 600 documents in this file,
which also represents the largest such collection yet made
for any country. Lists of inhabitants from the rest of
Europe (especially Scotland, Ireland, France, Germany,
Austria, Hungary, Italy, Belgium and Russia) and from
elsewhere (particularly Japan) are being added to the
collection, some of them in the ideographic form developed
for the purpose of exchange between different languages (see
HFPT, pp. 41 and 42). Unfortunately the English and Welsh
lists are concentrated in some areas (Kent, London,
Westmorland, Staffordshire) and rare or absent in others
(e.g. Lincolnshire, Oxfordshire, Cornwall, Cheshire), and
common at some dates (the 1690s and the 1790s) and not at
other times. Copies of the enumerators' books from the 1851,
1861, 1871 and 1881 censuses are being added to the
collection.

The original techniques for hand analysis were described
in Laslett's contribution to Wrigley (ed.), *An Introduction to
English Historical Demography*, 1966, modified and extended
in *HFPT* in 1972. The classificatory scheme for household
types printed in that volume (p. 31) has been developed into
the version in Table 17. The results for the listing of the
inhabitants of Clayworth are there presented, but the
scheme can be, and has been, used for hundreds of other
lists of various dates and from many countries.

FILE 4 – *Literacy (file closed in the mid-1970s)*

Returns from a random sample of 300 English parish
registers recording ability to sign the marriage register, by
sex and (where possible) by occupation, from the date 1754
when such signing was first required until the 1840s. Only
limited use of this file has been made here. A series of results
from this file have been published by Roger Schofield and
David Cressy, see especially Cressy, *Literacy and the Social
Order*, Cambridge, 1980.

FILE 5 – *Parameters*

Details of select ecological characteristics for every
community represented in Files 1–4, that is to say over
1200 English settlements.

Table 17: *Analysis of the kin composition of households – at Clayworth, Notts., 1676*

Household type	Class		Number of households	Proportion of all households (%)
1 Solitaries (singletons in households)	1a Given as widowed		3	3
	1b Given as non-married or of unknown marital status		4	4
		SUBTOTAL	7	7
2 No-family households (co-residents amongst whom no conjugal family unit can be discerned)	2a Co-resident siblings		1	1
	2b Other co-resident relatives		0	0
	2c Co-residents with no familial relationship given		0	0
		SUBTOTAL	1	1
3 Simple-family households (conjugal family units only)	3a Married couples without offspring		8	8
	3b Married couples with offspring		52	53
	3c Widowers with offspring		5	5
	3d Widows with offspring		13	13
		SUBTOTAL	78	79
4 Extended-family units (conjugal family units having kin-linked individuals)	4a Extension upwards (of which 0 have fathers and 2 mothers)		4	4
	4b Extension downwards (of which 0 have grandchildren only)		2	2
	4c Extension sideways (of which 0 have brothers only and 1 sisters only)		1	1
	4d Combinations of 4a–4c, or any other form of extension		2	2
		SUBTOTAL	9	9
5 Multiple-family households (two or more kin-linked conjugal family units)	5a Households with secondary units disposed upwards from head (of which also extended)			
	5b Households with secondary units disposed downwards from head (of which also extended)			
	5c Households with secondary units disposed sideways from head, member of parental generation being present (of which also extended in other directions)			
	5d *Frérèches* households with secondary units disposed sideways from head, no member of parental generation (of which also extended)			
	5e Combination of 5a–5d, or any other multiple household arrangement (of which also extended)			
		SUBTOTAL	—	—
6 Indeterminate	(Households where kin linkages are insufficient for classification in any category above)		0	0
		SUBTOTAL	0	0
			2	2
		SUBTOTAL	2	2
		TOTAL	98	100

Population 401

Notes to the text

In the Notes which follow, all titles are published in
London unless otherwise stated. Some are published in both
London and New York.

The following abbreviations are used instead of the titles
of journals:

EcHR	*Economic History Review*, second series
JIH	*Journal of Interdisciplinary History*
LPS	*Local Population Studies*
P and P	*Past and Present*
Pop Studs	*Population Studies*

CHAPTER 1 *English society before and after the coming
of industry*

1 See Sylvia Thrupp, *History of the Bakers' Company of
London*, Croydon, 1933, p. 17, etc.

2 'No baker should sell bread in his own house or shop,
but only in the open market, and only on Wednesday or
Saturday.' This was an immemorial rule of the London
bakers and was in full operation in Stuart times (see
Thrupp, *Bakers' Company*, p. 35), but it would be
unjustifiable to assume that it was the practice in all trades
and in all towns. Undoubtedly too some London tradesmen
lived in houses apart from their shops. See *The Inhabitants
of London in 1638*, edited by T. C. Dale for the Society of
Genealogists, 1931, and for shopping in the open air,
without wrappings, without even coins enough to pay, see
Dorothy Davis, *A History of Shopping*, 1966.

3 See Edmund S. Morgan, *The Puritan Family: Religion
and Domestic Relations in 17th-century New England*, New
York, 1966 (revised and enlarged; 1st edn, Boston, 1944),
especially p. 42 and references. In New England, as in Old,
wives often ran the family finances, but the most impressive
evidence of the managerial functions of officially subordinate
wives is found when the husband was imprisoned or
otherwise incapacitated. This can be seen in the letters
written by the wives of royalist gentlemen taken captive
during the English Civil Wars.

4   Indenture between William Selman, husbandman, his son Richard, and Thomas Stokes, broadweaver, of Wiltshire, signed in 1705. The wording is conventional and it is evident that its provisions were not always carried out, even as to residing with the master. We have found that the actual numbers of apprentices, formally so called, seem to have been somewhat exaggerated by historians, and indeed by contemporaries. Of 1739 males in the position of servants in the sample of 100 English parishes from Cambridge Group, File 3 (including nine London parishes) (see Peter Laslett, 'Size and structure of the household in England over three centuries', *Pop Studs*, 1969, XXIII, no. 2, 199–223) only 229, less than an eighth, were called apprentices. That 'servants' included the status of apprentice nevertheless is clear from all the sources, and especially from the city of Bristol in 1696. There up to 70 per cent of males called 'servant' in a taxation return were found to have been apprenticed; see Elizabeth Ralph and M. E. Williams, 'The inhabitants of Bristol in 1696', *Bristol Record Society Publications*, 1968, xxv, xxiii–xxiv.

5   Paper for Board of Trade, 1697, printed in H. R. Fox Bourne, *Life of John Locke*, 1876, II, pp. 377ff. The work, and the schooling, of English children at this period are well described with a mass of detail, from literary sources for the most part, by I. Pinchbeck and M. Hewitt, *Childhood in English Society*, I, *From Tudor Times to the 18th Century* (1972 (1969)).

6   For servants, see note 17 of Chapter 1, and for age at leaving home, see R. Wall, 'The age at leaving home', *Journal of Family History*, 3, no. 2, 181–202. The present interest in servants has sometimes led to an exaggeration of their numbers and of the proportion of all children who were at any one time in service. This always seems to have been a minority in England, at least in the sixteenth to eighteenth centuries, though a very large proportion of all children must have been servants at some time between maturity and marriage. It is a serious distortion to look on the institution of service as almost entirely a female affair, arising in the nineteenth century amongst the bourgeoisie.

7   There is evidence, however, that subordinate persons could quite easily conceive of a society without their social superiors, or even of disposing of such persons: see Chapter 8. Familistic ideology seems to have varied from area to area of traditional Europe, being particularly strong in England: see Peter Laslett, 'Family and household as work group and kin group', in *Famforms*. It is there insisted that by no means all, perhaps only a minority, can have lived in groups like that of a London master-baker at any time in England, even in the Middle Ages.

8   Grimm's *Fairy Tales* were first issued in German in 1812–14, but were translated into English at once, to swell the repertory of such literature already becoming popular. It may be significant in view of the origin of Marxist social protest in the same country at the same time that traditional industrial life seems to have been romanticized on the widest scale in Germany.

9   For the movement of servants between settlements and settlements, see pp. 75–7.

10   See the remarkable listing of the inhabitants of this community in the *Newdigate Papers* at the Warwick Record Office, C.R. 136, 12, pp. 64ff. (A full discussion of household and family in past time, with suggested definitions and principles of analysis, will be found in *HFPT*, ch. 1.) J. Hajnal, 'Two kinds of household formation system', in *Famforms*, describes the differences between western European especially English family households in the past, and those of China and India. He remarks on the paradox that in spite of these differences, they had a similar *average* size.

11   For the (often manufactured) permanence of noble family lines, see Chapter 10.

12   On the county musters see E. E. Rich, 'The population of Elizabethan England', in *EcHR*, 1950, II, 3, and for a very revealing record of one of them, John Smith of Nibley, *Men and Armour for Gloucestershire*, 1608, published 1902.

13   Cromwell commanded 26,000 or 27,000 men at Marston
Moor, and this must have been one of the largest organized
crowds ever to have assembled before Napoleonic times in
England. The greatest strength of the armed forces was
70,000 for a brief period under the Commonwealth; see
C. H. Firth, *Cromwell's Army*, 1902, p. 35. No doubt the
unorganized crowds which assembled in London during the
parliamentary crisis of the 1640s were of considerable size,
but little has been done on English evidence of this period
to rival George Rudé's study of *The Crowd in the French
Revolution*, Oxford, 1959.

14   On markets, market days and market areas, see Alan
Everitt, 'The marketing of agricultural produce', in
J. Thirsk (ed.), *The Agrarian History of England and Wales*,
IV, *1500–1640*, Cambridge, 1967. There is a list of schools in
W. A. L. Vincent, *The State and School Education, 1640–
1660, in England and Wales*, 1950, but Cressy insists that
their numbers at any time are very elusive: see David
Cressy, *Literacy and the Social Order: Reading and Writing in
Tudor and Stuart England*, Cambridge, 1980, pp. 164–74 etc.

15   For the builders see D. Knoop and G. P. Jones, *The
Medieval Mason*, Manchester, 1933, and various articles on
this theme. For large-scale industry and its organization,
various articles by J. U. Nef, especially that in the *EcHR*,
1934. For the miners, G. R. Lewis, *The Stannaries*, 1908;
J. W. Gough, *The Mines of Mendip*, Oxford, 1930; and
J. U. Nef, *The Rise of the British Coal Industry*, 2 vols,
1932.

16   *Institutional living and widowed persons*
The numbers, size and organization of almshouses instituted
between 1480 and 1660 are amongst the subjects dealt with
for London and select counties by W. K. Jordan in his
three important volumes on philanthropy during that period
– *Philanthropy in England*, 1959; *The Charities of London*,
1960; *The Charities of Rural England*, 1961. Few seem to
have contained more than a dozen or twenty inmates, but
in 1660 something like 1400 people may have been living in
such institutions in London. This was out of a population of
something like 400,000, and the rarity of institutional living

in the old world can be judged from the fact that in our
sample of 100 pre-industrial villages, only 335 people of a
total of some 70,000 were living in this way: see Laslett,
'Size and structure', p. 207. As for the situation of widowed
persons not in institutions, 74 per cent of all widowers
headed their own households, 18 per cent were in the
households of others, and 7 per cent were solitary. The
figures for widows are 58 per cent heading households,
24 per cent in the households of others and 14 per cent
solitary; compare *FLIL*, p. 204.

17 *Servants*
Servants made up 13·4 per cent of the total population of
our 100 villages (see *HFPT*, p. 152); 28·5 per cent of all
households had servants, and the sex ratio was 107, that is
to say there were 107 men and boys for 100 women and
girls. For the actual number of men and women in service in
England by age, see *FLIL*, Table 1–7, poor estimates
because the evidence is scanty. For much more reliable
figures from Denmark, see Hajnal, 'Household formation
system'. Ann Kussmaul, *Servants in Husbandry in Early
Modern England*, 1981, is the authoritative treatment of
male servants in agriculture.

18   See Laslett, 'Family and household', citing the work of
Charles Phythian-Adams, *Desolation of a City*, Cambridge,
1979. For the age at leaving for service, see Wall, 'Age at
leaving home', where it is emphasized that service before
the age of ten was very rare, that children left home at
various ages in their teens (boys before girls) and that some
stayed till marriage.

19   The quotation is from Richard Steele, *The
Husbandman's Calling*, 2nd edn, 1672, pp. 76 and 86.

20   *Farm family bye-employments*
The great importance to the budgets of modest working
families of activities pursued at home is clear from many
sources. Some (for example a remarkable listing in
Cambridge Group, File 3 for the village of Corfe Castle in
Dorset in 1790) actually list the pittances gained by wives,
teenage boys and girls, dependent widows, etc. 'Knits' is

the commonest description of the method of getting pennies. The desperate poverty of the countryside of late Victorian times was due in part to the disappearance of these rural bye-employments; for example Ridgmont in 1903, cited on p. 250.

21   Karl Marx and Friedrich Engels, *Manifesto of the Communist Party*, 1848, in *Selected Works*, Moscow, 1951, I, p. 35.

22   *Capitalism and industrialization*
The tendency of recent economic historians, especially those with a Marxist bent, has been to distinguish *industrial* capitalism, the capitalism associated with large-scale enterprise which first appeared early in the nineteenth century, from capitalism generally. The authoritative source for this view is Maurice Dobb, *Studies in the Development of Capitalism*, 1946. The transformation of family life referred to in the present work must be taken to mean the drastic reduction and now the virtual disappearance of the productive employment-providing functions of the household, the removal of the site of economic activity from the family dwelling.

23   See Steele, *Husbandman's Calling*, p. 104.

CHAPTER 2   *A one-class society*

1   The analysis of the ascription of status among the office-holders of Cheshire, extremely illuminating in many directions, is contained in Graham Kerby, 'Inequality in a pre-industrial society: a study of wealth, status, office and taxation in 17th-century Cheshire', PhD dissertation, Cambridge, 1983. See also Andrew Sharp, 'The English lay peerage and heraldic thinking during the Civil Wars and Interregnum', PhD dissertation, Cambridge, 1971, and his article 'Edward Waterhouse's view of social change in 17th-century England', *P and P*, 62, 1971. As for the title 'gentry' in the parish registers, it occurred in 2 per cent of all entries for eight rural parishes and for one town (Otley) between 1721 and 1740, May Pickles in *LPS*, 1976, 16.

'Professions' accounted for another 2 per cent in this
source. At Manchester in the earlier seventeenth century,
'gentry' was commoner. Between 1653 and 1655, 3·9 per
cent of 2380 burial entries contained some title like
'gentleman' or a higher status denomination, and the
addition of those marked 'Mr' or 'Mrs' brought the total
up to 11·3 per cent. There was a general tendency for titles
to be commoner in urban areas.

2   The Statute of Artificers, (5 Eliz. c. 4), para. IV, quoted
from R. H. Tawney and E. Power, *Tudor Economic
Documents*, 1924 (1951), I, p. 342, modernized.

3   Serjeant Thorpe, judge of assize for the Northern
Circuit, his charge to the Grand Jury at York Assizes,
20 March 1648, printed in *Harleian Miscellany*, II, 1744,
p. 12.

4   Gregory King's table, never published by that elusive
and unforthcoming author, was first printed in a book of
his friend Charles Davenant in 1699, and has been
reprinted many times since, in various versions. See *The
Earliest Classics*, Farnborough, 1973, which includes some
of King's workings for his *Observations*. The question
of the accuracy of King's often slapdash estimates is
discussed in that edition, but it has been a subject of debate
since then. Geoffrey Holmes ('Gregory King and the social
structure of pre-industrial England', *Transactions of the
Royal Historical Society*, 1977, 41–69) has shown how
backward looking and biased King was, and how he seems
deliberately to have played down certain figures for highly
conservative, political reasons. Peter Lindert and Geoffrey
Williamson ('Revising England's social tables, 1688–1867',
Dept. of Economics, University of California, Davis,
Working Paper Series No. 176, Sept. 1981) have replaced
his estimates with independent figures of their own, with
often discouraging results for those who would take King's
digits at face value. In the present text King's propositions
rather than his actual figures are the important thing, his
descriptions and the network of social relationships which
they imply.

5   See the very important article of D. C. Coleman, 'Labour in the English economy of the 17th century', in the *EcHR*, 1956, VIII, 3, for the implications of King's statements about decreasing and increasing the wealth of the Kingdom, i.e. the presence of transfer incomes on a large scale, see Peter Laslett, 'Household and family as work group and kin group', in *Famforms*.

6   Sir Thomas Smith, *The Commonwealth of England* (1560s), published 1583, edition of 1635, p. 66. The parish records of the seventeenth century make it clear that labourers did hold office as churchwardens and constables, and often attempted administrative tasks beyond their capacities as readers and writers. See particularly, Keith Wrightson, *English Society, 1580–1680*, 1982.

7   William Harrison, *Description of England*, 1577 etc., pp. 113–14.

8   Act of 12 Car. II. c. 9.

9   Christopher Hill, in the many considerations he has given to the subject since the 1940s (see note 1 of Chapter 8), seems to come to this conclusion, following Brough Macpherson (*The Political Theory of Possessive Individualism*, Oxford, 1962). E. P. Thompson apparently looks on the gentry and aristocracy of eighteenth-century England as an outstanding instance of a capitalist class in possession. For these views, and these developments of opinion, see R. S. Neale, *Class in English History*, Oxford, 1981, an interesting and useful book where the positions of such writers, along with those of Laslett, Perkin and others, are gone over with what may be called racy abandon. His comparison with the social structure of Tokugawa Japan seems to be peculiarly inappropriate, however.

10   No more general claim is made for the definitions of class and status in the text than that they seem to correspond to uses made of the concepts in the loose discussions of historians, particularly Marxian and post-Marxian historians. In technical Marxian analysis they

tended, at least before the change in emphasis recorded in the preceding note, to regard the emergent bourgeoisie of Stuart times as a class for 'itself', taking action, revolting or attempting to do so. Obviously if the common work-situation of individuals be taken as the critical characteristic of class ('class in itself') as for example by David Lockwood (see *The Blackcoated Worker*, 1958) or if 'the way a man is treated by his fellows' is taken to be its essence, as it is by T. H. Marshall (*Citizenship and Social Class*, Cambridge, 1950), it would be possible to identify many social classes in Stuart England. But none of them, it is being claimed, was likely ever to become a 'class for itself', that is to come into relation with other such classes, in such a way that collective group conflict, like the Civil War of 1642–8, could have been created.

11   In his very useful study of the gentry (*The Gentry: The Rise and Fall of a Ruling Class*, 1976) G. E. Mingay fails to include the nobility as part of the gentry and states that 'gentleman' was originally the description of the younger sons, brothers and grandsons of esquires. I have not seen these claims in any discussion of the topic by a Stuart author and I believe that usages described in the text were well established at the time.

12   See T. H. Hollingsworth, 'The demography of the British peerage', supplement to *Pop Studs*, XVIII, no. 2 (Nov. 1964). Nearly 40 per cent of peers' sons born between 1550 and 1674 married daughters of peers; this proportion fell to 25 per cent for peers born 1700–49. D. N. Thomas, 'The social origins of the marriage partners of the British peerage in the 18th and 19th centuries', *Pop Studs*, 1971, XXVI, n . 1, 99, shows that peers marrying outside their order chose mostly partners from the gentry, but married extensively into the bourgeoisie and the professional classes, sometimes even into the lower levels of society.

13   See Kerby, 'Inequality', and Sharp, 'English lay peerage' and 'Edward Waterhouse'. Kerby is particularly anxious to dispose of the belief that England was an estate society.

14   For a somewhat different view of the gentry and the general divide between the élite and the rest coming at the gentry line, see Kerby, 'Inequality', Mingay, *The Gentry*, and Wrightson, *English Society*, ch. 1 (with its references). They tend to stress the continuity of the social hierarchy rather more than is done in the text, playing down the sharp distinction between gentry and the rest. For Kerby there is nothing particularly special about the gentry as a social group; they were simply richer than most yeomen and poorer than most esquires, and individuals amongst them were frequently called by other than gentle names. In his view the distinctions so often insisted on existed much more clearly in the minds of persons like Gregory King and in those of historians than they did in the minds of seventeenth-century English people, especially of the poorer people.

15   6 and 7 William and Mary, c. 6. This Act, and the returns to which it gave rise up to the time of its repeal in 1705, are of great importance to English history, both demographic and sociological. The listings of inhabitants in Cambridge Group, File 3, on which so much has to be based, are commoner for the period 1695–1705 than for any other in pre-census times, and there is a danger that our view of pre-industrial social structure as a whole may for this reason (and because of the connected work over the same years of Gregory King, see note 4 of Chapter 2) be true of the 1690s only. The Act, its origin, its importance, its research possibilities, its workings, are authoritatively discussed by Professor Glass in 'Two papers on Gregory King', in D. V. Glass and D. E. C. Eversley (eds), *Population and History*, 1965.

16   See note 8 of Chapter 2. In the twelve first companies (Goldsmiths, Drapers, etc.) the assessment went like this: master £10 (equivalent to that for an esquire), liveryman £5 (equivalent to that for a gentleman – the liverymen were ex-masters or potential masters and of the same social standing), yeoman £3 (above a clergyman, £2, but below a gentleman).

17   *The poverty line in seventeenth-century England*
The families which Gregory King names as making up that

half of the population which was 'decreasing the wealth of
the kingdom' seem a rather miscellaneous assemblage:
seamen, 'labouring people and outservants', cottagers and
paupers, common soldiers and vagrants. Evidently King
was not anxious to be specific about the poor, and the
major interest in these descriptions is what they did not
include. He did not judge 'shopkeepers and tradesmen',
'artisans and handicrafts' to be in permanent poverty since
he places them above the 'decreasing' line, but this does
not mean that the carpenters, bricklayers, masons, thatchers,
weavers, coopers and so on were always out of poverty. It
seems much more likely that they were in poverty at certain
times of their lives, or in bad seasons, or for some weeks
even in good seasons, but not perpetually dependent in the
way that labourers, cottagers, paupers and the common
soldiery were. This was the pattern of the industrial
proletariat in the late nineteenth century and the early
twentieth century when they were studied by Rowntree and
Booth (see Chapter 11).

The statement in the text is true if King's estimates are
reliable. In an economy of the type he was describing any
person in receipt of a transfer income from the wealthier
people must surely be in need of such an income in order to
subsist, and this is the sense in which it seems best to
understand King's concept of 'increasing or decreasing' the
national wealth. It is very difficult to believe that such
transfers were taking place in order to equalize wealth, or to
add to the incomes of those who already had enough to
keep them out of poverty. No doubt such transfers did go
on in favour of the craftsmen who were sometimes liable to
poverty, but on balance craftsmen appear to have been
self-sufficient, which was perhaps why King did not think of
them as permanently among the decreasers. Compare Peter
Laslett, Introduction to *The Earliest Classics*.

18   Harrison, *Description of England*, p. 115.

19   William Lambarde, *Perambulation of Kent*, 1570, published 1576, reprinted at Chatham, 1826, p. 6, modernized.

20   Thomas Westcote, *A View of Devonshire in 1630*,
edited by G. Oliver and P. Jones, Exeter, 1845.

21   Thomas Wilson, *The State of England,* 1600, edited by F. J. Fisher, 1936 (1600), Camden Society publication Lii, p. 20.

22   See for example Sir John Doddridge, *Honors Pedigree,* 1652. The argument seems to have gone on since Elizabethan times, and Sir Thomas Smith took the minority view that apprenticeship did derogate from gentry.

23   *Urban gentry*
See *The Visitations of London, 1633, 1634 and 1635,* 2 vols, 1880–3. On merchants who had country houses at an earlier time, see Sylvia Thrupp, *The Merchant Class of Medieval London,* Ann Arbor, Mich., 1962, and on city/country dynasties, Sir Anthony Wagner, *English Genealogy,* Oxford, 1960, p. 141, etc. As for gentry resident in cities, 4 of the 67 families resident in the London parish of St Mary le Bow in 1695 of known status (74 families in all) were described as gentry, and 16 of 205 (255) in the similar parish of St Peter Mancroft, Norwich, in 1694. There were 91 gentlemen, 21 esquires, 8 knights and a baronet in Bristol in 1696. All these proportions are higher than the estimate for the population at large.

24   Westcote, *View of Devonshire,* p. 52. On working families, see Laslett, 'Household and family'.

25   *Some Considerations of the Consequences of Lowering of Interest,* 1692, *Works,* 1801, 5, p. 71.

CHAPTER 3   *The village community*

1   See A. M. Carr-Saunders, D. Caradog Jones and C. A. Moser, *A Survey of Social Conditions in England and Wales as Illustrated by Statistics,* Oxford, 1958 (using the 1951 census), pp. 50–5.

2   For the size of London on the eve of industrialization, see Roger Finlay, *Population and Metropolis: the Demography of London 1580–1650,* Cambridge, 1981, p. 51. The city had 50,000 people in 1500, 70,000 in 1550, 200,000 in 1600, 400,000 in 1650, 575,000 in 1700, 675,000 in 1750,

and 900,000 in 1800. Tokyo is reckoned to have numbered a
million people in the Tokugawa period, 1615–1868, and
Japan may well have been more urbanized in the great city
sense than any other country, since Kyoto and Osaka are
said to have numbered up to half a million. (Paper on *Town
and City in Pre-Modern Japan*, c. 1967, communicated by
Prof. R. J. Smith of the Department of Anthropology,
Cornell University.)

3 *Size of villages*
The Wingham area documents are in the Kent County
Record Office. The difficulty with them, as with all
problems of size of settlement, is the extent to which each
named place in fact represented an independent community
and not just an arbitrary area which existed for some
traditional or administrative reason. Certainly the sixteen
populations with less than 100 people, nearly half of the
sample, look rather suspect as villages, and some of them
may have been gentlemen's seats rather than settlements.
Nevertheless the distribution of settlements by size is
known to be usually pronouncedly skewed in a negative
direction, and in the nineteenth-century English censuses,
places of under 100 inhabitants were still common. In 1801,
of 100 named places, 14 were smaller than 100, the mean
size was 476 and the median 273. In 1871 the median was
still as low as about 380, and 12 per cent were smaller than
100. In both census years 15 per cent of the whole
population was living in settlements of less than median
size and in 1801 only a quarter in settlements of the order
of the English pre-industrial city centre, that is places of
3000 inhabitants and more. By 1871 this proportion had
more than doubled and was soon to treble.

4 The figures for London and other cities are based on
Finlay, *Population*, Table 1.1. For the smaller places see
Glass, 'Two papers on Gregory King', in D. V. Glass and
D. E. C. Eversley (eds), *Population and History*, 1965,
p. 186. His figures from 'other cities and market towns' are
much larger than Finlay's. The source excerpted there is a
manuscript notebook of King's called by Glass the Kashnor
Manuscript, and now in the National Library of Australia.
King's table (MS p. 2) is in the form of totals of *houses*, not

individuals, for each town and in the text of figures have
been converted into populations by the use of the multiple
4·45 persons to a house, the figure which Glass shows was
the one used by King himself.

5   See Pierre Goubert, *Beauvais et les Beauvaisis de 1600 à
1730*, Paris, 1960. On p. 255 he prints a list of the number
of *feux* in the thirty-five towns coming after the three
greatest from lists dating from 1718 and 1726. They have
been converted into the approximations given in the text by
multiplying by five. Professor Goubert tells me that in
France the urbanized population was nevertheless not so
much greater in proportion than it was in England. It was
the lack of an urban polity, of a city which could also be a
state, which marked out our country even more than the
small number of great urban centres.

6   E. A. Wrigley, 'A simple model of London's importance
in changing English society and economy, 1650–1750', in
P. Abrams and E. A. Wrigley (eds), *Towns in Society*,
Cambridge, 1978, p. 221. I am grateful to this writer for
help with urbanization at this period.

7   See Chapter 7, and *Bastardy*, pp. 63–4. Confirmation for
early-seventeenth-century London is to be found in
Finlay, *Population*, p. 149.

8   The figures for Norfolk parishes and for parishes in the
other counties referred to, come from Sir Henry Spelman,
*Village Anglicum, or a View of all the Cities, Towns and
Villages in England* (1656), 2nd edn, 1678.

9   For the influence of ethnic origin on the social system in
various areas of England see the work of George Homans,
English Villagers of the 13th Century, Harvard, 1942.

10   The contrast between Bottesford and Shepshed is
splendidly described in David Levine, *Family Formation in
an Age of Nascent Capitalism*, 1977. The exact relationship
between proto-industrial activity and demography or family
structure is by no means settled however.

11   For an authoritative discussion of enclosure and the voluminous literature on that subject see G. E. Mingay, *English Landed Society in the 18th Century*, 1963, especially pp. 179–88 and references. A wholly darker picture is painted by Keith Snell, in a forthcoming work based on settlement examinations.

12   See S. C. Powell, *Puritan Village: The Formation of a New England Town*, Middletown, Conn., 1963. The suggestion that the model for the New England township is to be found in the co-operative society of peasants in an open-field village was made as early as 1910 by William Cunningham; see *Common Rights at Cottenham and Stretham*, Camden Miscellany, xii, and references.

13   See Laslett, 'The gentry of Kent in 1640', *Cambridge Historical Journal*, 1948, ix, no. 2.

14   See W. G. Hoskins, 'Galby and Frisby', in *Essays in Leicestershire History*, Liverpool, 1950. Dr Hoskins also presents the social history of the much bigger village of Wigston Magna nearby (*The Midland Peasant*, 1957) until late in the seventeenth century as one dominated by substantial peasants and not by gentry.

15   For John Adams, see *Dictionary of National Biography*, and for his *Index Villaris* see Glass, 'Papers on Gregory King'.

16   As was the house at Goodnestone; see p. 65. The county histories give numerous examples of great houses out to let, e.g. Edward Hasted, *History of Kent*, 1782. For gentry in urban areas, see note 23 of Chapter 2, and for their distribution in a midland county, and their presence in the county town, Warwick, see P. Styles, 'The social structure of Kineton Hundred in the reign of Charles II', in *Studies in West Midland History*, Kineton, 1978.

17   The enquiry is known as the Compton census and gave rise to several documents now forming part of Cambridge Group, File 3. The full set of returns is in the course of publication by Ann Whiteman.

18   Compare the standard of 13·4 per cent for pre-industrial England: see note 17 of Chapter 1 and *HFPT*, pp. 150–7. Not all servants exchanged poor small households for larger, richer ones however: see p. 13.

19   Generalization about all 10,000 villages in the country as they were at the turn of the seventeenth to the eighteenth century is hazardous, especially in view of their differing economies and ecologies. Nevertheless the statements about the social structure of Goodnestone, Clayworth, the Kent villages, Ealing and so on seem to apply in general and with appropriate modulation to the following other places. Terling and Earls' Colne in Essex; Petworth in Sussex; Kirby Lonsdale in North Lancashire; Fenny Compton and Chilvers Coton in Warwickshire; Bilston in Staffordshire; St Bees in Cumberland; Grasmere in Cumberland (Wordsworth's Grasmere); Myddle in Shropshire; Poole, Corfe Castle and Puddletown in Dorset; Donhead in Wiltshire. These are settlements where it has been possible to make comparisons, either because their documentation has become available, generally a listing of inhabitants being part of it, or because work has been published on them since the 1960s, often both of course. Convincing counter examples are not known to me.

20   See Hasted, *Kent*, p. 815.

21   Between 1618 and 1628 mean household size at Cogenhoe varied between 4·92 and 5·11, and the actual size of the village between 150 and 185.

22   The great difference made to the social structure of a village community by a married parson is well illustrated by the position of the family of Christopher Spicer at Cogenhoe, whose establishment was the largest in the village from 1618–28, in the years when the manor house was vacant; compare also the position at Clayworth: see *FLIL*, ch. 2.

23   See Keith Wrightson and David Levine, *Poverty and Piety in an English Village: Terling 1525–1700*, 1979, especially pp. 103–6 and the table on p. 105, a unique

investigation of this important topic. In the view of the authors, their community, the village of Terling in Essex, was becoming progressively polarized between an élite, resembling that at Goodnestone, and the poor, mainly labourers and indigent craftsmen.

24   Listing published by K. J. Allison, *Bulletin of the Institute of Historical Research*, 1963. This listing is the earliest of English history to give a complete familial detail with ages.

25   See *FLIL*, Tables 2.16, 2.17, etc.

26   On the social structure of late-seventeenth-century London, see note 2 of Chapter 3 and references. The nine London parishes in Cambridge Group, File 3 have a mean of 27 per cent servants in the population, and of 66 per cent of households with servants. These proportions varied between 20·2 per cent and 48 per cent (St Andrew Wardrobe) to 35 per cent and 80·5 per cent (St Mary le Bow). These high percentages were not confined to the capital since almost 30 per cent of the population of the central, high-status parish of St Peter Mancroft, Norwich, were servants in 1694, and 58 per cent of households had servants.

27   See Henry Best, *Rural Economy in Yorkshire in 1641, Being the Farming and Account Books of Henry Best, of Elmswell in the East Riding of the County of York*, edited by C. B. Robinson, 1857 (1641), p. 93, modernized. We are not told whether every landholder in a village would have his own harvest celebration, or whether one large party served for the whole society. I believe that this last was the general rule, but practices no doubt varied from place to place and time to time. Descriptions like this one seem to be rare.

28   Witchcraft is now a much studied subject, which would take us beyond the scope of the present book. The authoritative treatment is, and is likely to remain, Keith Thomas, *Religion and the Decline of Magic: Studies in Popular Belief in 16th and 17th Century England*, 1971. But

there are other important studies including one by Alan Macfarlane, all of which are surveyed in relation to village life by Keith Wrightson, *English Society 1580–1680*, 1982, ch. 7.

29   For the practice of Easter communion, the duties of parishioners to attend and of the priest to refuse the cup to the sinful, and for making out of lists of communicants (which was required by the canons of the Oxford diocese) see S. A. Peyton, 'The Churchwardens' presentments in the Oxfordshire peculiars of Dorchester, Thame and Banbury', *Oxfordshire Record Society*, 1928, pp. xxxvi and xxxvii.

30   K. S. Inglis, *Churches and the Working Classes in Victorian England*, 1963.

31   There are occasional records of such meetings in schoolhouses where these existed.

32   See Powell, *Puritan Village*.

33   The files of the meetings of the justices of the peace of the counties at quarter sessions are full of references to the granting, abuse and withdrawal of licences to keep alehouses, but the number of inns mentioned are very small. Alehouses, their functions in the life of village and town society, their relationship with poverty and the threat of famine, their role as the site of relaxation and celebration for humble people, their liability to suppression by the established order, especially where it was Puritan, have received a lot of recent attention. See Wrightson, *English Society*, ch. 4 and the references, especially his own doctoral dissertation and the complementary (urban) study of Peter Clark.

34   Perhaps Gregory King; he preserved a copy of this listing of the inhabitants of Harefield in 1699, and it is to be seen amongst his papers in the Public Record Office, ref. T64/302. Keepers of London inns could be as rich as merchants with the title of Mr.

35 It is recorded by John Aubrey; see his *Brief Lives*, edited by O. L. Dick, 1949, p. 148.

36 Figures from *FLIL*, pp. 98–9.

37 Peter Laslett and John Harrison, 'Clayworth and Cogenhoe', in H. E. Bell and R. L. Ollard (eds), *Historical Essays 1600–1750, Presented to David Ogg*, 1963, p. 157. Extended and revised in *FLIL*, ch. 2.

38 The original article was extended in 1968 to include a similar study for two villages in France, department of Pas de Calais, in the later eighteenth century. Turnover was of the same order there, but slightly less. In *FLIL* the study was revised again, with slightly different figures replacing those first published. In Wrightson, *English Society*, ch. 2, there is a very interesting discussion of mobility in English seventeenth-century settlements, and the suggestion is made that it was decreasing as the seventeenth century went on.

39 The Clayworth documents do not include the Wawen estate records and we know nothing of how they ran their land. The best example known to me of a landowner who recorded such decisions is S. E. Fussell (ed.), *Robert Loder's Farm Accounts, 1610–20*, 1936.

40 E. Corbett, *A History of Spelsbury*, Banbury, 1962, p. 170.

41 John Smith of Nibley, *Men and Armour for Gloucestershire*, 1608, published 1902, contains many places where every male inhabitant of military age is given as 'servant' to the landlord.

42 For the influence of personal indebtedness on social solidarity amongst village neighbours, see Wrightson, *English Society*, pp. 52–3. The liveliest and most informative description of kinship within the village community and its importance in co-operation of every kind is by Miranda Chaytor: 'Household and kinship: Ryton in the late 16th and early 17th centuries', *History Workshop*, 10.

CHAPTER 4 *Misbeliefs about our ancestors*

1 The references here are to *Romeo and Juliet*, I, ii, lines 8–11; iii, lines 69–73; *The Tempest*, I, ii, lines 44 and 54.

2 See Chapter 7.

3 Dr Hollingsworth also communicated the details relating to Elizabeth Manners.

4 *Age at marriage*
Sample taken at random from vol. II of J. M. Cowper (ed.), *Canterbury Marriage Licences 1619–60*, Canterbury, 1894. Age at marriage, especially age at first marriage for women, has established itself as perhaps the most important single variable distinguishing demographic and familial regimes one from another, and much research is being done on its history. See R. B. Outhwaite (ed.), *Marriage and Society: Studies in the Social History of Marriage*, 1981, and his study, 'Age at marriage in England from the 17th to the 19th century', *Transactions of the Royal Historical Society*, 1972. See also J. Hajnal's famous article of 1965, with R. M. Smith, 'Some reflections on the evidence for the origins of the European marriage pattern', in C. Harris (ed.), *The Sociology of the Family*, 1980. Dr Smith is now directing a project on marriage and family formation at the Cambridge Group.

5 The figures cited come from the authoritative work of J. M. Tanner, the great expert on human growth and attempts to understand it in the past, *A History of the Study of Human Growth*, Cambridge, 1981, see Table 11.3. The subject is surveyed from the point of view of the history of social structure in *FLIL*, ch. 6, 'Age at sexual maturity in Europe since the Middle Ages', where the suggestion is made about a mean age of sixteen, or just below, being a historical norm in Europe before the end of the nineteenth century. In the most recent version of this chapter (French translation, Paris, 1984) the view is propounded that there was no *historical* development in this statistic before that time.

6   Mean age at menarche has been taken at 15·75 years for these rough estimates and the distribution normal with a standard deviation of 1·1 years. See *FLIL*, ch. 6, addendum.

7   *Child marriage*
I am indebted to Professor Muriel Bradbrook, sometime Mistress of Girton College, Cambridge, for all the literary references to child marriage, and the discussion of them is mainly hers. As for instances of child marriage rather closer to Shakespeare than Renaissance Tuscany, it is reported from the Massif Central in France that between 1578 and 1599 sixteen girls out of fifty were married before 18, and one at only 11: Jacques Dupâquier, *Population rurale du bassin parisien, 1670–1720*, 1982 (1979). She may perhaps have been like Susan Alford, for whom see the *Report and Transactions of the Devonshire Association for the Advancement of Science, Literature and Art*, Plymouth, 1894, XXVI, p. 181. The case of Lady Rowecliffe comes from A. Percival Moore, 'Marriage contracts or espousals in the reign of Queen Elizabeth', *Reports and Papers of Associated Architectural Societies*, 1909, XXX, 1, quoting Whitaker's *History of Craven*. His book is a valuable treatment of marriage in Elizabethan dramatic literature. The St Botolph registers are excerpted in T. R. Forbes, *Chronicle from Aldgate*, Yale, 1971; see pp. 37–8.

8   For a development of the argument about the use of literature in this way see Peter Laslett, 'The wrong way through the telescope: a note on the use of literary evidence in sociology and historical sociology', *British Journal of Sociology, 1976*, 27. The assumption that literature reflects social facts is rejected, and it is insisted that until literary sociology advances beyond its present state, the interpretation of imaginative writing in this way is a very uncertain undertaking. Further work on literature of a less fictitious character is in contemplation.

9   *Married brothers and sisters co-residing*
This law is borne out by all the listings of communities which we have so far examined: see *HFPT*. The chapters of this book show that the simultaneous presence of two married couples was rare in the northern part of

seventeenth-century France and eighteenth-century Holland
or Corsica, but seemingly rarest of all in England. For
further comparison with the continent, see *FLIL*, ch. 1,
and *Famforms, passim.*

10   Work of Mrs Jean Robin in progress at the Cambridge
Group. The complex families of the very poor seem to have
been the outcome not so much of the personal decisions of
their members as of the policy of those distributing poor
relief.

11   See e.g. James Tait (ed.), 'Lancashire quarter sessions
records, sessions rolls, 1590–1606', *Chetham Society,*
Manchester, 1917, pp. 56, 145, 247, 260, etc., and for the
splitting up of dwellings, see N. Goose, 'Household size and
structure in early Stuart Cambridge', *Social History,* Oct.
1980.

12   King reckoned 2–2½ per cent of all houses in the later
17th century were empty, and even more in London:
D. V. Glass, 'Two papers on Gregory King', in D. V. Glass
and D. E. C. Eversley, *Population and History,* 1965, p. 185.
Eight out of 117 houses were vacant at Harefield in 1699.
But a hundred years earlier housing was short, though with
no effect that we can see on household size and structure.

13   S. C. Ratcliff and H. C. Johnson, *Warwick Quarter
Sessions,* 5, *Warwick County Records,* 1939, p. 65.

14   For all these issues, about which very little more is so
far known, see *FLIL*, ch. 8 (the history of ageing and the
aged) and V. Brodsky Elliott, 'Mobility and marriage in
pre-industrial England', PhD dissertation, Cambridge, 1979,
with her contribution to Outhwaite, *Marriage and Society.*

15   See Chapter 10 and K. W. Wachter, E. A. Hammel and
Peter Laslett, *Statistical Studies of Historical Social
Structure,* 1978, ch. 7.

16   This work has been done at the Cambridge Group by
Professor E. A. Wrigley and Dr R. S. Schofield, analysing
aggregative returns for 404 Anglican parish registers

submitted by 230 local volunteers. Beginning in 1964 the task was completed in 1981 with the publication by Wrigley and Schofield of their monumental treatise, *The Population History of England, 1541–1871: A Reconstruction*, with contributions by J. E. Oeppen of the Cambridge Group and by Professor Ronald Lee, of the University of California, Berkeley. It will be evident to the reader that virtually all the demographic statistics given here come from that book, and are republished with the permission of its authors. The fascinating process of reconstruction whereby monthly totals of baptisms, marriages and burials in the aggregative returns were made to yield so rich a harvest of national historical demographic statistics is technical and complicated. It cannot be described or discussed here, and the reader is referred to the book itself for these purposes, and for the estimated accuracy of the figures which have been reproduced.

17   See Henry Best, *Rural Economy in Yorkshire in 1641, Being the Farming and Account Books of Henry Best, of Elmswell in the East Riding of the County of York*, edited by C. B. Robinson, 1857 (1641), pp. 116–17.

CHAPTER 5   *Births, marriages and deaths*

1   Expectations of life at various ages have been taken from the model life tables of A. J. Coale and P. Demeny in *Regional Model Life Tables*, Princeton, 1966, using model North, level 9 for the 1690s, level 24 for the 1980s.

2   See J. Dupâquier, E. Hélin, P. Laslett and others, *Marriage and Remarriage in Populations of the Past*, 1981, for further discussion and for comparative evidence. On widowers and the elementary demography of English widowhood, an illuminating paper by James E. Smith, 'Widowhood in earlier times', presented to the world demographic conference on records, Salt Lake City, August 1980.

3   The story of the Bacons, Loversages and Welters is from Peter Laslett and John Harrison, 'Clayworth and Cogenhoe',

in H. E. Bell and R. L. Ollard (eds), *Historical Essays 1600–1750, Presented to David Ogg*, 1963, extended and revised in *FLIL*, ch. 2. In many of the listings in Cambridge Group, File 3, one or two members of a household are found on parish relief, when the head is not. It is often an 'inmate', or a widowed relative, or even a parent of a spouse. Compare *FLIL*, chs 4 (on orphans) and 5 (on the elderly), and see R. M. Smith, *Land, Kinship and the Life Cycle* (in press), Introduction, for an illuminating discussion.

4   See Louis Henry, *Anciennes familles genèvoises*, Paris, 1956. The facts about recognizing family limitation are given in E. A. Wrigley, *Population and History*, 1969; see e.g. pp. 87–8.

5   See E. A. Wrigley, 'Family limitation in pre-industrial England', *EcHR*, 1966, xix, no. 1, 82–109.

6   For the insistence that contraception was the practice of only a minority at Colyton, the minority whose marriages in the later seventeenth century did not tend to be celebrated clandestinely, see E. A. Wrigley, 'Marital fertility in 17th century Colyton, a note', *EcHR*, 1978, xxxi, 429–36. The codification of English marital and nurturing behaviour, in comparison with Flanders, areas of France, Bavaria and elsewhere, is the work of Christopher Wilson. See his dissertation, 'Marital fertility in pre-industrial England', 1981 (copy at the Cambridge Group) and its references, e.g. John Knodel, 'Breast-feeding and population control', *Science*, 1977, cxcviii, 111–15.

7   This is the theme of a lecture delivered by the author at the Collège de France in Paris, 2 June 1982. Compare the work of Arthur Imhof on Protestants and Catholics in Germany and for nurturance among English Protestants, especially in America, Philip Greven, *The Protestant Temperament*, New York, 1977.

8   Figures for the dependency ratio are given in W and S, Table A3.1; see the discussion on pp. 216–19, 443ff, referring to misinterpretations arising from the figures of King.

9   *Childhood in pre-industrial society*
The quotation is from David Davies, *The Case of Labourers in Husbandry*, Bath, 1795, a passage communicated from Aberdeenshire in 1769. The accounts of childhood in question are those of Lloyd de Mause (see the collective volume, *The History of Childhood*, 1974, together with the journal of the same title, which is also the journal of psychohistory). Philippe Ariès, Lawrence Stone, Ivy Pinchbeck and Margaret Hewitt, J. H. Plumb ('The new world of childhood in the 18th century', reprinted in *The Light of History*, 1972). Alan Macfarlane (see his review of Stone's book in *History and Theory*, 18, 103–26), Keith Wrightson and Linda Pollock especially are those who have pronounced this view to be unsatisfactory. A study based on the analysis of hundreds of diaries and autobiographies by Linda Pollock is due in 1983: *Forgotten Children: Parent–Child Relationships 1500–1800*, Cambridge. See also John Gilles, *Youth and History*, 1974, and Randolph Trumbach, *The Rise of the Egalitarian Family*, 1978.

10   The impressive and ingenious explanatory model worked out for this purpose by Wrigley and Schofield will be found in their final chapters, 10 and 11.

CHAPTER 6   *Did the peasants really starve?*

1   See Pierre Goubert, *Beauvais et les Beauvaisis de 1600 à 1730*, Paris, 1960, ch. III, 'Structures démographiques' and especially section 3, 'Analyse des crises démographiques'. E. A. Wrigley, in *Population and History*, 1969, presents some of the numerical material in English, with an informative discussion.

2   The manuscript diary of John Locke is in the Bodleian Library and this volume is MS Locke F.5: see pp. 19–22. His English has been modernized. I cannot confirm his check on Alice George's account of Queen Elizabeth's journey to Worcester. She did go there in 1575 but not in 1588, as far as I can see.

3   Henry Best, *Rural Economy in Yorkshire in 1641, Being the Farming and Account Books of Henry Best, of Elmswell*

in the East Riding of the County of York, edited by
C. B. Robinson, 1857 (1641), pp. 42–3. The employment of
women as labourers in agriculture is described by Keith
Snell, e.g. in 'Agricultural seasonal unemployment, the
standard of living and women's work in the south and east,
1690–1860', *EcHR*, 1981, xxxiv.

4   For Bethnal Green, see Michael Young and Peter
Willmott, *Family and Kinship in East London*, 1959 (1957),
ch. IV. It has since been shown that although Preston
exhibited a similar pattern in 1851 (Michael Anderson,
Family Structure in 19th-Century Lancashire, Cambridge,
1971), Bethnal Green in that year decidedly did not. See
the dissertation in preparation at the Cambridge Group of
Martin Clarke.

5   John Graunt, *Natural and Political Observations upon the
Bills of Mortality*, 1662, etc., reprinted in *The Earliest
Classics*, Farnborough, 1973. The 'milch-women' were wet
nurses, and it is known that they were commoner in London
than anywhere else.

6   For a full description with examples of the classic French
crise de subsistance see Michael Drake in the Open
University course book, *Historical Demography, Problems
and Prospects*, Milton Keynes, 1974, pp. 89–110. He applies
it to the parish of Halifax in the harvest year of 1586–7
and demonstrates a crisis which fits the model. But he
concludes that 'a one-to-one relationship between food
supplies and mortality does not exist' (p. 104).

7   Scottish record office, Edinburgh, E 8/58 (s.d. 23 Feb.
1700). The passage translated from Goubert is on pp. 76–7,
slightly modified. The eating of roots, grasses and leaves
was not of itself a sign of famine, though commoner then
and the plants concerned generally less suitable. David
Dymond states in 'The famine of 1527 in Essex', *LPS*,
1981, 26, fn 19, 'that the roots of corn, parsley and dandelion
were eaten during the winter, while in the spring the fresh
leaves of hawthorn ("bread and cheese tree") or the young
shoots of bracken could supplement a meagre diet'.

8   I have modified this passage in the original text to take account of the observations of Andrew Appleby in *Famine in Tudor and Stuart England*, Stanford, 1978, pp. 115–18, where a fuller list of conditions to be satisfied by a crisis of subsistence will be found. It is now disputed whether infantile mortality is particularly associated with famine.

9   The registers of Ashton-under-Lyne, Lancashire, were published in 1927–8 by H. Brierley. Though marred by gaps, they contain exceptional information on such things as abortions and suicides, especially for the years 1596–1640. For burials in West Yorkshire, see Michael Drake, 'An elementary exercise in parish register demography', *EcHR*, 1962, LXV, no. 3. A better example of an English crisis of subsistence would have been Halifax at an earlier date in 1580–7; see note 6 of Chapter 6.

10   Quoted by Joan Thirsk in 'Industries in the countryside', in F. J. Fisher (ed.), *Essays in Honour of H. H. Tawney*, 1961. The Greystoke registers were edited by A. M. MacLean and published at Kendal in 1911: I have been unable to consult a copy in revising the text in 1982. The late Dr W. G. Howson, a pioneer of studies of this kind, drew my attention to this record: see his 'Plague, poverty and population in parts of North West England', *Transactions of the Historical Society of Lancashire and Cheshire*, 1960.

11   The St Margaret's registers were printed by A. M. Burke in *Memorials of St Margaret's Church, Westminster*, 1914, and causes of death are given between May and June 1557, with omissions and uncertainties. Mr J. F. Ede communicated the entry from the Wednesbury register.

12   This type of activity on the part of English governments and city fathers is summarized in E. Lipson, *The Economic History of England*, 9th edn, 1947, I, p. 302, etc.; II, pp. 419–48. Charles Phythian-Adams, *Desolation of a City: Coventry and the Urban Crisis of the Late Middle Ages*, Cambridge, 1979, says of Coventry, 'everything points to famine in the harvest year which began in 1520'. For

counting of people and corn stocks in the countryside in that decade and at other times, see note 28 of Chapter 5.

13   Chapter 8, 'Short term variation, some basic patterns': Chapter 9, 'Short term variations: vital rates, prices, weather', (a remarkable and decidedly econometric contribution to the book by Ronald Lee), and Appendix 10, 'Local mortality crises', constitute an entire and quite self-contained treatment of our topic.

14   The quotation is from *The Causes of the English Revolution*, 1972, third printing, 1975, p. 110. Stone's references reveal that his conclusions are based on 'two epidemics in one town (Northampton in 1605 and 1638) in which only *one-sixth* of the population died' (W and S, p. 686, fn. 97). Appleby's workings on mortality in 1585–9, 1595–9 and 1621–5 in fifteen Westmorland and Cumberland parishes show Greystoke to have been affected on all three occasions, as only one other parish was, though not always the most seriously (*Famine*, Figs 3–14). Calculation shows that in 1623 burials at Greystoke exceeded the forecast trend value by the required 3·36 standard errors (see p. 647) in each month from July to December – a severe crisis but by no means exceptionally severe. It is very important to notice that in the section headed 'The structure of local crisis mortality' (W and S, pp. 685–93) the crisis rate per century has been given in error as the decadal crisis rate. All mentions of the decadal crisis rate should therefore be understood to refer to that per century. Roger Schofield informs me that these amendments will be made in any future printing of the book.

15   *Mentions of death by starvation in English records*
The Latin phrase in the text is cited by Appleby, *Famine*, p. 148. David Palliser in 'Dearth and disease in Staffordshire, 1540–1670', in C. W. Chalklin and M. A. Havinden (eds), *Rural Change and Urban Growth*, 1974, p. 64, quotes a burial entry from the register of Rocester in that county dated 1618–19 for 'A suckerlesse pore woman destitute of maintenance'. The wording is almost identical with that of two of the Greystoke entries, but it is less specific. Other references are still more general

and do not attach to particular burials. They come from the 1590s and from town records. 'An old chronicler of Shrewsbury', according to E. M. Leonard, *The Early History of English Poor Relief*, 1900, pp. 123–4, fervently hoped in 1596 that God's 'chosen flocke perrishe not and die for want as many in all contries [i.e. counties, districts] in England die and go in great numbers miserably begging'. A frequently cited passage in the City records of Newcastle-on-Tyne in October 1597 ('Sundrey starving and dying in the streets and in the fields of lack of bread', Appleby, *Famine*, p. 10) and a record from Nantwich in Cheshire of 1595 ('Greate sicknesse by famine ensued and many poore died thereof', Palliser, 'Dearth and disease', p. 61) seem at present to complete the list. As for France, Pierre Goubert writes: 'La mention des causes de la mort sur les registres françaises de sèpulture est *rare*, mais existe: elle est presque toujours vague . . . "Famine" veut parfois dire seulement nourriture insuffisante, ou polluée, ou malsaine' (letter of September 1982).

16   Roger Schofield, 'The impact of scarcity and plenty on population change in England, 1541–1871', paper to the Conference on Hunger and History, Bellagio, July 1982, forthcoming in *JIH*. For Thompson's essay, *P and P*, 50.

17   Amartya Sen, *Poverty and Famine: An Essay in Entitlement Deprivation*, Oxford, 1981.

18   For prices, mortality, marriage and fertility, see W and S, Tables 9.8 and 9.6, with the relevant discussion. There are signs that only extremely high or very low mortality would affect nuptiality (383), which would confirm a conspicuous feature of the crisis of subsistence model. Prices did not affect fertility via nuptiality, mortality had a greater influence on births than prices did and all these effects went both up and down. The deaths of pregnant women were not an important factor.

19   Expectation of life at birth fell by three years in the later 1550s and by the same amount in the later 1720s, but the proportion of parishes undergoing crisis mortality did not reach 40 per cent in the first case or 30 per cent in the

second (W and S, Table A10.2 and p. 318). These are the
two highest proportions. A sample of 404 parishes is of
course less effective for studying geographical than temporal
variation and it must be remembered that not all of them
were always in observation, only about a quarter in the
1550s: see Tables 2.19 and A10.2.

20   This is repeatedly asserted in W and S and in
'Nutrition and disease: the case of London, 1550–1750',
JIH, 1975, vi, 1, Appleby demonstrates the point for that
city. For France, see J. Dupâquier, *La population française
au XVII et XVIII siècles*, Paris, 1979, pp. 42–50, where he
also propounds his revision of the theories of Meuvret,
Goubert and others on crises of subsistence. Dupâquier
believes that in France pestilence was much more important
than war and famine as a cause of mortality and of crisis,
and that the country was more like England in this respect
than Wrigley and Schofield allow. For the plague, see *The
Plague Reconsidered: A New Look at its Origins and Effects
in 16th and 17th century England*, Supplement to *Local
Population Studies*, 1977, where Schofield demonstrates how
the disease can be identified from a parish register in the
absence of cause of death from the records, using the case
of Colyton in 1645–6. See also the contribution by
J-N. Biraben of Paris, the leading authority, as to the still
open question of why plague disappeared from Europe in
the late eighteenth century. Compare with this Andrew
Appleby, 'The disappearance of the plague, a continuing
puzzle', *EcHR*, 1980, xxiii, and P. Slack, 'The
disappearance of the plague, an alternative view', *EcHR*,
1981, xxxiv. Appleby took the view that rats developed
immunity to plague, Slack believes that it was the
effectiveness of quarantine, though Biraben has still more
recently proposed a bacteriological explanation.

21   *Famine and infection*
Sen, *Poverty and Famine*, Appendix D, 'Famine and
mortality, a case study', p. 210. For the Irish famine see
the chapter by Sir William MacArthur, 'The medical
history of the famine', in R. Dudley Edwards and
T. Williams (eds), *The Great Famine*, Dublin, 1956. His
description of dysentery, typhus, scurvy and famine dropsy

reads very much as if it would fit in to English seventeenth-century food-related mortalities. The most thorough and useful medical analysis of these effects, though in twentieth-century west European populations, is a large two-volume work, *The Biology of Human Starvation*, by Ancel Keys and many others, 1951. Though some of its conclusions and suggestions seem incompatible with the treatise issued by the World Health Organization in 1968 (N. S. Scrimshaw, C. E. Taylor and J. E. Gordon, *Interactions of Famine and Disease*, Geneva) no reference is there made to the Keys volumes, a puzzle to the non-medical outsider.

22 The quotation is from Scrimshaw, Taylor and Gordon, *Interactions*, p. 15. It is Paul Slack, in his very useful study of 'Mortality crises and epidemic disease in England, 1485–1610', in Charles Webster (ed.), *Health, Medicine and Mortality in the 16th Century*, 1979, who refers to the synergistic relation and to 'mixed crises and famine crises'. Other local studies, apart from Howson, Palliser and Appleby, are C. D. Rogers, *The Lancashire Population Crisis of 1623*, Manchester, 1975; A. Gooder, 'The population crisis of 1727–30 in Warwickshire', *Midland History*, 1972, I, 4; N. T. Oswald, 'Epidemics in Devon, 1538–1837', *Transactions of the Devon Association for the Advancement of Science*, 1977; Victor Skipp, *Crisis and Development: An Ecological Study of the Forest of Arden, 1570–1674*, Cambridge, 1978; and for Scotland, T. C. Smout, 'Famine and famine relief in Scotland', in L. M. Cullen and T. C. Smout (eds), *Comparative Aspects of Scottish and Irish Economic and Social History*, Edinburgh, 1977; Rosalind Mitchison, 'The making of the old Scottish poor law', *P and P*, 1974, 63; and Michael Flinn (ed.), *Scottish Population History*, Cambridge, 1977, where Appendix A prints mortality indices by region, 1615–1852. Most of these accounts have been used in the text. See Roger Schofield's note appended to the notes for this chapter (p. 325) on the interpretation of demographic evidence in relation to famine.

23 See J. Menken, J. Trussell and S. Watkins, 'The nutrition fertility link: an evaluation of the evidence', with its references, *JIH*, 1981, xi, 3. The theorist of this relationship is Rose Frisch and her positions (see e.g.

'Nutrition, fatness and fecundity: the effect of food intake on reproductive ability', in W. H. Mosley (ed.), *Nutrition and Human Reproduction*, New York, 1978) are appraised by Menken *et al.* Some of them have been the subject of controversy, but these authors and other authorities agree that 'when food supplies are so short as to cause starvation there is little doubt that fertility is lowered'. Le Roy Ladurie's article (1979) is translated as 'Famine amenorrhea (17th–20th centuries)' in R. Forster and O. Ranum, *Biology of Man in History*, 1975. References to climatic history are given in W and S, though Appleby has subsequently made the suggestion that the crises, especially the food-related crises of the late sixteenth and early seventeenth centuries may have been due to a 'little ice age'. See his article in *JIH*, 1980, x, 4, 643–63.

24   Skipp, *Crisis and Development*, especially ch. 13. A long list of tables and figures in W and S is devoted to the relative severity of national and local crises, e.g. Tables 8.7–8.11, on percentage deviations from trend in real wages, birth, marriage and death rates; 8.12 and 8.13, on crisis years and crisis months; A10.1 and A10.2, with the remarkable figure A10.1, on proportions of parishes in crisis; and a whole succession of maps (Figs A10.2 to A10.14) delineating by month of the year settlements known to be touched in 1557–9, 1586–8, 1596–8, 1603–4, 1624–5, and so on. Crisis years and crisis months are identified for the whole country and allotted degrees of severity by a star system. It is possible therefore to place any year between the 1540s and the 1870s just where it belongs in respect of crisis mortality and of geographical intensity of local crises, though only for those settlements which happen to be represented in the sample of 404, in which Greystoke itself is present. Except in ch. 9, however, real wages, that is the ratio of wages to prices, are dealt with almost entirely. I have preferred to confine myself to wheat prices in this account, especially since the location, in the south, of the wage series, and its narrow base in building, cause so much dubiety; though see Appendix 9 in W and S.

25   For deaths by starvation in the capital as late as 1763, see James Boswell's *Johnson*, (ed.) Percy Fitzgerald,

printing of 1924, II, p. 374. Johnson was relaying
information from a London magistrate, Saunders Welch,
and probably had in mind a notorious case of three people
found dead of starvation in a deserted house. As for the
crisis of 1557 at Westminster, it may be justifiable to add
deaths due to flux and bloody flux and some fever deaths
which look like typhus, and even some from tuberculosis,
(Slack, *Crisis and Development*, p. 32) to make a total of
twenty-five deaths which were food-shortage-related. The
months of May and September were certainly crisis months
in this parish on the new criteria and the 'famine' deaths
took place in June (one), July (five), August (four) and
September (three). But then the sickness pattern changed,
and the 'new sickness' or burning ague, perhaps influenza,
but much less likely to be food-related, was present from
midsummer.

26   Appleby, *Famine* (see especially ch. 10), who is
followed by W and S. They add many other considerations
to his suggestions as to why the northerly, westerly, upland
pattern with its food-supply deficiencies ceased to be so
prevalent after the 1620s. In spite of the lamentable history
of the north-west, Devonshire and the south-west seems to
have been overall the most crisis-prone area of the country.

27   Palliser, 'Dearth and disease', p. 64, modernized. In
what follows in this chapter I am indebted not only to
Edward Thompson but to the studies of John Walter and
Keith Wrightson (Wrightson, *English Society 1580–1680*,
1982, especially ch. 6; Walter and Wrightson, 'Dearth and
the social order in early modern England', *P and P*, 1976,
71; Walter, 'Grain riots and popular attitudes to the law',
in John Brewer and John Styles (eds), *An Ungovernable
People*, 1980).

28   David Dymond in 'The famine of 1527 in Essex',
shows how *corn certificates* were drawn up for all the villages
in an Essex hundred in 1521 by a royal order to a local
commissioner. The population of each village and hamlet
was numbered, stocks of bread grains and drink grains (beer
was made of barley) determined, and the shortfall
calculated. His notes and references show that other

hundreds in Wiltshire and Kent were surveyed in the same year, and, which is most significant, that similar certificates were drawn up for two of the years in which we have seen that famine has been suspected, 1586–7 and 1623: see also Sir William Ashley, *The Bread of our Forefathers*, Oxford, 1928, Appendix IV. Further research might yield other indications that these practices, existing well before the Elizabethan Book of Orders, were part of long-established policy when famine was in the offing; compare R. H. Tawney and E. Power, *Tudor Economic Documents*, 1924, I, section 3, 'The corn trade and the food supply'. For such action in Scotland, see Mitchison, 'Old Scottish poor law'. The subject rapidly shades into that of national policy in respect of the import and export of corn in relation to the food needs of the country, a topic with a vast literature and on which R. B. Outhwaite is the authority: see e.g. 'Dearth and government intervention in English grain markets, 1590–1700', *EcHR*, 1981, XXIII, and 'Food crises in early modern England', *Proceedings of the 7th International Economic History Conference*, Edinburgh, 1978.

Movements of births and deaths in relation to famine: a note by Roger Schofield
It is sometimes alleged that if the numbers of births being registered fall at the same time as the numbers of deaths rise, this scissors movement can be taken to indicate that the mortality crisis was due to famine. For example Appleby writes, 'If it can be established that plague was definitely not present, amenorrhea [that is a fall in conceptions] becomes confirming evidence of famine'.[a] Unfortunately it was not just plague, but many other diseases too, that could temporarily depress fertility. If one takes the twenty years that witnessed the most severe upward swings in the national death rate (the earliest occurring in 1544 and the latest in 1762), sixteen of them witnessed a scissors movement with the birth rate falling below average. If one were then to conclude that these were famine years, one would be as likely to be mistaken as correct, for in eight of the sixteen years food prices were *below* average. Moreover, in five of the eight years in which food prices were above average the rise was less than 10 per cent, scarcely years of famine on a national scale.[b] Thus, in

the absence of independent evidence of the movement of food prices, a scissors movement in the birth and death series cannot be taken as conclusive evidence of a subsistence crisis; it is much more likely to have been produced by epidemic disease.

(*a*) Appleby, 'Disease or famine', *EcHR*, 1973, xxvi, 423. Rogers, in *Lancashire Population Crisis*, p. 6, accepts this opinion and takes a drop in conceptions as conclusive proof that famine was the cause of the heavy mortality that occurred in parts of Lancashire in 1623.
(*b*) W and S, Table 8.8 on p. 322, top panel (note that the column headings 'Real wage' and 'Death rate' should be transposed).

CHAPTER 7   *Personal discipline and social survival*

1   For a portrait of a contemporary village as a 'dying culture', see W. M. Williams, *The Sociology of an English Village: Gosforth*, 1956.

2   See J. Ruwet, in *Population*, 1954.

3   *Homosexuality, bestiality, etc.*
For acts of sexual incontinence, excommunication etc., and for the attitude of ordinary people towards such sexual offences, see any collection of cases from the archdeacons' court, and the following: R. A. Marchant, *The Church under the Law: Justice, Administration and Discipline in the Diocese of York, 1500–1640*, Cambridge, 1969; Paul Hair, *Before the Bawdy Court*, 1973; and G. R. Quaife, *Wanton Wenches and Wayward Wives: Peasants and Illicit Sex in Early 17th Century England*, 1979; Quaife discusses homosexuality on pp. 176–7. 'Buggery in the British Navy 1700–1861' (by Arthur N. Gilbert), 'London's sodomites: homosexual behaviour and urban culture in the 18th century' (by Randolph Trumbach), and 'Things fearful to name: sodomy and buggery in 17th-century New England' (by Robert Okes), (in the *Journal of Social History*, 1976, 10, 1, 72; 1977, 11, 1, 1; and 1978, 12, 2, 266) provide further evidence, along with Stone's book. For the definition of buggery, see Nelson's *Justice of the Peace*, 2 edn, 1707, pp. 115–16. The form of execution for the crime seems to

have differed from time to time; being buried alive, burnt or drowned are all mentioned. By the early 18th century it was a felony, which presumably meant death by hanging, and it was insisted that actual penetration must be proven. The paucity of cases makes one hope that the life of the homosexual was not in fact lived in terror of death.

4   See 'The Puritans and adultery: the Act of 1650 reconsidered', in Oswald Pennington and K. Thomas, *Puritans and Revolutionaries*, Oxford, 1978.

5   See E. A. Wrigley 'Marriage, fertility and population growth in 18th century England', in R. B. Outhwaite (ed.), *Marriage and Society: Studies in the Social History of Marriage*, 1981, pp. 163–4, for a demonstration that between the 1660s and the 1870s the seasonality of illegitimate conceptions was indistinguishable from that of legitimate conceptions. The relevant figures in W and S as to monthly conceptions in 1660 are in Table A2.4. Celebrations and holidays did sometimes leave such traces behind them, as did Christmas for English baptismal seasonality in the sixteenth century, though not later. For the implication that the laxity often held to be a dominant trait of Restoration culture cannot be said to 'reflect' sexual nonconformism, and for the bastardy rate of peers at the relevant time, see Peter Laslett, 'The wrong way through the telescope: a note on literary evidence in sociology and historical sociology', *British Journal of Sociology*, 1976, 27.

6   Edward Shorter introduced the idea of a sexual revolution in his *Making of the Modern Family*, 1975, and in associated studies. It is found in its least persuasive form in J. M. Phayer, *Sexual Liberation and Religion in 19th-Century Europe*, 1977, with reference to Bavaria. Alien as its argument seems to be to England, one English community as G. N. Gandy has shown in his dissertation of 1978 (DPhil, Oxford) did behave in the way Phayer describes for Bavarian communities, and it is not impossible that a rise in sexual nonconformism in the early nineteenth century was accompanied in some areas of England by an increase in religious fervour (evangelicalism), as Phayer might lead us to expect.

7   The number of acts of sexual intercourse likely to take place for any given conception presents a complex problem, requiring information about the timing of acts in relation to the point in the menstrual cycle when the woman ovulates. The relevant information is unlikely ever to be available for extramarital conception, especially in past time. In 1960 Tietz calculated that under our own conditions of physical well-being and within marriage the probability of pregnancy from a single act of coitus was about 1 in 50 (*Fertility and Sterility*, II, 1960). It must inevitably have been considerably lower between casual partners under less favourable, perhaps often the least favourable, conditions for conception.

8   The Registrar-General estimated in 1970 that nearly a third of illegitimates registered in April 1961 may have been born to married women. A study made by geneticists of 1417 white children about 1960 in the Detroit area showed that 1·4 per cent were demonstrably not fathered by their mother's husbands, although not admitted by those mothers to be illegitimate. The corresponding figure for 523 negro children was 8·9 per cent. See *FLIL*, p. 121. Bastards borne by married women are sometimes found in parish registers.

9   See James Tait (ed.), 'Lancashire quarter sessions records, sessions rolls, 1590–1606', *Chetham Society*, Manchester, 1917.

10   The quotations come from Quaife, *Wanton Wenches*, pp. 193–4, 157–8, 54 and 158 ('flitters' meant fragments).

11   See for example Richard Gough, *The History of Myddle*, edited by David Hey, 1981, pp. 102 (estate consumed by drink) and 133 ('he destroyed himself and his estate by drink'). For William Tyler, also a drunkard, and his escapades, see especially pp. 176–8, and for alehouses see Keith Wrightson, *English Society 1580–1680*, 1982, *passim*.

12   All these names appear in the attempt to sketch out a bastardy-prone sub-society, (*FLIL*, ch. 8) but the available evidence is not sufficient to demonstrate at all conclusively that the literary and artistic were more given to sexual

nonconformism than the rest of the élite. Lawrence Stone's capacious book (*The Family, Sex and Marriage in England 1500–1800*, 1977) assembles a vast body of evidence on their conduct, but in its shorter form (Penguin, 1981) he has abandoned the claim that what happened amongst the élite represented what everyone did.

13 Quaife, *Wanton Wenches*, pp. 183–5, 181–3 and *passim*. There was a bad hat amongst the parsons of Myddle who had a bastard by a Tyler girl. Quaife infers from his evidence, which it must always be remembered bears entirely on the actions of the notorious few whose conduct had offended local opinion, that all women were regarded as available by all men, especially the easily accessible, such as servants and sisters-in-law. But he will have little to do with the notions of Stone and Shorter as to the lovelessness of courtship and married life, pp. 243–9, or with the suggested sexual revolution in the eighteenth century. As with the issue of indifference to children (see p. 119) it seems best to note the superficiality of such theories and their skimpy scholarly foundations, whilst awaiting more materials and better analysis.

14 The somewhat unexpected confirmation for a year as late as 1911 is provided by N. R. Crafts, 'Illegitimacy in England and Wales', *Pop Studs*, 1982, 36, 2, 317–21, insisting that economics as well as locality should be taken into account in future versions of the courtship-intensity hypothesis. For the Lancashire figures before the nineteenth century, see *FLIL*, Tables 3.4–3.10, where some of the settlements have levels in the period 1381–1640 as high as those found in the period 1781–1820; the very large parish of Rochdale has a ratio of 6·0 per cent in the first and 5·9 per cent in the second period. But Lancashire was not one of the first ten counties in England in 1842 and between 1870 and 1902 it varied between 27th and 31st.

15 Martine Segalen, *Love and Power in the Peasant Family*, translated by Sarah Matthews, Oxford, 1983; see p. 21. For the Norman village with a bastardy-prone sub-society, see Jacques Dupâquier, *Population rurale du bassin parisien, 1670–1720*, 1982 (1979), p. 367 (40 per cent of all

illegitimates born to repeaters), and for the Italian one,
Paulo Viazzo in an address to the Cambridge Group, Oct.
1982 (over 60 per cent, 1851–1980).

16   *Marriage contracts and sexual intercourse*
See A. Percival Moore, 'Marriage contracts or espousals in
the reign of Queen Elizabeth', *Reports and Papers of
Associated Architectural Societies*, 1909, xxx, 1, 291,
modernized. No such overt admission of sexual intercourse
being the normal thing after a contract had been finally
settled has been found elsewhere in this authority from the
Leicestershire area, or from anywhere else in England.
Nevertheless the impression given by many of the marriage
cases so far published, especially those from the earlier
period (see e.g. the volume edited by James Raine for the
Surtees Society in 1845) is that cohabitation was assumed
after conclusion of the contract. The contract itself is
ordinarily in dispute in these proceedings: it is much less
frequently a question of whether intercourse took place.

**17   *A Mountain Chapelry, Being a Guide to the Parish of
Ulpha*,** written in 1934 by H. L. Hickes, and revised and
reprinted in 1950 and 1960 by B. S. Simpson. For Scottish
proceedings, see for example the *Sessions Book of the Parish
of Minnigaff*, privately printed in 1939 for the Marquis of
Bute, edited by Henry Payton.

18   For the quotation from Gouge, see *Domesticall Duties*,
1622, pp. 198–9, 202–3, and for that from Perkins, *Works*,
1618, 3, p. 672. Lawrence's book is entitled *Marriage by the
Morall Law of God Vindicated against all Ceremonial Laws
of Popes and Bishops destructive to Filiation, Aliment and
Succession and the Government of Families and Kingdoms*,
1680 (Wing L 690). There are English Puritan writers who
describe intercourse between contract and marriage as
sinful, however, and the views of a man like Lawrence look
quite exceptional.

19   See S. P. Menefee, *Wives for Sale*, Oxford, 1981, and
copious references especially to the researches of
E. P. Thompson: the passage from the *Ipswich Journal* is on
pp. 97–8 and the references to Kneller on p. 213. This
extraordinary book has a wealth of material on married life

but it is not presented in a manner suited to easy reference.
Jumping over a broom was undoubtedly a British
proletarian custom, which seems to have communicated
itself to the black slaves of the American continent. Thomas
Heath was cited to the Thame archdeacon's court (see
S. A. Peyton, 'The churchwardens' presentments in the
Oxfordshire peculiars of Dorchester, Thame and Banbury',
Oxfordshire Record Society, 1928, 184–5) for an offence
which, like many of the others, looks more like compensating
a husband for taking his wife as a mistress, perhaps
temporarily, than outright purchase.

20   The facts and figures about infanticide come for the
most part from an exhaustive but numerically somewhat
overcomplicated book by P. C. Hoffer and N. E. H. Hull,
*Murdering Mothers: Infanticide in England and New England,
1558–1803*, New York, 1981. For population control by
eliminating live babies in Japan, see T. C. Smith and others,
Nakahara, Stanford, 1977.

21   These calculations will be found in an appendix to
S. E. Sprott, *The English Debate on Suicide*, La Salle, Ill.,
1960. For the Ashton and Westminster registers see notes
9 and 25 of Chapter 6, and for the burial of suicides,
S. J. Steel and others, *National Index of Parish Registers*, I,
1968. The concept of anomie is becoming less popular with
sociologists in the 1980s. See C. Fairchilds, in the *Journal of
Social History*, Jan. 1982, 89, fn 5, with its reference to
C. O. Anderson, 'Did suicide increase with industrialization
in Victorian England?', 1980, 86, Anderson concludes that
it did not.

22   See Peter Laslett, 'Illegitimate fertility and the
matrimonial market', in Jacques Dupâquier and others,
Marriage and Remarriage in Populations of the Past, 1981.
It is suggested there that in view of the facts about
extramarital conception, fertility should be reckoned as a
function not of an individual's marital, but of her or his
procreative career. The arrival of the onset of procreative
union for whole populations as a delayed effect of real wage
fluctuations is discussed in the final chapter of W and S,
though marriage is the term used.

23   See Wrigley, pp. 181–2. He shows that the rise in prenuptial pregnancy in later eighteenth-century England must have been due to an increase in circumstances where the woman conceiving occasioned marriage, and that the rise was proportionately higher for younger women, whereas in France it was proportionately higher for older women.

24   See Barbara Laslett, 'The family as a public and private institution: an historical perspective', *Journal of Marriage and the Family*, 1973, 35, 480; Orvar Löfgren, 'Family and household among Scandinavian peasants', *Ethnologia Scandinavica*, 1974, 1, and Segalen, *Love and Power*. Privacy has been investigated for early colonial society (e.g. D. H. O'Flaherty, *Privacy in Colonial New England*, Charlottesville, 1972) but not for our own country.

CHAPTER 8   *Social change and revolution in the traditional world*

1   *The Good Old Cause: The English Revolution of 1640–60, its Causes, Course and Consequences, Extracts from Contemporary Sources*, by Christopher Hill and Edmund Dell, 1949, p. 19. Earlier statements of this character had been made during the 1930s (see A. L. Morton, *A People's History of England*) and by Hill himself in *The English Revolution*, 1940. In the rewritten introduction to the second edition of *The Good Old Cause* in 1969, the sentence is replaced with one to the effect that a bourgeois revolution is one which 'whatever the subjective intentions of the revolutionaries – had the effect of establishing conditions favourable to the development of capitalism', p. 20. The phrase 'seventeenth-century revolution' appears there instead of the references to the 1640s. The statements of 1980 are made in his chapter entitled 'A bourgeois revolution?' in J. G. A. Pococke (ed.), *Three British Revolutions, 1641, 1688, 1776*, Princeton, 1980.

2   Max Weber, *General Economic History*, translated by R. M. Knight, 1961, ch. 12, especially p. 132. Compare C. I. Hammer, 'Family and familia in early medieval Bavaria', *Famforms*, ch. 7, which contains examples of an

organization named *gynaecum* in the ninth century,
described as 'a woman's cloth workshop', with twenty-three
occupants in one case, twenty-four in another.

3 *The Pleasant History of Jack of Newbury*, in Deloney's
Works, edited by A. G. Mann, 1912. The passage seems first
to have been cited as evidence for the existence of factories
by George Unwin, who recognized that the tale was mainly
mythological, but called it 'not unacceptable as evidence',
Studies in Economic History, 1927, p. 193. See also
S. T. Bindoff in his Penguin History, *Tudor England*, 1969,
p. 123, though he is very tentative in his statements about
Jack of Newbury.

4 The original German was published by Peter Kriedte,
Hans Medick and J. Schlumbohm in 1977, translated under
the English title in 1981. See p. 60 and note 10 of
Chapter 3; and for discussion of proto-industrialization
generally in England, with references to the literature, see
Rab Houston and Keith Snell, 'Proto-industrialization:
theory and reality', in course of publication in the *Historical
Journal*. A comparative study of nineteenth-century
Bethnal Green, a notorious nineteenth-century proto-
industrial community, engaged in silk-weaving, with
silk-weaving and labouring households in the Essex
countryside, is in progress at the Cambridge Group by
Martin Clarke, and underlines the remarks made above
(p. 197) about the uncertainty of the effects of these production arrangements on demography and family structure.

5 See Peter Laslett, 'Household and family as work group
and kin group', in *Famforms*. The recognition of these
facts about familial ideology undoubtedly qualifies to some
extent the position taken up in Chapter 1 of the present book.

6 *The Law Book of the Crowley Ironworks* was edited by
M. W. Flinn in 1957 for the Surtees Society. The full
document is in the British Library, Add. MS. 34, 555, a
tedious but extremely important body of evidence.

7 See Lewis Coser, *The Function of Social Conflict*, 1956,
and especially the introductory chapter for the history of

conflict theory amongst the sociologists. An impressive discussion of the relevance of the critique of functionalism to historical sociology will be found in Philip Abrams, *Historical Sociology*, 1982.

8   Peter Laslett, Foreword to J. H. Hexter, *Reappraisals in History*, 1961. It has been complained that this suggestion reduces everything to the status of an improbable misfortune, but there is no point in denying the contingency even of epoch-making historical occurrences.

9   Thomas Hobbes, *Behemoth, The History of the Causes of the Civil Wars of England*, 2nd edn, 1682, opening sentences. An excellent guide to the unending discussion beginning in Hobbes's generation and continuing to ours has now been written: R. C. Richardson, *The Debate on the English Revolution*, 1977.

10   This is the tendency of Lawrence Stone's brilliant survey of *The Causes of the English Revolution*, 1972. It makes all the details of the struggle of the 1640s easier for the reader to understand, but does little to convince him that what happened then was social revolution in the sense required here. The seismic metaphor which Stone uses here and elsewhere to indicate a divide in the social and political fabric progressively widening over the generations, is an altogether unconvincing one.

11   Max Gluckman has presented this phenomenon in a succession of books and articles, of which perhaps the most important to our subject is *Order and Rebellion in Tribal Africa*, 1963; see e.g. the essay there on 'Succession and civil war among the Bemba'. The phenomenological tendency of most recent sociological theory would give little importance to the functions of conflict in perpetuation of social structure, simply accepting it as a perpetual circumstance.

12   See *Class and Class Conflict in Industrial Society* (1957), English edn, 1959.

13   Peter Laslett, 'Commentary on science in seventeenth-century England', in A. C. Crombie (ed.), *Scientific Change*, 1963, pp. 801–5.

14   It is only necessary to cite here the title of the latest in the long series of studies which have been devoted since the 1960s to social change, political violence, intellectual and cultural innovation in seventeenth-century England: 'When was the English Revolution?' by Angus Macinnes, *History*, 1982, 377. An attempt to list all of the sets of events in the seventeenth century in England which have been called revolutions, and of the fields of activity in which they are supposed to have occurred, has had to be abandoned: there are too many instances. The word is used in a bewildering number of ways, with few attempts at definition, and it becomes obvious that its only general significance is as an emphasizer. A study is in preparation on the confusion between time scales of change in various fields, and on the widespread disposition to suppose that all change takes place in political time.

CHAPTER 9   *The pattern of authority and our political heritage*

1   For Abigail see Peter Laslett 'Masham of Otes', in Peter Quennell (ed.), *Diversions of History*, 1954. Although households of gentry contained more resident kin than others (see Table 7 on p. 96) the great majority of them were simple family households like the rest. Jessica Gerard, in her PhD dissertation for London University, 1981, demonstrates this point for the nineteenth century from the largest sample of country-house families so far studied.

2   The standard exposition of deference is by Edward Shils, writing under that title in J. A. Jackson (ed.), *Social Stratification*, Cambridge, 1968. Use is made of that essay by Bob Jessup in *Traditionalism, Conservation and British Political Culture*, 1974, and by Howard Newby in *The Deferential Worker*, 1977. The theory is derived, however, from face-to-face attitudes, especially from employers in relation with their employees, rather than from the behaviour of subordinate masses like those characteristic of traditional England, though Keith Wrightson, *English Society 1580–1680*, 1982, does make use of the deprivation concept.

3   The proposition about witchcraft comes from Keith
Thomas, *Religion and the Decline of Magic: Studies in
Popular Belief in 16th and 17th Century England*, 1971. Not
all commentators look on witchcraft as displaced aggression,
and it must not be thought that rioting crowds in
traditional society usually consisted of the very poor. For
the case of a desperate, destitute man taking to highway
robbery, see J. H. Langbein, 'Albion's fatal flaws', *P and P*,
1983, 98, 97.

4   I owe almost all of what is said in the text about
catechizing and political socialization to Professor Gordon
Schochet of Rutgers University: for a full presentation see
his *Patriarchalism in Political Thought*, 1975. Schochet
makes no reference to the archdeacons' courts, the evidence
of which so S. A. Peyton claims ('The churchwardens'
presentments in the Oxfordshire peculiars of Dorchester,
Thame and Banbury', *Oxfordshire Record Society*, 1928,
xxxv) shows that catechizing was an irksome duty,
extensively neglected by the clergy in the seventeenth and
eighteenth centuries. The actual cases printed in the volume,
however, and certainly those from other areas, do not
entirely confirm this view.

5   William Fleetwood (Bishop of Ely), *Sermons*, 1737
(1705), pp. 232–3.

6   John Lilburne, *The Free Man's Freedom Vindicated*
(16 June 1646), pp. 11–12, slightly abbreviated and
modernized. See T. C. Pease, *The Leveller Movement*,
Washington, D.C., 1916, p. 128.

7   For transmission of attitudes by successive socialization
into families descended from each other and its possible
importance for the persistence of radical political beliefs
over time, see *Bastardy*, p. 222.

8   James Tyrrell, *Patriarcha non Monarcha*, 1681, first
pagination, p. 83. For this book and its relationship with
Filmer and Locke, see Peter Laslett (ed.), *Patriarcha, and
other Political Works of Sir Robert Filmer*, Oxford, 1949, and
Laslett (ed.), *Two Treatises of Government*, Cambridge, 1960,

1963, etc. The fact that Filmer codified common beliefs may account for his being little read, even at the time when the Whigs were burying him with their arguments. The Puritan colonists could not see their way to admitting women, children and servants to political rights. See Richard C. Simmons, 'Godliness, property and the franchise in Puritan Massachusetts', *Journal of American History*, Dec. 1968.

9   See A. S. P. Woodhouse (ed.), *Puritanism and Liberty*, 1951 edn, pp. 53, 60 (Ireton's appeal to the 5th Commandment) and 61. In *The Case of the Army Soberly Discussed* (Thomason Tracts E. 396, 10, 3 July 1647) it was argued that the law of nature giving all authority to the head of the family prevented 'the servants and prentices not yet free and children unmarried' then in the army from participating in such political activities. Some modern authorities, notably Brough Macpherson, in *The Political Theory of Possessive Individualism*, 1962, and other works, argue that the Levellers excluded all employed persons, that is the great majority of all males and the majority of all household heads, from the franchise. This would make them as élitist as Locke or Tyrrell, or more so. The contrary is argued by Laslett in an introduction to the works of Gregory King, *The Earliest Classics*, Farnborough, 1973, and in *FLIL*.

10   Peter Laslett, 'The gentry of Kent in 1640', *Cambridge Historical Journal*, 1948, IX, no. 2, 164. Alan Everitt has developed the theory in a series of publications, and since his work on *The Community of Kent and the Great Rebellion*, 1969, numbers of studies have appeared, for Suffolk, Lancashire, Yorkshire, Cheshire and other counties, a list too long for detailing here. Most of them will be found named in two studies critical of the theory, Clive Holmes, 'The county community in Stuart historiography', *Journal of British Studies*, 1980, XIX, and Christopher Hill, 'Parliament and people in 17th-century England', *P and P*, 1981, 92. Only Graham Kerby, in 'Inequality in a pre-industrial society: a study of wealth, status, office and taxation in 17th-century Cheshire', PhD dissertation, Cambridge, 1983, actually lists the numbers, social descriptions and wealth of those holding county office, who

might compose the county community. In his view such sets of persons should be thought of as 'constructive reference groups' rather than 'real collectivities'. It is perhaps worth insisting that the criterion of preferential county endogamy for a sense of county consciousness among the gentry was not part of the original analysis of Kent. It was recognized that the gentry would take their brides and bridegrooms from where it suited their familial and personal interest best, in spite of the fact that kinship was an important feature of gentry collaboration. Nor was it, nor need it be, claimed that the age of gentry families, that is the number of generations during which they had been seated in a county, was all-important to the strength of county community feeling.

11   Wrightson, *English Society*, p. 225. He uses the term 'the English Revolution' in this passage, however.

CHAPTER 10   *The politics of exclusion and the rule of an élite*

1   See David Cressy, *Literacy and the Social Order: Reading and Writing in Tudor and Stuart England*, Cambridge, 1980. Name-signing is regarded here as indicative of being able to read and so a good indicator of the upper band of full literacy. It is impossible to say what proportion of those able to sign would have the other attributes named in the text. The nature of literacy and its social significance have been much discussed, especially by Harvey Graff, who has provided excellent guides to the topic. See his *Literacy in History: An Interdisciplinary Research Bibliography*, New York, 1981, and a reader *Literacy and Social Development in the West*, Cambridge, 1981. His own views, and a critique, are contained in *The Literacy Myth*, New York, 1979.

2   It is significant that Alan Macfarlane concludes of Ralph Josselin, the Essex parson of the mid-seventeenth century, both that his kinship network was relatively restricted and that he turned for assistance to neighbours and friends rather than relatives – *The Family Life of Ralph Josselin, a Seventeenth-Century Clergyman: An Essay in Historical*

Anthropology, Cambridge, 1970. If this was true even of someone so much a part of literate society as Josselin, it would look as if those below him would have been much more cut off from their kindred. It is very difficult to imagine that the kinship network of a traditional English village can have been much more elaborate than the 'attenuated' set of relationships described by W. M. Williams in 1963 for his *West Country Village* during the 1950s, and in my view it was even less developed. Compare Miranda Chaytor, 'Household and kinship: Ryton in the late 16th and early 17th centuries', *History Workshop*, 1980, 10.

3   See David Levine, 'Education and family life in early industrial England', *Journal of Family History*, 1979, 4, 4. He calls into question here many of the assumptions about the importance of literacy to 'modernization' and to the quality of intellectual life, the naiveté of which has led Graff to talk of 'the literacy myth': see the works cited in note 1 of Chapter 10.

4   See Peter Clark, 'The ownership of books in England, 1560–1640: the example of some Kentish townsfolk', in Lawrence Stone (ed.), *Schooling and Society*, Baltimore, 1976.

5   See Peter Laslett, 'Scottish weavers, cobblers and miners who bought books in the 1750s', LPS, 1969, 3. Of 398 persons recorded as subscribing to a serious theological work published in 1757, 120 were weavers, 8 were tailors, 6 were smiths and 2 were coal-heavers. Of 606 persons subscribing to a similar book two years later 242 were weavers and 34 were shoemakers. Compare R. E. Jones in *LPS*, 1979, 23.

6   See K. W. Wachter, E. A. Hammel and Peter Laslett, *Statistical Studies of Historical Social Structure*, 1978. The calculation for the *samurai* was made on figures supplied by Professor Yamamura of Washington State University. In *Balancing on an Alp*, Cambridge, 1981, Robert Netting describes a society where patrilines appear to have been more durable than those of the English baronets, though see the foreword to that book by Peter Laslett. For

surviving heirs among groups of children of the same father, see E. A. Wrigley, 'Fertility strategy for the individual and the group', in Charles Tilly (ed.), *Historical Studies in Changing Fertility*, Princeton, 1978. See also R. M. Smith, *Land, Kinship and the Life Cycle* (in press).

7 Thomas Wilson, *The State of England*, edited by F. J. Fisher, 1936 (1600), p. 24, modernized and slightly abbreviated.

8 M. C. Bradbrook, *Shakespeare, the Poet and his World*, 1978, especially p. 9. The facts about Newton's family and its literacy will be found in the *Dictionary of National Biography* and in the National Trust guide to Woolsthorpe Manor, 1980.

List of authorities

All titles are published in London unless otherwise stated.

Abrams, Philip and Wrigley, E. A. (1978) *Towns in Society: Essays in Economic History and Historical Sociology,* Cambridge.

Appleby, Andrew (1978) *Famine in Tudor and Stuart England,* Stanford.

Ariès, Philippe (1962 (1960)) *Centuries of Childhood,* translated by Robert Baldick. Original: *L'Enfant et la vie familiale sous l'ancien régime,* Paris, 1960.

Best, Henry (1857 (1641)) *Rural Economy in Yorkshire in 1641, Being the Farming and Account Books of Henry Best, of Elmswell in the East Riding of the County of York,* edited by C. B. Robinson.

Chamberlayne, Edward (1702 (1669)) *Angliae Notitia: or the Present State of England.*

Chaytor, Miranda (1980) 'Household and kinship: Ryton in the late 16th and early 17th centuries', *History Workshop,* 10.

Clayworth, Rector's Book (1910) *The Rector's Book of Clayworth, Notts.,* edited by Harry Gill and E. L. Guilford, Nottingham.

Cressy, David (1980) *Literacy and the Social Order: Reading and Writing in Tudor and Stuart England,* Cambridge.

Dobb, Maurice (1946) *Studies in the Development of Capitalism.*

Drake, Michael (1974) *Historical Demography: Problems and Prospects* (Open University course book).

Dupâquier, Jacques (1982 (1979)) *Population rurale du bassin parisien, 1670–1720.*

Everitt, Alan (1967) 'Farm labourers', in Thirsk, J. (ed.) (1967) *The Agrarian History of England and Wales,* IV, *1500–1640,* Cambridge.

———— (1967) 'The marketing of agricultural produce', in Thirsk, J. (ed.) (1967) *The Agrarian History of England and Wales,* IV, *1500–1640,* Cambridge.

Finlay, Roger (1981) *Population and Metropolis: the Demography of London, 1580–1650,* Cambridge.

Fleetwood, William (1737 (1705)) 'The relative duties of

parents and children, husbands and wives, masters and servants', in *Compleat Collection of Sermons*.

Furnivall, F. (1897) *Child Marriages, Divorces and Ratifications*, etc.

Glass, D. V. (1965) 'Two papers on Gregory King', in Glass, D. V. and Eversley, D. E. C. (eds), (1965) *Population and History*.

Goubert, Pierre (1960) *Beauvais et les Beauvaisis de 1600 à 1730*, Paris.

Gouge, William (1622) *Of Domesticall Duties*.

Gough, Richard: see Myddle.

Hajnal, J. (1965) 'European marriage patterns in perspective', in Glass, D. V. and Eversley, D. E. C. (eds) (1965) *Population and History*.

——————— (1983) 'Two kinds of household formation system', in *Famforms*.

Hammel and Laslett (1974): see Laslett, Peter.

Hasted, Edward (1782) *History of Kent*, Canterbury.

Hexter, J. H. (1963 (1961)) *Reappraisals in History*.

Hill, Christopher (1961, etc.) *The Century of Revolution*, Edinburgh.

——————— (1967) *Reformation to Industrial Revolution*.

Hollingsworth, T. H. (1964) 'The demography of the British peerage', supplement to *Pop Studs*, XVIII, no. 2, Nov. 1964.

Kerby, Graham (1983) 'Inequality in a pre-industrial society: a study of wealth, status, office and taxation in 17th-century Cheshire', PhD dissertation, Cambridge.

Keys, Ancel (with others) (1951) *The Biology of Human Starvation*, 2 vols, Oxford.

Kussmaul, Ann (1981) *Servants in Husbandry in Early Modern England*, Cambridge.

Laslett, Peter (1948) 'The gentry of Kent in 1640', *Cambridge Historical Journal*, IX, no. 2.

——————— (1961) Foreword to Hexter, J. H. (1963 (1961)) *Reappraisals in History*.

——————— (1963) with Harrison, John, 'Clayworth and Cogenhoe', in Bell, H. E. and Ollard, R. L. (eds) *Historical Essays, 1600–1750, Presented to David Ogg*, p. 157. Extended and revised in *FLIL*, chapter 2.

——————— (1963) 'Commentary on scientific change', in Crombie, A. C. (ed.), *Scientific Change*, p. 801.

Laslett, Peter (1966) 'The study of social structure from
listings of inhabitants', in Wrigley, E. A. (ed.) (1966)
English Historical Demography.
———————— (1969) 'Size and structure of the household in
England over three centuries', *Pop Studs*, XXIII, no. 2,
199.
———————— (1969) 'Scottish weavers, cobblers and miners
who bought books in the 1750s', *LPS*, no. 3, 7.
———————— (1972) with Wall, Richard, *Household and
Family in Past Time: Comparative Studies in the Size and
Structure of the Domestic Group over the Last Three
Centuries in England, France, Serbia, Japan and Colonial
North America, with Further Materials from Western
Europe*, Cambridge (abbreviated to *HFPT*).
———————— (1973) with Oosterveen, Karla, 'Long-term
trends in bastardy in England', *Pop Studs*, XXVII, no. 2,
255.
———————— (1973) Introduction to *The Earliest Classics*
(works by John Graunt and Gregory King with a
manuscript notebook of King's), Farnborough.
———————— (1974) with Hammel, E. A., 'Comparing
household structure over time and between cultures',
Comparative Studies in Society and History.
———————— (1976) 'The wrong way through the telescope: a
note on literary evidence in sociology and historical
sociology', *British Journal of Sociology*, 27.
———————— (1977) *Family Life and Illicit Love in Earlier
Generations*, Cambridge (abbreviated to *FLIL*).
———————— (1978) with Wachter, K. W. and Hammel, E. A.,
Statistical Studies of Historical Social Structure
(development of the theory of household composition and
social mobility in relation to demography and of other
theories propounded in this volume).
———————— (1979) 'Family and collectivity', *Sociology and
Social Research*, 63.
———————— (1980) with Oosterveen, Karla, and Smith,
Richard M., *Bastardy and its Comparative History*
(international comparisons in the historical development
of illegitimacy and prenuptial pregnancy) (abbreviated to
Bastardy).
———————— (1983) with Wall, R. and Robin, J., *Family
Forms in Historic Europe*, Cambridge (chapter on

'Household and family as work group and kin group') (abbreviated to *Famforms*).

Levine, D. (1977) *Family Formation in an Age of Nascent Capitalism*.

Macfarlane, Alan (1970) *The Family Life of Ralph Josselin, a Seventeenth-Century Clergyman: An Essay in Historical Anthropology*, Cambridge.

———— (1977) with Harrison, S. and Jardine, C., *Reconstructing Historical Communities*, Cambridge.

Macpherson, C. B. (1962) *The Political Theory of Possessive Individualism*, Oxford.

Mingay, G. E. (1976) *The Gentry: The Rise and Fall of a Ruling Class*.

Moore, A. Percival (1909) 'Marriage contracts or espousals in the reign of Queen Elizabeth', *Reports and Papers of Associated Architectural Societies*, xxx, 1.

Morgan, Edmund, S. (1966) *The Puritan Family: Religion and Domestic Relations in 17th-Century New England*, New York (Revised and enlarged; original: Boston, 1944).

Myddle, *The History of Myddle* (1701) by Richard Gough, edited by David Hey, 1981.

Neale, R. S. (1981) *Class in English History*, Oxford, 1981.

Outhwaite, R. B. (ed.) (1981) *Marriage and Society: Studies in the Social History of Marriage*.

Peyton, S. A. (1928) 'The churchwardens' presentments in the Oxfordshire peculiars of Dorchester, Thame and Banbury', *Oxfordshire Record Society*.

Phythian-Adams, Charles (1979) *Desolation of a City: Coventry and the Urban Crisis of the Late Middle Ages*, Cambridge.

Pinchbeck, I. and Hewitt, M. (1972 (1969)) *Childhood in English Society*, i, *From Tudor Times to the 18th Century*.

———— (1973) ii, *From the 19th Century to the Children Act, 1948*.

Powell, C. L. (1917) *English Domestic Relations, 1487–1653*, New York.

Powell, S. C. (1963) *Puritan Village: The Formation of a New England Town*, Middletown, Conn.

Quaife, G. R. (1979) *Wanton Wenches and Wayward Wives: Peasants and Illicit Sex in Early 17th-Century England*.

Richardson, R. C. (1977) *The Debate on the English Revolution*.

Rowntree, B. S. (1922 (1901)) *Poverty: A Study of Town Life.*

Runciman, W. G. (1966) *Relative Deprivation and Social Justice.*

Schochet, G. J. (1975) *Patriarchalism in Political Thought,* Oxford.

Schofield, R. S. (1973) 'Dimensions of illiteracy, 1750–1850', *Explorations in Economic History,* 10, no. 4, 437.

Schofield, R. S. (1981): see Wrigley, E. A.

Sen, Amartya (1981) *Poverty and Famine,* Oxford.

Smith, John, of Nibley (1902 (1608)) *Men and Armour for Gloucestershire.*

Smith, R. M. (in press) *Land, Kinship and the Life Cycle.*

Smith, Sir Thomas (1906 (1583)) *The Commonwealth of England,* edited by L. Alston, Cambridge.

Steele, Richard (1672 (1668)) *The Husbandman's Calling.*

Stone, Lawrence (1977) *The Family, Sex and Marriage in England, 1500–1800.*

Tait, James (ed.) (1917) 'Lancashire quarter sessions records, sessions rolls, 1590–1606', *Chetham Society,* Manchester.

Tanner, J. M. (1981) *A History of the Study of Human Growth,* Cambridge.

Thirsk, J. (ed.) (1967) *The Agrarian History of England and Wales,* IV, *1500–1640,* Cambridge.

Thomas, Keith (1971) *Religion and the Decline of Magic: Studies in Popular Belief in 16th and 17th Century England.*

Titmuss, R. M. (1962) *Income Distribution and Social Change.*

Wachter, K. W. with Hammel, E. A. and Laslett, P. (1978) *Statistical Studies of Historical Social Structure.*

Wall, R. (1978) 'The age at leaving home', *Journal of Family History,* 3, no. 2, 181.

———— (1983) with Robin, J. and Laslett, P., *Family Forms in Historic Europe,* Cambridge (abbreviated to *Famforms*).

Willmott, Peter: see Young, Michael.

Wilson, Thomas (1936 (1600)) *The State of England,* edited by F. J. Fisher, Camden Society publication Lii.

Wrightson, Keith (1982) *English Society 1580–1680.*

Wrightson, Keith, and Levine, David (1979) *Poverty and Piety in an English Village: Terling 1525–1700.*

Wrigley, E. A. (ed.) (1966) *An Introduction to English Historical Demography* (with contributions by E. A. Wrigley on 'Family reconstitution', D. E. C. Eversley, Peter Laslett etc.).

——————— (1966) 'Family limitation in pre-industrial England', *EcHR*, xix, no. 1.

——————— (1969) *Population and History* (published simultaneously in London, New York, in France, Italy, Germany, Spain and Holland in the appropriate languages).

——————— (1978) 'A simple model of London's importance in changing English society and economy, 1650–1750', in Abrams, Philip, and Wrigley, E. A. (1978) *Towns in Society: Essays in Economic History and Historical Sociology*, Cambridge.

——————— (1981) with Schofield, R. S., *The Population History of England, 1541–1871: A Reconstruction* (abbreviated to W and S).

——————— (1981) 'Marriage, fertility and population growth in 18th century England', in Outhwaite, R. B. (ed.) (1981) *Marriage and Society: Studies in the Social History of Marriage*.

Young, Michael, and Willmott, Peter (1959 (1957)) *Family and Kinship in East London*.

Zagorin, Perez (1982) *Rebels and Rulers 1500–1660*, 2 vols, Cambridge.

Index